NIK LEVER

Animation Magic
with Visual Basic 5™

Get in touch – we'd like to hear from you!

Your opinion counts

If you have any comments about this book – positive or negative, long or short – please send them in. We want to refine our books according to the needs of our readers, so do tell us if there is something that you would like to see in future editions of this book. Your input could well appear in print! We genuinely appreciate it when people take the time to contact us, so every month we give away a free Prentice Hall computer book for the most helpful and comprehensive comments.

Please feel free to cmail me personally with your comments:

feedback@prenhall.co.uk

Or you can write to me:

Jason Dunne
Prentice Hall
Campus 400
Maylands Avenue
Hemel Hempstead
Herts.
HP2 7EZ
United Kingdom

Please note that Prentice Hall cannot serve as a technical resource for questions about hardware or software problems.

We would also love to hear your ideas for new books, whether it is just for a book that you want to see in print or one you intend writing yourself. Our guide for new authors can be found in the back of this book.

Thanks for choosing Prentice Hall.

Jason Dunne
Acquisition Editor, Prentice Hall

jdunne@prenhall.co.uk

NIK LEVER

Animation Magic

with Visual Basic™ 5

LEARNING TO PROGRAM

Prentice Hall

London New York Toronto Sydney Tokyo Singapore
Madrid Mexico City Munich Paris

First published 1997 by
Prentice Hall Europe
Campus 400, Maylands Avenue
Hemel Hempstead
Hertfordshire, HP2 7EZ
A division of
Simon & Schuster International Group

© Prentice Hall 1997

Typeset in 10/12pt Century
by PPS, London Road, Amesbury, Wilts.

Printed and bound in Great Britain by The Bath Press, Bath

Library of Congress Cataloging-in-Publication Data

Available from the publisher

British Library Cataloguing in Publication Data

A catalogue record for this book is available from
the British Library

ISBN 0–13–842296–6

1 2 3 4 5   01 00 99 98 97

Trade marks
Microsoft, Windows and Visual Basic 5 are registered
trade marks of Microsoft Corporation.

To Andrew and Sophie

ACKNOWLEDGEMENT

Special thanks to my wife Pam for her patience and tolerance while I was writing this book. There is a great deal of work involved in writing a book and this one is an after-hours project which demanded almost all my 'free' time for six months.

CONTENTS AT A GLANCE

CONTENTS IN FULL

ABOUT THE AUTHOR

Nik Lever was born in Bolton, Lancashire, in 1958. He was just too old for college when he decided to study computers; so instead he studied animation and has produced animation for advertising films, TV series and for training since 1980.

His fascination with computers began in 1983 when he bought a Sinclair Spectrum computer, with 48K of memory, no disk storage (it required a cassette tape recorder to store and load programs and it did this very unreliably) and an 8 colour display. This computer was used to drive the rostrum camera at the company where Nik worked. Using a program written in Sinclair Basic and some bits of electronics he soldered together, the computer helped to create professional animation films for nearly five years. It is remarkable what you can do with 48K if you're careful!

Since then he has developed a regular computer museum, filled with Amiga units and old PCs. Computers come and go more quickly than the fashion industry changes clothes.

Computers and animation came together for Nik in 1993 when the company he runs, Catalyst Pictures, began to develop bespoke multi-media projects for business clients.

Nik is currently doing a maths degree with the Open University. He is married with two children, Andrew (born 1989) and Sophie (born 1991), and his hobbies include sailing, when he can spare the time.

INTRODUCTION

Many artists and designers are finding that they are having to learn a little computer programming to add interactivity to a web site or multimedia presentation. This book is written with just those people in mind.

'You need to be a teenage genius or have a degree in computer science to program.' – *False*.

'Most books that teach programming have really boring examples.' – *True*.

So what's so special about this book?

For the novice programmer the language of choice is Visual Basic, as it provides all the tools necessary to begin programming under Windows. However, most of the training guides use examples that explain simple database manipulation and text editing, and for many people this is not exactly riveting stuff!

This is the book that I looked for five years ago when I moved from Amiga to PC programming. Games dominated Amiga software; the PC, however, was a different animal. The most widely used types of PC software were and still are word processors and database management systems. The operating system most users chose was Windows, but it was widely considered that fast animation and Windows did not go together. Consequently, the information available for games and animation programming on the PC concentrated on DOS programs. This may have been a convenience for the programmers, but it has given thumping headaches to many game players, fighting to get the software to run on their computer. If you have struggled with interrupts and DMAs then you know what I mean. The public want games that work with Windows. This book is a journey of discovery to show you how to provide those games and how to add fast animation to multimedia titles.

Who is this book for?

This book assumes that you are familiar with Windows 95. You must understand how to move files around using Explorer, and how to run applications. This book assumes NO programming knowledge whatsoever. If you have never used Visual Basic then you will be able to understand the examples in the book. New concepts are fully explained as they are introduced, and for those who have never used Visual Basic there is an introduction to this development tool in Appendix A.

The book is written with the following people in mind.

- **Beginner:** You have never programmed before in your life. Well you have come to the right place. Here you will learn structured programming with fun examples that will keep you entertained and wanting to learn more.
- **Designer:** You have probably tried Director and found it inadequate in some respects, but never considered Visual Basic because you felt it dealt mainly with databases. You will soon realise that everything you can do with Director you can do with Visual Basic, not least because you can use Director as an ActiveX Control within your Visual Basic application! You will also learn how to use VBScript to enliven your web pages. It is time you got to grips with object-orientated code, and this is the book for you.
- **Hobbyist:** You want to write games for fun and to distribute on the web; or you may want to develop fun things for the kids. Everything you need is here, including lots of sprites that you can use in your own programs.
- **Professional:** You know your Visual Basic inside out. You can talk WorkSpaces and RecordSets with the best of them, but you have never used animation in your programs because you thought it was difficult to implement. You are, however, aware that even Microsoft's own operating system uses animations as part of its user interface (flying files in the file copy dialog). In about 3 hours with this book, and the enclosed Sprite ActiveX Control, you can pep up your program and add those extra touches that clients are beginning to expect.

The structure of this book

The book is divided into four parts. Part 1 is for beginners to programming. If you already know about data structures, the class implementation with Visual Basic and object-orientated code techniques, then you can safely skip this section.

Part 2 explains how animation is done and describes how you can use Visual Basic to develop the tools you will need to create the images required for animation.

Part 3 uses various types of computer game to explore animation techniques. This section introduces the enclosed Sprite ActiveX Control, and has some advanced techniques that will only be understood by those beginners who have studied the book from the beginning. Professionals should find this a most interesting section.

Part 4 discusses how you can use Visual Basic 5 to create ActiveX controls that you can use as part of a web page. The emphasis in this section is on the use of animation in a web page.

Installing the example programs

Before you can use the software in this book you need to run the set-up program that is on the CD. This transfers approximately 1Mb of programs to your hard drive. These include a dynamic link library that is used in the early part of the book and an ActiveX control that is used later.

All the examples in the text are included on the CD, but the setup program does not transfer them to your hard drive. You are encouraged to explore the contents of the CD using Explorer and to run the programs straight from the CD.

Warning! Warning! Warning!

Almost all the example programs require your computer to be set up with a 256 colour display. Failing to do this will generate GPF (General Protection Faults) and the code will not run. This will do no damage to your computer, and to correct the problem simply go to Control Panel|Display|Settings and make sure that you have selected 256 colours as the colour resolution. If you prefer to work at a higher colour depth then try the examples to see if you like them and check the 'Readme' on the CD to find out about getting a version of the Sprite ActiveX Control that will work in 16-bit and 24-bit colour depths. There are no versions of the Sprite ActiveX Control that will work in colour depths below 256 colours.

If you find an example that you want to use in your own program, you can use any of the codes by simply copying the code to a new folder on your hard drive. Using Explorer, highlight the files that you have copied and right click on the blue area.

You will see that Read Only is on check. Click on this to uncheck the box and click OK. If you forget to do this then Visual Basic will be unable to write to these files as you edit them. CD files are all marked Read Only.

Typographic conventions

Headline

This is a headline title

Code is set out like this
```
Dim i as integer,
For i =0 To 20
    debug.print ''Hello''
Next
⏎ wrapped code line
```

TIP

An example program to help learn

NOTE

HOW DO THEY WORK? – 1:

PART ONE

The Sorcerer's Apprentice

CHAPTER 1

Hello world – Animation in your first program

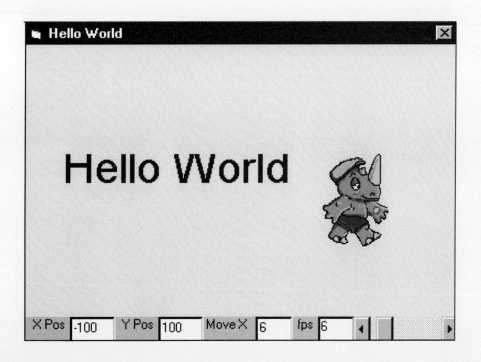

If this is your first book on programming then you might wonder why this first chapter involves a simple program that writes 'Hello World' on the screen. The reason is, as any seasoned programmers out there will know, that just about every manual on programming starts out with just such a program. But in this book we aim to be more fun, so we will do the whole thing as a cartoon!

NOTE

If you are already a proficient programmer and want to learn animation tricks then move straight to Part 3.

What is programming?

Programming involves writing instructions that tell the computer how to behave. These instructions vary depending on the language you are using. Although there are differences, there are also lots of similarities between programming languages. The more Visual Basic you learn the easier you will find it if you decide to learn another programming language such as C++. As we get further into the book we will also discuss pseudo code. This is a style of code that gives general computer instructions – it is not the instructions of any specific language, but a kind of Esperanto for computers. It is then the programmer's job to convert this into the language being used.

I hope that you are sitting at your computer as you read this. You can work through the example by opening Visual Basic and loading the project file 'Hello.vbp'. Before we go through the detail, pop the CD in the drive and find 'Chap01\Hello.exe'. You will need to have a full 32-bit version of Visual Basic set-up on your machine and to have run the set-up program discussed in the introduction for the program to run properly. Now run the program – the little cartoon rhino walks across the screen revealing 'Hello World' as he passes by. Having crossed the screen he pops back in at the left, the words are cleared and the action repeats.

Altering the animation

Try altering the value in the edit box labelled 'MoveX'. Smaller values make him move very slowly across the screen, higher values have the opposite effect. Changing 'MoveX' between 1 and 15 gives reasonable results. If you try a negative value, then, you've guessed it, he walks backwards. With a value around −6 you have a moonwalking rhino! Now try adjusting the frames per second (fps) value. This is achieved by moving the scroll bar, on which the value is restricted to between 1 and 50 fps. Finally, try altering the 'YPos' edit box. This moves the rhino up and down the screen.

HOW DO THEY WORK? – 1:

Describing a point on the screen

Before we look at the code, a brief word about Cartesian co-ordinates. A rather remarkable Frenchman in the 17th century almost reinvented geometry. Before Descartes, geometry included what could be achieved with a straight edge and a compass. Descartes translated geometrical ideas into algebra. You do not need a great deal of maths for the examples in this book, but a little is helpful. Descartes's big idea was to invent graphs. With a graph you can place a point and give it a value. The idea of a point on a graph is very important to understand as you will use this in every program in this book, so lets look at a diagram.

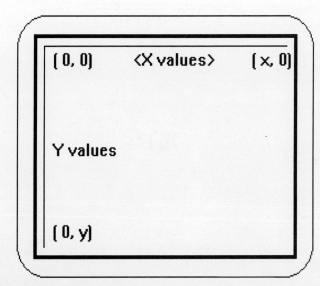

Diagram 1.1

Your computer screen is made up of small dots, called pixels, each of which has a colour value. Although each single pixel can only be one colour, a whole screen full of pixels creates the pictures you see on your computer screen. It is the role of every computer animation programmer to manipulate those pixels to create new images that entertain and challenge the user. For most Windows screens the value that represents the distance across the screen (the X position) gets bigger as you move from left to right. The value that represents the distance down the screen (the Y position) gets bigger as you move down the screen. I hope that with the 'Hello.exe' program you experimented by altering the X and Y values, to get a feel for the effect of bigger and smaller values. Now we can describe any position on the screen using just two numbers. For example (320, 240), that is 320 across and 240 down, is the centre of a 640 × 480 VGA screen. You may be wondering how we tell the computer what colour to display at that pixel; if you are, then you are definitely of the right material to write fast animation code. But, fear not if you had not even considered how to display colours at the pixel level, because we have a long way to go before we need to consider code in such detail.

Cartoons

Most people have some idea about how animation is created. The common vision involves lots and lots of drawings flashing past the viewer's eyes. Here is a very brief introduction to animation.

Hopefully, you have tried altering the fps value and the MoveX value in the example program. Animation is an illusion; rapidly changing similar pictures confuses the eye into believing the picture itself has life. Here are the pictures that make up the moving rhino.

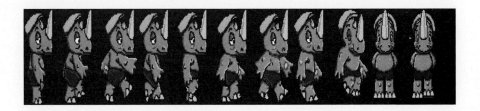

There are just 8 different images in the walk; having reached number 8, the walk continues by returning to image 1. If you are worried about your own capabilities to draw then perhaps you could glance at

Chapter 7 which explains many tricks you can use when creating artwork for animation. Alternatively, the CD contains lots of images like the one above that you can use in your own games. High-quality TV animation uses around 12 drawings per second; feature animation uses twice that number, 24 drawings per second. The example program uses a frame rate of just 6 drawings per second by default, but even at this rate an acceptable appearance of movement is conveyed.

How do we use the drawings?

Using Visual Basic there are no obvious ways to add moving animations to the screen. In the example program I have included a special module that adds these functions to your own projects. I have deliberately written the module using the minimum of confusing calls to the Windows API.

NOTE

Underlying Windows itself are libraries of functions that are available to the programmer that allow you to add functionality not available within Visual Basic itself. These additional functions are referred to as the Windows API (Application Programmer's Interface).

I want to make the code as easy to understand as possible, and I will be explaining in detail what is happening in the code at every stage. I hope that by the end of this book you will be in a position to reinvent all my code, and considerably improve it for your own programs. You may find dissenters who say that Visual Basic is not suitable for game writing. They might argue that you will have to write it in C + + and assembler. It's true that to get the best possible performance this is definitely the case, but computers are getting faster, and with a P75 or better you can afford to waste a little processor time. It is much more important that you can learn the techniques and skills that are required. Your programs will still run faster than you might expect. In the later chapters I will cover faster and more sophisticated methods, but lets build on some simpler experimentation.

Opening your first project

Run Visual Basic. Open the file 'Ex01A.vbp'. In the declarations section of the form are two variables that have global scope. In programming you will often need to decide whether a variable has local or global scope. If you have never encountered the idea of a variable, the next chapter covers all the concepts. A variable is like a pigeon hole where you can store some information to use later. If it is global then anyone can look at the pigeon hole; if it is local then only your best friends can look and after looking they discard the contents of the pigeon hole.

```
Dim intFrame As Integer, intXRhino As Integer
```

The next section of code looks after the initialisation of the form. In Visual Basic windows are referred to as 'forms'. An application usually has three distinct stages, initialisation, main loop and termination. In Visual Basic this is the case and a Form_Load event is usually the best place to put the initialisation code. Lots of the techniques that will be covered throughout this book are illustrated for the first time in this sub-routine. Windows programming involves adding code to events. An event is something that happens while the program is running. To give you an idea of what I mean, think about a program that you often use. One of the first events will be the window opening on your screen. Having opened, the program will do different things whether the mouse is over a toolbar button, or a menu. All the different actions that the user can make are events. In Visual Basic the possible events that Windows is checking for are given their own possible sub-routines. A sub-routine is a short section of code with a specific purpose. It is not necessary to add code to all these events, or even any of these events, but it is usually by adding code to certain events that the main user interface is built.

In the example program, most of the action revolves around picture controls. Visual Basic has lots of different types of control, all with different functionality. The picture control unsurprisingly is the place to store pictures.

In this example we use the following controls:

picHidden

This is used to draw all the screen changes before the viewer sees them. The changes from one frame to the next involve several independent drawing functions. If the viewer sees all these then he or she can see a half-finished result. Obviously this is undesirable and is avoided by doing all the drawing off screen, then, only when you are happy with the result, you copy it to the screen.

picBackground

This is used to hold the contents of the background behind the moving animation. It is important to be able to restore the background as the animation moves, otherwise a trail of bits of the animation would be left behind.

picSprite

The moving bits of a game are often called sprites, the detail of what is involved in creating a sprite is covered in the following chapters. This control stores the picture that holds all the images.

picSpriteMask

To put an irregularly shaped image on the screen using the standard Windows API calls, involves the use of a mask. This control is used to store the mask. In the subsequent chapters we use a special library to avoid the need to create masks. From Part 3 onwards all the graphic operations are done using a special control called an ActiveX control that makes things even easier. The techniques adopted in this chapter are plain Visual Basic with nothing added and nothing taken away, the idea being to show the different approaches you can make to generating animation using Visual Basic.

The initialisation routine

Most of the codes in the Form_Load sub-routine cover the sizing of these picture controls. The way the computer deals with these pictures will change, dependent on the value of AutoRedraw. This sub-routine ensures that the controls have the correct value for AutoRedraw. Again the full details of this are given later in the book. The sub-routine concludes by initialising the values of a sprite. Do not worry if all this code is confusing, all the details will be covered when it is essential that you understand. For now just use the code like a black box that does the job for you.

```
Private Sub Form_Load()
    'Initialise the size of the hidden picture buffer
    'to the size of the form
    picHidden.Width = ScaleWidth
    picHidden.Height = ScaleHeight
    picHidden.AutoRedraw = True
```

```
'Set up the background picture with the size and text
picBackground.Width = ScaleWidth
picBackground.Height = ScaleHeight
picBackground.FontSize = 30
picBackground.Print
picBackground.Print
picBackground.Print ''Hello World''
picBackground.AutoRedraw = True
'Make sure the picture size for the sprite bitmaps
'is OK.
picSprite.AutoSize = True
picSpriteMask.AutoSize = True
'Set up initial sprite details
intXRhino = -100
intFrame = 0
SpriteCode.Sprite(0).intX = intXRhino
SpriteCode.Sprite(0).intY = Val(txtYpos.Text)
SpriteCode.Sprite(0).intWidth = 60
SpriteCode.Sprite(0).intHeight = 88
SpriteCode.Sprite(0).lngPicHDC = picSprite.hDC
SpriteCode.Sprite(0).lngMaskHDC = picSpriteMask.hDC
hsbFps.Value = 6
End Sub
```

Using a timer

Animation using Visual Basic is often achieved using a timer control. Timers are part of the standard toolbox that comes with Visual Basic. The main property of a timer is the value "interval", in milliseconds. Here is a little table of the number of occasions the timer is called per second for different interval values. The relationship between the calls per second and the interval is given by these equations:

Calls per second = 1000/Interval (Interval must not be 0)
Interval = 1000/Calls per second (Calls per second must not be 0)

Interval	Calls per second
1000	1
500	2
250	4
200	5
100	10
50	20

Nothing confuses computers quite so much as dividing by zero, so in this example I use a scroll bar which restricts the range of values for the 'fps' to between 1 and 50, therefore 'Calls per second' is never zero.

TIP

Data validation is an important issue. One of the chief benefits of object-orientated programming is the ability to validate all data that is sent to an object.

In the code for the Timer event (Public Sub Timer1_Timer ()), the first call is to a special function that is included in the special module SpriteCode which is saved on the CD as 'hello.bas'. This module has the functions necessary to move and draw animated sprites.

When used in the code, MoveSprite must be followed by five numbers which should have the following values:

```
Public Sub MoveSprite intIndex, intX, intY, intRow, intCol
```

The picture that includes the images that make up the animated sprite is divided into a grid. In the current example there is 1 row and 11 cols. In the above diagram of the moving rhino you will see that there are 11 pictures of the rhino in a line. By choosing the correct row and column the programmer has control over the picture displayed.

Parameters:

intIndex	This keeps track of which sprite we are dealing with
intX	The X co-ordinate of the top left corner of the sprite
intY	The Y co-ordinate of the top left corner of the sprite
intRow	The row from which the image is taken
intCol	The column from which the image is taken

In this code we are only using one sprite, the rhino, which has an index value 0. The position across the screen is given by the variable 'intXRhino'. The position down the screen is given by the value in the YPos edit box. 'Val(txtYpos.Text)' is a function that gets the value from that edit box. The row is always 0 since there is only one row in the animation picture. Finally, 'intFrame' is another variable that has the value for the 'Col' number in the picture. For the walk this needs to be a number between 0 and 7. After calling MoveSprite, the value for intXRhino is updated. This has the effect of moving the rhino across the screen. When you experimented with changing values for 'MoveX', you were increasing or decreasing the amount that intXRhino changed from one frame to the next. Having updated intXRhino, the code then checks whether the rhino has walked off the screen at the right. If it has, then it is repositioned at the left of the screen and the visible area is cleared of the words 'Hello World'. 'ScaleWidth' is the width of the current window, when intXRhino is bigger than this width, the rhino must have reached the right of the screen. If you are still confused by this idea, then try putting different values in the XPos and YPos edit boxes on the example; observing the effect will quickly cement this idea in your head. Using x and y positions to dictate where an image is placed on the viewer's screen is so important that I am probably overstressing it, but without fully understanding this idea you will quickly get stuck as you work through further examples.

Choosing the image to display

The next line increases the value of the displayed frame. You may be wondering about the function of 'Mod 8'; this limits the values of the variable 'intFrame' to between 0 and 7. So the line

```
intFrame = (intFrame + 1) Mod 8
```

has the following effect:

The pigeon hole that is called 'intFrame' may have the value 7 at the moment. The code tells the computer to add 1 to the current value, so now intFrame is 8. We now divide 8 by 8 and save the remainder, which in this case is 0. Table 1.1 gives the results of that line of code for different values of intFrame and, as you can see, the value is limited as required.

Table 1.1		
intFrame	intFrame+1	(intFrame + 1) Mod 8
0	1	1
1	2	2
2	3	3
3	4	4
4	5	5
5	6	6
6	7	7
7	8	0
8	9	1
9	10	2
10	11	3

Redrawing the user's display

Finally, the code tells the computer to show the result on the screen. You may wonder why the call to MoveSprite did not show itself on the screen. In this example it would have been all right to do just that, but in most games you will be moving more than one sprite. It is much better to move all the sprites in a picture control off screen, then, when they have all moved, show the new positions to the player. Techniques of minimising the areas on the screen that need to be redrawn will be introduced later in the book, although this presentation of the sprite functions acts as a very early introduction. UpdateScreen draws all the changes to the viewer's screen that are necessary.

```
Private Sub Timer1_Timer()
  'Move the rhino sprite
  SpriteCode.MoveSprite 0, intXRhino, Val(txtypos.Text), 0,
intFrame
  intXRhino = intXRhino + Val(txtmovex.Text)
  'If off screen right reposition at the left
  If intXRhino > ScaleWidth + 40 Then
    Cls
    intXRhino = -50
  End If
  'Cycle through the 8 animation frames
  intFrame = (intFrame + 1) Mod 8
  'Send the changes to the desktop screen
  SpriteCode.UpdateScreen
End Sub
```

Review

That covers the Visual Basic example quite fully, except to encourage you to play with the values in the Form_Load sub-routine that are given to SpriteCode.Sprite(0).iWidth and SpriteCode.Sprite(0).iHeight. These determine the width and height of the animation image. If they have different values from those in the code, then random bits of the animation images are displayed. We will return to these ideas later but it is useful to realise that you are simply displaying a small section of the animation frame shown above, and the value held in intWidth and intHeight determines whether this relates sensibly to the animation picture or whether the result is nonsense.

If you are new to any kind of programming, then lots of the ideas in this chapter will seem strange and unfamiliar. This is understandable; the idea is to give you a short and rapid introduction. The road from here will use many of the same techniques with many more examples and explanations. Below is a short quiz and a summary of what I hope you will have learnt by this stage. If any of the information in the summary is confusing, then I would suggest reviewing the chapter, before continuing.

QUIZ

1. How do you position a sprite on the screen?
Answer: By setting the X position and the Y position of the top left corner of the sprite.

2. Can I use a variable to store information that is important to the program?
Answer: Yes.

3. What is the Windows API?
Answer: A set of functions that you can use with Visual Basic and other programming languages to extend their functionality.

4. What is the result of (20 Mod 6)?
Answer: 2. Mod gives the remainder after integer division.
*20/6 = 3, 6 * 3 = 18, 20 − 18 = 2.*

Summary

- Programming involves unambiguous written instructions. In game programming these instructions often simply control the on screen displays of the computer.
- Variables store important values that the program uses regularly.
- The screen is built up of pixels
- All pixels have a position across the screen – the x position and a position down the screen – the y position
- A sprite is a moving image on your computer screen.

CHAPTER 2

What is a sprite? – Learning about data structures

Computer programming is about the manipulation of data structures, which is probably as clear as mud. But when you read that again after studying this chapter, you will say, 'Give me a data structure. I want to do some manipulating!'

What is a variable?

You probably know by now that computers are basically stupid. They are as clever as an amoeba. To get them to do as you wish you will need to do rather more than just say, 'I want a spaceship whizzing along that I can steer around meteorites and boulders'. The first step is to understand the concept of a variable. When your program is running you want places to store important information: the score; how many lives you have left; your position on the screen. To do this you tell the program that you want to allocate some space for this information and you give it a name that you will be able to use to update the information stored or simply to find out what is currently stored there.

NOTE

If you are very new to Visual Basic then I recommend spending a happy half hour with Appendix A to familiarise yourself with the event-orientated nature of this style of programming and simply to give you an awareness of where to find the various subroutines and functions that we will be using along the way.

Creating a simple game

Suppose that you want to create a kids' arithmetic program. You want to be able to allow the kids to view two numbers that they will need to add, subtract, multiply or divide. We can call the first number 'num1' and the second 'num2'. In the program we would put

```
Dim num1 As Integer, num2 As Integer
```

This tells the program to create space for two integer numbers. An integer on Visual Basic 4.0 can contain any number between $-32,768$ and $32,767$. Why does this range not run from $-30,000$ to $30,000$? This is a good question, and the reason is partly attributed to how computers work and partly attributed to history.

NOTE

The 'How do they work?' sections contain more in-depth detail than is strictly necessary. If you just want to get started, then by all means omit them. But, if you read all the text then review them, you just might find them useful.

HOW DO THEY WORK? – 2:

Binary computers

When you break it right down, computer data can either be 1 or 0. I told you that computers are not clever. Now here is the best part: if you add $1 + 1$, what do you get ? No, you don't get 2, you get 0. That is because a single bit of computer information can only be 1 or 0. If it is 1 already, then adding 1 simply changes that bit to 0. In electronic component terms a bit is a flip-flop gate. The analogy is that the light is either on or off; it is never part on or part off. So a 1 bit computer would not be very useful to anyone.

'Have you finished that spreadsheet yet?'
'Yes the answer is 1 again!'

Now the history lesson: early computer builders decided that counting up to 1 was not very useful so they put 4 of these bits together in such a way that when bit 1 changed from 1 to 0, it added one to bit 2. Bit 2 was similarly connected to bit 3 and so on. So the consequence of adding 1 repeatedly, created a sequence of 1 and 0 as follows:

Bit	4 3 2 1	Result of adding 1
	0 0 0 0	...
	0 0 0 1	Bit 1 changes to 1
	0 0 1 0	Bit 1 changes to 0 causing bit 2 to change to 1
	0 0 1 1	Bit 1 changes to 1
	0 1 0 0	Bit 1 changes to 0 causing bit 2 to change to 0 causing Bit 3 to change to 1
	0 1 0 1	etc.

To keep track of the values, the 0 and 1 data is given weights. In bit 1 a 1 is worth 1; in bit 2 a 1 is worth 2; in bit 3 a 1 is worth 4; and in bit 4 a 1 is worth 8. So the data 1010 is $(1 \times 8) + (0 \times 4) + (1 \times 2) + (0 \times 1) = 10$. That is the binary number system and that is how all digital computers operate.

Soon computers started using 8 bits of data, which gave a maximum value of 255. That is,

$$128 + 64 + 32 + 16 + 8 + 4 + 2 + 1 = 255.$$

Another way of describing it is:

$$2^7 + 2^6 + 2^5 + 2^4 + 2^3 + 2^2 + 2^1 + 2^0.$$

(2^4 is simply a short way of saying $2 \times 2 \times 2 \times 2$, 2 multiplied by itself 4 times.)

Sorry about the maths, but there is really very little more maths to have to do. Do not feel that computer programming is full of mathematics; it really isn't. So how is a negative number described? Most often, when using an integer value in computer code, a negative value has the highest bit set to 1. So if it was an 8-bit computer the range of values would be between -128 and 127, that is $-(2^\wedge 7)$ to $(2^\wedge 7) - 1$. A 16-bit value can take the range $-(2^\wedge 15)$ to $(2^\wedge 15) - 1$, and that is $-32,768$ to $32,767$. That, therefore, is where the range of values of a Visual Basic integer datatype stem from.

Just to complete the terminology, 8 bits make a byte and 2 bytes make a word. So, hopefully, now you know why the values are so strange. As an exercise, what is the range for a 32-bit signed integer?

Answer: $-(2^\wedge 31)$ to $(2^\wedge 31) - 1$, $-2,147,483,648$ to $2,147,483,647$.

Example: Ex02A

Now may be a good time to run the program example for this chapter. On the CD you will find a folder called 'Chap02'. Look in the folder and open the 'Ex02A.vbp' project file. This project contains two files, 'Ex02A.frm' and 'Sprites.bas'.

NOTE

The examples use files that must be transferred to your hard drive using the set-up program. Your computer must be set to 256 colours.

The 'Sprites.bas' file is used in every project in Part 1 of this book. It simply contains the declarations for a dynamic link library that the set-up program placed in your system folder. If you have no idea what a dynamic link library is, then fear not, the journey has just begun.

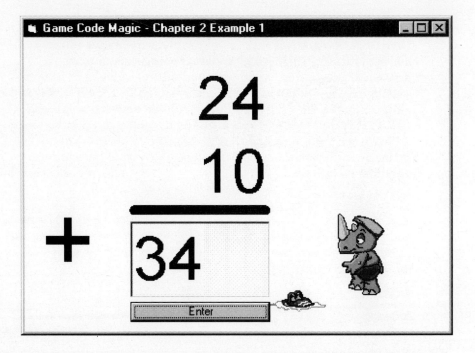

In this simple example program you are presented with a screen that includes two numbers and a box for entering the answer. The arithmetic operation is shown as '+' at the left. Enter a value, then press the 'Enter' button. If you were correct then the rhino from Chapter 1 came in from the right, jumped up and walked out again. When the rhino exits the numbers are replaced by new numbers and you can try again. If you got the answer wrong, then the crocodile bites the rhino's bottom and he turns round looking rather concerned; the answer you gave is replaced by the correct answer and the rhino walks off again. The other three arithmetic operations are included, simply click on the '+' to see it change to a '−', a '×' and a '/' symbol. If you have been paying close attention you will have tried the program with a division, and although you entered the correct number the crocodile still bit the rhino. Why? Is it a bad piece of programming? Well, no. It is an example of the difference between integer values and numbers with a decimal point, which are called *floating-point numbers* in computer terminology. Why not use floating point values for all your number variables? The answer is that there is a speed advantage using integers, and as you are often simply using a variable to count up or down, an integer gives all the information you will need.

Using floating-point numbers

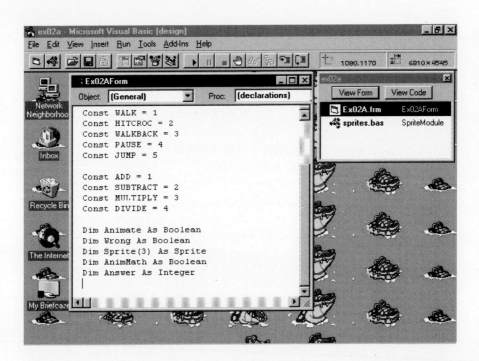

Now let's try to see how we can fix this problem. Here is a listing of the '(General) – (declarations)' section of the Ex02A.frm file. To get to it make sure that the project explorer window is in view. Use 'View|Project explorer' from the menu if it is not visible. Highlight 'Ex02A.frm Ex02AForm' and click the 'View Code' icon. The screen should look similar to the screen grab shown above. If you are not looking at the '(General) – (declarations)' section then click the arrow at the right of the object box and a list of objects will be shown. Select '(General)' and in the Proc box click the arrow and select '(declarations)'. The code will be as listed below:

```
Option Explicit

Const RHINO = 0
Const CROC = 1
Const MATH = 2

Const WALK = 1
Const HITCROC = 2
```

```
Const WALKBACK = 3
Const PAUSE = 4
Const JUMP = 5

Const ADD = 1
Const SUBTRACT = 2
Const MULTIPLY = 3
Const DIVIDE = 4

Dim Animate As Boolean
Dim Wrong As Boolean
Dim Sprite(3) As Sprite
Dim AnimMath As Boolean
Dim Answer As Integer
```

The problem is in choosing an integer value for Answer. Change 'Integer' to 'Single' and run the program again. The division now works, but the answer can sometimes be too long for the text box. The best way to fix this for a kids' program is to avoid divisions that do not have integer solutions. Using code to make decisions is covered in Chapter 4 where, in addition, we show how to validate data, ensuring that the numeric values that are offered are more suited to the program. At this stage do not worry about all the rest of the code which is operating the movement of the cartoon characters. The techniques will be fully covered in later chapters.

Using constants

You will have noticed, in the listing above, the use of the word 'Const'. This is used to declare a constant. So just as you can create space for a variable you can also create space for a value that does not vary. It is good coding practice to use constants for those parts of your program in which you may use an actual number rather than a variable.

There are two main benefits to giving a number a name and a value in the declarations section, then using the name in the rest of your code. First, the code becomes easier to understand and, second, it is easier to alter. Suppose you have decided that the maximum number of sprites that you are going to use is 6. Through your code you use the number 6 when looping through procedures that check on collisions and movement. If you then decide that you need another two more sprites, you will need to search for each instance that you have used the number 6 to refer to the maximum number of sprites. If to begin with you had used a constant, you could simply make this small alteration:

```
. . .
Const MAX_NUM_SPRITES = 8 'Change the number
. . .
```

Code that is easy to change is good code. It is a standard coding convention that constants use uppercase with an underscore character between words. Remember, there are no spaces between words. For a short discussion of standard coding conventions see Appendix B.

Adding a score box to the example

First, add a label box in the top right corner with the following properties. If you are unsure how to add controls then a quick tour of Appendix A will help out.

Table 2.1 Label 1 properties

Property	Value	Comment
Alignment	2	Centred
BackColor	&H000008	Black
Font	Arial	
charset	0	
weight	400	Normal
size	27.75	
underline	0	False
italic	0	False
strikethrough	0	False
ForeColor	&H0000FF00&	Green
Height	855	Sizes in Twips
Left	4080	Sizes in Twips
Top	360	Sizes in Twips
Width	2415	Sizes in Twips

In the project explorer window, highlight 'Ex02A.frm Ex02AForm' and click the 'View Code' icon. Add the code between the markers.

```
. . .
Dim Animate As Boolean
Dim Wrong As Boolean
Dim Sprite(3) As Sprite
Dim AnimMath As Boolean
Dim Answer As Single
'> > > > > > > > > > > > > > > > > > > > > > > > > > > > > >
'          ADD HERE
'> > > > > > > > > > > > > > > > > > > > > > > > > > > > > >
Dim Score as integer
'> > > > > > > > > > > > > > > > > > > > > > > > > > > > > >
'          END ADD
'> > > > > > > > > > > > > > > > > > > > > > > > > > > > > >

Private Sub cmdEnter_Click()
. . .
  If Val(txtAnswer.Text) = Answer Then
    Wrong = False
'> > > > > > > > > > > > > > > > > > > > > > > > > > > > > >
'          ADD HERE
'> > > > > > > > > > > > > > > > > > > > > > > > > > > > > >
    Score = Score + 1
    Label1.Caption = Str(Score)
'> > > > > > > > > > > > > > > > > > > > > > > > > > > > > >
'          END ADD
'> > > > > > > > > > > > > > > > > > > > > > > > > > > > > >
  Else
    Wrong = True
  End If
End Sub
```

Now when you run the program the value of Score is increased if the answer is correct – that is, if it is not Wrong, which brings us to another type of variable. During the last century a fascinating gentleman called George Boole (1815–1864) spent much of his life considering, and in many ways inventing, a logical language. The ideas he pioneered are much used in computer programming. The structured logic that he created is called Boolean logic and in Visual Basic there is a variable type called a Boolean. This can be only be either True or False. It is used in the code above to pass information to another part of the program.

NOTE

George Boole's book **The Laws of Thought,** *published in 1854 by Macmillan and Co., established the whole theory of Boolean Logic which we will meet often throughout this book.*

'Wrong' is a Boolean variable which is declared in the '(General) – (declarations)' section of the code. So now we have Integers, Singles (floating-point numbers) and Booleans. To complement the Single type is a Double type and to complement the Integer type which in some computer languages is called a short, is a Long. If you put 8 bits of information together you have a byte. In Visual Basic a byte is unsigned, that is, it cannot be a negative number.

Table 2.2 presents a list of the numeric and logic types in Visual Basic.

Table 2.2 Numeric and logic types in Visual Basic		
Type	**Storage size**	**Range of possible values**
Byte	1 byte	0 to 255
Boolean	2 bytes	True or False.
Integer	2 bytes	−32,768 to 32,767.
Long (long integer)	4 bytes	−2,147,483,648 to 2,147,483,647.
Single (floating-point)	4 bytes	Positive and negative numbers – accuracy is not critical
Double (floating-point)	8 bytes	Positive and negative numbers – accuracy is critical
Variant (with numbers)	16 bytes	Any numeric value up to the range of a Double.

Just to complete the set, there is a datatype that comes with Visual Basic called a Variant. If you do not state the type of variable you require, it is created as a Variant. Notice that the Variant type takes up 8 times the space of an integer. Computers with lots of memory can cope, but the speed at which the calculations are done within your computer are also affected. When you write animation programs you want speed, so keep the data type as small as possible and, if possible, avoid floating point.

How does the computer manipulate text?

Now we know that a computer is basically a machine that can count. So how does it store text and pictures and sounds and video? Hold on, one thing at a time. Let's start with text. Long ago a committee tried to determine how a terminal computer could store text information. They decided on a code. Now you and I would give 'a' the value of 1 and 'b' the value of 2, etc. But that is not what they did. They gave 'a' the value 97! Thankfully you will hardly ever have to think about

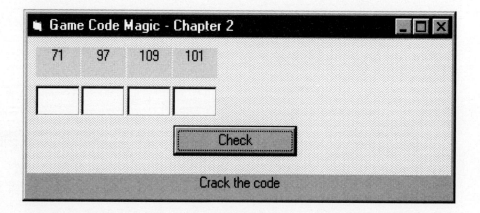

what number represents a letter because Visual Basic does all the thinking for you, but to help get the idea of how a letter is stored in memory as a number, try the little program 'Ex02C'. Open the project file as usual and run the program. A set of text boxes has numbers above. Look in Appendix F for the ASCII codes, look at the number and the box below it and enter the letter which has that ASCII code. If you get them right the status bar will say 'Well done' and repeat the word. If you get them wrong it will say 'No – the word is' and give the correct word. You tell Visual Basic that the variable you are considering is not a number but text, by declaring it as a 'String' – that is, a string of characters. You can then compare two text variables to see if they are the same. There are many other operations that you can use with strings, but that will be considered later.

Creating arrays of variables

Often you will need to deal with sets of information. You may have 25 meteorites all plunging through space. You could create the variables for these as follows:

```
. . .
Dim m1XPos As Integer, m1YPos As Integer
Dim m2XPos As Integer, m2YPos As Integer
. . .
Dim m25XPos As Integer, m25YPos As Integer
```

But now to manipulate them you will need to handle each one
individually. If your program could deal with the meteorites as a set it
would be much more efficient. The answer is to use an array.

```
. . .
Dim mXPos(25) As Integer, mYPos(25) As Integer
. . .
```

Now you have a list of 25 variables for the X position of the meteorite
and 25 variables for the Y position. To access each one you use:

```
. . .
mXPos(1) = 22
mYPos(10) = 132
. . .
```

The numbers 1 and 10 can be any value in the range of your array, so
in this example, it could be a number up to 25. But even better, the
value in the brackets could be another variable.

```
Dim i As Integer

i = 6
mXPos(i) = 22
mYPos(i) = 132
i = 12
mXPos(i) = 312
mYPos(i) = 290


. . .
```

Now when you are able to use the commands that control the looping
of your program you will be able to deal with all the meteorites from
the same code loop. In this example you have used two arrays, one for
the X positions and one for the Y positions. It would be nice to be able
to keep these together since they both refer to the same object, a
meteorite. In the next section we will look at how you can combine
variables to create your own datatypes.

Creating your own datatypes

Now you know the main ways in which Visual Basic can store variables. Sometimes it is useful to combine the variables into a unit. In most of the examples in this book we are using a module in the code called 'Sprites.bas'. If you open 'Ex02B.vbp' you will see it in the project explorer window. Highlight it and click the 'View Code' icon.

There is only a '(General) – (declarations)' section. Ignore all the 'declare' statements, as these will be described fully later. The code is as follows:

```
. . .
Type Sprite
    X As Integer
    Y As Integer
    MoveX As Integer
    MoveY As Integer
    Frame As Integer
    Action As Integer
    Index As Integer
    Count As Integer
End Type
```

The Visual Basic syntax for declaring your own datatype is to start with the word 'Type' then the name you will use, in this case 'Sprite', followed by the various parts that will be included, and finally 'End Type'. This has not created a sprite datatype, it has simply told the computer what one will be when you do decide to use one. To declare a sprite you put:

```
. . .
Dim MySprite As Sprite
```

The word 'MySprite' can be any descriptive word. Just as you were able to create an integer, now you can create a sprite. The computer would allocate 16 bytes of memory space for your sprite; that is, two bytes for each of the eight integers it contains. To access the individual bits you use the name that you used for your descriptive word, a full stop, then the name of the part of the sprite you want to access.

```
. . .
Dim i As Integer

MySprite.X = 100 'This sets the X value of the sprite to 100.
i = MySprite.Action 'This gets the value of the sprite's Action
   'integer and puts it in the variable that was created called i.
```

How the user defined datatype sprite is used

The main code that manipulates the sprites is in the timer procedure.

```
Private Sub Timer1_Timer()
  Dim i As Integer

  For i = 0 To 2
    If i = RHINO And Animate Then
      Select Case Sprite(i).Action
      Case WALK:
        Sprite(i).X = Sprite(i).X + Sprite(i).MoveX
        Sprite(i).Frame = (Sprite(i).Frame + 1) Mod 8
        If Sprite(i).X < 300 Then
          Sprite(i).MoveX = 0
          Sprite(i).Frame = 21
          If Wrong Then
            Sprite(i).Action = HITCROC
          Else
            Sprite(i).Frame = 28
            Sprite(i).Action = JUMP
            Sprite(i).MoveY = −13
          End If
        End If
      Case PAUSE:
        Sprite(i).Count = Sprite(i).Count − 1
        If Sprite(i).Count = 0 Then
          Sprite(i).Action = WALKBACK
          Sprite(i).Frame = 8
          Sprite(i).MoveX = 5
        End If
      Case WALK_BACK:
        Sprite(i).X = Sprite(i).X + Sprite(i).MoveX
        Sprite(i).Frame = ((Sprite(i).Frame + 1) Mod 8) + 8
        If Sprite(i).X > 450 Then
          'Start again
```

```
        Animate = False
        NewNumbers
        Sprite(i).Y = 180
        Sprite(i).MoveX = -5
        Sprite(i).Frame = 0
        Sprite(i).Action = WALK
      End If
    Case HITCROC:
      If Sprite(i).Frame < 24 Then
        Sprite(i).Frame = Sprite(i).Frame + 1
      End If
    Case JUMP:
      If Sprite(i).Frame < 31 Then
        Sprite(i).Frame = Sprite(i).Frame + 1
        Sprite(i).Count = 10
      ElseIf Sprite(i).Count Then
        Sprite(i).Count = Sprite(i).Count - 1
        Sprite(i).Y = Sprite(i).Y + Sprite(i).MoveY
        Sprite(i).MoveY = Sprite(i).MoveY + 3
      Else
        Sprite(i).Action = WALKBACK
        Sprite(i).MoveX = 5
      End If
    End Select
  End If
  If i = CROC And Sprite(RHINO).Action = HITCROC Then
    Sprite(i).Frame = Sprite(i).Frame + 1
    If Sprite(i).Frame = 5 Then
      Sprite(RHINO).Count = 30
      txtAnswer.Text = Str(Answer)
      Sprite(RHINO).Action = PAUSE
      Sprite(i).Frame = 0
    End If
  End If
  If i = MATH And AnimMath Then
    Sprite(i).Frame = Sprite(i).Frame + 1
    If (Sprite(i).Frame + 1) Mod 8 = 0 Then
      Sprite(i).Frame = (Sprite(i).Frame + 1) Mod 32
      AnimMath = False
      NewNumbers
    End If
  End If
```

```
    MoveSprite Sprite(i).Index, Sprite(i).X, Sprite(i).Y,
Sprite(i).Frame
  Next
  UpdateStage
End Sub
```

OK, don't panic, I know that there are lots of commands in the listing that you are not yet familiar with. For now we will look at a small section

```
. . .
    Sprite(i).Y = 180
    Sprite(i).MoveX = −5
    Sprite(i).Frame = 0
    Sprite(i).Action = WALK
. . .
```

You are probably confused by the use of Sprite(i). If you look again at the '(General) – (declarations)' section of 'Ex02B.frm' then you will see the following:

```
. . .
Dim Sprite(3) As Sprite
. . .
```

Just as you can create arrays of integers and strings, you can also create arrays of your very own datatypes. In this declarations section we create three sprites in an array of sprites. The rest of the small section of code just shows how to alter the values of sections of the user datatype for an array. The actions are all declared in the declarations section as numbers. So the code

```
. . .
    Sprite(i).Action = WALK
. . .
```

sets the value of Sprite(i).Action to 1, not to a string of text 'WALK'.

When to decide on the size of your arrays

Sometimes it is possible to be sure of the size of an array throughout the program. In this case you can use the syntax we have already used. In other programs you may only know how big an array will be when the program is running. If this is the case then in the declarations section you do not give a size to the array. The example 'Ex02D.Vbp' is a quick example of resizing arrays at run time using the Visual Basic statement 'ReDim'. If you made the mistake of giving a size to your array in the declarations section of your code, then you will get an error message. Similarly, if you start using the array before you give it a size with 'ReDim' then you will get an error because Visual Basic has not created any space for the data.

```
. . .
    Dim j As Integer
    j = Int(Rnd() * 30)
    ReDim Numbers(j)
. . .
```

In the code sample above taken from 'Ex02D.frm' an array of integers was declared but not dimensioned in the '(General) – (declarations)' section of the code. The second line generates a random number up to 29 and the array is recreated with the new randomly generated size.

Are you ready to do some data manipulation?

This chapter began with 'Computer programming is about the manipulation of data structures'. that is, creating space for data and manipulating the contents. Hopefully that makes more sense now than it did at the beginning. Here is a small quiz to test your knowledge.

NOTE

To simplifiy the listings in this chapter I chose not to use the code conventions in Appendix B. However, all subsequent chapters will use the code conventions, which means that an integer will have 'int' before the variable name. Now would be a good time to look at Appendix B.

QUIZ

1. a, b and c are integers. a = 11, b = 5, c = a/b. Does c = 5, c = 5.5 or c = 6

Answer: c = 5. Integers take the value of a calculation that does not include a decimal point.

2. In the declarations section of your code is the following:
      Const FALL = 12
Can you do the following later in the code: FALL = 14?
Answer: No. Once created a constant must stay the same throughout the program.

3. In the declarations section of your code is the following:
      Dim Meteorite(10) As Sprite
Assuming that you have the module 'Sprite.bas' as part of the project, how do you set the sixth meteorite to a position on screen of (200, 100)?
Answer: Meteorite(6).X = 200   Meteorite(6).Y = 100

4. If the declarations section has the code 'Dim XPosition(12) As Integer', can you use the code 'ReDim XPosition(20)' later in the program?
Answer: No. if you want to resize the array at run time you should have used 'Dim XPosition() As Integer', in the declarations section. There is no value for the number of members in the array.

Summary

In this chapter you discovered:

- Datatypes, Byte, Integer, Long, Single, Double, Variant, String.
- The use of constants in your code.
- How to create constants using the Visual Basic statement Dim.
- How to create sets of variables of a particular type called arrays.
- How to resize your arrays as the program is running.
- How to create your own data types using the statement 'Type ... End Type'.
- How to manipulate the contents of a user defined data type.

CHAPTER 3

At your command – Introducing some syntax

Having read the previous chapter, you now know how to create a space in memory for a variable, how to alter the contents of that variable and how to create sets of variables called arrays. Now we must look at the way your program flows. Often you will need the computer to execute a section of code repeatedly. In this chapter we look at how you can write programs that can loop.

The various options

Sometimes you will know how many times you need to loop. If this is the case then you can use

```
Private Sub Form_Load()
    Dim intIndex As Integer

    For intIndex = 1 To 10
        Debug.Print intIndex
    Next End Sub
```

This little example starts by creating an integer type variable which the programmer has called 'intIndex'.

NOTE

Variables can have any name the programmer thinks is useful. There would be no problem calling the integer in the example 'Sophie', if that was what the programmer required. Programming style is in many ways the choice of the programmer, and in Appendix B you can find out what are regarded as 'standard' conventions for writing code. These conventions are simply to help you, and other people who read your code, to understand what the code is doing. They do not affect the way in which your code operates. However, it is a sad reality that no one who writes code gets everything right first time; correcting the errors, or debugging, forms a large part of writing code. In this respect variables with understandable names are easier to identify.

This variable is used in a 'For ... Next' loop. This means that the code between the line 'For intIndex = 1 To 10' and 'Next' is repeated. The first time the code is executed with 'intIndex' having the value 1; the second time 'intIndex' takes the value 2, the third time 3 and so on. Everytime it loops back the variable 'intIndex' is increased by 1. In this example the debug object is used and it will contain a list of the numbers from 1 to 10.

TIP

The debug object is very useful for seeing what your code is doing. Use it to print values of variables in your program at key moments in the execution of the code.

This is a very common way of using a 'For ... Next' loop. But, there is more complexity available if required. See if you can work out what the next short code does.

```
Private Sub Form_Load()
   Dim intIndex As Integer

   For intIndex = 1 To 10 Step 2
      Debug.Print intIndex
   Next End Sub
```

Instead of the list of numbers in the debug window being 1, 2, 3, 4, 5, 6, 7, 8, 9, 10, the list is 1, 3, 5, 7, 9 because 2 is added to index each time the code loops.

```
Private Sub Form_Load()
   Dim sngIndex As Single

   For sngIndex = −5 To 5 Step 0.7
      Debug.Print sngIndex
   Next
   Debug.Print

End Sub
```

This example is to show that the variable in the control loop does not have to be an integer. If you make it a Single (a decimal number or floating point number) then the variable can take on non-integer values. This code section gives the following result in the debug window:

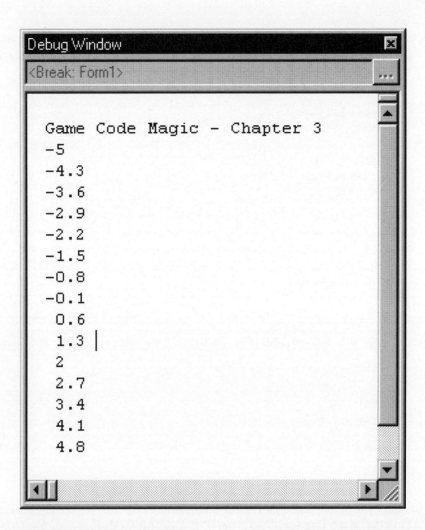

```
Debug Window                                    ⊠

<Break: Form1>                              ...

    Game Code Magic - Chapter 3
    -5
    -4.3
    -3.6
    -2.9
    -2.2
    -1.5
    -0.8
    -0.1
     0.6
     1.3  |
     2
     2.7
     3.4
     4.1
     4.8
```

If you worked it out, then give yourself a pat on the back.

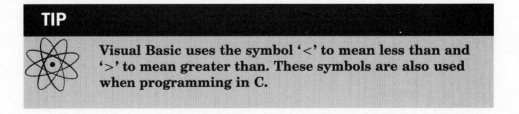

TIP

Visual Basic uses the symbol '<' to mean less than and
'>' to mean greater than. These symbols are also used
when programming in C.

Now see if you can predict what the following code would put in the
debug window:

```
Private Sub Form_Load()
  Dim sngIndex As Single

  For sngIndex = 1 To 10 Step 0.6
    Debug.Print sngIndex
    If sngIndex > 5 Then Exit For
  Next End Sub
```

Did you get 1, 1.6, 2.2, 2.8, 3.4, 4, 4.6, 5.2 ? Yes, 'Exit For' is a useful way of getting out of a loop if a certain condition is realised. So now you have a useful tool for creating loops. The initial number and the final number in the loop can themselves be variables, just like this:

```
Private Sub Form_Load()
  Dim intIndex As Integer, intFirst As Integer, intLast As Integer

  For intIndex = intFirst To intLast
    Debug.Print intIndex
  Next
  Debug.Print
End Sub
```

Here a variable is used to start and end the loop.

What would the debug window show?

When the variables 'intFirst' and 'intLast' are created by Visual Basic they are given the initial value 0. Consequently 'intFirst' and 'intLast' are both equal to zero in the above code. For this reason the loop is executed once with variable 'intIndex' being assigned the value 0. The debug window simply shows 0.

It is good programming practice to assign values to variables as near to their use in code as possible. In this example the variables 'intFirst' and 'intLast' are assigned values just prior to their use in the control loop.

```
Private Sub Form_Load()
  Dim intIndex As Integer, intFirst As Integer, intLast As Integer

  intFirst = 5
  intLast = 10

  For intIndex = intFirst To intLast
    Debug.Print intIndex
  Next
  Debug.Print
End Sub
```

This time the debug window would show 5, 6, 7, 8, 9, 10.

The increment does not have to be an integer value; nor does the increment have to be positive.

```
Private Sub Form_Load()
  Dim sngIndex As Single, sngFirst As Single, sngLast As Single,
  sngDelta as Single

  sngFirst = 10
  sngLast = 3
  sngDelta = −0.6

  For sngIndex = sngFirst To sngLast Step sngDelta
    Debug.Print sngIndex
  Next
  Debug.Print
End Sub
```

Here we use variables for all three parts of a 'For ... Next' construction. The result in the debug window will be 10, 9.4, 8.8, 8.2, 7.6, 7, 6.4, 5.8, 5.2, 4.6, 4, 3.4. Given such a useful construction tool, why would you want any alternative? Sometimes it is important to be able to alter the control variable during the control loop in an uneven way. If you are using a 'For ... Next' construction, it is usually bad programming practice to manipulate the control variable during the loop. For example, in

```
For intIndex = 1 To 20
    Debug.Print intIndex
    intIndex = intIndex * 2
Next
```

'intIndex' is incremented by the control loop and is altered during the loop. This technique is discouraged. In all the 'For ... Next' instructions the index parameter was increased or decreased by the same amount each time the code looped.

Here is an alternative example:

```
Private Sub Form_Load()
  Dim intIndex As Integer

  intIndex = 2
  Do While (intIndex < 200)
    intIndex = intIndex * intIndex
    Debug.Print intIndex
  Loop
End Sub
```

In this loop the 'Do While ... Loop' construction is used because 'intIndex' is repeatedly multiplied by itself. The loop is tested at the beginning to see if 'intIndex' is less than 200.

TIP

It is a frequent requirement of code to check if one value is bigger or smaller than another. For Visual Basic, this would be written as:
a<b   True if a is less than b.
a>b   True if a is greater than b.

As long as 'intIndex' is less than 200 the loop repeats.

An alternative way to write this code puts the test at the end of the loop.

```
Private Sub Form_Load()
  Dim intIndex As Integer

  intIndex = 2
  Do
    intIndex = intIndex * intIndex
    Debug.Print intIndex
  Loop While (intIndex < 200)
End Sub
```

You may think that both versions do the same thing, and in this instance they do.

At some point you may want a section of code to execute at least once regardless of the check condition, and that is the time to put the test at the end of the loop.

The last of the loop constructions is similar to 'Do While ... Loop'. This time the 'While' is replaced by 'Until'.

```
Private Sub Form_Load()
  Dim index As Integer

  index = 2
  Do
    index = index * index
    Debug.Print index
  Loop Until (index > 200)
End Sub
```

In the 'While' version you are checking that a test is still true. In the 'Until' version you are checking that a test is still false.

Another way to perform loops is by the use of 'While ... Wend', but as this offers no more than can be done with 'Do While ... Loop' and you are advised not to use it.

Example Ex03A

We shall now look at some proper examples. In this first example
'Ex03A.vbp', multiple sprites are generated at run time, depending on
the value in a text box control.

If you run the program you will see some buckets walking along on the
screen. You can alter the number of buckets by entering a value
between 1 and 20 in the text box and pressing the 'Enter' button. The
screen is regularly redrawn to create the animation. When it is
redrawn the following code is executed. Again do not worry that some
of the code uses instructions that will be strange to you. Concentrate
on the 'For ... Next' loop. Here the loop goes through each bucket in
turn, updating the frame displayed and the position of the sprite.
When all the buckets have been repositioned the screen is redrawn
using the 'UpdateStage' command.

NOTE

In this section of code the two commands 'MoveSprite' and 'UpdateStage' are not part of Visual Basic, they are calls to a dynamic link library 'Sprites.dll'. This should be in your Windows System folder, or the code will fail. Check the introduction for how to make sure the code examples work on your machine. The details of all the subroutines and functions in the dynamic link library are given in Appendix D.

```vb
Private Sub Timer1_Timer()
  Dim i As Integer

  If intNumBuckets = 0 Then Exit Sub
  For i = 0 To intNumBuckets - 1
    Bucket(i).X = Bucket(i).X + Bucket(i).MoveX
    If Bucket(i).X > 450 Then
      Bucket(i).MoveX = -5
      Bucket(i).Frame = 0
      Bucket(i).Action = 64
    End If
    If Bucket(i).X < -50 Then
      Bucket(i).MoveX = 5
      Bucket(i).Frame = 0
      Bucket(i).Action = 0
    End If
    Bucket(i).Frame = (Bucket(i).Frame + 1) Mod 8 +
    Bucket(i).Action
    MoveSprite Bucket(i).Index, Bucket(i).X, Bucket(i).Y,
    Bucket(i).Frame
  Next
  UpdateStage
End Sub
```

NOTE

If you are very hot on code conventions then you will notice that I have not used data type prefixes for the members of the user data type Sprite. I feel that using prefixes for member variables makes the code more difficult to read. Here I broke with the convention to make the code easier to read.

Mandelbrot set generator

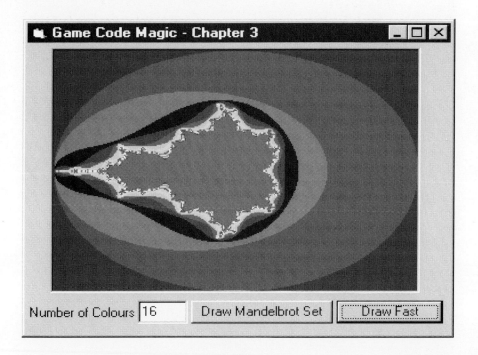

The other example program is 'Ex03B.vbp'. This is a Mandelbrot set generator; that is, one of those fractal things. It uses a 'Do While . . . Loop' to determine what colour to use for every pixel in a picture control. It is rather slow in Visual Basic because of the calculations it entails. I have included a 'Draw Fast' button which calls a command that is written in 'c'. You will find that it executes much more quickly. This is a short introduction to a later chapter in which we discuss how you can speed up sections of your program by linking to code written in another language. This does not mean that learning Visual Basic is a waste of time; on the contrary, much of the complexity of Windows programming is taken care of by the use of Visual Basic, but when you need to speed things up, you can. In that way you get the best of both worlds.

The Visual Basic code is

```
Private Sub cmdDraw_Click()
    Dim sngA As Single, sngB As Single, sngP As Single, sngQ As
    Single
```

```
  Dim sngPnew As Single, sngQnew As Single, sngAdelta As Single,
sngBdelta As Single                                                    ↵
  Dim intX As Integer, intY As Integer, intIteration As Integer
  Dim intXmid As Integer, intYmid As Integer
  Dim lngColour As Long, intNumColours As Integer

  intNumColours = Val(txtlngColours.Text)
  If intNumColours < = 0 Then intNumColours = 1
  If intNumColours > 255 Then intNumColours = 255

  picMandelBrot.ScaleMode = 3
  sngAdelta = 4 / picMandelBrot.ScaleWidth
  sngBdelta = 4 / picMandelBrot.ScaleHeight
  picMandelBrot.Scale (−2, −2)–(2, 2)
  picMandelBrot.Cls

  Screen.MousePointer = 11
  For sngA = −2 To 2 Step sngAdelta
    For sngB = −2 To 2 Step sngBdelta
      sngP = 0
      sngQ = 0
      intIteration = 0
      Do While (p * sngP + sngQ * sngQ < 4) and (intIteration <
intNumColours)                                                         ↵
        sngPnew = sngP * sngP - sngQ * sngQ + a
        sngQnew = 2 * sngP * sngQ + b
        sngP = sngPnew
        sngQ = sngQnew
        intIteration = intIteration + 1
      Loop
      lngColour = &H1000000 + intIteration
      picMandelBrot.PSet (a, b), lngColour
    Next
  Next
  Screen.MousePointer = 0
End Sub
```

Here you will find many points of detail that you have learned already.
The 'Dim' statements at the beginning of the procedure create lots of
different variables, then the number of colours is set using information
from the on-screen text box. (The way this is done will be explained
later.) The picture control that is used to receive all the drawing is set
up to suit the code. (The details of this will also be covered later.)
Finally, the mouse pointer is changed to an hour glass using
'Screen.MousePointer = 11'.

The MousePointer property

You can change the appearance of the mouse cursor to certain styles that are always available. These are shown in Table 3.1.

Table 3.1 Mouse Pointer properties		
Constant	**Value**	**Description**
ccDefault	0	(Default) Shape determined by the object
ccArrow	1	Arrow
ccCross	2	Cross (cross-hair pointer)
ccIbeam	3	I beam
ccIcon	4	Icon (small square within a square)
ccSize	5	Size (four-pointed arrow pointing north, south, east, and west)
ccSizeNESW	6	Size NE SW (double arrow pointing northeast and southwest)
ccSizeNS	7	Size N S (double arrow pointing north and south)
ccSizeNWSE	8	Size NW, SE
ccSizeEW	9	Size E W (double arrow pointing east and west)
ccUpArrow	10	Up arrow
ccHourglass	11	Hourglass (wait)
ccNoDrop	12	No Drop
ccArrowHourglass	13	Arrow and hourglass (only available in 32-bit Visual Basic)
ccArrowQuestion	14	Arrow and question mark (only available in 32-bit Visual Basic)
ccSizeAll	15	Size all (only available in 32-bit Visual Basic)
ccCustom	99	Custom icon specified by the MouseIcon property

At this stage the code is ready to draw the set using two 'For ... Next' loops for the positions down and across the screen and a 'Do While ... Loop' to determine the colour.

HOW DO THEY WORK? – 3:

An introduction to palettes

The libraries on the CD are designed to be used with a computer that is set up to have 256 colours. These 256 colours can be chosen from a palette of over 16 million colours.

Each Visual Basic program can have its own palette, which consists of a series of RGB values. An example of an RGB value is 128, 0, 0. Here the value for red is 128 which is half the maximum value of 255. So the colour shown would be a medium red, since the values for blue and green are 0. The colour also has an index value. The 256 colours can be chosen by using the index.

Your table of values would be something similar to:

Colour index	Red	Green	Blue
0	0	0	0
1	128	0	0
2	0	128	0
3	128	128	0
4	0	0	128
...			
254	255	255	0
255	255	255	255

Windows usually insists that the first and last 10 colours, termed 'static colours', have specific values.

Colours can be specified in three ways:

1 *RGB value*   Here you give a Long value which is split up into 4 bytes:

Byte	3	2	1	0
Value	0	Blue	Green	Red

(The value of over 16 million colours comes from all the different ways you can combine the colours: 256*256*256 = 16,777,216). If the colour does not exist in the palette it is created by *dithering* (dithering is a technique of combining different coloured pixels to help suggest a colour that is not available in the current palette) colours from the palette. (It actually only uses the static 20 colours, but more of that later.)

2 *Colour index*

Byte	3	2	1	0
Value	1	0	0	Index

Here you know that your palette contains 256 colours and you specify the colour by choosing the index for that colour.

3 *Solid RGB*

Byte	3	2	1	0
Value	2	Blue	Green	Red

A scan is made for the nearest colour in the palette to the RGB value. It is this that is used rather than a dithered version of the static colours. If your palette does not contain anything close then the result may be quite different from that expected.

Using palettes with Windows is a confusing and difficult subject. In Chapter 17 you will find a full explanation of how to deal with palettes in your programming. This short description is simply to help explain the strange code

```
colour = &H1000000 + intIteration
```

This is a method of telling Windows that the colour you want is an index to the colour, not an actual colour, and by this method you get a solid colour. Try removing &H1000000 from the line and see the effect. An alternative method of choosing colours is to use the Visual Basic RGB function, which is similar to using option 1 above. More often, however, you will want a colour from a palette you have set.

Setting the palette for a control can be quite difficult. The easy way to set the palette of the Visual Basic controls 'Form' and 'Picture Box' is to load a picture into the control at design time. The picture can be a small white bitmap; it is the palette the bitmap contains that justifies its use, not the picture. If this is all terribly confusing then you are in good company. Palettes are difficult to understand, but you will do well to learn about their use.

Never use an unconditional jump

Visual Basic includes a command that you should try not to use. 'Goto' is usually regarded as unnecessary. The traditional programming attitude is that you can always write your code without using it. The command allows your program to jump from one place to another, but it is always best to use another construction.

The next stage in our journey is learn how the computer can be instructed to make decisions, but first you should try this little quiz.

QUIZ

1. Here is a short section of code that will not work. Can you detect the error?

```
Dim intIndex As Integer

Do While (intIndex < 20)
    debug.print ''Hello''
Loop
```

Answer: The value of 'intIndex' is not altered in the loop, so 'index' will stay as 0. Since 0 is less than 20 the condition will always be true and the code will loop for ever.

2. What will be displayed in the debug window using this section of code?

```
Dim intIndex As Integer

For intIndex = 10 to −10
    debug.print intIndex
Next
```

Answer: Just '10', because on the second loop intIndex = 11 and 11 is greater than −10, so the loop terminates.

3. In the code for question 2, what is the instruction to list the values from 10 to −10?
Answer: Follow the −10 with 'Step −1'. Now index is decreased every time and the test is for index being less than −10, not greater than −10.

4. You want a loop to always execute at least once. Which of the constructions described in this chapter should you use?
Answer: 'Do ... Loop While ()'. The test should be at the end of the loop, ensuring that it will always execute at least once.

Summary

In this chapter you learnt about using loops in your code.

- 'For ... Next'. If you add 1 to your counter and you know how many loops.
- 'For ... Next Step'. If you add other than 1 to your counter.
- 'Do While ... Loop'. Test for true condition. Variable is altered non-linearly.
- 'Do ... Loop While'. Loop always executes once. Otherwise as above.
- 'Do Until ... Loop'. Test for false condition. Variable is altered non-linearly.
- 'Do ... Loop Until'. Loop always executes once. Otherwise as above.
- A short introduction to palettes was included.

CHAPTER 4

Making decisions – The choice is yours

So far we have considered how to create variables in your programs to store important information. We have covered how to create control loops to repeat sections of code. While looking at the 'Do While ... Loop' construction, we encountered conditional execution, i.e. code whose execution is dependent on a test. In this chapter we will look in detail at how you can write programs that make decisions.

True or false?

For Visual Basic the world is a simple place. A thing can be either true or false, with none of the hazy half truths that make up the world in which we live. In fact as far as Visual Basic is concerned, True is the value -1 and False is the value 0. Try to work out what the following little code section would place in the debug window:

```
Dim i As Integer

i = -1
If i Then Debug.Print ''It's True!''
i = 0
If i Then Debug.Print ''It's False!''
```

The construction 'If . . . Then' does precisely what you would expect. First it tests the expression that follows 'If'. Should this expression be True, then the code that follows 'Then' is executed, if the expression is found to be False, then the code is skipped. A gold star if you realised that the second text would not be printed. By making i=0 any code that is looking for the result of a decision will evaluate the result to 'False'. Confused? Try this next bit of code:

```
Dim i As Integer

i = 11000
If i Then Debug.Print ''It's True!''
i = 0
If i = 0 Then Debug.Print ''It's False!''
```

There's a slight twist here. Instead of setting i to −1 it is set to 11000, yet it still prints 'It's True!' because any value other than 0 is True. So why did I say above that True is −1? When Visual Basic sets a Boolean variable to True, it gives it the value −1, but to use expressions to make decisions you only need to take a non-zero value. When you are learning to write code you will probably want to test for a specific value, and a test should be done like this:

```
Dim i As Integer

i = 30
If i = 30 Then Debug.Print ''i is equal to 30''
If i > 20 Then Debug.Print ''i is greater than 20''
If i < 50 Then Debug.Print ''i is less than 50''
If i < > 20 Then Debug.Print ''i does not equal 20''
If i > = 30 Then Debug.Print ''i is greater than or equal to
30''
If i < = 30 Then Debug.Print ''i is less than or equal to 30''
```

Here all the options that you can use in your programs are covered. You can test for equivalence, less than or greater than, less than or equal to, greater than or equal to, or not equal to. With these simple test you can make a great number of decisions.

Combining decisions

Sometimes you need to perform multiple tests. When tests are combined you will make use of Boolean algebra. Whoops, that sounds like more maths to me! Boolean algebra is wonderfully simple: no complicated equations with funny looking symbols. Boolean algebra uses words like And, Or and Not, and is used as follows:

(test 1) And (test 2)   True if both test 1 and test 2 are true
(test 1) Or (test 2)   True if either test 1 or test 2 is true
Not (test 1)   True if test 1 is false

Now that's simple, isn't it? To help you understand it better, here are a few examples:

```
Dim intA As Integer, intB As Integer, intC As Integer

intA = 100
intB = 200
intC = 300

'Here the first test is False and the second test is True
'Using Or if either test is True then the combined result is True
If (intA > intB) Or (intB < intC) Then
    Debug.Print ''One or both of the tests are True''
Else
    Debug.Print ''Neither test is True''
End If
'The Debug window will display ''One or both of the tests are True''
'Since ( intA > intB ) is False and ( intB < intC ) is True
'False Or True = True

'Here using And, the combined tests are True only when both tests
are True
If ( intA > intB ) And ( intB < intC ) Then
    Debug.Print ''Both of the tests are True''
Else
    Debug.Print ''One or both of the tests are False''
End If
'The Debug window will display ''One or both of the tests are False'
'Since ( intA > intB ) is False and ( intB < intC ) is True
'False And True = False
```

```
'Using Not, the result of the test is reversed.
If Not ( intA > intB ) Then
    Debug.Print ''intA is less than intB''
Else
    Debug.Print ''intA is greater than intB''
End If
'The Debug window will display ''intA is less than intB''
'Since ( intA > intB ) is False
'Not False = True
```

Using logic decisions to ensure good data

Remember in Chapter 2 we looked at a kids' arithmetic program that created problems that sometimes required answers to 25 decimal places. Clearly that data was unsuitable for the users. If you run 'Ex04A.vbp' then you will see that this has been corrected. Most of the corrections are in the section of code shown below.

```
Sub NewNumbers()
    Dim intNum1 As Integer, intNum2 As Integer, i As Integer

    If Sprite(MATH).Frame = DIVIDE Then
      'Must be division operation
      i = Rnd() * 10 + 1 ' Generate a number between 1 and 10
      intNum2 = Rnd() * 10 + 1 'Generate a number between 1 and 10
      intNum1 = intNum2 * i
    Else
      intNum1 = Rnd() * 30 + 1 'Generate a number between 1 and 30
      If Sprite(MATH).Frame = MULTIPLY Then
        'Limit multiplication to 1 to 10
        intNum2 = Rnd() * 10 + 1 'Generate a number between 1 and 10
    Else
        intNum2 = Rnd() * 30 + 1 'Generate a number between 1 and 30
    End If
    If intNum1 < intNum2 Then
        'Avoid negative numbers by making sure intNum1 is bigger
        'than intNum2
        i = intNum1
        intNum1 = intNum2
        intNum2 = i
    End If
  End If
```

```
lblintNum1.Caption = Str(intNum1)
lblintNum2.Caption = Str(intNum2)
txtAnswer.Text = '' ''
If Loaded Then
   txtAnswer.SetFocus
End If

End Sub
```

First we look at the arithmetic operation by checking what Frame number the MATH sprite is on.

NOTE

Uppercase characters are used to represent Const values. These are set as the program is first loaded and cannot be changed while the program runs.

Remember that with this program you can click on the '+, −, ×, /' signs. Clicking on the sign changes it to the next in the list. This value is used to display the correct picture. Finding the operation that is currently being displayed is simply a matter of checking the frame the sprite is displaying. To make the code easier to read, these key pictures have been given Const values with recognisable names. This is a good programming convention and is highly recommended when writing your own code.

If the current operation is division then it is important that the result of the division is an integer. First an integer 'i' is given a random value between 1 and 10.

TIP

The Visual Basic function Rnd gives a value between 0 and 1. To get an integer value between certain values use this syntax:

Int(Rnd*(HighValue − Low Value + 1) + Low Value)

This multiplies the floating point value that is between 0 and 1 by the scale you need, then adds the lowest value to the result; the whole operation is finally converted to an integer value.

The variable 'intNum2' is then given a value between 1 and 10, and, finally, the two numbers are multiplied together to give the value for variable 'intNum1'.

'i × intNum2 = intNum1'

is another way of saying

'intNum1 / intNum2 = i'

which is what we need.

Another decision is made, later in the code, concerning the maths operation 'multiply'. Here the range for the variable is limited to 1 to 10 while, for addition and subtraction, the range goes up to 30.

Finally a test is made to check whether 'intNum1' is less than 'intNum2'. If so, then the order of the numbers is reversed: 'intNum1' becomes 'intNum2' and vice versa. The values of the variables 'intNum1' and 'intNum2' are put into the on-screen controls to enable the user to see them. The old answer is cleared away, and if the form is visible the focus is set to the 'txtAnswer' control.

What is focus?

When you use the keyboard with Windows, the results of your typing can be directed towards many different on-screen controls. Ensuring that the correct control receives the keyboard messages is part of the programmer's responsibility when writing programs for Windows. With Visual Basic it is easy to direct the keyboard towards a particular control using the method 'SetFocus'. This technique can be used with lots of Visual Basic's standard controls.

A more complicated example

Hopefully, the code in the above example was quite easy to follow. If you are new to programming then, firstly, well done for staying with it so far. You have learnt a great deal in these first few chapters and you are nearly in a position to start writing your own example programs using the techniques that have been described. Of course, there is much more to learn before you can write your own interactive animation programs, but many of the concepts build on the information you have already learnt.

Example Ex04B

Open the example 'Ex04B.vbp'. This program is a simple little game
where you try to knock a bucket off a wall. Run the program, click on
the ball at the bottom of the screen and stretch out the line while
continuing to press the left mouse key. You are directing the trajectory
of the ball. The longer the line, the further the ball will go. The line
needs to be below the ball to make the ball go up towards the bucket.
You now have some idea of how the program works. This may not
exactly be earth shattering, but we still have a long way to go!

The declarations section of the code contains important variables and
useful constants.

```
(General) – (declarations)
Dim sprBucket As Sprite
Dim sprBall As Sprite
Dim intXPos As Integer, intYPos As Integer
Dim intXTarget As Integer, intYTarget As Integer
Dim blnClick As Boolean, blnShoot As Boolean
```

```
Const WALK_RIGHT = 0
Const TURN_LEFT = 1
Const CLIMB = 2
Const INTO_CLIMB = 3
Const SMALL_FALL_RIGHT = 4
Const BIG_LAND_RIGHT = 5
Const POUR = 7
Const WALK_LEFT = 8
Const TURN_RIGHT = 9
Const SMALL_FALL_LEFT = 10
Const BIG_LAND_LEFT = 11
Const FALL_LEFT = 13
Const FALL_RIGHT = 14
```

I have used the Form_Load event to do most of the initialisation of
variables. Most programs require some form of initialisation. The broad
picture for program execution is: declare global variables, initialise
variables and objects, loop, clean-up before terminating, end.
Sometimes the largest part of the code is in the initialisation section.
Here we initialise the animation and the two sprites used, the
'sprBucket' and the 'sprBall'.

```
Private Sub Form_Load()
   Width = 400 * Screen.TwipsPerPixelX
   Height = 350 * Screen.TwipsPerPixelY
   'Initialise the animation, see Appendix C for details
   InitAnimation hDC, App.Path + ''\bricks.bmp''
   sprBucket.Index = InitSprite(App.Path + ''\bigbuck.bmp'', 0, 0,
   48, 48)
   sprBall.Index = InitSprite(App.Path + ''\sprBall.bmp'', 192,
   250, 16, 16)
   sprBucket.X = 10
   sprBucket.Y = 30
   sprBucket.MoveX = 5
   sprBucket.Action = WALKRIGHT
   sprBall.X = 192
   sprBall.Y = 250
End Sub
```

After initialisation the program will wait for user input. The interface
used here requires code in the mouse events. If a click is done on the
Form then the program must respond. We use the Form_MouseDown
event to test whether the click is on the static 'sprBall'. Notice that the

Form_MouseDown is followed by a list of variables. These variables 'Button, Shift, X' and 'Y' give you, the programmer, lots of information that you can use. The 'X' and 'Y' are the current position of the mouse relative to the Form. The long list of 'less than' and 'greater than' tests for X and Y uses these values to check whether the mouse cursor coincides with 'sprBall'.

If so, then a Boolean variable 'blnClick' is set to 'True' for use in future tests. A variable used in this manner is often called a flag. The use of DrawMode and DrawStyle set the properties necessary to create the stretchable line as you move the mouse. Finally the variables intXPos, intYPos, intXTarget and intYTarget are loaded with the current mouse position.

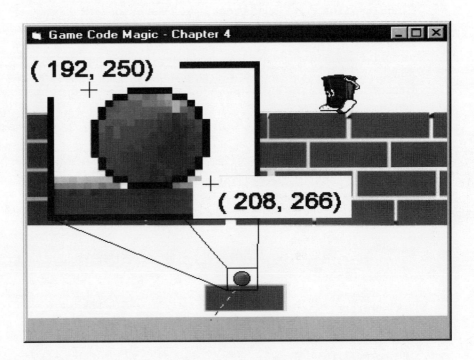

```
Private Sub Form_MouseDown(Button As Integer, Shift As Integer, X
As Single, Y As Single)
    If X > 192 And X < 208 And Y > 250 And Y < 266 Then
        blnClick = True
        DrawMode = 6
        DrawStyle = 2
        intXPos = X
```

```
      intYPos = Y
      intXTarget = X
      intYTarget = Y
   End If
End Sub
```

We can now examine what happens when the mouse is moved. Here we use the Form_MouseMove event. First we test the Boolean variable 'blnClick'. If it is not True the code is ignored and nothing is done; if 'blnClick' is True then the code in the 'If ... Then ... End If' section is executed. Because we set the DrawMode and DrawStyle in the Form_MouseDown event we are not drawing with colours. Instead we are drawing by inverting what is already on the screen. If it is white it becomes black, and vice versa; by repeating the drawing of the line we can get back to what was originally on the screen. The 'Line' method draws lines on the screen from the co-ordinates in the first set of brackets to the co-ordinates in the second set. Here we draw the line that we drew previously to clean up the screen, then take the new mouse position and draw the line again. This technique can be used for stretching boxes, which you may have seen used in paint programs for selecting areas. We store the current mouse positions so that they can be reused next time this event is executed.

```
Private Sub Form_MouseMove(Button As Integer, Shift As Integer, X
As Single, Y As Single)
   If blnClick Then
      Line (intXPos, intYPos)-(intXTarget, intYTarget)
      intXTarget = X
      intYTarget = Y
      Line (intXPos, intYPos)-(intXTarget, intYTarget)
   End If
End Sub
```

The last step in the use of the mouse is to clean up after the button is released. Again we check that 'blnClick' is set before executing the code. We draw the line to clean up the screen. Change the DrawMode and DrawStyle back to the defaults, set 'blnClick' to false and set the initial parameters for the movement of the 'sprBall' sprite. To enable us to move the 'sprBall' another Boolean variable is used, 'blnShoot'.

```
Private Sub Form_MouseUp(Button As Integer, Shift As Integer, X As
Single, Y As Single)
    If blnClick Then
        Line (intXPos, intYPos)-(intXTarget, intYTarget)
        intXTarget = X
        intYTarget = Y
        DrawMode = 13
        DrawStyle = 0
        blnClick = False
        sprBall.MoveX = (intXPos — intXTarget) / 2
        sprBall.MoveY = (intYPos – intYTarget) / 2
        blnShoot = True
    End If
End Sub
```

The Timer event

The Timer event contains most of the code that controls the way the
sprites are drawn on the screen. The 'sprBucket' can be performing
one of many different 'Actions' and different tests are required,
dependent on its current 'Action'. Visual Basic has a useful way to
move through different choices using the construction 'Select Case ...
Case ... End Select'.

Using 'Select Case'

To use 'Select Case' take a variable, in this instance
'sprBucket.Action', then test for certain values of this variable. The
section of code that executes is dependent on the test. You should read
through this section very carefully to see how tests are used to check
for the sides of the window, and to test whether it has landed on the
ground.

After 'sprBucket' is moved, then 'sprBall' is considered. The sprite
'sprBall' should only be moved when 'blnShoot' is set to True, so the
first test checks the value of this variable. If 'sprBall' is moving then a
test is made to see if it is off screen. When the 'sprBall' is sent off
screen it is reset to the start position and 'blnShoot' is reset to False.

The final test concerns the collision with the 'sprBucket', here another
of the functions in the 'Sprite.dll' dynamic link library is used. This

function 'CollisionCheck' requires the 'Index' values of two sprites and returns True if they are touching and False otherwise. When they are touching, the 'sprBall' must have hit the 'sprBucket', so parameters are set to inform the program that the 'sprBucket' should now fall either to the left or to the right depending on the current direction of the 'sprBucket'. The routine finishes by moving the sprite 'sprBall' and redrawing the stage.

NOTE

The 'Sprite.dll' function CollisionCheck takes a third argument. This is a Boolean value. If this is set to False the function simply tests for intersections of the two sprites' bounding rectangles. If the value is set to True then a full pixel test is done.

```
Private Sub Timer1_Timer()
  Select Case sprBucket.Action
  Case WALK_RIGHT:
    If sprBucket.Y > 100 Then
      If sprBucket.X > 400 Then
        sprBucket.Action = WALK_LEFT
        sprBucket.MoveX = -5
        sprBucket.Y = 30
      End If
    ElseIf sprBucket.X > 320 Then
      sprBucket.MoveX = 0
      sprBucket.Action = TURN_LEFT
      sprBucket.Frame = 0
    End If
  Case TURN_LEFT:
    If sprBucket.Frame = 15 Then
      sprBucket.MoveX = -5
      sprBucket.Action = WALK_LEFT
    End If
  Case WALK_LEFT:
    If sprBucket.Y > 100 Then
      If sprBucket.X < -50 Then
        sprBucket.Action = WALK_RIGHT
        sprBucket.MoveX = 5
        sprBucket.Y = 30
      End If
```

```
    ElseIf sprBucket.X < 10 Then
      sprBucket.Action = TURN_RIGHT
      sprBucket.MoveX = 0
      sprBucket.Frame = 0
    End If
  Case TURN_RIGHT:
    If sprBucket.Frame = 79 Then
      sprBucket.Action = WALK_RIGHT
      sprBucket.MoveX = 5
      sprBucket.Frame = 0
    End If
  Case FALL_RIGHT:
    sprBucket.MoveY = sprBucket.MoveY + 1
    If sprBucket.Y > 200 Then
      sprBucket.Action = BIG_LAND_RIGHT
      sprBucket.MoveX = 0
      sprBucket.MoveY = 0
    End If
  Case FALL_LEFT:
    sprBucket.MoveY = sprBucket.MoveY + 1
    If sprBucket.Y > 200 Then
      sprBucket.Action = BIG_LAND_LEFT
      sprBucket.MoveX = 0
      sprBucket.MoveY = 0
    End If
  Case BIG_LAND_LEFT:
    If sprBucket.Frame = 95 Then sprBucket.Action = BIG_LAND_LEFT
+ 1
    End If
  Case BIG_LAND_LEFT + 1:
    If sprBucket.Frame = 103 Then
      sprBucket.Action = WALK_RIGHT
      sprBucket.MoveX = 5
    End If
  Case BIG_LAND_RIGHT:
    If sprBucket.Frame = 47 Then sprBucket.Action = BIG_LAND_
RIGHT + 1
    End If
  Case BIG_LAND_RIGHT + 1:
    If sprBucket.Frame = 55 Then
      sprBucket.Action = WALK_LEFT
      sprBucket.MoveX = -5
    End If
  End Select
  sprBucket.X = sprBucket.X + sprBucket.MoveX
```

```
    sprBucket.Y = sprBucket.Y + sprBucket.MoveY
  If sprBucket.Action < FALL_LEFT Then
    sprBucket.Frame = (sprBucket.Frame + 1) Mod 8 +
sprBucket.Action * 8                                    ↵
    'Debug.Print sprBucket.Frame
  End If
  MoveSprite sprBucket.Index, sprBucket.X, sprBucket.Y,
sprBucket.Frame                                         ↵
  If blnShoot Then
    sprBall.X = sprBall.X + sprBall.MoveX
    sprBall.Y = sprBall.Y + sprBall.MoveY
    sprBall.MoveY = sprBall.MoveY + 3
    If sprBall.Y > 310 Or sprBall.X < -20 Or sprBall.X > 410
Then
      blnShoot = False
      sprBall.MoveX = 0
      sprBall.MoveY = 0
      sprBall.X = 192
      sprBall.Y = 250
    End If
    b = CollisionCheck(sprBall.Index, sprBucket.Index, True)
    If b Then
      sprBucket.MoveY = 1
      If sprBucket.Action < WALK_LEFT Then
        sprBucket.MoveX = 2
        sprBucket.Action = FALL_RIGHT
        sprBucket.Frame = 33
      Else
        sprBucket.MoveX = -2
        sprBucket.Action = FALL_LEFT
        sprBucket.Frame = 81
      End If
    End If
    MoveSprite sprBall.Index, sprBall.X, sprBall.Y, sprBall.Frame
  End If
  UpdateStage

End Sub
```

Tidying up

The other two code sections tidy up some problems that you may have
noticed in earlier chapters. If you put something over the window

containing the animation and then moved this window away, the area
of the sprite stage underneath the covering window will show up as
blank. This is part of Windows' operating system. We will explain
Windows, events and messages in much more depth later, but for now
the simple function DrawFullStage, if entered in the Form_Paint
event, will correct any problems. This was deliberately omitted in
earlier programs to enable you to see more clearly how Windows draws
the screen. Try to return to those earlier programs and add this simple
function.

The final function necessary whenever you use the sprite library is
'CloseAnimation'. This is essential, since a considerable amount of
memory management is contained in the code. This memory is
returned to Windows when you call 'CloseAnimation'.

```
Private Sub Form_Paint()
   DrawFullStage
End Sub
Private Sub Form_Terminate()
   CloseAnimation
End Sub
```

Making it harder

You probably found it very easy to hit the 'sprBucket' in the previous
example. We now look at how to make the game much more difficult.
The problem is that you can shoot the 'sprBall' with terrific force and
almost guarantee hitting the 'sprBucket'. If you could limit the power
with which the sprite 'sprBall' is projected, then hitting the sprite
'sprBucket' would not be so easy. The limit needs to occur only when
the parameters for 'sprBall.MoveX' and 'sprBall.MoveY' are set. Try
adding this to the existing example:

```
Private Sub Form_MouseUp(Button As Integer, Shift As Integer, X As
Single, Y As Single)
   If blnClick Then
      Line (intXPos, intYPos)-(intXTarget, intYTarget)
      intXTarget = X
      intYTarget = Y
      DrawMode = 13
      DrawStyle = 0
      blnClick = False
```

```
        sprBall.MoveX = (intXPos — intXTarget) / 2
        sprBall.MoveY = (intYPos — intYTarget) / 2
    '> > > > > > > > > > > > > > > > > > > > > > > > > >
    '      ADD HERE
    '> > > > > > > > > > > > > > > > > > > > > > > > > > >
        If sprBall.MoveY < —31 Then sprBall.MoveY = —31
    '> > > > > > > > > > > > > > > > > > > > > > > > > > >
    '      END ADD
    '> > > > > > > > > > > > > > > > > > > > > > > > > > >
        blnShoot = True
    End If
End Sub
```

Now the sprite 'sprBall' only just arrives at the sprite 'sprBucket', so you need to be more accurate. But it is still quite easy.

Creating a barrier

Finally we introduce a third sprite that acts as a barrier to prevent the sprite 'sprBucket' being hit. If you run 'Ex04C.exe' you will notice that the third sprite goes backwards and forwards, making a clear shot more difficult. See if you can work out a way to start the game with the simplest version and make it harder and harder to hit the 'sprBucket' by limiting the possible shots from the 'sprBall' and making more and more obstructions. (Hint: use an array for the blocks and redimension it after each successful hit of the sprite 'sprBucket'.)

QUIZ

1. Write down what would appear in the debug window using this section of code:

```
Dim a As Integer, b As Integer, c As Integer, d As Integer

a = 10
b = 15
c = 26
d = 7
```

```
If a Then Debug.Print ''Hello, hello, hello.''
If a > b Then Debug.Print ''What are you doing my lad?''
If (c / d = Int(c / d)) Then Debug.Print ''The early bird''
If (a > b) Or (b < c) Then Debug.Print ''How are you today?''
```

Answer: 'Hello, hello, hello. How are you today?'

2. You have two sprites and you want to print 'Hit!' in the debug window when they collide. Using the sprite library, how would you do this?
Answer:

```
Dim b As Boolean

b = CollisionCheck(Sprite1.Index, Sprite2.Index, False)
If b Then Debug.Print ''Hit!''
```

The final argument for CollisionCheck can be True or False. If True a more accurate test is done.

3. You want to allow the user to create a stretchable line. What DrawMode do you need to set?
Answer: DrawMode = 6

4. Using the code listing, what causes the sprite 'sprBall' to bounce?

```
Dim b As Boolean

b = CollisionCheck(Sprite1.Index, Sprite2.Index, True)
If b Then sprBall.MoveY = sprBall.MoveY * b
```

Answer: In the code b is given the value −1 or 0. If −1 then 'sprBall.MoveY' is multiplied by −1. This has the effect of inverting its value, giving the appearance of a bounce.

Summary

In this chapter you built on your growing knowledge of programming by making decisions in the code using Boolean algebra.

- You learnt that expressions are True if they have a value and False if they are zero.
- The 'If ... Then ... End If' construction was used to test many different expressions.
- Combinations of True and False expressions were evaluated using the connecting operators 'And' and 'Or' and the negation operator 'Not'.
- You used 'If ... Then ... End If' to control the play performance of a small game.

CHAPTER 5

Building blocks – Sub-routines and functions

If you were writing a computer program that simulated the movement of cars through a city, the number of options could be as great as the number of cars. Trying to keep track of all the cars using 'For Next' loops or 'If Then' constructions could get very confusing. This chapter explains how, with experience and a great deal of skill, programmers have developed ways of generating code that make it easier to create and repair complex programs.

What is a sub-routine?

Visual Basic is superbly structured. I first started writing code using a Sinclair Spectrum. This lovely machine had a Z80 processor, in fact the same processor as a Nintendo Gameboy. It had 48K of RAM and an operating system built into a ROM chip that used just 16K. Compare that with Windows 95, which has an average installation of around 80MB – a mere 5000 times the size!

NOTE

For our American readers, the UK experienced low-cost computers in the early 1980s due, mainly, to two companies, Sinclair and Acorn. The Sinclair Spectrum computer formed the cornerstone for many professional UK game programmers. Learning the ins and outs of a simple graphics interface and a relatively simple assembler language, they pushed a basic machine to its limits.

The Spectrum had a basic interpreter built into the ROM chip. This version of Basic required the use of line numbers and was about as unstructured as computer code could be. You, on the other hand, are learning to program using an environment that simply cries out structure. This is a tremendous improvement.

Two questions must first be answered: what is a sub-routine and why is it useful?

A sub-routine is a section of code that is complete in itself and looks after one part of the program. All the sections of code that you have used up to this point in this book are either sub-routines or functions, because the use of Visual Basic requires a *structured* program. If you were writing a DOS program, you could write the whole program to start at the beginning and work its way through to the end. With Visual Basic, you write code that will be executed when the Form loads, when a control is clicked, when a timer gets called or when a control gets focus. This is a highly structured approach and moves you towards the ultimate in structured programming: object-orientated code. It took me a long time to see the difference, and I have tried to explain the difference to people who are still programming ROM chips for washing machines, and they cannot see what the fuss is about, so I am going to labour this point again.

Structured and unstructured code

Let us assume that twenty meteorites are heading towards your poor unsuspecting spaceship. If the responsibility for moving a meteorite and testing for a collision could be turned into a one-line instruction 'MoveMeteorite index', where index is the number of the meteorite in the code, then adjusting the performance of a meteorite would be easy. If you had to increase or decrease the number of meteorites, this too would be easy. If, however, the movement of the meteorites is in a complicated control loop, then changing the parameters or number of meteorites is much more difficult. At this point let me introduce you to pseudo-code, which is a style of code that cannot be written directly into any computer language, but is useful when you are designing a complicated control sub-routine, since it can quickly help you to identify any potential problems.

```
Sub MoveMeteorite (index As Integer)
     Move meteorite in x and y direction
     Test whether meteorite is off screen if so then return
     Test for collision with spaceship, if so then inform the main
program
     Inform main program that this meteorite has moved and needs
     redrawing
End Sub
```

Let's walk through this simple code. First the sub-routine begins with a name; the purpose of the name is to allow this code to be called from elsewhere in the program.

```
Sub Timer()
     For intIndex = 1 to intNumMeteorites
          MoveMeteorite intIndex
     Next
End Sub
```

The 'MoveMeteorite' sub-routine updates the x and y co-ordinates for the meteorite. The full code would need to know the velocity of the meteorite. The sprite data type that we have been using in our code to date uses the structure

```
Type Sprite
   X As Integer
   Y As Integer
   MoveX As Integer
   MoveY As Integer
   Frame As Integer
   Action As Integer
   Index As Integer
   Count As Integer
End Type
```

By creating a 'Sprite' variable the MoveX and MoveY parameters can be used to store the x and y velocities of the sprite. In the meteorite example, if the meteorites were created as sprite variables then the programmer could use information stored in the MoveX and MoveY parameters to decide how fast the meteorite is moving.

The next line in the pseudo-code segment is a test to see if the meteorite is off screen. If it, is then it cannot have hit the spaceship, so that's the end of one problem and we can move on to the next. Then we test for a collision. Now it would be ideal if we could inform the spaceship that it has been hit, and even better if we could tell the spaceship who did the hitting.

This is one style of programming, and you can program in the style that suits you, but the best programmers in the world, with a great deal of experience, have learnt that the more modular you can make your code then the more chance it will work as the complexity of your programs snowballs. Taking the example further, we could have a sub-routine to move the spaceship; this could test if 'Action' had been set by another sprite to 'HIT' and, if so, then perhaps the programmer could have used the 'Count' parameter to tell the spaceship which sprite did the hitting. Hopefully, you have now grasped the idea of modularity.

The other big idea concerns passing data to sub-routines and functions.

Passing information to sub-routines and functions

After the name of the sub-routine or function comes a list, in brackets, of the data being passed. In your program, variables have what is called *scope*. The variables declared in the '(General) – (declarations)' section have Form scope, this means that the variables are accessible from all the sub-routines and functions in that Form. If a variable with the same name as one in the '(General) – (declarations)' section is used in a sub-routine or function in that Form, then its value will be known. If, however, the variable is declared at the beginning of a sub-routine or function, then only that sub-routine or function knows the value of that variable. Additionally if the sub-routine or function is called for a second time, then the variable is recreated a second time, and no information is retained from the first time the sub-routine or function was called. If you need to retain the information stored in a variable from one call of the sub-routine or function to the next, then declare the variable as 'Static'. In this case it is created when the sub-routine or function is first called and is not deleted until the program terminates.

Your sub-routines or functions can also use the variables passed to them to control the way they execute.

Returning information from sub-routines or functions

Here we finally find the difference between a sub-routine and a function. To return information from a sub-routine you will need to alter the contents of a Form or Project level variable. You declare Form variables in the '(General) – (declarations)' section of a Form, and Project level variables in the '(General) – (declarations)' section of a Module.

TIP

By default, variables in a Form are 'Private' to that Form and cannot be read from another Form or Module. You can change this by declaring them as 'Public'. By default variables in a Module are 'Public' but you can change them by declaring them as 'Private'.

You can do the same with a function, but additionally you can return a value from the function, as follows:

```
Function Add (intNum1 As Integer, intNum2 As Integer) As Integer
    Add = intNum1 + intNum2
End Function
```

Given that a function like the one above exists in your program, then to add two numbers you could use the following technique:

```
Dim intResult As Integer

intResult = Add (12, 6)
Debug.Print intResult
```

Here the answer '18' would be printed in the Debug window.

By using the function name as the name of a variable in the function, the value assigned to the function name becomes the one returned from the function. When the function is used in another section of code, it acts as a black box, hiding any complexity but returning the desired result. Sometimes functions only return a value to indicate whether they performed correctly or not. In this case they should be declared as Boolean, then they can return the value True or False.

```
Function DidItWork() As Boolean
```

How did the frog cross the road?

You have probably realised that I like modularity in programs – so much so that I have included with this book a library of useful functions and sub-routines that get used again and again. When I first started writing the book I intended that this module would be written in Visual Basic, as in fact is the example in Chapter 1. Since then the examples have all used functions and sub-routines in the special library 'Sprites.dll' which should be in your 'Windows\System' folder. The reason was mainly speed of execution, but the principle is the same; that is, the same functions are used from one program to another. The whole structure of this special library of functions and sub routines is covered in later chapters and summarised in Appendix C, but now I hope you are ready to explore some of the details.

```
Declare Sub ShowDib Lib ''Sprites.dll'' _
  (ByVal hdcDest As Long, ByVal strFilename As String, ByVal intX As
  Long, ByVal intY As Long)
Declare Function InitAnimation Lib ''Sprites.dll'' _
  (ByVal hdcDest As Long, ByVal strFilename As String) As Boolean
Declare Sub CloseAnimation Lib ''Sprites.dll'' ()
Declare Function InitSprite Lib ''Sprites.dll'' _
  (ByVal strFilename As String, ByVal lngX As Long, ByVal lngY As
Long, _
  ByVal lngWidth As Long, ByVal lngHeight As Long) As Long
Declare Function ClearSprite Lib ''Sprites.dll'' _
  (ByVal lngIndex As Long) As Boolean
Declare Function NewBackground Lib ''Sprites.dll'' _
  (ByVal strFilename As String, ByVal blnKeepSprites As Boolean) As
Boolean
Declare Sub MoveSprite Lib ''Sprites.dll'' _
  (ByVal lngIndex As Long, ByVal lngX As Long, ByVal lngY As Long,
  ByVal lngFrame As Long)
Declare Function CloneSprite Lib ''Sprites.dll'' _
  (ByVal lngIndex As Long, ByVal lngX As Long, ByVal lngY As Long)
  As Long
Declare Sub UpdateStage Lib ''Sprites.dll'' ()
Declare Function GetSpriteActive Lib ''Sprites.dll'' _
```

```
    (ByVal lngIndex As Long) As Boolean
Declare Function DrawFullStage Lib ''Sprites.dll'' () As Boolean
Declare Function CollisionCheck Lib ''Sprites.dll'' _
    (ByVal lngSprite1 As Long, ByVal lngSprite2 As Long, ByVal
    blnAccurate As Boolean) As Boolean
Declare Function PasteSprite Lib ''Sprites.dll'' _
    (ByVal lngIndex As Long, ByVal lngX As Long, ByVal lngY As Long,
    ByVal lngFrame As Long) As Boolean
```

This is a listing of all the declarations for the functions in the library 'Sprites.dll'. Notice how each function has a name that attempts to explain the purpose of that function. If the declaration is for a function then it must have a return value. For example, the function 'PasteSprite' takes three parameters (or arguments) when it is called. Firstly, the index number of a sprite, then its position x and y, and finally the frame number to use. The function returns True if it was successful and False if it failed for whatever reason.

In the example program 'Ex05A.exe' you will find a simple frogger game. It is actually quite difficult to get the frog across the road because the frog jumps up before jumping across, so it is quite easy to hit a car if you are not careful. I soon became adept at it and managed to get him across a few times, so I'm sure that you will do a lot better than I.

This picture of the frog animation frames shows that the frog stretches out a long way before jumping.

```
(General) — (declarations)
Option Explicit

Dim sprFrog As Sprite
Dim sprCar(10) As Sprite

Const KEY_UP = 38
Const KEY_DOWN = 40
Const KEY_LEFT = 37
Const KEY_RIGHT = 39

Const WALK_LEFT = 1
Const WALK_RIGHT = 5
Const JUMP = 9
```

Just a few constants and two sprites declared in the form declarations section. These variables have form scope, which means we can refer to them anywhere in the rest of the code for this form. It is generally agreed that variables should have minimum scope to ensure maximum portability, so try to avoid too many variables in the (General) – (declarations) section. You could pass the variables as a parameter of a function or subroutine instead. If this is still a little hazy, then worry not, you are just experiencing the clouding of the brain which is a standard feature of computer programming and can be cured by a short break! When you return, refreshed, the fog will start to clear.

Did you enjoy your break? Remember me? We were discussing subroutines, functions and parameter passing. Look at the following sub-routine that Visual Basic creates for you. It comes complete with two parameters, 'KeyCode' and 'Shift'. In the code that I added to this function I test for the KeyCode only. The test is there to check if the arrow keys are pressed. The nice easy names KEY_LEFT and so on are the constants declared in the declarations section. I hope you agree that they make much more sense in the code than the use of the numbers 37–40 that they represent. In the code the 'sprFrog' attributes for action and movement are updated according to the key pressed. This sub-routine is called many times as the key is pressed, not just once.

```
Private Sub Form_KeyDown(KeyCode As Integer, Shift As Integer)
  Select Case KeyCode
  Case KEY_LEFT:
    sprFrog.Action = WALK_LEFT
    sprFrog.MoveX = -10
    sprFrog.MoveY = 0
  Case KEY_RIGHT:
    sprFrog.Action = WALK_RIGHT
    sprFrog.MoveX = 10
    sprFrog.MoveY = 0
  Case KEY_DOWN:
    If sprFrog.Action < > JUMP Then
      sprFrog.MoveY = 0
      sprFrog.Frame = 8
      sprFrog.Action = JUMP
      sprFrog.MoveX = 0
    End If
  End Select
End Sub
```

The KeyUp code is called only once as the key is released.

```
Private Sub Form_KeyUp(KeyCode As Integer, Shift As Integer)
  If sprFrog.Action < > JUMP Then
    sprFrog.MoveX = 0
    sprFrog.MoveY = 0
    sprFrog.Action = 0
  End If
End Sub
```

As usual the Form_Load event is used to initialise the animation and variables. No doubt you are now realising that lots of the examples use the same simple set-up procedures.

```
Private Sub Form_Load()
  Dim i As Integer

  InitAnimation hDC, App.Path + ''\bg.bmp''
  sprFrog.index = InitSprite(App.Path + ''\sprFrogs.bmp'', 0, 0,↵
64, 85)
  sprCar(0).index = InitSprite(App.Path + ''\sprCars.bmp'', 0, 0,↵
93, 60)
```

```
        sprCar(0).y = 60
        sprCar(0).MoveX = 10
        sprCar(0).Frame = 1
        sprCar(1).index = CloneSprite(sprCar(0).index, 0, 0)
        sprCar(1).x = 280
        sprCar(1).y = 60
        sprCar(1).MoveX = 10
        sprCar(1).Frame = 1
        For i = 2 To 3
          sprCar(i).index = CloneSprite(sprCar(0).index, 0, 0)
          sprCar(i).x = 280 * (i - 2)
          sprCar(i).y = 120
          sprCar(i).MoveX = -10
          sprCar(i).Frame = 0
        Next
        sprFrog.x = 180
        sprFrog.y = -30
        Width = 400 * Screen.TwipsPerPixelX
        Height = 300 * Screen.TwipsPerPixelY
    End Sub
```

The most complicated code is found, as usual, in the listing for the
Timer event. The timer code is executed as often as the timer interval
dictates. In the examples, the timer interval is set to 50, that is, 50
milliseconds; so theoretically it is executed 20 times a second. I say
theoretically because it is heavily dependent on the computer you use
to run the examples and, particularly, on your graphics card.

```
    Private Sub Timer1_Timer()
      Dim i As Integer, b As Boolean, blnFrogHit As Boolean

      Select Case sprFrog.Action
      Case WALK_LEFT:
        sprFrog.Frame = (sprFrog.Frame + 1) Mod 4
        If sprFrog.x = 0 Then sprFrog.MoveX = 0
      Case WALK_RIGHT:
        sprFrog.Frame = (sprFrog.Frame + 1) Mod 4 + 4
        If sprFrog.x > 360 Then sprFrog.MoveX = 0
      Case JUMP:
        sprFrog.Frame = sprFrog.Frame + 1
```

```
      If sprFrog.Frame = 11 Then sprFrog.MoveY = 15
      If sprFrog.Frame = 15 Then
        sprFrog.MoveY = 0
        sprFrog.Frame = 0
        sprFrog.Action = 0
      End If
      If sprFrog.y > 250 Then
        'Back to start
        sprFrog.MoveX = 0
        sprFrog.MoveY = 0
        sprFrog.Action = 0
        sprFrog.Frame = 0
        sprFrog.x = 180
        sprFrog.y = -30
      End If
    End Select
    sprFrog.x = sprFrog.x + sprFrog.MoveX
    sprFrog.y = sprFrog.y + sprFrog.MoveY
    MoveSprite sprFrog.index, sprFrog.x, sprFrog.y, sprFrog.Frame
    bsprFrogHit = False
    For i = 0 To 3
      sprCar(i).x = sprCar(i).x + sprCar(i).MoveX
      If sprCar(i).x > 430 Then
        sprCar(i).x = -100
      ElseIf sprCar(i).x < -100 Then
        sprCar(i).x = 420
      End If
      b = CollisionCheck(sprFrog.index, sprCar(i).index, True)
      If b Then bsprFrogHit = True
      MoveSprite sprCar(i).index, sprCar(i).x, sprCar(i).y,
  sprCar(i).Frame
    Next


    If bsprFrogHit Then
      'sprFrog hit
      PasteSprite sprFrog.index, sprFrog.x, sprFrog.y, 16
      sprFrog.x = 180
      sprFrog.y = -30
      sprFrog.MoveY = 0
      sprFrog.Frame = 0
      sprFrog.Action = 0
    End If
    UpdateStage
End Sub
```

Now I will explain some of the stranger code in this subroutine:

```
sprFrog.Frame = (sprFrog.Frame + 1) Mod 4
```

When you look through the chapters about animation you will see that animation is an illusion maintained by quickly changing static drawings. The drawing that is chosen for the 'sprFrog' sprite is stored using the value of 'sprFrog.Frame'. Many of the animations cycle, that is they loop back to a certain 'Frame' then repeat. The code adds 1 to the 'Frame', divides the answer by 4, and saves the remainder. If this is confusing try doing a list of what would happen starting at 0. (You should get 0,1,2,3,0,1,2,3, etc.)

Much of the remainder of the code is a 'Select Case ... End Select' construction, executing certain sections as the 'sprFrog' performs different actions.

```
MoveSprite sprFrog.Index, sprFrog.X, sprFrog.Y, sprFrog.Frame
```

Finally, the 'sprFrog' is moved using the 'MoveSprite' sub-routine. This is from the 'Sprites.dll' and takes four parameters, which should be fairly obvious from the example. A word of warning, you will not see any changes on the screen when you call MoveSprite. The design of the sprite library requires a call to UpdateStage to transfer the changes to the user's screen. Move all the sprites in the timer event before finally calling UpdateStage.

```
b = CollisionCheck(sprFrog.Index, sprCar(i).Index, True)
```

Collision checking is done using the function 'CollisionCheck'. The final parameter in this example is True, and this is required for pixel accurate collision checking.

When would you use inaccurate collision checking?

Sometimes when collision checking it is sufficient to test whether the rectangle that surrounds one sprite intersects with the rectangle that surrounds another. This type of test is often sufficient and is much faster to execute. In this example the 'sprFrog' images are quite small inside a sea of white, which, for the 'sprFrog' sprite, is the transparent colour. Collision checking based on bounding rectangles would in this case lead to quite misleading results. If you want to see what I mean, try changing the True to False and running the example again. If you succeed in getting the frog across the road you are a genius! I designed this function to enable you to use it either way; it returns True if there is a collision between the two sprites that are passed in the first two parameters.

```
PasteSprite sprFrog.Index, sprFrog.X, sprFrog.Y, FROG_SPLAT
```

Another useful function in the library is PasteSprite. This makes a permanent copy of your sprite at the x and y positions given and with the 'Frame' number passed as the fourth parameter. In this case the constant FROG_SPLAT, set to 16, is used. The purpose of this function is to avoid having to generate lots of copies of the frog as he is run over. This would use lots of system resources in order to let you, the programmer, bring him back to life. Clearly in this case this is not going to happen, so it is better to paste a copy of the splattered frog, then keep the moving 'sprFrog' sprite. We will be covering sprites, animation and screen drawing techniques in more detail in later chapters.

By using functions and sub-routines that can be reused, the code for this example is very short, hiding a lot of complexity just below the surface. This is the aim of well-structured code.

QUIZ

1. A programmer using the library 'Sprites.dll' uses the following code, but is disappointed and frustrated when she doesn't see any movement on the screen. What went wrong?

```
Sub Timer1_Timer()
  MySprite.X = MySprite.X + MySprite.MoveX
  MySprite.Frame = (MySprite.Frame + 1) Mod 8
  MoveSprite MySprite.Index, MySprite.X, MySprite.Y,
  MySprite.Frame
End Sub
```

Answer: There is no call to UpdateStage so the changes are not transferred to the user's screen.

2. If you need to return a value from a procedure should you use a sub-routine or a function?

Answer: A function can return a value, a sub-routine does not.

3. If you declare a variable in the declarations section of a Form, can you use that variable in another module?

Answer: Not unless you declare the variable as Public.

4. If a sprite has a very irregular shape and you need to check for collisions, should the last parameter of CollisionCheck be True or False?

Answer: True

Summary

In this chapter you learnt to use sub-routines and functions in you own programs to improve the structure of you code.

- You learnt about some new functions in the 'Sprite.dll' library. CollisionCheck and PasteSprite
- You learnt about the scope of variables.
- Sub-routines can be past parameters or arguments, but do not return any information.
- Functions can be past parameters or arguments and can return information.

CHAPTER 6

OOP's – So what is object-orientated programming?

Starting with the fourth version, Visual Basic moved one step closer to being a true object-orientated programming language. 'So what?' I hear you say, 'I want to learn how to create interactive animation'. The truth is that a million programmers can't all be wrong. This is something you need to learn before you can decide just how deep you want to go. Microsoft would have you go very, very deep, and we will try to follow. Here we go, hold on tight; this is going to be quite a ride.

When computers first began the evolution from soldering irons in laboratories to the high street stores, they introduced a new word. If you could travel back in time and said 'Software' to an average man in the street 20 years ago, you would have received a blank look and he would have shuffled off thinking he had met some kind of maniac.

NOTE

When software really began is the subject of debate. Perhaps Charles Babbage's calculating engines used software of a kind over 100 years ago. Perhaps the most realistic candidate for the first Software is the virtual machine invented by Alan Turing just over 50 years ago. The Turing machine could be programmed with basic instructions and perform different tasks dependent on the program.

In principle, software design has been developed over the last 30 years. Despite these notable earlier pioneers. It is fair to say that the development process is far from complete and that new directions will evolve as computers evolve.

NOTE

Platform independence is the hot topic of the moment. Most software has been written for a specific set of hardware and will not run on any other. The language Java developed by Sun is designed for platform independence. It works through the principle of a virtual computer.

I come from an art and design background, and most artists think they are very creative and that computer programmers are just people in anoraks who need to get a life. The truth is, the creativity that has gone into the development of tight logical languages to instruct machines is easily equal to the creativity that is present in most of the more immediately obvious creative art forms. All this creative endeavour has been pointing in one direction: towards robust code that is modular and as reusable as possible.

Already in this book you have moved from using basic variables to inventing your own procedures, functions and sub-routines. Visual Basic forces you as a programmer to concentrate on breaking up the programming task into small segments, then developing the code for those segments. This is a step in the direction of object-orientated programming. The controls you add to the Forms you create are mostly perfect examples of 'objects'. For example, 'Picture Control' has properties of size, picture displayed, scale mode and so on. The control can also respond to events such as a mouse click, being redrawn and so on. Finally, the 'Picture Control' has methods that you as a programmer can use. One of the most useful methods is 'PaintPicture'. This method allows you as a programmer to replace the current picture with a copy or resized version of another picture with total flexibility over positioning. The Visual Basic controls wrap up the data types and sub-routines into one complete object. Can you see any advantage in this as a programmer?

Writing code that you can reuse

The big advantage is *reuse*. You can use a Picture Control in every program you create. And it is not necessary to write code to control how pictures are displayed, down to each individual pixel. All you have to do to display a picture is copy one from another control using an assignment operator – an equals sign.

NOTE

Using '=' as the assignment operator is not as obvious as you might think. The line of code

    a = a + 1

is a perfect example. Clearly if 'a' is a variable with the value 4, then 4 does not equal 5. What you are doing with the statement is declaring that you want 'a', which is currently equal to 4, to be equal to 5 in all future events. You are assigning a new value, not making a mathematical revelation that 4 now equals 5.

By making your code modular you are speeding up program development and improving your ability to maintain your programs. If you write your own control to display fast-moving sprites, you can then use this in program after program, and if you improve the way the control is written to get that bit of extra performance then you can quickly transform all the other programs by simply replacing the control.

Is Visual Basic object orientated?

This is something of a debate. To be fully object orientated requires three principles.

Encapsulation

- Data and functionality are wrapped up together in a black box.
- Do you fully understand how your video works down to the last detail?
- Can you use your video to record programs?

By limiting the access to the fine detail of the way your video works you are not limited in the way you choose to operate the machine. If you had to solder capacitors every time you used the video you probably would never use it. This black box technology is the idea behind Encapsulation.

You could easily build Encapsulation into a module. Access to the internal data of an object can be restricted by the programmer, which is why Visual Basic now has private and public data and procedure statements. It took me a long time to understand the importance of this. Take, for example, the dynamic link library that you have been using through the book. The library has lots of data members to which you have no access. If you did have access you could easily crash your computer by placing data into an area of memory that is looking after something else. This would not be your error; it would be the error of the library in allowing you access to do such a damaging thing. By making your data accessible only by routines that you write, these embarrassing events are avoided. Other benefits are data validation. If, instead of allowing a programmer to access the variables in your class, you forced that person to use functions to change the variables, then you can use those functions to check that the changes are not going to lead to catastrophe. In addition, the functions you create to allow other programmers to alter the member variables of your class can perform additional maintenance services.

Inheritance

Visual Basic has a weakness in this area. If you write in C++ (to be discussed later) you can create something called a *class*. Let us assume that you create a class to display a picture. This class may have the following data types:

pBits as Memory address of bitmaps data, width as integer, height as integer

and procedures

LoadPicture, ShowPicture and so on.

You could use this class to create another class called a sprite. As the new class would inherit all the behaviours of the parent class, loading and displaying pictures would be immediately available. Now you could add functionality to display the picture with transparent bits – that is, rather than being a rectangle it can be irregularly shaped like a person or a car. Perhaps you would choose to add yet another class that inherits all the functionality of the sprite class but also offers the ability to look after moving and displaying itself based on such properties as its target values for X and Y.

Polymorphism

Having created a base class, this could be used as the foundation of differing kinds of new classes. Polymorphism concerns the ability to evolve in differing ways from the same base class or classes.

To resume . . .

So now we have the principles of object-orientated programming

1 Modular programming is reusable and easy to maintain.
2 Objects become black boxes that are more robust when used by teams of programmers, and are more maintainable.
3 An object can inherit all the characteristics of a parent, then head off in its own direction.
4 Offspring need not all be the same.

From Visual Basic 4, the concept of a class has been introduced to the language. Visual Basic 5 takes it a step further. Controls in Visual Basic that you can add to the toolbox are all OLE or ActiveX controls and in Part 3 of this book you will use the 'Sprite.ocx', a OLE control. In Part 4 you will learn how you can create your own controls using Visual Basic 5. The ideas behind OLE, object linking and embedding will be fully discussed in a later book, but I hope in this book to have given you the commitment to learn about classes. It can be a frustrating journey, but once learnt you will realise that it was time well spent.

Creating a bucket class

In this example we start to build a game. The game involves cartoon buckets climbing ladders and walking along platforms to reach a bath that needs to be filled. Each level will require you to fill the bath against a clock, the bucket itself will need to be filled from a tap and a fall will spill some of the water in the bucket.

Open 'Ex06A.vbp' and take a look at the file called 'BucketClass'. The functionality of the program is still limited to help illustrate the concepts. Running the program should create seven buckets that fall until they land at the bottom of the window. Further movement is to walk left and right. Clicking on a bucket allows you to drag it until the left mouse button is released, at which point it falls back.

Each bucket is created as datatype BucketClass. Just as the controls that come with Visual Basic have properties, events and methods, the BucketClass has properties events and methods.

When you declare a 'New BucketClass' the first thing that happens is that the Class_Initialize method is called. The following shows what happens when the Bucket is created; I have placed 'c_' in front of the variables that have class scope; that simply lets me know that these variables are available throughout the class.

```
Private Sub Class_Initialize()
  If Rnd() > 0.2 Then
     c_index = InitSprite(App.Path + ''\bbucket.bmp'', 0, 0, 48,
48)
     c_width = 48
     c_height = 48
  Else
     c_index = InitSprite(App.Path + ''\sbucket.bmp'', 0, 0, 32,
32)
     c_width = 32
     c_height = 32
  End If
  'Default action
  c_action = WALK_RIGHT
  c_frame = 0
  c_x = 10
  c_y = 10
  c_movex = 5
  c_movey = 0
  c_water = 100
End Sub
```

First, the random function 'Rnd' is called to decide if this is going to be a large or a small bucket. Then the picture is set and the 'InitSprite' function is called. The result of this function is stored in the class member variable 'c_index', to be referred to later when necessary. The member variables 'c_width' and 'c_height' are then set to determine the number of pixels for the sprite's height and width. Finally the default action, frame, position and movement are defined, again using member variables. These member variables cannot be set from outside the class; they are set and accessed using property procedures. If this is still vague then try using

```
clsBucket(1).c_x = 4
```

in the form code. You will get a message saying

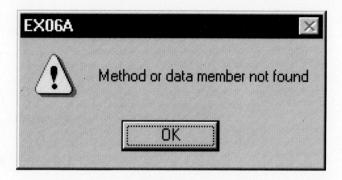

This is because the member variable 'c_x' is not available to your code in the form. To access this member variable you must use

```
clsBucket(1).X = 4
```

This then uses the property method

```
Public Property Let X(i As Integer)
    c_x = i
End Property
```

So why not simply declare the member variable 'c_x' as public and avoid the need to have property methods?

Encapsulation. You are in control. You decide when and how the data can be manipulated. You can write code to check on the suitability of the revised value. You can reject new values if unsuitable. If you are learning about programming as part of a course or part of a team of programmers then you will quickly see the need to use black box code; if you are a lone programmer then it will not be as clear. Suppose that you write a class module that you want to use and reuse. Perhaps the internal behaviour of the code that was once so clear will become hazy. You will then appreciate the techniques involved. Programming technique is not learnt overnight, it is the combination of research and experience. You may choose to use only a limited amount of classes in your code. As you become more confident with your code, you may choose to use C++ for your code. If you have learnt to use classes in Visual Basic then the methodology of C++ will be all the clearer and will become simply a matter of learning a new syntax, rather than a completely new technique.

Here is the '(General) – (declarations)' section of the bucket class.

```
Private c_index As Integer, c_x As Integer, c_y As Integer
Private c_width As Integer, c_height As Integer, c_action As
Integer
Private c_count As Integer, c_movex As Integer, c_movey As Integer
Private c_frame As Integer, c_drag As Boolean, c_water As Integer

Const WALK_RIGHT = 0
Const TURN_LEFT = 1
Const CLIMB = 2
Const INTO_CLIMB = 3
Const SMALL_LAND_RIGHT = 4
Const BIG_LAND_RIGHT = 5
Const POUR = 7
Const WALK_LEFT = 8
Const TURN_RIGHT = 9
Const SMALL_LAND_LEFT = 10
Const BIG_LAND_LEFT = 11
Const FALL_LEFT = 13
Const FALL_RIGHT = 14


Const STAGE_RIGHT = 350
Const STAGE_LEFT = 10
Const STAGE_FLOOR = 265
```

Notice again the use of 'Const' values to allow the code to be more
easily read and to allow the code to be altered more easily.

Each class can have properties, methods and events. You create your
own properties by adding 'Get' and 'Set' procedures to your code. Just
type in 'Public Property Set' then the name of the property that you
need to create, use '(variable as datatype)'. If you are still shaky on
procedures and returned datatypes then review the last chapter. The
alternative 'Get' returns a value for your program to use.

```
Public Property Set Y(i As Integer)
   c_y = i
End Property

Public Property Get Y() As Integer
   Y = c_y
End Property
```

The majority of the functionality of the BucketClass comes form the Move method. Here a 'Select ... Case' construction is used as usual to decide how the bucket should be moved.

```
Public Sub Move()
  Select Case c_action
  Case WALK_RIGHT
    c_frame = (c_frame + 1) Mod 8
    If Not c_drag Then
      c_x = c_x + c_movex
      c_y = c_y + c_movey
      If c_x > STAGE_RIGHT Then
        c_action = TURN_LEFT
        c_movex = 0
        c_frame = TURN_LEFT * 8
      End If
      If c_y < (STAGE_FLOOR - c_height) Then
        c_movey = c_movey + 1
        If c_movex > 0 Then
          c_movex = c_movex - 1
        End If
      ElseIf c_y > (STAGE_FLOOR - c_height) Then
        'Do nothing if bucket is on floor
        c_y = STAGE_FLOOR - c_height
        If c_movey > 10 Then
          c_action = BIG_LAND_RIGHT
          c_frame = BIG_LAND_RIGHT * 8
        Else
          c_action = SMALL_LAND_RIGHT
          c_frame = SMALL_LAND_RIGHT * 8
        End If
        c_movex = 0
        c_movey = 0
      End If
    End If
  Case TURN_LEFT
    c_frame = c_frame + 1
    If c_frame = 15 Then
      c_action = WALK_LEFT
      c_movex = -5
      c_frame = WALK_LEFT * 8
    End If
  Case CLIMB
  Case INTO_CLIMB
```

```
Case SMALL_LAND_RIGHT
   c_frame = c_frame + 1
   If c_frame = SMALL_LAND_RIGHT * 8 + 7 Then
     c_action = WALK_RIGHT
     c_movex = 5
     c_frame = WALK_RIGHT * 8
   End If
Case BIG_LAND_RIGHT
   c_frame = c_frame + 1
   If c_frame = BIG_LAND_RIGHT * 8 + 15 Then
     c_action = WALK_LEFT
     c_movex = -5
     c_frame = WALK_LEFT * 8
   End If
Case POUR
Case WALK_LEFT
   c_frame = (c_frame + 1) Mod 8 + WALK_LEFT * 8
   If Not c_drag Then
     c_x = c_x + c_movex
     c_y = c_y + c_movey
     If c_x < STAGE_LEFT Then
       c_action = TURN_RIGHT
       c_movex = 0
       c_frame = TURN_RIGHT * 8
     End If
     If c_y < (STAGE_FLOOR - c_height) Then
       c_movey = c_movey + 1
       If c_movex > 0 Then
         c_movex = c_movex - 1
       End If
     ElseIf c_y > (STAGE_FLOOR - c_height) Then
       c_y = STAGE_FLOOR - c_height
       If c_movey > 10 Then
         c_action = BIG_LAND_LEFT
         c_frame = BIG_LAND_LEFT * 8
       Else
         c_action = SMALL_LAND_LEFT
         c_frame = SMALL_LAND_LEFT * 8
       End If
       c_movey = 0
       c_movex = 0
     End If
   End If
Case TURN_RIGHT
   c_frame = c_frame + 1
```

```
      If c_frame = TURN_RIGHT * 8 + 7 Then
        c_action = WALK_RIGHT
        c_movex = 5
        c_frame = WALK_RIGHT * 8
      End If
    Case SMALL_LAND_LEFT
      c_frame = c_frame + 1
      If c_frame = SMALL_LAND_LEFT * 8 + 7 Then
        c_action = WALK_LEFT
        c_movex = −5
        c_frame = WALK_LEFT * 8
      End If
    Case BIG_LAND_LEFT
      c_frame = c_frame + 1
      If c_frame = BIG_LAND_LEFT * 8 + 15 Then
        c_action = WALK_RIGHT
        c_movex = 5
        c_frame = WALK_RIGHT * 8
      End If
    Case FALL_LEFT
    Case FALL_RIGHT
    End Select

    MoveSprite c_index, c_x, c_y, c_frame
End Sub
```

You may have noticed that the code checks for the value of the
member variable 'c_drag'. This value is set when the method 'Drag' is
called.

```
Public Function Drag(X As Single, Y As Single)
  c_drag = True
  c_x = Int(X)
  c_y = Int(Y)
End Function



Public Function EndDrag()
  c_drag = False
End Function
```

This method overrides the main way of altering the position of the sprite and replaces it with a new call. The use of 'Drag' is terminated using the method 'EndDrag'.

Using the new class

It is for the main form to look after creating and manipulating this new class, so now we will look at the code involved.

NOTE

Just as you declare variables in your code before you use them. So you must declare an instance of a class before using it. When creating an instance of an object you must use the 'New' key word.

Dim myObject As New clsMyClass

```
(General) – (declarations)
Option Explicit

Dim clsBucket(6) As New BucketClass
Dim sprPlatform(10) As Sprite
Dim sprButton(10) As Sprite

Dim IntNumBuckets As Integer
Dim intNumPlatforms As Integer
Dim intDragSpriteIndex As Integer
Dim intDragBucket As Integer
Dim intDragPlatform As Integer
```

The new code here is the declaration involved to create a bucket class object. It uses the extra word 'New'. This creates what is called an 'instance' of the class 'BucketClass' which can then be referred to using the name following the Dim statement.

Most of the once-only code goes into the form load event as usual.

NOTE

The form load event takes place before the form is drawn on the screen. Watch this since in the graphics-orientated programs that we are writing it is sometimes easy to assume that drawing in the form load event will be seen by the user. This is not the case when the form has its AutoRedraw property set to false. This property dictates the persistence of the screen data. Animation requires this property to be set to false to speed the performance. But this means we have to take extra care that the form is painted on the screen correctly. This is the principal reason for using the 'paint' event for a call to 'DrawFullStage'.

When dealing with animation it is usually best to refer to all co-ordinates in pixel values. To ensure this the ScaleMode for the form must be set to 3. Other options are more suited to proportional fonts and graphs. When resizing the form you need to use the width and height. Resizing does not occur by using the ScaleHeight and ScaleWidth properties; new values in these simply alter the ScaleMode to 'user' or 0. The problem is that calls to 'Width' and 'Height' must be in 'Twips' – a ScaleMode that is referenced when ScaleMode is equal to 1. To resize the form in pixels you need to multiply the number of pixels in the X direction (wide) by 'Screen.TwipsPerPixelX', this converts pixels to Twips as required by the property 'Width'. Similarly, any change in the height is done by multiplying the new pixel height by 'Screen.TwipsPerPixelY' and calling the 'Height' property.

```
Private Sub Form_Load()
Dim i As Integer

 InitAnimation hDC, App.Path + "\bg.bmp"
 sprButton(0).Index = InitSprite(App.Path + "\buttons.bmp", ↵
10, 273, 28, 27)
 sprPlatform(0).Index = InitSprite(App.Path + ↵
"\vertplts.bmp", −100, 100, 34, 100)
 sprPlatform(1).Index = InitSprite(App.Path + ↵
"\horzplts.bmp", −100, 0, 84, 20)
 Width = 410 * Screen.TwipsPerPixelX
 Height = 350 * Screen.TwipsPerPixelY
 For i = 1 To 9
```

```
      sprButton(i).Index = CloneSprite(sprButton(0).Index, 0, 0)
      MoveSprite sprButton(i).Index, i * 30 + 10, 273, i
   Next
   For i = 1 To 6
      clsBucket(i).X = Int(Rnd() * 300) + 5
      clsBucket(i).Y = Int(Rnd() * 200) + 5
   Next
   intNumPlatforms = 2
   intNumBuckets = 7
   Timer1.Enabled = True
   'make sure we are using pixel values
   ScaleMode = 3
End Sub
```

The functionality to move the buckets by clicking on them is created using the Mouse_Down, Mouse_Move and Mouse_Up events.

The Mouse_Down event sets the index of a bucket that has been clicked if the function HitTest returns a value. This index is checked against the index values of the buckets. When the correct bucket is found the current value of 'i' is stored in the variable 'intDragBucket' and the sub-routine terminates.

```
Private Sub Form_MouseDown(Button As Integer, Shift As Integer, X
As Single, Y As Single)
   Dim i As Integer

   If intDragSpriteIndex = 0 Then
      intDragSpriteIndex = HitTest(X, Y)
      If intDragSpriteIndex Then
         For i = 0 To intNumBuckets - 1
            If intDragSpriteIndex = clsBucket(i).Index Then
               intDragBucket = i
               intDragPlatform = 0
               Exit For
            End If
         Next
      End If 'Hit sprite
   End If 'First hit test
End Sub
```

The value stored in 'intDragBucket' is used to call the method 'Drag' of the class 'BucketClass'. If this is all getting too confusing then have a short break and return refreshed. This exercise is about passing parameters to functions and methods, and it is essential that you are familiar with this way of working. This is extremely difficult, but the fog *will* lift as soon as sub-routines, functions, properties, methods and events are all second nature. What's that outside the window? Surely not a flying pig!

```
Private Sub Form_MouseMove(Button As Integer, Shift As Integer, X
As Single, Y As Single)
    If intDragBucket Then
      clsBucket(intDragBucket).Drag X, Y
    End If
End Sub
```

The Mouse_Up event is used to terminate dragging.

```
Private Sub Form_MouseUp(Button As Integer, Shift As Integer, X As
Single, Y As Single)
    If intDragBucket Then clsBucket(intDragBucket).EndDrag
    intDragSpriteIndex = 0
    intDragBucket = 0
    intDragPlatform = 0
    End If
End Sub
```

So after all the hard work, here is the benefit; the Timer event is now trivial. Just a call to move each bucket. The responsibility for moving the bucket is left to the bucket itself. Can you now see how this will make collision checking and maintenance easier?

```
Private Sub Timer1_Timer()
    Dim i As Integer

    For i = 0 To 6
      clsBucket(i).Move
    Next
    UpdateStage
End Sub
```

Review

In the first section of this book you have moved from simple variables to much more complex constructions called classes. You have learnt the importance of modular program design. All the time you are looking to create code that can be reused to make the programming cycle easier. Hopefully you have had fun on the way. It has been necessary to maintain your interest in this part, because there is so much to learn.

The next section of the book covers artwork creation. Animation and computer programming are remarkably similar: when you program games you are creating a world that you can control, and animation is also about creating worlds that you can control. Putting the two together allows for an interactive world of your creation. Now you know something of the art of code creation, you are ready to explore how to create the artwork for your sprites.

QUIZ

1. If 'c_length' is a private member of class 'Boat', then how can you access this value from a form?

Answer: Use

```
Public Property Get Length() As Integer
    Length = c-length
End Property
```

2. If 'c_length' is a private member of class 'Boat', how can you set the value of this variable from a form?

Answer:

```
Public Property Let Length(i As Integer)
    c_length = i
End Property
```

3. The class 'Boat' sails across the sea using values stored in the member variables 'c_x' and 'c_y'. Using a method 'Move', how do you create this in the class?

Answer:

```
Public Sub Move(X As Integer, Y As Integer)
    c_x = X
    c_y = Y
End Sub
```

4. Using the method 'Move' created in the previous question, how can you move the boat to (100, 200) in a form?

Answer:

```
boat.Move 100, 200
```

Summary

In this chapter you learnt about the main techniques of object-orientated programming.

- Encapsulation – black box code: you decide what others can do with your code.
- Inheritance – one black box can add new functionality to another black box.
- Polymorphism – same black box can be the parent of non-identical children.

Visual Basic allows you to use some of these ideas with the use of class modules.

PART TWO

The Magic Box

CHAPTER 7

Animation Art – It's life, but not as we know it

When creating interactive animation – the main concern of this book – programming is only part of the problem. The other challenge is to produce the pictures that form the animation. In this chapter we look briefly at the techniques that you can use to create the necessary artwork. You may not feel able to create this art: 'I can't draw', or '3D animation packages are so complicated', may be your reaction. If you want to be part of the team making the next Disney feature then you will need to be able to draw exceptionally well. If you want to create the next blockbuster game then you will need a team of 3D animators. If, however, you want to provide interesting and inventive art solutions for your next epic game, then stay tuned.

It's all done with mirrors

In the later half of the nineteenth century audiences were entertained with magic lantern shows. By using simple movements of the slides that made up the show, very simple animations were created that fascinated those watching. Creating a convincing illusion of movement on a two-dimensional screen required more technology than was then available.

Movement

NOTE

Run 'Ex07.exe' and press the 'Moving Still' button for this demonstration

Our eyes are amazing at detecting all forms of movement – objects or animals – even at a distance. The examples for this chapter are designed to just watch, and now is the time to try movement spotting. In this clip a small section of camouflage is moved briefly then stops. Once stationary it is incredibly difficult to spot, then, when it moves again, it is glaringly obvious. Our ability to recognize movement and patterns helps enormously when we view animated drawings.

Victorian toys

To capture and recreate movement was an obsession of many inventors as the last century drew to a close. Victorian developments included the Praxinoscope and the Zoetrope. One used mirrors, the other a slot as a shutter. (Press the Zoetrope button to see a demonstration.) The shutter is needed to break up the images being sent to the eye into small sections of time. Our eyes and brain are incredible but still have their limits. Send them still pictures fast enough and similar enough and the eye will try to create movement from the images. Just as we saw movement in the moving camouflage, we will see movement in the seemingly similar drawings. This is a demonstration of persistence of vision. There is nevertheless a limit to how fast our brain can decode the information it is receiving from our eyes.

As the nineteenth century came to an end technology continued to develop and the tricks of the Zoetrope were better understood. Taking photography, clear nitrate (a transparent plastic material), and mechanical sophistication, the Lumière brothers (Louis Lumière 1864–1948, Auguste Lumière 1862–1954) in France, invented cinema. George Méliès (1861–1938) took it further with his marvellous *Le Voyage dans la Lune* (A trip to the moon, 1902).

From a fairground spectacle to an international art form

From a fairground spectacle a new and dominant art form was created. Detractors at the time dismissed it as transitory and ephemeral. I wonder if that has a resonance with the reader. I hear that computer game play is ephemeral – a 90-day wonder. I don't think so. As today's generations get older, the technology yet more sophisticated and the developers mature, so we will be looking at an art form every bit as important as cinema. Try to think of yourselves as part of this pioneering spirit. I personally consider D.W. Griffith as the mould breaker for cinema. At first, cinema was restricted by its own technology: no colour, no sound. But, within the restrictions Griffith developed the fundamentals of film technique. Departing dramatically from stage performance, he directed his actors to move *towards* the camera rather than side to side, he introduced intercutting between long, medium and close-up shots and introduced editing techniques to indicate the passage of time. Computer entertainment, like cinema, involves a marriage of technology and art.

The other individual that I would rank with Griffith, Lumière and Méliès in the birth of cinema would be the inventor of the zoom lens, one of the most influential pieces of movie hardware.

In creating your animation art think of the invention that motivated these pioneers and particularly think new. You are actively involved in creating a new medium; do not just repeat old ideas, invent new ones.

Your first animation

Press the 'Frog' button on the demonstration for this chapter. This opens a new screen, where we can examine in detail the animation of the frog from Chapter 5. This animation uses just 12 different drawings to create the four actions necessary for the frog. In the game the frog needs to walk left and right, jump and get splattered. Try pressing the action buttons to review what the actions look like at a much increased size.

This section of animation is selected for economy rather than skill to show what can be made from just a few drawings. You may choose to use a 3D rendering animation package to create your animation art, the techniques of economy are still very useful. Games that load quickly without making endless demands on the hardware of the user are still attractive to audiences. I am sure there are still many Windows users who have a sneaky game of Solitaire in a quiet moment. The frog animation breaks down into a standard pose, a side walk, a jump and a splat.

Tens, not hundreds, of drawings

One of the first myths that I would like to explode is that animation needs thousands of different images. Here is a cartoon sprite that uses just 12. Now you may not feel like creating your own artwork and may be tempted to skip this chapter, but before you do, here are my top ten tips for interactive animation artwork.

1   Try to keep your sprites small, they will be drawn more quickly.
2   If an animation needs to change direction, use lots of frames.

3　Anticipate an action before doing it.
4　If drawing, use paper, not a computer.
5　Animation needs registration, keep the blitters in the right place.
6　Colour them to stand out from the background
7　Make all your sprite artwork share the same palette.
8　Apply stretch and squash to the animation
9　Always have a return position
10　Keep it simple.

Whether you create the art by drawing or by any other method, the top ten tips are still applicable. So we will look at each in turn.

1 Try to keep your sprites small, they will be drawn more quickly

If computers were fast enough to redraw the whole screen 25 times a second then you would be viewing great big video clips on your computer, not small ones. An average computer can cope with redrawing an area 320 × 240 about 20 times a second. You may have played DOS games that seem to redraw the whole screen very quickly and this is true. The trick is that they have set up the screen to only use 320 pixels across and between 200 and 240 pixels down. Windows needs 640 × 480 as a minimum and since you are learning to program you probably are comfortable with your computer and have it set-up to be at least 800 × 600. This means that you are only able to update a section of this screen fast enough to experience smooth animation. This is not a problem, it is more of a challenge. Try to develop games that do not require a full screen update many times a second. The 'Sprite.ocx' control that you will be using for the remainder of the book carefully considers all the movement going on and draws to the screen the smallest possible amount to keep the user's screen up to date. This technique is called the *dirty rectangle technique*. Instead of drawing the whole window it just redraws the area that is the combination of where the sprite was last drawn and where it is now.

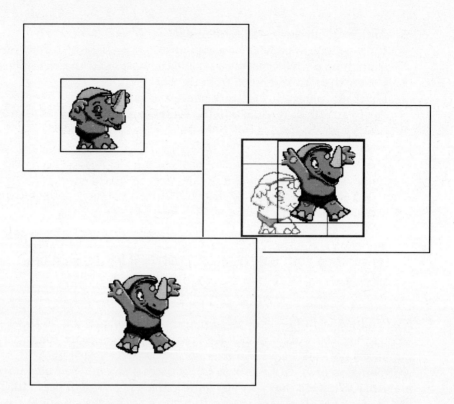

From the diagram you can see that in order to update the user's screen, simply drawing a new sprite frame at every new position would leave a trail of old frames on the screen. Calculating the combined area of the old and new positions means that when the sprite is redrawn the screen is correct. Perhaps you can see from this that big animation frames with large movements require more of the user's screen to be redrawn. If, then you create the animation, you intend to make use of the 'Sprite.ocx' control, then you will need to put all the frames together in a grid on one picture.

The program 'GridPics.exe' – which is the main topic of the next chapter and is in the utility folder on the CD – can help you make a big picture from lots of small ones.

2 If an animation needs to change direction, use lots of frames

Animation is as much about timing as it is about the look of an individual frame. Beautiful artwork can easily be destroyed by bad timing. When producing artwork for a Windows game it is reasonable to plan for around ten screen updates per second. I have produced many CD-ROM projects where the update rate is less, 8 fps as a minimum. When producing cartoon animation for television it is usual to use only 12 fps and the result is quite smooth.

> **NOTE**
>
>
> **My own choice of a highly influential animator is Richard Williams, who spent most of his working life producing animation for advertising from a studio in Soho, London. He did not like an update rate of 12 fps, known in theatrical and TV animation fields as shooting on twos, since film has an update rate of 24 fps. Richard Williams regarded it as moving still drawings, sensing the stationary poses between updates. You may be less critical.**

Whatever update rate you use, the issue of timing is still critical. Suppose you are moving a spaceship that needs to appear to have considerable dimensions. This body would have a great deal of momentum. Forcing it to slow to a halt and reverse direction would require both time and a great effort. On this scale the situation is obvious; it is rather more difficult to spot in a more general case like the frog jumping. In order to improve the feel of the animation, the frog does not jump directly; instead the frog compresses to anticipate the action of jumping, good fluid animation could use as many as 12 drawings just for this compression, and at film rates this would be just half a second. Having set up the jump the frog can now leap a considerable distance. But before falling it is as well to pack in some extra drawings. This is always the case: on a change of direction, point the change with additional drawings.

3 Anticipate an action before doing it

This follows on naturally from the previous tip. If it is possible in the run of the game to anticipate, then do it. For example, the head pops around the door before the rest of the body follows. If you are setting up a gag then a wrinkled lipped character could show his head around the corner of the door; now wait for at least 2 seconds for the audience to react, don't destroy the impact by going off too soon. In most computer games you do not have the filmic luxury of intercutting a close up, so the wait can be even longer than you would choose on film. Finally after the lingering wait he walks out and we can see that he is out of place in a gorilla outfit. Now, if a real gorilla walked in immediately it would not raise a response; if, however, you use a sound effect off stage and our hero looks even more anxious, then this just helps to explain the situation and helps build anticipation.

4 If drawing, use paper, not a computer

This is my Luddite principle.

NOTE

The Luddites were an organisation devoted to destroying machines as England became industrialised nearly 200 hundred years ago. It is commonly used to indicate someone who is reluctant to accept developments in technology.

Having been a professional animator since 1980, I consider drawing with a computer to be as natural as swimming 100 metres under water with both hands tied behind my back. The truth is I cannot stand it. If you choose to draw, and I don't expect that many of you will, then get a light box – that is, construct a box containing a small fluorescent tube and place a sheet of translucent plastic over the light. When you put paper on this box it is illuminated from below rather than from above. In this way it is possible to see through several layers of paper. The idea of onion skinning that is surfacing in some more recent computer paint packages owes its birth to this simple tool.

Once you have your light box buy the best pencil sharpener you can afford, and you will be able to get a very good electric one for as little as the cost of 4 MB of ram. The only other thing you will need is paper and a registration device. You could get official punched animation paper, which is punched with two long holes and one circular hole. To use this kind of paper you will need an animation peg bar. You can, however, get just as good results using the standard two-hole punch for school files and some thin paper. Make a holding device for the two-hole punch paper by drilling small holes into the translucent plastic and buying some thin dowel to plug these holes.

5 Animation needs registration, keep the blitters in the right place

Another important factor when creating animation is the registration that you use. If the artwork is allowed to shift when it should stay in one place the illusion will be immediately ruined. For nearly all the artwork on the CD, I used a very simple system. A single cross allowed me to line up the artwork using the 'gridpics' tool. The technique is as follows:

- Create the artwork using an animation peg bar for registration.
- Place a single cross in the same place on each drawing.
- Import the drawings into the 'gridpic' package.
- Reposition the drawings so the cross is in the same place for each drawing. Using the arrow keys moves the active drawing by a single pixel.
- Drag a bounding rectangle around the artwork and move through the drawings to make sure nothing runs off the edge.
- Finally decide how many columns and rows you want for your drawings.
- Clicking 'make grid' will create the combined picture for you to use with the 'Sprite.ocx' control.

6 Colour them to stand out from the background

The relative balance of animation and background is what the user will see on the screen. Make sure it works well.

7 Make all your sprite artwork share the same palette

Most users are still viewing your game on a computer screen that can show at most 256 colours.

NOTE

 See Chapter 17 for more explanation of how palettes work.

You can use a package like Paint Shop Pro (it's on the CD) to ensure that all the artwork for a game has a common palette. To create the palette in the first place, use 24-bit artwork; copy sections of all the artwork onto the same picture until this picture has a version of nearly every colour that you will use in the game. Now reduce the colour depth of this picture. If you then save the palette for this picture, you can apply this palette to all the artwork in the game. When you remap a picture select 'nearest colour' for all the sprite artwork, otherwise Paint Shop Pro will try make the sprites' transparent colour look more like the actual colour by *dithering*. When you eventually display this sprite, the artwork will be surrounded by random pixels.

Another trick is to use oversize scanning. If you need animation that is, say, 100 × 100 pixels, scan the artwork at 500 × 500 pixels. Flood fill areas of colour up to a boundary, again using Paint Shop Pro. This artwork can then be resampled down to the right size, and hey presto, no jagged edges. You will however be left with the problem of fringing colours when you use a single transparent colour. If you are creating a cartoon that has a black line, then try surrounding the animation with dark grey before resampling. Replacing the dark grey with white before reducing the colour depth to 256 colours should help reduce the fringing and the artwork quality within the transparent colour will be gorgeous. One final point about transparency: the 'Sprite.ocx' control takes the colour in the top left pixel to be the chosen transparent colour. Be aware of this when controlling the transparent areas of your sprite.

8   Apply stretch and squash to the animation

When a ball hits the floor, it compresses before recovering its spherical shape and bouncing away from the floor. This observation from life is something that you can use in your animation. When an arm bends the overall volume remains the same but the arm fattens, displaying muscles. Try to keep volumes the same but shape can alter radically. Extremes of stretch and squash are often a feature of the wonderful cartoons that bear the name Tex Avery. In the days before Disney made animation strictly for kids, Tex was producing cartoons to delight more grown-ups than school children.

9   Always have a return position

Games that use lots of beautiful animation are often rightly criticised for a lack of game play. The designers have thought too linearly when creating their masterpiece. I know this is not a mistake that you will make, but just in case, the tip is: Have a master position, and whatever animation you do, return to this position.

10   Keep it simple

You are learning; Rome wasn't built in a day, so keep it simple. Don't use 100 drawings when 20 will do. The user will value speed of loading and game play over elegant animation movements that are only used once.

But, I can't draw

Don't worry. If you have a video camera and a card for your PC to input video, then try setting up a couple of lights and using Plasticine or Plastalena. You can get terrific results using this technique.

The keys to success with plasticine

Make sure your camera is very rigid. Professionally, the cameras are mounted on stands that could withstand a punch from a boxer and not move. If you cannot reach that standard then don't worry, just make it as rigid as possible

Support the plasticine inside with a skeleton made of wire. In this form it will stand up to the remodelling that you will be doing to create all the positions for your game. Try to avoid lights appearing to come from every angle. Use directional lights from one angle and diffused lights from elsewhere. When shooting models for the TV, wooden frames that are covered with tracing paper are used to diffuse the light and disguise the direction of the shadow.

When the animation is shot you will need to strip it from the background to place it over the background of your choice. You will need a colour in the background that is even and does not reflect back into the model. Try to get as much space as possible between the model and this coloured background. Light the background independently of the model. This type of animation is sometimes called 'Stop-frame' animation as you shoot a stationary frame and move the image before shooting the next frame.

Another simple approach that does not require drawing skills is the use of cut outs. Look through magazines for interesting pictures, cut them out and move them on a scanner to create simple walks and other movements. The technique can give entertaining and highly original results.

Live action as animation

If you have a video camera and a good stand for the camera then try a technique pioneered by Norman McClaren at the National Film Board of Canada. Norman won an Oscar for an animation film he produced that involved no drawing at all. Instead he worked real people holding a pose while he shot a frame of film, then they moved to a new position where he shot another pose. When he played the film back at speed the people seem to move in a strange and unnatural way. This worked very well in the film he was creating called 'Neighbours' where the stupidity of war is exemplified by two feuding neighbours, who fight to be the owner of a beautiful flower that grows on the boundary of their properties.

Props as animation

The same film maker used similar techniques to bring to life a chair and a table. While studying at the Glasgow School of Art he created a film which has influenced a thousand pop videos. He imbued life into inanimate objects. Your objects could be Lego bricks, drinks cans or microchips. Simply move them slightly, shooting one frame at a time, and grab the result. Then use a paint package and 'gridpics' to organise them for the 'Sprite.ocx' control.

Puppets

I often favour the use of rod, glove or string puppets. Again you can shoot the results into the camera using a video camera and an input card. Alternatively you may have a digital camera which would allow you to create the images. Any method getting the images into your computer is fine. Any technique that you use is fine. Never feel intimidated by the craft. Terry Gilliam, of Monty Python fame, created terrific animations using the most basic of equipment and the most limited of budgets. He has since produced elaborate and expensive live action films, and not all of these later works are improvements on the rough and ready animations that he created in his early career.

Recommendations

This chapter is a brief introduction to the techniques involved in animation. If this is an area of real interest then I can recommend only one book. For nearly 2000 years mathematicians relied on Euclid's *Elements* for their knowledge of mathematics. *The Illusion of Life* by Frank Thomas and Ollie Johnston is the animation equivalent. Regardless of the technique that you choose to use, a deep study of this book will be both rewarding and informative. I cannot recommend it enough. Go out and buy it!

Another very popular approach is to use 3D computer graphics packages to create rendered animations that you can use in your game. There are many choices when using 3D graphics. Professionally we use 3D Studio and Lightwave 3D which are both fast and robust. Animation Master is another useful 3D graphics program which is available for under £500. Watch for offers in computer magazines; there are often demos available that will help you to decide which package to choose. 3D ray tracing is very demanding on hardware, but 3D boards are becoming available that make the processes more interactive. Where previously you had to wait to see a test render, render views that show the model in a great deal of complexity are instantly redrawn as changes are made using OpenGL libraries. 3D Studio Max provides this level of functionality, but you would be looking at around £5000 minimum for software and hardware, which is obviously outside the budget of most people.

Animation is fun to do and very rewarding. Don't feel that you are only able to use artwork created by someone else in your games. Using one of the techniques covered in this chapter you can start to create your own animations and develop a style that is distinctively your own.

QUIZ

1. To create fluid animation for a computer game, what is the minimum number of images per second?
Answer: At least 8 frames per second; ideally 12 or more.

2. To make your animation seem to have more weight, do you use more drawings, or less, as the action changes direction?
Answer: More.

3. If you are using stop-frame animation how do you prepare the animation for use as a sprite?

Answer: The animation must be shot against an even colour that is not a part of the animation. In this way you can use a paint package to provide a consistent and flat colour behind the animation. This colour can be made transparent when you use the 'Sprite.ocx' control or the 'Sprite.dll' library.

4. Should you create the animation initially the size that you will need in the game?

Answer: No, produce it oversize and use a paint package to resample it to a smaller size. This will result in an improvement in the quality of the artwork.

Summary

- You don't need to be able to draw to create animation.
- To use the 'Sprite.ocx' control you need to prepare your pictures in a grid using 'gridpics.exe' on the CD.
- Your animation should all use the same palette if possible.
- Try to use as few frames as possible since more frames mean a slower load time for the user, and can result in a lack of game play.

CHAPTER 8

Your toolbox – Making tools with Visual Basic

While writing programs you will need to use many different tools. Often those tools will be available from software shops, or the web. But sometimes the tool that you need will not exist. This chapter is about using Visual Basic to write your own tools.

Most of the examples in this book so far have used a dynamic link library called 'Sprite.dll'. This library contains special functions that add to the existing functionality of Visual Basic to extend the programming environment in a way that is suited to animation programmers. The example in this chapter, however, uses just the controls, properties, functions and events that are available in the standard version of Visual Basic 5.0. This example is intended to help familiarise you with the richness available in the programming environment that comes with each version of Visual Basic. We use no calls to the Windows API and no custom controls that are not already available on your computer.

What is the Windows API?

Windows is designed to allow programmers like yourself to greatly improve their own programs by using the functions that Windows uses when it is running. You can add Windows functions to your own programs by declaring them either in a separate module or declaring them in a form module as 'Private'. 'Private' means that that function can only be used from the module in which it is declared. If you are still confused by 'scope' then I recommend that you review Chapter 2. The declaration tells Visual Basic how to pass information to the function and how to retrieve the information that is returned. An example is:

```
Declare Function BitBlt Lib ''gdi32'' (ByVal hDestDC As Long, ByVal
x As Long, ByVal y As Long, ByVal nWidth As Long, ByVal nHeight As
Long, ByVal hSrcDC As Long, ByVal xSrc As Long, ByVal ySrc As Long,
ByVal dwRop As Long) As Long
```

'BitBlt' is a very popular function for graphics-orientated programmers. Many experienced programmers have a love–hate relationship with the function 'BitBlt'. The reason for the love is that it works in just about every circumstance and every computer; it is hated because it can be slow. It is sometimes slow because it is a general-purpose function with error checking and accommodates just about every mistaken use that could ever be thrown at it. It also looks after transfers between device contexts that can have different palettes. More information about palettes and device contexts is given in Chapter 17.

You may find the long declaration very intimidating. It is really much simpler than it looks. First we learn that this is a function, it could be a sub-routine in which case there would be no returned value. If this is confusing then you may like to review Chapter 5 which looks at how sub-routines and functions behave. After deciding whether we have a sub-routine or a function, Visual Basic is told where to look for this function, in this case in the dynamic link library 'gdi32'. This would often be 'xxx.dll', the name of a dynamic link library file. If the library is given without a path then it must be one of the paths included in the DOS path list. It is common to place the '.dll' file in the 'Windows\System' directory.

Now we come to the issue of passing parameters by reference or by value. The simple advice is, pass them 'ByVal'. By this method you are passing the parameter in such a way that it has a value to the function being called. If the value is manipulated in the calling function, then your version of the value remains the same. If, however, you call by reference, which is the default for Visual Basic, then you are in actual fact passing a pointer to the variable. Remember that variables are little areas of memory, pigeon holes, set aside by the programmer to use in the program. Each of these pigeon holes has a unique address, the value of the memory location. When you pass by reference you pass the memory location number and the type of variable to expect to find there. This is a very confusing issue and represents the biggest obstacle for programmers learning to use programming languages like C.

NOTE

Each of the variables that the function requires is included in the declaration list. In this way all the functions and sub-routines that are available to Windows are also available to the Visual Basic programmer.

Remember the beginning of Chapter 2: 'Computer programming is about the manipulation of data structures'? Does that feel any better now? NO! Oh dear, well in this chapter you will learn how to use a standard box of Visual Basic features to manipulate your data.

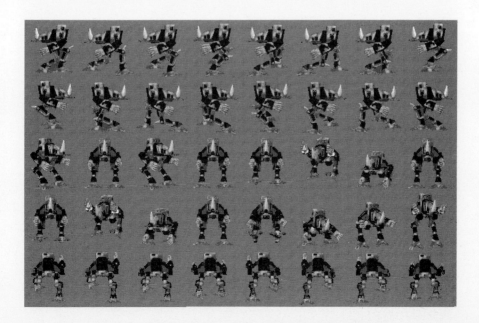

The purpose of the example is to prepare artwork created by a paint package, or a 3D computer program, into a format that is required by the 'Sprite.dll' library or the 'Sprite.ocx' control; that is, a grid of pictures all on one standard Windows bitmap, a '.bmp' file.

When you use a computer graphics program you often use a format for the output of 320 × 240. This may be much bigger than your artwork. To use the libraries included with this book, you need to get as many pictures as possible in the smallest space possible with no overlaps. This is a job for a computer and an ideal task to create your own special tool. This type of tool needs to be functional, but you don't have to worry about too much error checking since you will be either using the tool yourself or overseeing whoever does use it.

The GridPic specification

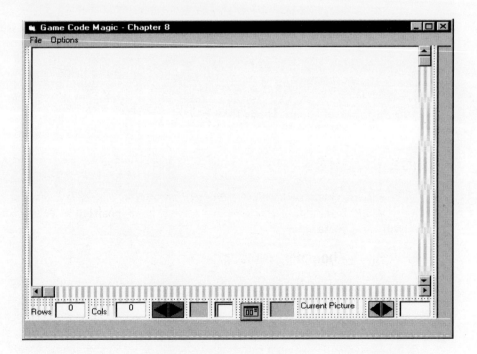

Before you start any programming job I recommend spending some time writing a specification. What do you want the program to do? The most basic specification would include:

- Initialisation
- User input
- Data manipulation
- User output
- Termination

For this program the user can load pictures, move each picture in turn, view and manipulate a bounding rectangle, create an array of the pictures in a chosen format, and save the result.

Loading pictures

Only the standard Windows bitmap format is supported, that is files with the '*.bmp' extension. We need to be able to load many of these. In the specification we will allow for the selection of all the pictures in a particular directory or folder. We will allow the user to add to the currently loaded pictures. If we were producing a complete program then the software would allow the user to delete some or all of the currently loaded pictures and support extensive error correction if the user incorrectly chose to load the wrong format. This example stops short of this detail. This is a tool for programmers, not a fully idiot protected final program. It is useful to understand the difference. Writing programs that allow the user easily, conveniently and robustly to manipulate data, is the aim of all programmers. The robustness can often be the hardest part of the specification.

Moving pictures

Having loaded the pictures, we wish to be able at a simple mouse click to view the selection of pictures and adjust their position in relation to a bounding rectangle.

Altering the bounding rectangle

One of the aims with this program is to allow the user to adjust the region that bounds and clips the bitmap. Perhaps the animation is not easily contained and needs to be moved frame by frame. This is a feature of the program. The bounding rectangle is displayed throughout and clicking on the top left corner or the top right corner allows the user to adjust this bounding rectangle.

Making the array of pictures and saving the result

The aim of the program is to allow the user to create an array of pictures and save the result.

Having drawn up a list of specifications, the next step is to attempt to decide on the Visual Basic controls required for its implementation.

- To hold the array of loaded pictures: A control array of picture box controls
- To move from picture to picture: a spin control.
- To load the pictures: a menu call that opens a special dialog box.
- To manipulate the loaded pictures: a picture control displaying them as icons.
- To move through the loaded pictures: a scroll control.
- To adjust the format of the final result: a spin control.
- To save the final picture: a common dialog box as used by most Windows programs.

To further develop the specification, try to write in simple English how to respond to the events that will occur in the lifetime of your program and the functions that your program will call. A common approach is to use PDL (Programming Design Language) which works far better than flow charts for most programmers.

The 'LoadPictures' call could become

```
LoadPictures
    open a dialog to retrieve the file paths of the chosen files
        Offer the ability to do nothing or load many pictures
Create the controls that will hold the newly loaded material.
        If there are controls to load then decide whether to delete the
        old controls.
        Load the pictures into the controls. Analyse possible load
        errors and inform the user if appropriate.
```

This simple list of English instructions is an attempt to remain abstract about the problem. Never start by writing code, always start by analysing the problem and fully understanding how to implement the specification. You would always use a plan before building a house. Always plan your software construction.

Using a special dialog box for user input

I chose to use a special dialog box, that is a window other than the usual form that is loaded in the code for the purpose of special user input or output, for the picture loading. The use of a special dialog box allowed for multiple loading of pictures. This is very likely to be the choice of the user. The application only becomes useful when several pictures are loaded.

LoadForm – a special dialog box for loading multiple pictures

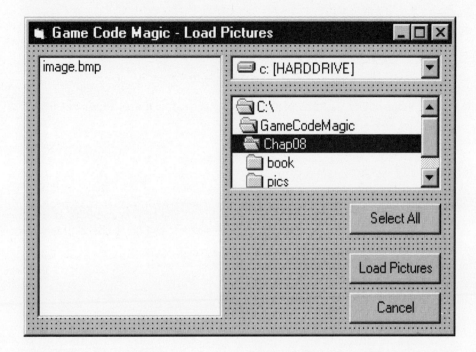

The chosen form has a drive control. This is a special control that allows the user to select a drive. There is also a directory list, which again the user can select with the mouse. Finally, a file list box is included that allows the user easily and efficiently to explore and select files.

The implementation

First the simple stuff:

```
Private Sub Form_Load()
   left = (Screen.width - width) / 2
   top = (Screen.height - height) / 2
End Sub
```

This places the dialog box in the centre of the user's computer screen when it is loaded.

Selecting all the files in a file list box

This achieved with a simple control loop.

```
Private Sub cmdAll_Click()
  Dim i As Integer

  For i = 0 To fleList.ListCount − 1
    fleList.Selected(i) = True
  Next
End Sub
```

A file list box has a special property that is the number of entries in the list. If the list was:

file1.txt
file2.txt
file3.txt

then 'ListCount' would be 3. The first selection is index 0. If the file list box had been given the name 'fleList' to select these files you could use:

fleList.Selected(0) = True
fleList.Selected(1) = True
fleList.Selected(2) = True

In the code, a 'For ... Next' construction is used when the 'Select All' button is clicked. The code iterates through all the files in the current directory and chooses to select them all.

```
Private Sub cmdCancel_Click()
  Unload LoadForm
End Sub
```

It is always good programming practice to allow the user to step back without doing anything. The 'Cancel' button provides the perfect implementation for this. If the user decides the time is not right to load the pictures then nothing is done by unloading this special dialog box.

The 'Load Pictures' command button

```
Private Sub cmdLoad_Click()
  Dim i As Integer, intNumSelected As Integer, intIndex As Integer
  Dim blnFirst As Boolean
```

```
    'Check to see if any are selected
    For i = 0 To fleList.ListCount - 1
      If fleList.Selected(i) Then
        intNumSelected = intNumSelected + 1
      End If
    Next
    'If some selected then prepare to load them
    If intNumSelected Then
      'now load new controls
      For i = GridPicForm.NumPics To intNumSelected +
GridPicForm.NumPics - 1
        If i Then Load GridPicForm.picImage(i)
        GridPicForm.picImage(i).AutoSize = True
        GridPicForm.picImage(i).AutoRedraw = True
        End If
      Next
    Else
      LoadForm.Visible = False
      Exit Sub
    End If
    'load picture into new control
    intIndex = GridPicForm.NumPics
    blnFirst = True
    For i = 0 To fleList.ListCount - 1
      If fleList.Selected(i) Then
        If right(dirList.Path, 1) = ''\'' Then
          GridPicForm.picImage(intIndex).Picture =
LoadPicture(dirList.Path + fleList.List(i))
        Else
          GridPicForm.picImage(intIndex).Picture =
LoadPicture(dirList.Path + ''\'' + fleList.List(i))
          'Debug.Print dirList.Path + ''\'' + fleList.List(i)
        End If
        intIndex = intIndex + 1
      End If
    Next
    GridPicForm.NumPics = GridPicForm.NumPics + intNumSelected
    GridPicForm.vsrIcons.Max = GridPicForm.NumPics
    GridPicForm.vsrIcons.Value = 0
    GridPicForm.vsrIcons_Change
    LoadForm.Visible = False
End Sub
```

The code attached to the 'Load Pictures' button is much more complicated. We can look at this a bit at a time. First the 'local' variables are defined. Next the current list is looped through to see if a selection has been made. If a selection has been made then the picture controls that will be used to store the individual pictures are systematically loaded. At this stage these controls do not have the pictures loaded, they are simply empty controls ready to receive the pictures. Certain properties of the controls are set.

TIP

When dynamically creating controls at run time the programmer must set the required properties. When loading the control the default properties are not the same as the defaults at design time.

The picture controls must have 'AutoSize' and 'AutoRedraw' set to True. If no pictures were selected then the form is set to invisible and the sub-routine is terminated. It is good programming practice to use the true section of a 'If ... Then ... Else ... End If' construction, for the default case. Here it was decided that the user was more likely to choose to load pictures than not.

In the next section of code the selected items from the list are used for the picture loading. It is here that a complete program would error check for appropriate data. The user could have chosen unsuitable files. The file list has a filter set to only show '*.bmp' files, so a very primitive error check has been used. This filter is set at design time. Look at the properties list for the file list control to see how this has been set.

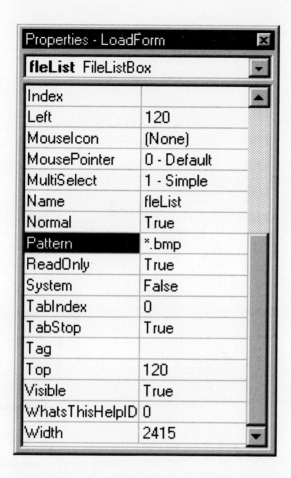

The pattern property is set to '*.bmp'.

Synchronising drive, directory and file list controls

When using the file list, directory list and drive list, they must be synchronised. This is very easy; you simply add the following code to their change events:

```
Private Sub dirList_Change()
   fleList.Path = dirList.Path 'When directory changes, set file
path.
End Sub
```

```
Private Sub drvList_Change()
   dirList.Path = drvList.Drive 'When drive changes, set directory
path.
End Sub
```

Main form declarations

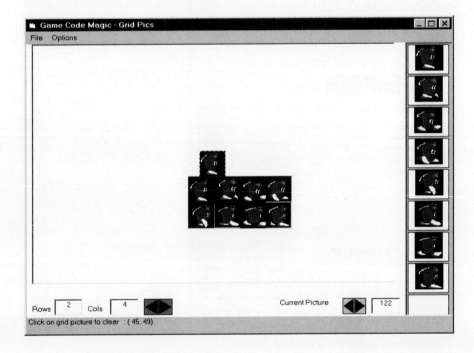

```
GridPicForm
(General) – (declarations)
Public intNumPics As Integer
Public intFirstIcon As Integer
Dim intShowPic As Integer

Private Type Pos
   left As Integer
   top As Integer
   init As Boolean
End Type

Private Type Rect
   left As Integer
```

```
   top As Integer
   right As Integer
   bottom As Integer
End Type

Dim posPic(300) As Pos
Dim posMovePic As Pos
Dim rctCutRect As Rect
Dim rctDragRect As Integer

Const TOPLEFT = 2
Const BOTTOMRIGHT = 3
```

Here two special types are created, a few module level variables and
two constants. As usual the Form Load event is used for one-off
initialisation. Form sizing and positioning and setting the display for
the miniature picture strip up the left hand side are all performed as
part of the Form_Load event.

```
Private Sub Form_Load()
   Dim i As Integer
   width = 640 * Screen.TwipsPerPixelX
   height = 480 * Screen.TwipsPerPixelY
   left = (Screen.width - width) / 2
   top = (Screen.height - height) / 2
   picIcons.AutoRedraw = True
   For i = 0 To 480 Step 60
      picIcons.PaintPicture picBorder.Picture, 0, i
   Next
   picBigPic.DrawStyle = 2
   picBigPic.DrawMode = 6
   rctCutRect.left = 100
   rctCutRect.top = 100
   rctCutRect.right = 300
   rctCutRect.bottom = 300
   intNumPics = 0
End Sub
```

The Form Resize event is used to make sure that the bounding
rectangle is displayed.

```
Private Sub Form_Resize()
  picBigPic.Line (rctCutRect.left, rctCutRect.top) –
  (rctCutRect.right, rctCutRect.bottom), , B
End Sub
```

The form includes a big picture control that acts as the main display. It is here that the manipulation of the pictures takes place and the bounding rectangle is determined. The miniature picture control at the left is for extending the functionality of the program at a later date. The current program does not allow the user to alter the order of the picture. This control is intended to provide the interface for such functions. At the bottom of the screen are two spin controls to allow the user to select the loaded pictures and to determine how they will be laid out on the final grid picture. 16 pictures could be laid out in the following way:

Rows	Columns
1	16
2	8
4	4
8	2
16	1

This control allows you to select the option that suits the program that you are creating.

The Form Activate event is used to set these controls after the load pictures form has been used. As the main form is reactivated, so the following code executes:

```
Private Sub Form_Activate()
  If intNumPics Then
    txtRows.Caption = 1
    txtCols.Caption = intNumPics
    mnuMakeGridPic.Enabled = True
    vsrIcons.Max = intNumPics
    If Not posPic(intShowPic).init Then
      posPic(intShowPic).init = True
      posPic(intShowPic).left = (picBigPic.ScaleWidth –
          picImage(intShowPic).ScaleWidth) / 2
      posPic(intShowPic).top = (picBigPic.ScaleHeight –
          picImage(intShowPic).ScaleHeight) / 2
```

```
    End If
    picBigPic.PaintPicture picImage(intShowPic).Picture,
            posPic(intShowPic).left, posPic(intShowPic).top
    picBigPic.Line (rctCutRect.left, rctCutRect.top) —
(rctCutRect.right, rctCutRect.bottom), , B
    End If
End Sub
```

The most interesting operation here is the use of Visual Basic's 'PaintPicture' method. All picture controls and forms can use this method. Instead of replacing the picture with another picture using the assignment operator ('='), the PaintPicture method allows you to replace a section of a picture by a section of another. The method takes a large number of parameters, but these are quite simple to follow.

```
object.PaintPicture picture, x1, y1, width1, height1, x2, y2,
width2, height2, opcode
```

Firstly, the source picture is defined, then the position for the destination picture and its width and height. Next the position for the source picture is defined and the size of the section being used. Finally, a code is used to determine the type of operation taking place. For now, simply leave this parameter out, the result will be to copy the two pictures. By adjusting the parameters for the source and destination width and height it is possible to stretch or shrink the picture.

'PaintPicture' is an extremely useful method that was only introduced to Visual Basic in version 4.0. Before that you were required to use a Windows API function.

Using menus

If this is the first time you have used a menu in a Visual Basic program then you may need a little explanation of how they work. Menus are created with the Menu Editor which is next to the 'properties' button on the toolbar. Just like the 'properties' button the 'Menu Editor' button is only available when the form is displayed.

Using the Menu Editor

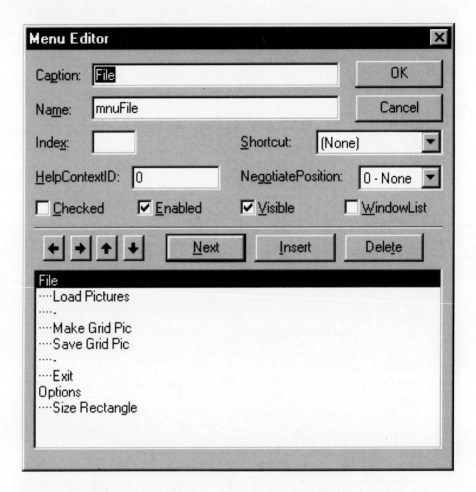

Enter a word in the caption box. This will be the word actually
displayed in the menu. Make sure you enter a name for this selection.
It is the name given to the selection that is used in the code. In
addition, you can set details such as whether the selection is enabled;
if it is not enabled then it will be displayed in greyed out form in the
menu. A selection can also be part of an array of choices if they are
connected. If this is the case then set the index values in the same
order as they appear in the menu. Whether a caption appears on the
main menu or a sub-menu is determined by its indent. Use the arrow
buttons to adjust the ideating for a selection. Finally close the box to
confirm the menu. The menu options will now be available in code as
below:

```
Private Sub mnuLoadPics_Click()
   Load LoadForm
   LoadForm.dirList.Path = App.Path
   LoadForm.Show 1
End Sub
```

This simple code loads the Load Pictures form we discussed earlier.

When the application first loads the 'MakeGridPic' option on the menu, and the 'SavePicture' options are disabled – that is, there are no pictures loaded to use to make the grid picture and so, obviously, there is no grid picture to save – the form activate code is used to enable 'mnuMakeGridPic' when the value of 'intNumPics' is greater than 0. This is the code that executes when this selection is chosen:

```
Private Sub mnuMakeGridPic_Click()
   Dim i As Integer, x As Integer, y As Integer
   Dim cx As Integer, cy As Integer
   Dim intDestX As Integer, intDestY As Integer, intDestWidth As
Integer, intDestHeight As Integer                               ↵
   Dim intSrcX As Integer, intSrcY As Integer

   If txtRows.Caption = ''1'' Then
      i = MsgBox(''Only one row?'', vbYesNo, ''GridPics Message'')
      If i = vbNo Then Exit Sub
   Else
      i = MsgBox(txtRows.Caption + ''rows and'' + txtCols.Caption
+ ''columns'', vbYesNo, ''GridPics Message'')                   ↵
      If i = vbNo Then Exit Sub
   End If
   'must be OK
   'Load picture into control to set palette for the device context
   picGridPic.Picture = picImage(0).Picture
   'Make sure all painting goes to the persistent bitmap
   picGridPic.AutoRedraw = True
   cx = rctCutRect.right — rctCutRect.left
   cy = rctCutRect.bottom — rctCutRect.top
   picGridPic.width = cx * Val(txtCols.Caption) *
Screen.TwipsPerPixelX                                           ↵
   picGridPic.height = cy * Val(txtRows.Caption) *
Screen.TwipsPerPixelY                                           ↵
  x = 0
  y = 0
```

```
For i = 0 To intNumPics − 1

  If Not posPic(i).init Then
    posPic(i).init = True
    posPic(i).left = rctCutRect.left
    posPic(i).top = rctCutRect.top
  End If

  If rctCutRect.left < posPic(i).left Then
    intDestX = x + posPic(i).left − rctCutRect.left
    intSrcX = 0
    intDestWidth = cx − (posPic(i).left − rctCutRect.left)
  Else
    intDestX = x
    intSrcX = rctCutRect.left − posPic(i).left
    intDestWidth = cx − intSrcX
  End If

  If rctCutRect.top < posPic(i).top Then
    intDestY = y + posPic(i).top − rctCutRect.top
    intSrcY = 0
    intDestHeight = cy − (posPic(i).top − rctCutRect.top)
  Else
    intDestY = y
    intSrcY = rctCutRect.top − posPic(i).top
    intDestHeight = cy − intSrcY
  End If

  picGridPic.PaintPicture picImage(i).Picture, intDestX,
intDestY, intDestWidth,_intDestHeight, intSrcX, intSrcY,
intDestWidth, intDestHeight
    x = x + cx
    If x > picGridPic.ScaleWidth Then
      x = 0
      y = y + cy
    End If
  Next
  'Show the result
  picGridPic.left = (Screen.width − picGridPic.width) / 2
  picGridPic.top = (Screen.height − picGridPic.height) / 2
  picGridPic.Visible = True

  mnuSaveGridPic.Enabled = True
  lblStatus.Caption = ''Click on grid picture to clear''
End Sub
```

It may look a little daunting but taken a bit at a time you will be able to understand what is going on.

As usual the code begins by declaring the local variables to be used in this sub-routine. Then the values in the rows and columns boxes are confirmed. One of two message boxes is used for the confirmation. If only 1 row is chosen then the first box is displayed. I chose to use this as the default since this is what will happen if the user does not alter the rows and columns spin control. A message box is displayed using the function 'MsgBox'. This function takes three parameters: first, the displayed caption; second, the type of box, in this case a yes–no box having just two buttons; third, the caption for the window. The message box can return a value which can be used to control program flow. In this case if the user says no then the sub-routine is exited.

It is essential that the receiving picture shares the same palette as the individual pictures. This is done by setting the picture property for the receiving picture 'picGridPic' to the first of the individual pictures. The AutoRedraw property is then set to True to ensure that all the picture copying that takes place will be saved in memory. 'cx' and 'cy' store the width and height of the bounding rectangle. It is important to resize the 'picGridPic' control to the size of the bounding rectangle multiplied by the number of rows and columns, and the next section of code does just that.

Having initialised these important parameters the individual pictures are taken in turn and copied in the correct position to the 'picGridPic' control. The position of the top left corner of the small picture dictates how it should be copied, the details are set up in the variables 'intDestX', 'intDestY', 'intSrcX', 'intSrcY', 'intDestWidth' and 'intDestHeight'. The destination position targets are updated at the end of the loop. If the x setting exceeds the width of 'picGridPic' then it must be time to move to the next line down, so x is reset and y is increased by the bounding rectangle height which has previously been stored in the variable 'cy'.

Once the copying is finished the 'picGridPic' control is positioned in the centre of the screen and is set to be visible. The enabled property of the menu selection 'Save GridPic' is set to True. Finally, a label control is used as a status bar, and is filled with a text message.

Saving the picture

The code to save the picture is very simple:

```
Private Sub mnuSaveGridPic_Click()
    Dim filename As String

    cmnDialog.ShowSave
    SavePicture picGridPic.Image, cmnDialog.filename
End Sub
```

This uses a Common Dialog control, which is a standard extension that comes with Visual Basic. To make sure it is part of the current project, use the Tools menu option and select Custom Controls. Make sure that Microsoft Common Dialog Control is checked.

Using the Common Dialog Control

Simply set the properties that you require.

Properties - GridPicForm	☒
cmnDialog CommonDialog	▾
Color	&H00000000& ▲
Copies	0
DefaultExt	
DialogTitle	Save Picture
FileName	image.bmp
Filter	Pictures (*.bmp)|*.bmp
FilterIndex	0
Flags	0
FontBold	False
FontItalic	False
FontName	
FontSize	8
FontStrikeThru	False
FontUnderLine	False
FromPage	0
HelpCommand	0
HelpContext	0
HelpFile	
HelpKey	
Index	
InitDir	app.path
Left	4200 ▼

In this example I have set the caption to 'Save Pictures', the filename to 'Image.bmp', the filter to 'Pictures (*.bmp)|*.bmp' and the 'InitDir' to 'App.Path'. The file name is the default name that will appear in the dialog box so that the user can save the picture simply by clicking the enter key. The filter is a little more complicated. Windows presents a filtered choice of files in a directory based on the filter. To define a filter two sections are used: the first section is simply what is displayed to the user, which, by convention, shows a descriptive word followed by the three letter extension in brackets. It can be any text as this is only a convention. The second part following '|' is the actual DOS extension, which must be accurate. In the example the only files that can be used are '.bmp' so there is only one type of filter. The filter could be a choice of several options, for this to work the filterindex property is also used to set the filter.

If the filter is 'Pictures (*.bmp)|*.bmp|All Files (*.*)|*.*' and the filterindex is set to 1, then the dialog box would display the second option as the first option has index 0.

To display the dialog box the method 'object.ShowSave' is used, where 'object' is the name of your Common Dialog Control. This displays the standard Windows 95 save dialog box. When the user selects the appropriate file and presses save this, of course, does not have the effect of saving the appropriate file. Instead the dialog box filename is set, which is all the Common Dialog box is used for – to get user input. It is then your job as programmer to use the filename for your own save routine. Here the Visual Basic function 'SavePicture' is used. This takes two parameters, the picture that is being saved and the filename under which it is being saved.

Allowing the user to manipulate the pictures

The main picture control responds to mouse clicks in one of two ways. Either the user can move the bitmap, or the user can drag the bounding rectangle. I chose to select between the two with a menu option of size rectangle.

```
Private Sub mnuSizeRect_Click()
   picBigPic.Line (rctCutRect.left − 2, rctCutRect.top − 2) −
(rctCutRect.left + 2, rctCutRect.top + 2), , BF         ↵
   picBigPic.Line (rctCutRect.right − 2, rctCutRect.bottom − 2) −
(rctCutRect.right + 2, rctCutRect.bottom + 2), , BF      ↵
   rctDragRect = 1
```

```
        lblStatus.Caption = ''Click to drag rectangle''
    End Sub
```

The main thing here is setting the value of 'rctDragRect' to 1. 'rctDragRect' is a module scope variable that is used as a *flag* – that is, the value of the variable is never used directly, it is only used in order to select options in other sections of the code.

Here is the MouseDown event, the code that is executed once when the mouse is pressed while over this control.

```
Private Sub picBigPic_MouseDown(Button As Integer, Shift As
Integer, x As Single, y As Single)
   If rctDragRect Then
      rctDragRect = 0
      picBigPic.Line (rctCutRect.left − 2, rctCutRect.top − 2) −
(rctCutRect.left + 2, rctCutRect.top + 2), , BF
      picBigPic.Line (rctCutRect.right − 2, rctCutRect.bottom − 2)
−(rctCutRect.right + 2, rctCutRect.bottom + 2), , BF
      lblStatus.Caption = ''Bounding Rectangle ('' +
Str(rctCutRect.left) +'', ''+ _
         Str(rctCutRect.top) +'') − ('' + Str(rctCutRect.right)
+'', ''+_
         Str(rctCutRect.bottom) +'') ['' + Str(rctCutRect.right −
rctCutRect.left)_
         +'', ''+ Str(rctCutRect.bottom − rctCutRect.top) +'')''
      If x > (rctCutRect.left − 4) And x < (rctCutRect.left + 4)
And_
         y > (rctCutRect.top − 4) And y < (rctCutRect.top + 4) Then
         'Clicked in top left
         rctDragRect = TOPLEFT
      ElseIf x > (rctCutRect.right − 4) And x < (rctCutRect.right
+ 4) And_
         y > (rctCutRect.bottom − 4) And y < (rctCutRect.bottom +
4) Then 'clicked in bottom right
         rctDragRect = BOTTOMRIGHT
      End If
      Exit Sub
   End If
   If x > posPic(intShowPic).left And_
      x < (posPic(intShowPic).left +
picImage(intShowPic).ScaleWidth) And_
      y > posPic(intShowPic).top And_
      y < (posPic(intShowPic).top +
picImage(intShowPic).ScaleHeight) Then
      posMovePic.left = x
```

```
        posMovePic.top = y
        posMovePic.init = True
    End If
End Sub
```

Here if 'rctDragRect' is set to 1 then the first 'If' statement results in true so it is the bounding rectangle that can be moved. The code checks if the click is near the top left of the bounding rectangle or the bottom right. If it is near neither then there is no action. If it is near the top left then the value for 'rctDragRect' is set to the constant 'TOPLEFT', if it is near the bottom right then the value for 'rctDragRect' is set to the constant 'BOTTOMRIGHT'. If 'rctDragRect' was not set then the code that follows is executed which allows the user to move the pictures. Parameters are stored in the module level user datatype 'posMovePic'. A MouseDown event is an initialisation procedure to set up details for the 'MouseMove' event that occurs many times a second.

```
Private Sub picBigPic_MouseMove(Button As Integer, Shift As
Integer, x As Single, y As Single)
  If rctDragRect Then
    picBigPic.Line (rctCutRect.left, rctCutRect.top) –
(rctCutRect.right, rctCutRect.bottom), , B
    Select Case rctDragRect
    Case TOPLEFT
      rctCutRect.left = x
      rctCutRect.top = y
    Case BOTTOMRIGHT
      rctCutRect.right = x
      rctCutRect.bottom = y
    End Select
    lblStatus.Caption = ''Bounding Rectangle ('' +
Str(rctCutRect.left) +'', ''+_
        Str(rctCutRect.top) +'') – ('' + Str(rctCutRect.right)
+'', ''+ _
        Str(rctCutRect.bottom) +'') ['' + Str(rctCutRect.right –
rctCutRect.left)_
        +'', ''+ Str(rctCutRect.bottom – rctCutRect.top)
+'')''
    picBigPic.Line (rctCutRect.left, rctCutRect.top) –
(rctCutRect.right, rctCutRect.bottom), , B
    Exit Sub
  End If
  If posMovePic.init Then
    posPic(intShowPic).left = posPic(intShowPic).left +
(x – posMovePic.left)
```

```
    posPic(intShowPic).top = posPic(intShowPic).top +
(y - posMovePic.top)                                    ↵
    picBigPic.Cls
    picBigPic.PaintPicture picImage(intShowPic).Picture,
posPic(intShowPic).left, posPic(intShowPic).top          ↵
    picBigPic.Line (rctCutRect.left, rctCutRect.top) -
(rctCutRect.right, rctCutRect.bottom), , B               ↵
    posMovePic.left = x
    posMovePic.top = y
  End If
End Sub
```

The 'MouseMove' event only generates changes if either the value of 'rctDragRect' is set to certain values or 'posMovePic.init' is set to True. The elastic bounding box is created by setting drawing parameters for the picture control to

```
    picBigPic.DrawStyle = 2 'Dotted line
    picBigPic.DrawMode = 6 'Invert
```

Using these parameters any line will be dotted and drawing the line twice will wipe it from the screen. So the line is drawn first using the old value, then values are updated to reflect the mouse movement and the box redrawn.

It is usual with MouseMove code to use the MouseUp event to terminate the actions.

```
Private Sub picBigPic_MouseUp(Button As Integer, Shift As Integer,
x As Single, y As Single)
  posMovePic.init = False
  rctDragRect = 0
  picBigPic.SetFocus
End Sub
```

Simply setting the values for 'rctDragRect' and 'posMovePic.init' stops the MouseMove code from functioning.

A further detail that I chose to use in the original specification is to allow the user to move the pictures in small, single pixel increments using the arrow keys. Here the KeyDown event is used. To make sure that the 'picBigPic KeyDown' event is called the 'picBigPic' control needs to have focus. When a control has focus, keyboard events are sent to that control by Windows. This is how you can have 20 text boxes on the screen and the correct one receives the keyboard input. The KeyDown code is as follows:

```
Private Sub picBigPic_KeyDown(KeyCode As Integer, Shift As Integer)
  lblIcons.Caption = KeyCode
  Select Case KeyCode
  Case 37
    posPic(intShowPic).left = posPic(intShowPic).left - 1
  Case 38
    posPic(intShowPic).top = posPic(intShowPic).top - 1
  Case 39
    posPic(intShowPic).left = posPic(intShowPic).left + 1
  Case 40
    posPic(intShowPic).top = posPic(intShowPic).top + 1
  End Select
  picBigPic.Cls
  picBigPic.PaintPicture picImage(intShowPic).Picture,
posPic(intShowPic).left, posPic(intShowPic).top
End Sub
```

The code for the spin controls should be easy to follow. They have two events, up and down.

```
Private Sub spnButton_SpinDown()
  intShowPic = intShowPic - 1
  If intShowPic < 0 Then intShowPic = 0
  picBigPic.Cls
  If Not posPic(intShowPic).init Then
    posPic(intShowPic).init = True
    posPic(intShowPic).left = (picBigPic.ScaleWidth -
picImage(intShowPic).ScaleWidth) / 2                        ↵
    posPic(intShowPic).top = (picBigPic.ScaleHeight -
picImage(intShowPic).ScaleHeight) / 2                       ↵
  End If
  picBigPic.PaintPicture picImage(intShowPic).Picture,
posPic(intShowPic).left, posPic(intShowPic).top            ↵
  picBigPic.Line (rctCutRect.left, rctCutRect.top) -
(rctCutRect.right, rctCutRect.bottom), , B                 ↵
  lblIcons.Caption = intShowPic
End Sub


Private Sub spnButton_SpinUp()
  intShowPic = intShowPic + 1
  If intShowPic > (intNumPics - 1) Then intShowPic = intNumPics - 1
  picBigPic.Cls
  If Not posPic(intShowPic).init Then
    posPic(intShowPic).init = True
```

```
      posPic(intShowPic).left = (picBigPic.ScaleWidth -
    picImage(intShowPic).ScaleWidth) / 2                    ↵
      posPic(intShowPic).top = (picBigPic.ScaleHeight -
    picImage(intShowPic).ScaleHeight) / 2                   ↵
    End If
    picBigPic.PaintPicture picImage(intShowPic).Picture,
  posPic(intShowPic).left, posPic(intShowPic).top          ↵
    picBigPic.Line (rctCutRect.left, rctCutRect.top) -
  (rctCutRect.right, rctCutRect.bottom), , B               ↵
    lblIcons.Caption = intShowPic
  End Sub


  Private Sub spnGrid_SpinDown()
    If Val(txtRows.Caption) > 1 Then
      txtRows.Caption = Str(Val(txtRows.Caption) - 1)
      txtCols.Caption = Str(Int(intNumPics / Val(txtRows.Caption)))
      If Val(txtRows.Caption) * Val(txtCols.Caption) < intNumPics
  Then                                                     ↵
        txtCols.Caption = Str(Val(txtCols.Caption) + 1)
      End If
    End If
  End Sub


  Private Sub spnGrid_SpinUp()
    If Val(txtRows.Caption) < intNumPics Then
      txtRows.Caption = Str(Val(txtRows.Caption) + 1)
      txtCols.Caption = Str(Int(intNumPics / Val(txtRows.Caption)))
      If Val(txtRows.Caption) * Val(txtCols.Caption) < intNumPics
  Then                                                     ↵
        txtCols.Caption = Str(Val(txtCols.Caption) + 1)
      End If
    End If
  End Sub
```

Finally the film strip is manipulated using the scroll bar. All the code is in the Change event. Here the pictures that are stored in memory are scaled down to fit the film strip. Their display position is based on the current value for the scroll bar. Scroll bars are very useful and easy to set to different maximum values. As the user moves the scroll bar, the value for the scroll bar changes and the Change event is called.

```
  Public Sub vsrIcons_Change()
    Dim width As Integer, height As Integer
```

```
picIcons.ScaleMode = 3
For i = 0 To 480 Step 60
  picIcons.PaintPicture picBorder.Picture, 0, i
Next
For i = vsrIcons.Value To intNumPics - 1
  picImage(i).ScaleMode = 3
  If picImage(i).width > picImage(i).height Then
    picIcons.PaintPicture picImage(i).Picture, _
      14, 29 + 60 * (i - vsrIcons.Value) - 25 /
picImage(i).ScaleWidth * picImage(i).ScaleHeight, _
      50, 50, 0, 0, picImage(i).ScaleWidth, _
      picImage(i).ScaleHeight
  Else
    picIcons.PaintPicture picImage(i).Picture, _
    38 - 25 / picImage(i).ScaleHeight * picImage(i).ScaleWidth,
    5 + 60 * (i - vsrIcons.Value), 50, 50, 0, 0,
picImage(i).ScaleWidth, _
      picImage(i).ScaleHeight
  End If
Next
End Sub
```

This program displays a certain degree of functionality. It is intended to be useful when using the 'Sprite.ocx' control and to illustrate how you can use Visual Basic to create your own tools. Visual Basic hides a great deal of the complexity involved in providing a graphical user interface, while maintaining a great deal of flexibility.

QUIZ

1. Before you start to write the code, what should be the first part of creating an application program?

Answer: Write a specification detailing how to initialise the application, input data, respond to events, output data and safely terminate the application.

2. Flow charts are sometimes used to analyse a program before coding. What is an alternative and preferred technique?

Answer: Use PDL (Programming Design Language) natural language instruction written to help understand how the programming task can be broken into elements.

3. When using a file list box control, how do you ensure that the list only includes text files?

Answer: Set the pattern property to '.txt'.*

4. If a picture box control has its AutoRedraw property set to False, can you use PaintPicture and then save the results?

Answer: No. If the AutoRedraw property is set to False then all drawing goes to the screen. If the control is not visible then this drawing will not happen so the results cannot be saved. If the control is visible then the changes have not been done to the persistent bitmap and, again, the changes cannot be saved.

Summary

In this chapter you learnt how to use many of the controls that come with Visual Basic to harness this power for your own programs. Along with Appendix A this chapter provides a tutorial in how to use Visual Basic for programs other than games and multimedia. The ideas can be used to create programs that rely on a complicated user interface for their functionality.

PART THREE

Game Magic

CHAPTER 9

Platform games – Jump to it!

Fast animation, together with user control, is essential for a platform game, and this chapter shows how Visual Basic can be used to create fast animated graphics for that type of game.

The Sprite ActiveX Control

This chapter introduces a new control for your Visual Basic toolbox: The 'Sprite.ocx' control. This was added to your computer when you ran the set-up program for the sample programs, so if you still haven't run 'set-up' then the programs will not run.

TIP

**If you have not used 'set-up' but still want to run the
program, then follow these instructions:**

**1 Copy 'Sprite.ocx', directly from the Sprocx
    directory to your Windows system folder.**
2 Use the run option from 'Start'.
3 In the dialog box type 'RegSvr32 Sprite.ocx'.
**4 You should get a dialog box saying that the control
    has been registered.**
**This is not necessary if you have run 'set-up' as the
control will already be registered.**

To add a sprite control to your project, chose 'Tools' from the menu
and select 'Custom Controls'.

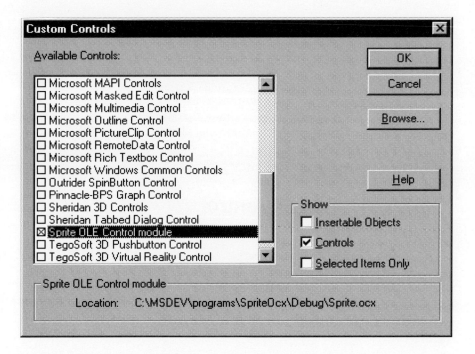

Make sure that Sprite OLE Control Module is checked. If you selected
the right module then your new toolbox will look like this:

The icon at the bottom is the sprite control. Clicking on this and dragging a box will give a display similar to:

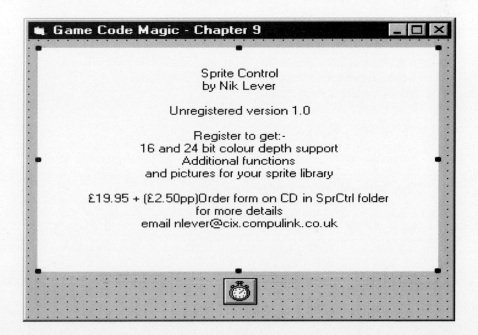

The Sprite ActiveX Control properties

The control has the following properties:

Name   The name you use in code to refer to the control.
Visible   The control is only visible when this property is set to True.
Enabled   The control is only enabled when this property is set to True.
AutoSize   If AutoSize is True then loading a background will resize the control to the size of the background.
Width   The control can be resized with Width when AutoSize is false.
Height   The control can be resized with Height when AutoSize is false.
Left   The left position on the destination Form.
Top   The top position on the destination Form.
Fps   The frames per second that will be used by the Sprite.

There is also a controls timer to generate Timer events.

The Sprite ActiveX Control methods

Many of the methods are similar to the functions that you can use in the dynamic link library.

```
UpdateStage()
CreateSprite(strPicName, intWidth, intHeight)
HitTest(intX, intY)
MoveSprite(intIndex, intX, intY, intFrame)
DeleteSprite(intIndex)
CloneSprite(intSrcIndex, intX, intY)
CollisionCheck(intSprite, intSprite2, blnAccurate)
PasteSprite(intIndex, intX, intY, intFrame)
LoadBackground(strBgFilename, blnKeepSprites);
PlaySoundFile(strSndFilename)
PlayMusicFile(strMusicFilename)
DrawFullStage()
```

For full details of the use of these methods see Appendix D.

The Sprite ActiveX Control events

Click   Generated when the control is clicked.
DoubleClick Generated when the control is clicked twice quickly.
KeyDown   Generated when the keyboard is used while the sprite control has the focus.
KeyUp   Generated when a key is released while the sprite control has focus.
MouseDown Generated when the mouse is clicked on the sprite control.

MouseMove   Generated when the mouse is moved over the sprite control.

MouseUp   Generated when the mouse button is released over the sprite
               control.

Timer   Generated periodically dependent on the fps property value. A
               fps of zero pauses the control and no Timer events occur.

OLE 2.0 and ActiveX controls

The sprite control shares most of the same functions that you have
been using in the dynamic link library. It is easier to use than the
library since you do not have to make sure that the function
declarations are present. An ActiveX control uses OLE 2.0 technology.
What's that? Basically it is a way for modular programs to talk to
other modular programs; it is a client server type of code. Perhaps as
you develop your programming skills you would like to learn more
about OLE 2.0. If so, there is really no better place to start than at
Microsoft's web site. If you point your browser at www.microsoft.com
and enter the 'For Developers Only' area, there is a mass of
information to help in your education process.

Using the control

Even if your program uses a simple coloured background, you will still
need to provide a background as this provides the control with the
information it needs for the colour palette. Remember that your
application can have only one palette at a time and the sprite control
sets the system palette to the nearest possible representation of your
background colours, given the current state of your computer.

TIP

For information on palettes, see Chapter 18.

It is possible for applications to pinch colours for their own use, and for
this reason, when working with animation and Windows, you are
advised to close down all other running applications to ensure that you
get first choice of the colours available. The area of palettes is very
confusing and I am still sometimes tripped up. So take this simple
advice: just run Visual Basic when developing using the sprite control.
If you have problems while no other programs are running, you can
blame me!

Sprite1.LoadBackground strBgFilename As String, blnKeepSprites As Boolean. (The term Sprite1 can be any name you choose for the control in your project.)

To load a background give the control a path name for the '.bmp' file that you wish to load. It **MUST** be a 256 colour '.bmp', saved with no compression (that is, RGB encoded not RLE encoded).

NOTE

If you register the control, you will be able to load 16, 256 and 16 million colour bitmaps, using either '.bmp" or '.gif' extensions. The '.gif' option is particularly useful when developing for Internet applications. Also you can save and load all the data for a game in one compressed unit.

```
Sprite1.LoadData ''mygame.sdt''
```

will load the background, sprites and set the game to the state the game was in when you use the sister function

```
Sprite1.SaveData ''mygame.sdt''
```

The parameter 'blnKeepSprites' is also used if you are changing the background during play. If you set this Boolean value to False then all sprites are deleted when you replace the background. If you set it to True then the sprites are retained and remapped to the new colour palette.

Full details of the use of the sprite control are included in Appendix D. Here is a summary of the methods.

If you have used the dynamic link library then most of the methods should be familiar. If not then have a quick look at the appendix and the back cover flap which provides a more detailed summary of the methods available.

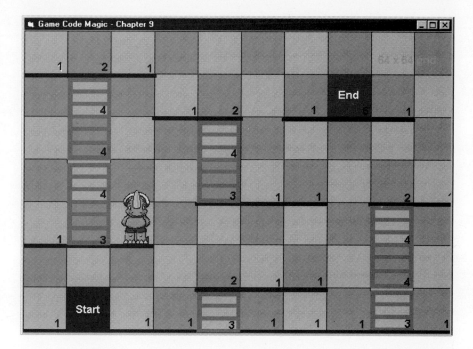

The first step is to create a simple background. Here I have shown how the background conforms to a 64 × 64 grid. This simple structure helps when we move on to the next stage of making the on-screen display understand how the world is made up.

Example Ex09A

Open and run example 'Ex09A.vbp'. This very simply allows you to move the character with the arrow keys. The character has no understanding of the way he should relate to the background. Before we add that detail let's take a look at the code so far.

```
Option Explicit

'Croc 96 × 61
'Rhino 80 × 91
'Bee 50 × 30
'Bat 87 × 67
'Snake 95 × 44
'Spider 33 × 26
```

```
Private Declare Function GetAsyncKeyState Lib ''user32'' (ByVal
vKey As Long) As Integer

Private Type Anim
   x As Integer
   y As Integer
   Index As Integer
   MoveX As Integer
   MoveY As Integer
   Action As Integer
   Frame As Integer
   Count As Integer
End Type

Dim Rhino As Anim

Const KEY_LEFT = 37
Const KEY_UP = 38
Const KEY_RIGHT = 39
Const KEY_DOWN = 40

Const STAGE_LEFT = 10
Const STAGE_RIGHT = 550
Const STAGE_TOP = 10
Const STAGE_BOTTOM = 360

Const RHINO_LEFT = 0
Const RHINO_RIGHT = 8
Const RHINO_STOP = 17
Const RHINO_FOOT = 19
Const RHINO_LAND = 25
Const RHINO_HURRY = 27
Const RHINO_JUMP = 29
Const RHINO_CLIMB = 32
```

Notice how we now are using a user-defined type 'Anim', which is basically just the old 'Sprite' user-defined type in the '(General) – (declarations)' section. I was a little concerned that if the control was called a sprite control, things could begin to get confusing, so the characters are now labelled 'Anim'.

You may be wondering about the strange declaration for 'GetAsyncKeyState'. As you know about focus, you will be aware that the events associated with a key press can be sent to only one control. We need to read the keyboard and respond just prior to redrawing the display. I decided that rather than use the KeyUp and KeyDown events associated with the sprite control, it was more intuitive to use the Windows API call 'GetAsyncKeyState'. You call this function with the parameter of the key that you want to examine. If the key is down then it returns a value, otherwise it returns 0.

To keep the code easier to read the code goes into a new sub-routine. This sub-routine alters the contents of the rhino's MoveX and MoveY parameters, dependent on the current key press.

```
Private Sub CheckKey()
  If GetAsyncKeyState(KEY_LEFT) Then
    Rhino.MoveX = Rhino.MoveX - 1
    If Rhino.MoveX < -10 Then Rhino.MoveX = -10
    Rhino.MoveY = 0
    Rhino.Count = 0
  ElseIf GetAsyncKeyState(KEY_RIGHT) Then
    Rhino.MoveX = Rhino.MoveX + 1
    If Rhino.MoveX > 10 Then Rhino.MoveX = 10
    Rhino.MoveY = 0
    Rhino.Count = 0
  ElseIf GetAsyncKeyState(KEY_UP) Then
    Rhino.MoveY = Rhino.MoveY - 1
    If Rhino.MoveY < -10 Then Rhino.MoveY = -10
    Rhino.MoveX = 0
    Rhino.Count = 0
  ElseIf GetAsyncKeyState(KEY_DOWN) Then
    Rhino.MoveY = Rhino.MoveY + 1
    If Rhino.MoveY > 10 Then Rhino.MoveY = 10
    Rhino.MoveX = 0
    Rhino.Count = 0
  Else
    Rhino.MoveX = 0
    Rhino.MoveY = 0
  End If
End Sub
```

Notice that the use of constants rather than numbers for the keys being examined helps the readability of code.

Again as usual the 'Form_Load' event covers once-only initialisation.

```
Private Sub Form_Load()
  Width = 640 * Screen.TwipsPerPixelX
  Height = 480 * Screen.TwipsPerPixelY
  Left = (Screen.Width — Width) / 2
  Top = (Screen.Height — Height) / 2
  Sprite1.AutoSize = True
  Sprite1.Left = 0
  Sprite1.Top = 0
  Sprite1.LoadBackground App.Path + ''\bg.bmp'', False
  Rhino.Index = Sprite1.CreateSprite(App.Path + ''\rhino.bmp'',
80, 91)                                                        ↵
  Rhino.X = 200
  Rhino.Y = 200
End Sub
```

The sprite control's Timer event

Most of the code that you will add to a project will control the sprite control's Timer event. The 'Sprite.dll' that you used in Part 1 of the book used a timer control to trigger the animation. With the sprite control the timer is built in.

As soon as the program starts the timer is created with a default speed of 15 frames per second. I chose to use frames per second rather than millisecond intervals, probably because frames per second is more familiar to me as my background is in film animation. To speed the control up set the 'fps' (frames per second) property to a higher number. You will need a very simple program with very small sprites and an excellent computer to achieve rates around 50 fps. Setting the control to a higher refresh rate than 50 will achieve nothing since internally it is capped to 50 fps. (A basic data validation check: Setting a refresh rate of 0 will pause the control; in fact it will cancel the internal timer. Negative rate changes are ignored; they do not disable the control, they simply do nothing. The previous 'fps' value is retained.)

Here is the code for the sprite control's Timer event.

```
Private Sub Sprite1_Timer()
  CheckKey

  If Rhino.MoveX = 1 Then
    Rhino.Action = RHINO_RIGHT
  Rhino.Frame = RHINO_RIGHT
```

```
ElseIf Rhino.MoveX = -1 Then
    Rhino.Action = RHINO_LEFT
    Rhino.Frame = RHINO_LEFT
  ElseIf Rhino.MoveY = 1 Then
    Rhino.Action = RHINO_CLIMB
    Rhino.Frame = RHINO_CLIMB
  ElseIf Rhino.MoveY = -1 Then
    Rhino.Action = RHINO_CLIMB
    Rhino.Frame = RHINO_CLIMB
  ElseIf Rhino.MoveX = 0 And Rhino.MoveY = 0 And Rhino.Action <>
RHINO_STOP And Rhino.Action <> RHINO_HURRY Then              ↵
    Rhino.Action = RHINO_STOP
  End If

  Select Case Rhino.Action
  Case RHINO_LEFT
    Rhino.Frame = Rhino.Frame + 1
    If Rhino.Frame > RHINO-LEFT + 7 Then Rhino.Frame = RHINO_
LEFT                                                        ↵
  Case RHINO_RIGHT
  Rhino.Frame = Rhino.Frame + 1
  If Rhino.Frame > RHINO_RIGHT + 7 Then Rhino.Frame = RHINO_
RIGHT                                                       ↵
  Case RHINO_CLIMB
    Rhino.Frame = Rhino.Frame + 1
    If Rhino.Frame > RHINO_CLIMB + 7 Then Rhino.Frame = RHINO_
CLIMB                                                       ↵
  Case RHINO_STOP
    Rhino.Frame = RHINO_STOP
    Rhino.Count = Rhino.Count + 1
    If Rhino.Count = 100 Then
      Rhino.Count = 0
      Rhino.Action = RHINO_HURRY
      Rhino.Frame = RHINO_HURRY
    End If
  Case RHINO_HURRY
    Rhino.Frame = RHINO_HURRY + 1
    Rhino.Count = Rhino.Count + 1
    If Rhino.Count = 20 Then
      Rhino.Count = 0
      Rhino.Action = RHINO_STOP
      Rhino.Frame = RHINO_HURRY
    End If
  End Select
```

```
Rhino.X = Rhino.X + Rhino.MoveX
If Rhino.X < STAGE_LEFT Then Rhino.X = STAGE_LEFT
If Rhino.X > STAGE_RIGHT Then Rhino.X = STAGE_RIGHT
Rhino.Y = Rhino.Y + Rhino.MoveY
If Rhino.Y < STAGE_TOP Then Rhino.Y = STAGE_TOP
If Rhino.Y > STAGE_BOTTOM Then Rhino.Y = STAGE_BOTTOM

Sprite1.MoveSprite Rhino.Index, Rhino.X, Rhino.Y, Rhino.Frame
Sprite1.UpdateStage
End If
End Sub
```

Already, without adding any understanding of the world that the main control sprite inhabits, the code is getting very messy and difficult to maintain. At this stage it is important to step back and examine exactly what is required and how best to introduce more modularity to the code.

Thinking through the design process

Objectives

- The control sprite will understand the world that it inhabits.
- The actions of the control sprite will be under user control.
- Enemy sprites need to be avoided or neutralised to get from Start to Exit.
- Time is important.
- Enemy sprites will reduce the life force for the control sprite.

Time and life force are easy to implement. Each call of the sprite control's Timer event can reduce the current time, and when it reaches zero the level can terminate. For life force we will add a new feature to the 'Anim' datatype. This will be preset to a certain value on initialisation and if it reaches zero then again the level will terminate.

NOTE

Never check for a particular value when you are more interested in an inequality. What do we mean by that? Well, suppose that you have a variable that stores the current time, and suppose that this variable is reduced each time the Timer event is called. Do not check when this variable reaches zero. Your code may be in error and may miss the unique circumstance when the variable reaches zero. Instead, check for when the variable is less than zero as the variable will be less than zero more often than it will be exactly zero. Use this strategy whenever you can as it will prevent many elusive bugs in your code. If you check for an equality rather than an inequality, then check and recheck your logic to make sure that for any possible instance of the program this equality will occur. If the variable is decreased twice before a test occurs then the program may never find a positive test of an equality test. Remember, check for an inequality, not an equality, whenever possible.

The other major considerations require a way in code to interpret the world. You probably spotted the numbers given to certain squares in the background that you saw in the first example. Loading these numeric values will allow the program code to understand how the rhino needs to respond to his current location on screen.

Example Ex09B

Now let's look at an improvement on the first program. Open 'Ex09B.vbp' and run it to see the difference. Now the character has some knowledge of the surroundings.

Here is the code to load the world data. This is a simple ASCII file – that is, a text file that can be created with Notepad or any word processor if the file is exported as text only. I recommend using Notepad, you can be assured that no formatting information is saved if you use Notepad and it comes with every version of Windows.

The world data file

The world data file uses line 1 to store the number of rows in the world, and line 2 the number of columns. Each subsequent line has the actual data with each cell divided by a space. Here is the 'world.dat' file used in the example.

```
7
10
1 2 1 0 0 0 0 0 0 0
0 4 0 1 2 0 1 6 1 0
0 4 0 0 4 0 0 0 0 0
0 4 0 0 3 1 1 0 2 1
1 3 1 0 0 0 0 0 4 0
0 0 0 0 2 1 1 0 4 0
1 5 1 1 3 1 1 1 3 1
[End]
```

Each value represents the type of area on the screen. A ladder has the code 4.

Code	Type
0	No platform
1	Platform
2	Top of ladder
3	Bottom of ladder
4	Ladder
5	Start
6	End

Each area represents a 64-pixel square region of the background picture, so there is a correlation between the world data array and the background picture.

If you are unfamiliar with using files then the code used to load the world data may be confusing. Let's examine this bit by bit.

```
Sub LoadWorld()
    Dim intRow As Integer, intCol As Integer
    Dim intFileNum As Integer, intRows As Integer, intCols As Integer
    Dim strTemp As String, lngNewPos As Long, lngOldPos As Long

    intFileNum = FreeFile

    Open App.Path + ''\world.dat'' For Input As intFileNum
```

```
    Line Input #intFileNum, strTemp
    intRows = Val(strTemp)
    Line Input #intFileNum, strTemp
    intCols = strTemp

    For intRow = 0 To intRows - 1
      Line Input #intFileNum, strTemp
      lngOldPos = 1
      lngNewPos = 1
      'Debug.Print
      For intCol = 0 To intCols - 1
        lngNewPos = InStr(lngNewPos, strTemp, '' '')
        If lngNewPos = 0 Then lngNewPos = Len(strTemp)
        World(intRow, intCol) = Val(Mid(strTemp, lngOldPos,
  lngNewPos - lngOldPos))
        lngNewPos = lngNewPos + 1
        lngOldPos = lngNewPos
        'Debug.Print World(intRow, intCol);
      Next
    Next

    Close intFileNum
  End Sub
```

This sub-routine starts, after creating some local variables, by using
the Visual Basic function 'FreeFile' to get the number of the next free
file. The return value is stored in the variable 'intFileNum' and used
in the call to 'Open' a file. The 'Open' statement has several
parameters. In this example, the first parameter is a path name; next
the type of data involved is given (this will be 'Input', that is, the file
contains information the program wants to input). The final parameter
is the 'intFileNum' previously stored. Because of the way we have
opened the file we can use 'Line Input' to receive data. 'Line Input'
retrieves text information until the new line and line feed characters
are received. 'Line Input' takes two parameters, the opened file
number and a string variable. If the contents of the string variable
need to be converted to a numeric value then use the 'Val' statement
to convert the result. In this example 'Rows' is set then 'Cols'. The
contents of these variables together with a new statement 'InStr' are
used for the rest of the data. 'InStr' is a string comparison function
that returns a position if the comparing strings are found, and 0
otherwise. Here we are checking for spaces. The position of the space is
used to determine the value of the text between the spaces. No error
checking is included in the example program, as this is not sufficiently
robust to allow user input. In this example the supplied program

provides the data, so error checking can be minimal. Any opened files must be closed when they have been used.

Analysing possible program states

The control sprite has several actions and user input is restricted dependent on its current action and location. In the third and final example a minimal sprite collision-checking routine will be covered.

Here is a table of control sprite actions, legal key presses, and legal world codes.

Possible actions	Key Press	Legal world codes
Walk left	Left arrow	1, 2, 3, 5, 6
Walk right	Right arrow	1, 2, 3, 5, 6
Climb up	Up arrow	3, 4
Climb down	Down arrow	2, 3, 4
Land	None	1, 2, 3, 5, 6
Stop	None	1, 2, 3, 5, 6
Hurry	None	1, 2, 3, 5, 6
Fall	Left or Right arrow	0, 4
Jump	Up arrow	1, 2, 5, 6

Any interactive program has a surprising number of possible states, and developing a code for every possible program state is challenging. The more modular you can develop the code, the more likely it will be that you can finally cover every possibility.

In this example I chose to put most code into the key events. However, the rhino action of falling or landing is covered separately since these actions are not under the total control of the user. Here is the new Timer event.

```
Private Sub Sprite1_Timer()
   Dim Key As Integer

   Key = CheckKey

   Select Case Key
   Case KEY_LEFT
      RhinoKeyLeft
```

```
        Case KEY_RIGHT
          RhinoKeyRight
        Case KEY_UP
          RhinoKeyUp
        Case KEY_DOWN
          RhinoKeyDown
        Case Else
          RhinoKeyNone
        End Select

        If Rhino.Action = RHINO_FALL Or Rhino.Action = RHINO_LAND Then
          RhinoFallOrLand
        End If

        Sprite1.MoveSprite Rhino.Index, Rhino.X, Rhino.Y, Rhino.Frame
        Sprite1.UpdateStage
    End Sub
```

First a call to test the keyboard. The CheckKey function has been streamlined to do just what it says, check the keyboard. No manipulation to global data is much better programming practice, as this keep the code that manipulates data in one place.

Dependent on the key press a call is made to a specific, key dependent sub-routine. Falling and landing are covered separately. Finally the Rhino sprite is moved and the stage is updated to reflect the changes.

```
    Private Function CheckKey() As Integer
      'Returns one of the arrow keys if pressed or zero

      If GetAsyncKeyState(KEY_LEFT) Then
        CheckKey = KEY_LEFT
      ElseIf GetAsyncKeyState(KEY_RIGHT) Then
        CheckKey = KEY_RIGHT
      ElseIf GetAsyncKeyState(KEY_UP) Then
        CheckKey = KEY_UP
      ElseIf GetAsyncKeyState(KEYDOWN) Then
        CheckKey = KEY_DOWN
      Else
        CheckKey = 0
      End If

    End Function
```

Using the data stored in the world array

Before we look at the keyboard dependent routines, let's look at a
function that each one calls.

```
Function CheckWorld() As Integer
    Dim intCol As Integer, intRow As Integer
    Dim intYoffSet As Integer, intXoffSet As Integer

    If Rhino.MoveX Then
        If Rhino.MoveX < 0 Then
            intXoffSet = CHECK_LEFT
        Else
            intXoffSet = CHECK_RIGHT
        End If
    Else
        intXoffSet = CHECK_MIDDLE
    End If

    If Rhino.MoveY <= 0 Or Rhino.Action = RHINO_CLIMB Then
    intYoffSet = CHECK_BOTTOM
    Else
        intYoffSet = CHECK_TOP
    End If

    intCol = Int((Rhino.X + intXoffSet) / 64)
    intRow = Int((Rhino.Y + intYoffSet) / 64)
    If intCol < 0 Then intCol = 0
    If intRow < 0 Then intRow = 0

    CheckWorld = World(intRow, intCol)

    #If RhinoDebug Then
        ShowData CheckWorld, intRow, intCol
    #End If
End Function
```

Notice that this function converts the control sprite's current position
into the correct row and column of the world data array. It is very
important with this routine that the correct information is returned. If
the cells were 1 pixel wide and high and the control sprite was only 1
pixel wide and high, then this function would not have to cover the
various conditions that are used. The problem is overlapping. In the
example each cell is 64 × 64 pixels and the rhino sprite is 80 × 91

pixels. When the rhino is walking left, we need to do a different test for world data than when the rhino is walking right.

Walking left

When the rhino is walking left we are much more interested in whether the bottom right corner of the rhino intercepts the top left corner of a cell. So we test whether the rhino is moving left. If the rhino is moving left then the movement vector '(Rhino.MoveX, Rhino.MoveY)' must have Rhino.MoveX < 0'.

Similar tests ensure that the return value of this function is as useful as possible. The strange code at the end of the function is how you can set-up conditional compilation.

Using conditional code

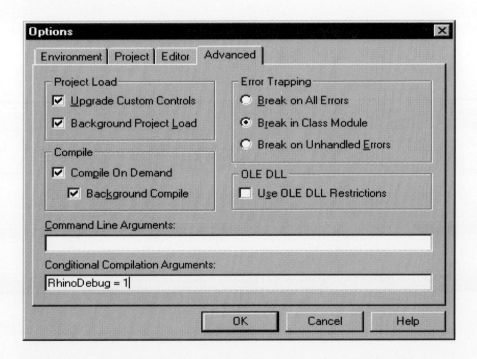

Choosing the 'Tools\Options' menu brings up this dialog box. Click the advanced tab. In the bottom edit box you can enter values for constants. This example defines 'RhinoDebug = 1'. Now the code between the '#If ... #Else ... #End If' is conditional on the value given to this constant. It is a simple matter to switch between your debug version and the final run time version. Altering the value of the constant to zero will ensure that the '#If' test fails and the code does not execute.

Debugging

My debugging routine simply writes a caption with lots of useful information when the program is running.

```
Sub ShowData(intWorld As Integer, intRow As Integer, intCol As
Integer)
   Caption = ''Rhino ('' + Str(Rhino.X) + '', ''
       + Str(Rhino.Y) + '') World: ('' + Str(IntRow) + '', ''_
       + Str(IntCol) + '') = '' + Str(IntWorld) + '' Current
Action:''_
       + Str(Rhino.Action) + '' Move data ('' + Str(Rhino.MoveX)
+_
       '', '' + Str(Rhino.MoveY) + '')''
End Sub
```

The keyboard routines

Now let's take a look at the keyboard dependent routines.

```
Sub RhinoKeyDown()
   Dim intCurrentCell As Integer

   intCurrentCell = CheckWorld

   Select Case Rhino.Action
   Case RHINO_CLIMB
     If intCurrentCell > 1 And intCurrentCell < 5 Then
     Rhino.MoveY = Rhino.MoveY + 1
     If Rhino.MoveY > 10 Then Rhino.MoveY = 10
     Else
       'Bottom of ladder
       Do
         Rhino.Y = Rhino.Y - 1
         intCurrentCell = CheckWorld
```

```
      Loop Until (intCurrentCell = 3)
        Rhino.MoveY = 0
      End If
      Rhino.Y = Rhino.Y + Rhino.MoveY
      Rhino.Frame = (Rhino.Frame - 1) Mod 8 + Rhino.Action
    Case Else
      Rhino.MoveY = 1
      Rhino.MoveX = 0
      Rhino.Action = RHINO_CLIMB
      Rhino.Frame = RHINO_CLIMB
  End Select

    If Rhino.Y > STAGE_BOTTOM Then Rhino.Y = STAGE_BOTTOM

End Sub
```

The only possible event for the down arrow is to allow the rhino to climb down a ladder if the current world position allows. The up arrow is a little more complicated.

```
Sub RhinoKeyUp()
  Dim intCurrentCell As Integer

  If Rhino.Action = RHINO_JUMP Then
    If Rhino.Frame < RHINO_JUMP + 2 Then
      Rhino.Frame = Rhino.Frame + 1
    End If
    Rhino.X = Rhino.X + Rhino.MoveX
    Rhino.Y = Rhino.Y + Rhino.MoveY
    Rhino.MoveY = Rhino.MoveY + 4
    If Rhino.MoveY > 0 Then Rhino.Action = RHINO_FALL
    Exit Sub
  End If

  intCurrentCell = CheckWorld

  If intCurrentCell = 3 Or intCurrentCell = 4 Then
    Select Case Rhino.Action
    Case RHINO_CLIMB
      Rhino.MoveY = Rhino.MoveY - 1
      If Rhino.MoveY < -10 Then Rhino.MoveY = -10
      Rhino.Y = Rhino.Y + Rhino.MoveY
      Rhino.Frame = (Rhino.Frame + 1) Mod 8 + Rhino.Action
    Case Else
      Rhino.MoveY = -1
```

```
        Rhino.MoveX = 0
        Rhino.Action = RHINO_CLIMB
        Rhino.Frame = RHINO_CLIMB
      End Select
    Else
      Select Case Rhino.Action
      Case RHINO_CLIMB
        Do
          Rhino.Y = Rhino.Y + 1
          intCurrentCell = CheckWorld
        Loop Until intCurrentCell <> 2
        Rhino.Y = Rhino.Y - 1
        Rhino.MoveY = 0
        Rhino.Action = RHINO_STOP
        Rhino.Frame = RHINO_STOP
        Rhino.Count = 0
      Case Else
        If intCurrentCell Then
          Rhino.Action = RHINO_JUMP
          Rhino.Frame = RHINO_JUMP
          Rhino.MoveY = -20
        End If
      End Select
    End If
  End Sub
```

First a jump is tested and the rhino position and frame are updated if
this is the action. Jump has priority, so after the updating the sub-
routine is exited without running the subsequent code.

Now the world position is checked using the special function
'CheckWorld'. If the rhino is on a ladder then 'intCurrentCell' value
will be 3 or 4. Check the picture of the background and you will see
that these are the only two possible values for a ladder. If the current
cell value is not 3 or 4 then the rhino must either be allowed to jump
or the key press is ignored.

```
  Sub RhinoKeyLeft()
    Dim intCurrentCell As Integer

    intCurrentCell = CheckWorld
```

```
Select Case Rhino.Action
Case RHINO_JUMP
   If Rhino.Frame < RHINO_JUMP + 2 Then
      Rhino.Frame = Rhino.Frame + 1
   End If
   If Rhino.MoveX > 0 Then Rhino.MoveX = 0
   Rhino.MoveX = Rhino.MoveX - 1
   Rhino.X = Rhino.X + Rhino.MoveX
   Rhino.Y = Rhino.Y + Rhino.MoveY
   Rhino.MoveY = Rhino.MoveY + 4
   If Rhino.MoveY > 0 Then Rhino.Action = RHINO_FALL
Case RHINO_RIGHT
   Rhino.Action = RHINO_LEFT
   Rhino.MoveX = 0
   Rhino.MoveY = 0
Case RHINO_LEFT
   If intCurrentCell And ((Rhino.Y + CHECK_TOP) Mod 64) < 4 Then
      'Walk OK
      Rhino.MoveX = Rhino.MoveX - 1
      If Rhino.MoveX < -10 Then Rhino.MoveX = -10
      Rhino.X = Rhino.X + Rhino.MoveX
      If Rhino.X < STAGE_LEFT Then Rhino.X = STAGE_LEFT
      Rhino.Frame = ((Rhino.Frame + 1) Mod 8) + RHINO_LEFT
   Else
      Rhino.Action = RHINO_FALL
   End If
Case RHINO_STOP
   Rhino.Action = RHINO_LEFT
End Select
End Sub
```

Aligning the control sprite to the grid

Two techniques are used to ensure the sprite is aligned to the grid
when stationary. First, when climbing, a test is made for the top of a
cell with value 2. When it is exceeded then 1 is added to the current
rhino y position. This moves the rhino down by one pixel. This loop
repeats until the current cell has value 2. This aligns the rhino to the
bottom of a cell with value 2.

```
Do
   Rhino.Y = Rhino.Y + 1
   intCurrentCell = CheckWorld
Loop Until intCurrentCell <> 2
```

Another technique is to test for the result of a modular arithmetic function. Remember that 'mod' gives the remainder of integer division.

9 mod 4 = 1, that is 9 − Int(9/4)

An example of this from the code is

((Rhino.Y + CHECK_TOP) Mod 64) < 4

This is a test for the rhino being within 4 pixels of the base of a cell. Sometimes this is used with an alignment routine that uses this modular arithmetic function to adjust as well as test the rhino's position.

All techniques for alignment need to be heavily tested to ensure they have the correct result for every possible variant of program state.

```
Sub RhinoKeyRight()
   Dim intCurrentCell As Integer

   intCurrentCell = CheckWorld

   Select Case Rhino.Action
   Case RHINO_JUMP
      If Rhino.Frame < RHINO_JUMP + 2 Then
         Rhino.Frame = Rhino.Frame + 1
      End If
      If Rhino.MoveX < 0 Then Rhino.MoveX = 0
      Rhino.MoveX = Rhino.MoveX + 1
      Rhino.X = Rhino.X + Rhino.MoveX
      Rhino.Y = Rhino.Y + Rhino.MoveY
      Rhino.MoveY = Rhino.MoveY + 4
      If Rhino.MoveY > 0 Then Rhino.Action = RHINO_FALL
   Case RHINO_LEFT
      Rhino.Action = RHINO_RIGHT
      Rhino.MoveX = 0
      Rhino.MoveY = 0
   Case RHINO_RIGHT
      If intCurrentCell And ((Rhino.Y + CHECK_TOP) Mod 64) < 4 Then
         'Walk OK
         Rhino.MoveX = Rhino.MoveX + 1
         If Rhino.MoveX > 10 Then Rhino.MoveX = 10
```

```
      Rhino.X = Rhino.X + Rhino.MoveX
      If Rhino.X > STAGE_RIGHT Then Rhino.X = STAGE_RIGHT
      Rhino.Frame = ((Rhino.Frame + 1) Mod 8) + RHINO_RIGHT
    Else
      Rhino.Action = RHINO_FALL
    End If
  Case RHINO_STOP
    Rhino.Action = RHINO_RIGHT
  End Select
End Sub
```

Remember to consider the option of no legal keyboard input.

The code that executes when no key is pressed is quite elaborate:

```
Sub RhinoKeyNone()
  Dim intCurrentCell As Integer

  intCurrentCell = CheckWorld

  If (intCurrentCell = 0 Or intCurrentCell = 4) And Rhino.Action
<>
RHINO_CLIMB Then
    Rhino.Action = RHINO_FALL
    Exit Sub
  End If

  Select Case Rhino.Action
  Case RHINO_JUMP
    If Rhino.Frame < RHINO_JUMP + 2 Then
      Rhino.Frame = Rhino.Frame + 1
    End If
    Rhino.X = Rhino.X + Rhino.MoveX
    Rhino.Y = Rhino.Y + Rhino.MoveY
    Rhino.MoveY = Rhino.MoveY + 4
    If Rhino.MoveY > 0 Then Rhino.Action = RHINO_FALL
  Case RHINO_CLIMB
    Rhino.Y = Rhino.Y - 1
    intCurrentCell = CheckWorld
    Rhino.Y = Rhino.Y + 1
    Rhino.MoveX = 0
    Rhino.MoveY = 0
    If ((Rhino.Y + CHECK_TOP) Mod 64) < 4 And intCurrentCell = 3 ↵
Then
      Rhino.Action = RHINO_STOP
```

```
      Rhino.Frame = RHINO_STOP
      Rhino.Count = 0
   End If
Case RHINO_FALL
   'ignore
Case RHINO_STOP
   Rhino.MoveX = 0
   Rhino.MoveY = 0
   Rhino.Count = Rhino.Count + 1
   If Rhino.Count = 100 Then
      Rhino.Frame = 27
   ElseIf Rhino.Count = 105 Then
      Rhino.Frame = 28
   ElseIf Rhino.Count = 150 Then
      Rhino.Frame = 27
   ElseIf Rhino.Count = 155 Then
      Rhino.Frame = RHINO_STOP
      Rhino.Count = 0
   ElseIf Int(Rhino.Count / 5) = Rhino.Count / 5 And Rhino.Count
< 100 Then
      Rhino.Frame = RHINO_STOP − (Rhino.Frame = RHINO_STOP)
   End If
 Case Else
    Rhino.Count = 0
    Rhino.Frame = RHINO_STOP
    Rhino.Action = RHINO_STOP
 End Select
End Sub
```

Most of the code covers the frame to display. The rhino taps his foot and gestures if the user does nothing. The 'Anim' data member 'Count' is used as a check for the loop. If 'Count' reaches the value 100 then a second wait animation is displayed. This alternative animation is a gesture to get the user to hurry up.

So what is the program lacking?

Well lots. There are no enemies, no power-up icons and no end of level. The code is designed to be illustrative rather than complete. But, to add some interest here is another example.

Example Ex09C

Run 'Ex09C.vbp', which adds three more characters to the screen: a
spider, a snake and a crocodile. The sub-routine that contains the code
to move these sprites is:

```
Sub MoveAnimals()
  If Spider.Count Then
    Spider.Count = Spider.Count − 1
    Spider.Y = −40
  Else
    Spider.Frame = (Spider.Frame + 1) Mod 5
    Spider.X = Spider.X + Spider.MoveX
    If Spider.Y < 230 Then Spider.Y = Spider.Y + 10
    If Spider.X > 400 Then Spider.MoveX = −4
    If Spider.X < 257 Then Spider.MoveX = 4
  End If

  Select Case Snake.Action
  Case SNAKE_LEFT
    If Snake.X < 385 Then
      Snake.Action = SNAKE_TURN_RIGHT
      Snake.MoveX = 0
    Else
      Snake.Frame = (Snake.Frame + 1) Mod 3 + SNAKE_LEFT
      Snake.x = Snake.X + Snake.MoveX
    End If
  Case SNAKE_TURN_LEFT
    Snake.Frame = Snake.Frame + 1
    If Snake.Frame = 5 Then
      Snake.Action = SNAKE_LEFT
      Snake.MoveX = −4
    End If
  Case SNAKE_RIGHT
    If Snake.X > 510 Then
      Snake.Action = SNAKE_TURN_LEFT
      Snake.MoveX = 0
    Else
      Snake.Frame = (Snake.Frame + 1) Mod 3 + SNAKE_RIGHT
      Snake.X = Snake.X + Snake.MoveX
    End If
  Case SNAKE_TURN_RIGHT
    Snake.Frame = Snake.Frame − 1
    If Snake.Frame = 3 Then
```

```
            Snake.Action = SNAKE_RIGHT
            Snake.MoveX = 4
        End If
    End Select

    Bee.Frame = (Bee.Frame + 1) Mod 3
    Bee.X = Bee.X — Int(Rnd() * 10)
    Bee.Y = Bee.Y + Int(Rnd() * 10 — 5)
    If Bee.X < 0 Then
    Bee.X = 640
    Bee.Y = Int(Rnd() * 400 + 80)
    End If

    Sprite1.MoveSprite Snake.Index, Snake.X, Snake.Y, Snake.Frame
    Sprite1.MoveSprite Bee.Index, Bee.X, Bee.Y, Bee.Frame
    Sprite1.MoveSprite Croc.Index, Croc.X, Croc.Y, Croc.Frame
    Sprite1.MoveSprite Spider.Index, Spider.X, Spider.Y,
    Spider.Frame
End Sub
```

The only unusual use in this code is the 'Spider.Count' test. The only animal that you can destroy in the program is the spider. Jump on him and after a sound effect the spider will disappear until 'Spider.Count' is decreased to zero. The spider then drops in from the top of screen.

The sprite control's Timer event is extended to cover this collision checking

```
Private Sub Sprite1_Timer()
    Dim Key As Integer

    Key = CheckKey

    Select Case Key
    Case KEY_LEFT
        RhinoKeyLeft
    Case KEY_RIGHT
        RhinoKeyRight
    Case KEY_UP
        RhinoKeyUp
    Case KEY_DOWN
        RhinoKeyDown
    Case Else
        RhinoKeyNone
    End Select
```

```
    If Rhino.Action = RHINO_FALL Or Rhino.Action = RHINO_LAND Then
        RhinoFallOrLand
    End If


    MoveAnimals
    If Rhino.X > STAGE_RIGHT Then Rhino.X = STAGE_RIGHT
    If Rhino.X < STAGE_LEFT Then Rhino.X = STAGE_LEFT
    Sprite1.MoveSprite Rhino.Index, Rhino.X, Rhino.Y, Rhino.Frame
'/////////////////////////////////////
'Note Collision checking
'/////////////////////////////////////
    If Spider.Count = 0 And Sprite1.CollisionCheck(Rhino.Index,
Spider.Index, True) Then
        If Rhino.MoveY > 0 Then
            Sprite1.PlaySoundFile App.Path + ''\sound3.wav''
            Spider.Count = 100
        Else
            Sprite1.PlaySoundFile App.Path + ''\sound2.wav''
        End If
    End If
'/////////////////////////////////////
'Collision checking end
'/////////////////////////////////////

    Sprite1.UpdateStage
End Sub
```

Now the program is looking more like a platform game. To become a full game you will need to

- Add collision checking for every animal.
- Test for the end of level.
- Add power-up icons on the screen.
- Give the rhino a life variable that is decreased when he is in a collision with another animal.

The single biggest difference from a fast commercial platform game is the lack of background scrolling. The problem here is the speed with which Windows can copy the entire screen. Remember that when you play a DOS platform game the screen resolution is usually 320×200. With Windows the minimum screen resolution is more than four times that number of pixels. It can be done: you can force your games to take over the whole screen and reset the resolution. The new Windows Game SDK, Direct X 2.0 (probably, version 4 by the time you are reading this), allows you to do just that. Before you can deal with this

level of programming you need to be a competent C++ programmer.
These advanced techniques must wait for another book.

Finally

If you are tired of cute little cartoons (and who can blame you) then try
'Ex09D.exe'. Surprisingly, this is exactly the same code as 'Ex09C.exe',
the only change is the artwork. What a difference this makes to the
overall look of the program. Instead of cute cartoons, here we have
robots and sci-fi. At the computer level, the pictures are just arrays of
pixels that are copied in rectangles to the screen.

QUIZ

**1. What Windows function is useful for getting keyboard input just
when you want it?**
Answer: GetAsyncKeyState

**2. Why must you sometimes test a sprite's position from a top
corner and, at another time, from a bottom corner?**
*Answer: Because a sprite has dimension; you are sometimes
interested in an intersection at the feet, other times at the head.*

**3. A sprite is moved with the following code but the user sees no
change. Why?**

```
Sprite1.MoveSprite Dog.Index, Dog.X, Dog.Y, Dog.Frame
```

*Answer: There is no call to 'Sprite1.UpdateStage'. Any changes are
not shown until this function is called.*

**4. To achieve DOS type speeds using Windows, Microsoft has
developed a new library. What is it called?**
Answer: DirectX

Summary

In this chapter you saw how to use the Sprite ActiveX Control supplied with this book.

- You used the control to create a simple platform example with world data checking and collision checking.
- You learnt about new ways to get keyboard input for your programs.
- You used sound in the examples for the first time.
- You saw the difference that artwork makes to the same code.

CHAPTER 10

Puzzle games – It makes you think

This chapter introduces the use of sprites in a classic puzzle game. The graphic images were created using a 3D computer graphic program.

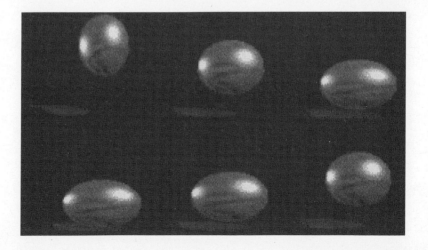

Before we begin, try running 'Ex10B.exe'. The usual caveats apply, you must have Visual Basic set-up on your computer and the sprite control must be registered in the Windows registry.

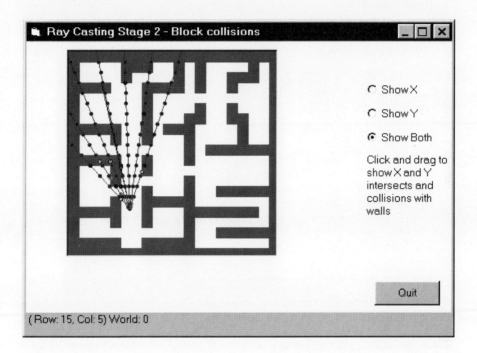

I am sure you will have seen a similar game. The game has three levels: In the first level, bouncing around the pyramid using the arrow keys changes the colour of the blocks from yellow to green. If you succeed without falling off the edge too many times then you move on to level 2. Here you have a baddy that you must avoid. Any collision with the baddy and you are deducted one life. If you manage to colour the blocks red then you reach level 3. Now there are two baddies, the only difference being that the new baddy knows where you are and is chasing you. If you succeed in the final colouring then well done.

Before we look at how the final version of the game is coded, we will look at a simpler version.

Example Ex10A

In this first version, we are interested only in providing the movement of the ball. The code needs to check for legal moves, some areas of the screen are not legal positions for the ball to bounce and this needs to be identified.

Initialisation

I hope that this simple initialisation code is becoming familiar.

```
Private Sub Form_Load()
  Width = 640 * Screen.TwipsPerPixelX
  Height = 480 * Screen.TwipsPerPixelY
  Left = 0
  Top = 0
  Sprite1.AutoSize = True
  Sprite1.LoadBackground App.Path + ''\bg.bmp'', False
  Sprite1.Left = 0
  Sprite1.Top = 0
  Ball.Index = Sprite1.CreateSprite(App.Path + ''\ball.bmp'',
99, 74)
  Sprite1.Fps = 18
  Ball.X = 255
  Ball.Y = 20
  Sprite1.PlayMusicFile App.Path + ''\music.mid''
  SetGrid
  Do
  Loop Until CheckKey = 0
End Sub
```

The only unusual bit is the check for a clear keyboard before completing the procedure. I was getting problems from spurious keyboard checks and decided this was a simple fix.

There is also a call to 'SetGrid'. The code uses an array of integers to store the possible legal moves and details of the current state of the pyramid.

```
Sub SetGrid()
  ReDim BoxGrid(6, 6)
  BoxGrid(0, 0) = 9
  BoxGrid(0, 1) = 9
  BoxGrid(0, 3) = 9
  BoxGrid(0, 4) = 9
```

```
      BoxGrid(0, 5) = 9
      BoxGrid(1, 0) = 9
      BoxGrid(1, 1) = 9
      BoxGrid(1, 4) = 9
      BoxGrid(1, 5) = 9
      BoxGrid(2, 0) = 9
      BoxGrid(2, 4) = 9
      BoxGrid(2, 5) = 9
      BoxGrid(3, 0) = 9
      BoxGrid(3, 5) = 9
      BoxGrid(4, 5) = 9
   End Sub
```

The use of 'ReDim' is a quick way to reset an array to zero. In order to use this statement you must dimension the array initially with no parameters for its size.

```
   Dim BoxGrid() As Integer
```

If you put dimensions in-between the brackets, the use of 'ReDim' will generate a run time error.

Certain values for the array are given the value 9. This is checked in code and, if found, the program knows that an illegal move has occurred.

Translating the balls position to this array requires the use of:

```
   If BoxGrid( (Ball.X — 15)/100, (Ball.Y — 15)/64) = 9 then
   DeadBall
```

This code uses the fact that the horizontal movement from one square to another is 100 and that the first square is not at the very edge of the screen. The vertical movement is divided by 64 to provide the correct conversion.

Table 10.1 shows the array values after SetGrid.

Table 10.1

		Columns					
		0	1	2	3	4	5
Rows	0	9	9	**0**	9	9	9
	1	9	9	0	0	9	9
	2	9	0	0	0	9	9
	3	9	0	0	0	0	9
	4	0	0	0	0	0	9
	5	0	0	0	0	0	0

Let's just test a possible Ball position (255, 20). Using the above code we first deduct 15 from the x and y positions (240, 5) then divide by 100 and 64 for the x and y values respectively; that is, (240/100, 5/64). Since the array is integer values we ignore the decimal places of the calculation; that is, the result is (2, 0) not (2.4, 0.08). The value for that position of the grid is marked on the table, zero. This is a legal position. If, however, the ball is at (205, 20) then the calculation would give (Int(205 − 15)/100, Int(20 − 15)/64) or (1, 0). This cell of the grid has value 9, an illegal move.

The 'CheckKey' function

The code uses the 'CheckKey' function to set up the movement of the ball. Any movement around the game world must be done in horizontal movements of 50 pixels and vertical movements of 64 pixels. I used a very simple way of achieving this by setting the MoveX and MoveY parameters to 7 and 9 respectively. There are 7 movements of these increments

```
7 * 7 = 49
7 * 9 = 63
```

Since the resulting arithmetic is 1 pixel out, we would develop an accumulated error. The addition of a single pixel to both the X value and the Y value ensures correct alignment. Obviously the movement can be in either direction and the appropriate key checks set-up the correct direction for the movement.

```
Private Function CheckKey() As Integer
    'Returns one of the arrow keys if pressed or zero
```

```
    If GetAsyncKeyState(KEY_LEFT) Then
       CheckKey = KEY_LEFT
       Ball.X = Ball.X - 1
       Ball.Y = Ball.Y - 1
       Ball.MoveX = -7
       Ball.MoveY = -9
       Ball.Count = 7
    ElseIf GetAsyncKeyState(KEY_RIGHT) Then
       CheckKey = KEY_RIGHT
       Ball.X = Ball.X + 1
       Ball.Y = Ball.Y + 1
       Ball.MoveX = 7
       Ball.MoveY = 9
       Ball.Count = 7
    ElseIf GetAsyncKeyState(KEY_UP) Then
       CheckKey = KEY_UP
       Ball.X = Ball.X + 1
       Ball.Y = Ball.Y - 1
       Ball.MoveX = 7
       Ball.MoveY = -9
       Ball.Count = 7
    ElseIf GetAsyncKeyState(KEY_DOWN) Then
       CheckKey = KEY_DOWN
       Ball.X = Ball.X - 1
       Ball.Y = Ball.Y + 1
       Ball.MoveX = -7
       Ball.MoveY = 9
       Ball.Count = 7
    Else
       CheckKey = 0
       Ball.Count = 0
       Ball.MoveX = 0
       Ball.MoveY = 0
    End If

End Function
```

The Timer event

Since the ball can only move in blocks, the control functionality need only check the keyboard when this alignment is reached. The code uses the value of 'Ball.Count' to determine whether a keyboard read is necessary. Also as a fun touch, whenever the ball displays frame 0 of the animation we play a sound effect of a bounce.

```
Private Sub Sprite1_Timer()
  Dim intKey As Integer, intRow As Integer, intCol As Integer
  Dim blnOutOfRange As Boolean

  intTime = intTime + 1
  Ball.Frame = (Ball.Frame + 1) Mod 6
  If Ball.Frame = 0 Then Sprite1.PlaySoundFile App.Path +
''\bounce.wav''

  If Ball.Count Then
    Ball.X = Ball.X + Ball.MoveX
    Ball.Y = Ball.Y + Ball.MoveY
    Ball.Count = Ball.Count - 1

    If Ball.Count = 0 Then
      intRow = (Ball.Y - 15) / 64
      intCol = (Ball.X - 15) / 100
      If intRow < 0 Or intRow > 5 Or intCol < 0 Or intCol > 5 Then
        'illegal move
        blnOutOfRange = True
        DeadBall
      ElseIf BoxGrid(intRow, intCol) = 9 Then
        DeadBall
      ElseIf BoxGrid(intRow, intCol) = 0 Then
        Total = Total + 1
        BoxGrid(intRow, intCol) = 1
        Sprite1.PasteSprite Diamonds, Ball.X + 13, Ball.Y + 33,
Level
        Sprite1.MoveSprite Diamonds, -200, -200, 0
        Sprite1.PlaySoundFile App.Path + ''\paint.wav''
        If Total = 21 Then
          EndLevel
        End If
      End If
      #If BallDebug Then
        If blnOutOfRange Then
          Caption = ''Out of range''
        Else
          Caption = ''Ball ('' + Str(Ball.X) + '', '' +
Str(Ball.Y) + _
            '') Grid ('' + Str(intRow) + '', '' + Str(intCol) +
_
            '') = '' + Str(BoxGrid(intRow, intCol))
        End If
      #End If
```

```
    End If
  Else
    intKey = CheckKey
  End If
  Sprite1.MoveSprite Ball.Index, Ball.X, Ball.Y, Ball.Frame
  Sprite1.UpdateStage
End Sub
```

When the value of 'Ball.Count' is greater than zero the ball is moved using the current values of 'MoveX' and 'MoveY'. The 'Ball.Count' is then decreased by 1. If this results in zero then checks are made for a legal or illegal move. If the move is illegal – that is, the value for row or column is out of range or the current 'BoxGrid' array value is 9 – then the sub-routine 'DeadBall' is called; if not then a check is made to see if this block has been visited before. If it has then the array value will be 1; if it has not then the current value for the array for that block is set to 1 and the value for 'Total' is increased by 1. If the value for 'Total' reaches 21 then the player has completed a level and the sub-routine 'EndLevel' is called.

'DeadBall' and 'EndLevel'

In this example you have an infinite number of lives. All that the DeadBall routine does is fire a sound effect and reposition your ball at the top of the grid.

```
Sub DeadBall()
  Sprite1.PlaySoundFile App.Path + ''\fall.wav''
  Ball.X = BALL_START_X
  Ball.Y = BALL_START_Y
End Sub
```

If you clear a level then you get a message box. The Visual Basic statement for message boxes takes a variable number of arguments. The first argument is the displayed message; the next is a variable that defines the buttons that are displayed; and finally, if required, a title for the message box.

Message boxes can return a value to the program. The second use of 'MsgBox' shows how this is done. If the user wants to play again then the background is reloaded to clear the screen. This time the background is loaded with the second argument set to True, which ensures that the loaded sprites are retained and remapped to the new background. Since this is simply the same background as before, the effect should be fairly minimal.

```
Sub EndLevel()
  MsgBox ''Well Done. You clear it in'' + Str(time / Sprite1.Fps)
+
''Seconds'', vbOKOnly, ''Cubics''
  SetGrid
  Level = Level + 1
  If Level = 3 Then
    result = MsgBox(''That's all for now. Play Again?'', vbYesNo,
''Cubics'')
    If result = vbYes Then
      Sprite1.LoadBackground App.Path + ''\bg.bmp'', True
      Sprite1.UpdateStage
      Level = 0
    Else
      End
    End If
  End If
  Total = 0
End Sub
```

I am sure you agree that more of a challenge is required. In the second
example we add bad sprites, a timer and a finite number of lives.

Example Ex10B

Initialisation

The new version of the Form Load event creates several new sprites;
notice also the use of 'CloneSprite'. The numbers displayed for the
current time are all sprites that use the same pictures. To save
memory you can create a sprite from an existing sprite. The function
takes three arguments: first the index of the source sprite, then the
initial X and Y positions. Quite often you may not need to use initial X
and Y positions, so simply put 0 for these two arguments.

```
Private Sub Form_Load()
  Dim i As Integer

Width = 640 * Screen.TwipsPerPixelX
  Height = 480 * Screen.TwipsPerPixelY
  Left = 0
  Top = 0
  Sprite1.AutoSize = True
  Sprite1.LoadBackground App.Path + ''\bg.bmp'', False
```

```
   Sprite1.Left = 0
   Sprite1.Top = 0
   Ball.Index = Sprite1.CreateSprite(App.Path + ''\ball.bmp'',
99, 74)
   Cone.Index = Sprite1.CreateSprite(App.Path + ''\cone.bmp'',
99, 68)
   Tube.Index = Sprite1.CreateSprite(App.Path + ''\tube.bmp'',
99, 79)
   Diamonds = Sprite1.CreateSprite(App.Path + ''\diamonds.bmp'',
100, 57)
   Numbers(0) = Sprite1.CreateSprite(App.Path + ''\text.bmp'',
20, 28)
   For i = 1 To 5
     Numbers(i) = Sprite1.CloneSprite(Numbers(0), 0, 0)
   Next
   Sprite1.Fps = 18
   Ball.X = 255
   Ball.Y = 20
   Ball.Lives = 5
   Sprite1.MoveSprite Cone.Index, −200, −200, 0
   Sprite1.MoveSprite Tube.Index, −200, −200, 0
   Sprite1.MoveSprite Diamonds, −200, −200, 0
   Sprite1.PlayMusicFile App.Path + ''\music.mid''
   SetGrid
   Do
   Loop Until CheckKey = 0
End Sub
```

The new Timer event

The new variable 'intTime' is used to display a counter, rather than display the time on every call of the timer event. I choose to update it just one time in 5. The test for equality of an integer division and a floating-point division provides a quick way to control the number of times a call is made.

So now we have two new routines 'ShowTime' and 'MoveBaddies'. Also, if the level is higher than 0, then the baddies are moved and collisions are tested.

```
Private Sub Sprite1_Timer()
   Dim intKey As Integer, intRow As Integer, intCol As Integer
   Dim blnOutOfRange As Boolean

   intTime = intTime + 1
```

```
If Int(intTime / 5) = intTime / 5 Then
  ShowTime
End If
Ball.Frame = (Ball.Frame + 1) Mod 6
If Ball.Frame = 0 Then Sprite1.PlaySoundFile App.Path +
''\bounce.wav''

MoveBaddies

If Ball.Count Then
  Ball.X = Ball.X + Ball.MoveX
  Ball.Y = Ball.Y + Ball.MoveY
  Ball.Count = Ball.Count - 1
  If Ball.Count = 0 Then
    intRow = (Ball.Y - 15) / 64
    intCol = (Ball.X - 15) / 100
    If intRow < 0 Or intRow > 5 Or intCol < 0 Or intCol > 5 Then
      'illegal move
      blnOutOfRange = True
      DeadBall
  ElseIf BoxGrid(Row, Col) = 9 Then
    DeadBall
  ElseIf BoxGrid(Row, Col) = 0 Then
    Total = Total + 1
    BoxGrid(Row, Col) = 1
    Sprite1.PasteSprite Diamonds, Ball.X + 13, Ball.Y + 33,
Level
    Sprite1.MoveSprite Diamonds, -200, -200, 0
    Sprite1.PlaySoundFile App.Path + ''\paint.wav''
    If Total = 21 Then
      EndLevel
    End If
  End If
  #If BallDebug Then
    If blnOutOfRange Then
      Caption = ''Out of range''
    Else
      Caption = ''Ball ('' + Str(Ball.X) + '', '' +
Str(Ball.Y) + _
        '') Grid ('' + Str(Row) + '', '' + Str(Col) + _
        '') = '' + Str(BoxGrid(Row, Col))
    End If
  #End If
  End If
Else
  intKey = CheckKey
```

```
      End If

    If Level > 0 Then
      Tube.Frame = (Tube.Frame + 1) Mod 6
      Sprite1.MoveSprite Tube.Index, Tube.X, Tube.Y, Tube.Frame
      If Sprite1.CollisionCheck(Tube.Index, Ball.Index, True) Then
DeadBall
      If Level > 1 Then
        Cone.Frame = (Cone.Frame + 1) Mod 6
        Sprite1.MoveSprite Cone.Index, Cone.X, Cone.Y, Cone.Frame
        If Sprite1.CollisionCheck(Cone.Index, Ball.Index, True) Then
DeadBall
      End If
    End If
    Sprite1.MoveSprite Ball.Index, Ball.X, Ball.Y, Ball.Frame
    Sprite1.UpdateStage
End Sub
```

If you missed it in the previous chapter then '#If ... Then ... #End If'
provides a way to produce sections of code that execute, dependent on
compilation conditional arguments. Check out the previous chapter for
details.

Moving the Bad Guys

Now that the code is moving three sprites, I decided to put the code for
the non-control sprites in a separate sub-routine.

The baddies move with the same restriction that is placed on the ball.
The allowed increments are + or − 50 for the horizontal value and +
or − 64 for the vertical value. The value of the sprites 'Count' variable
is tested to decide whether to move the sprite or not. A new move for
the 'Tube' is set up randomly. If the tube ends in an illegal position
then the tube position is reset. When setting up a new move for the
'Cone' the current position of the ball is considered. The new
parameters for 'Tube.MoveX' and 'Tube.MoveY' ensure that the cone
moves closer to the ball. Having moved to the new position the baddy
bounces briefly until the count test evaluates to True.

```
  If Tube.Count < Level * 10 − 40 Then
```

Notice that the variable level is used in the test.

The following is a table of the tested value depending on the value of 'Level':

Level	Level * 10–40
0	−40
1	−30
2	−20

As the game progresses this test evaluates to True faster and faster. This very simple device makes the levels progressively harder. If you use code like this in your program then make sure that the test will always have the effect you are aiming for.

If we continue the table

Level	Level * 10–40
3	−10
4	0
5	10

Now a problem will occur in your code: this section of code only executes when the value of 'Count' is already zero and the loop decreases the value. As soon as level 4 is reached the code will immediately evaluate to True. So the effect of increasing difficulty would need more careful coding.

```
Sub MoveBaddies()
   Dim intOffsetAs Integer, intBallPosAs Integer, intRow As Integer,
intCol As Integer

   If Tube.Count > 0 And Level > 0 Then
      Tube.X = Tube.X + Tube.MoveX
      Tube.Y = Tube.Y + Tube.MoveY
      Tube.Count = Tube.Count − 1
      If Tube.Count = 0 Then
         intRow = (Tube.Y − 15) / 64
         intCol = (Tube.X − 15) / 100
         If intRow < 0 Or intRow > 5 Or intCol < 0 Or intCol > 5 Then
            'illegal move
```

```
            Sprite1.PlaySoundFile App.Path + ''\fall.wav''
            Tube.X = 255
            Tube.Y = 150
         ElseIf BoxGrid (intRow, intCol) = 9 Then
            Sprite1.PlaySoundFile App.Path + ''\fall.wav''
            Tube.X = 255
            Tube.Y = 150
         End If
      End If
   Else
      'Move to new square
      'Hunting out the ball
      Tube.Count = Tube.Count − 1
      If Tube.Count < Level * 10 − 40 Then
         Tube.Count = 7
         If Rnd < 0.5 Then
            Tube.MoveX = 7
            Tube.X = Tube.X + 1
         Else
            Tube.MoveX = −7
            Tube.X = Tube.X − 1
         End If
         If Rnd < 0.5 Then
            Tube.MoveY = 9
            Tube.Y = Tube.Y + 1
         Else
            Tube.MoveY = −9
            Tube.Y = Tube.Y − 1
         End If
      End If
   End If
End If

If Cone.Count > 0 And Level > 1 Then
   Cone.X = Cone.X + Cone.MoveX
   Cone.Y = Cone.Y + Cone.MoveY
   Cone.Count = Cone.Count − 1
   If Cone.Count = 0 Then
      intRow = (Cone.Y - 15) / 64
      intCol = (Cone.X - 15) / 100
      If intRow < 0 Or intRow > 5 Or intCol < 0 Or intCol > 5 Then
         'illegal move
         Sprite1.PlaySoundFile App.Path + ''\fall.wav''
         Cone.X = 255
         Cone.Y = 250
      ElseIf BoxGrid (intRow, intCol) = 9 Then
```

```
                    Sprite1.PlaySoundFile App.Path + ''\fall.wav''
                    Cone.X = 255
                    Cone.Y = 250
                End If
            End If
        Else
            'Move to new square
            'Moving towards the Ball
            Cone.Count = Cone.Count - 1
            If Cone.Count < Level * 10 - 60 Then
                Cone.Count = 7
                If Cone.X < Ball.X Then
                    Cone.MoveX = 7
                    Cone.X = Cone.X + 1
                Else
                    Cone.MoveX = -7
                    Cone.X = Cone.X - 1
                End If
                If Cone.Y < Ball.Y Then
                    Cone.MoveY = 9
                    Cone.Y = Cone.Y + 1
                Else
                    Cone.MoveY = -9
                    Cone.Y = Cone.Y - 1
                End If
            End If
        End If

    End Sub
```

Displaying the current game time

This code converts the current 'intTime' value to a string; that is, an integer to text. 1234 is the number one thousand two hundred and thirty-four, and '1234' is a string of characters. The difference is sometimes difficult to understand, but by converting the number to a string it is easier to find out what the value is for each digit.

Visual Basic has many useful functions for dealing with strings, and the following routine shows two of the most useful.

'Format' takes two parameters: a number and a string detailing information about how the string is to be formatted. In this example '000000' means that if the value of the number is only 345, for example, then the string would be '000345'. Zeros are added to the left of the string to make sure that it is 6 characters in length. Format can be very useful when preparing to display high score tables and timer details. The 'MoveSprite' call takes the 6 number sprites and displays them with the six characters in the 'strNewTime' string. 'Mid' is another useful string function which takes three parameters: the name of the variable that is being used for extraction, the start character for the extraction, and the number of characters to extract.

```
Sub ShowTime()
   Dim strNewTime As String

   strNewTime = Format(Time, ''000000'')
   For i = 1 To 6
      Sprite1.MoveSprite Numbers(i − 1), 50 + 20 * i, 16,
Mid(strNewTime, i, 1)
   Next
End Sub
```

The new 'DeadBall' and 'EndLevel' routines

If a ball has entered an illegal position off the pyramid or has collided with a baddy then the 'DeadBall' routine is called. Here a check is made for the available lives of the player. If there are no lives remaining then a simple message box is displayed to ask whether the player wishes to continue. By calling the Visual Basic function 'MsgBox' with 'vbYesNo' as the second parameter, the displayed box will have 'Yes' and 'No' buttons. Once the player has clicked one of the buttons we can test for the result of the 'MsgBox' function. If the player chose 'vbYes' then the board is reset; if not, then application terminates.

```
Sub DeadBall()
   Sprite1.PlaySoundFile App.Path + ''\fall.wav''
   Ball.X = 255
   Ball.Y = 20
   Ball.MoveX = 0
   Ball.MoveY = 0
   Ball.Lives = Ball.Lives − 1
   Sprite1.PasteSprite Numbers(0), 620 − Ball.Lives * 34, 15, 10
   If Ball.Lives = 0 Then
      result = MsgBox(''Ooops you just died. Play again?'', vbYesNo,
''Cubics'')
```

```
        If result = vbYes Then
          'Reset stage
          Ball.Lives = 5
          SetGrid
          Total = 0
          Level = 0
          Tube.X = -200
          Cone.X = -200
          Sprite1.LoadBackground App.Path + ''\bg.bmp'', True
          Sprite1.MoveSprite Tube.Index, Tube.X, Tube.Y, Tube.Frame
          Sprite1.MoveSprite Cone.Index, Cone.X, Cone.Y, Cone.Frame
          Sprite1.DrawFullStage
        Else
          End
        End If
      End If
  End Sub
```

In this example there are only three levels and this simple code sets up the alternative levels. Use is made of a global variable 'Level' to decide in code the stage of the game.

```
  Sub EndLevel()
    MsgBox ''Well Done. You clear it in'' + Str(Time / Sprite1.Fps)
    +
  ''Seconds'',
  vbOKOnly, ''Cubics''
    SetGrid
    Level = Level + 1
    If Level = 3 Then
      result = MsgBox(''That's all for now. Play Again?'', vbYesNo,
  ''Cubics'')
      If result = vbYes Then
        Sprite1.LoadBackground App.Path + ''\bg.bmp'', True
        Sprite1.UpdateStage
        Level = 0
      Else
        End
      End If
    End If
    Total = 0
  End Sub
```

Creating your own programs

Using the techniques in this chapter you can easily create other programs:

Plumbing against the clock   You could create a grid structure with tiles made from sprites that can only be connected in one way. This must be done against the clock before the water is turned on.

Square peg in a round hole   Create a sprite made from a square peg. Have sliding rows to make the legal move from the square peg to a square hole. The rows can move while the peg moves. If the peg lands on a round hole then create a dead peg routine.

These are just two quick ideas to get you started. Hopefully by now you are confident with ideas of your own. The sprite control is easy to use and you can quickly put together a little program. The important thing is have fun.

QUIZ

1. You want to display a score in which the display looks like a mechanical counter. How would you implement it?

Answer: Store a counter that is updated every time the sprite control's Timer event is triggered. Use the Visual Basic 'Format' function to convert this value into a string, then parse the string using 'Mid' to find the value of each digit. Use this information to control the display of a sprite that contains just numbers.

2. You want to receive a simple 'Yes' or 'No' from the player. How would you implement this?

Answer: Use the Visual Basic 'MsgBox' function, with 'vbYesNo' as the second parameter. Test the returned value of the function for 'vbYes'.

3. You are having problems with the sprite control not showing correctly when it has been covered by another window. How do you fix this?

Answer: Place "Sprite1.DrawFullStage" in the Forms Paint event (where 'Sprite1' is the name you have given to your sprite control).

4. Why do we use "Screen.TwipsPerPixelX" when resizing the form?

Answer: If you attempt to resize a form by assigning a value to the form's width property, then it must be specified in Twips. Since the sprite control is using pixels as its scale mode you need to convert between Twips and pixels. The screen object has two properties that you can use for this: 'TwipsPerPixelX' and 'TwipsPerPixelY'.

Summary

In this chapter we looked for the first time at displaying useful game time and status information.

- We saw how to use handy Visual Basic string statements to control how text information can be displayed.
- The Visual Basic 'MsgBox' function was explained.
- We added life parameters to our 'Anim' type.

CHAPTER 11

Simulation – Megalomania made easy

Computers are often used to simulate real world conditions. Programmers can then experiment by varying the parameters of the computer model. This technique is used by business to study how transport and warehousing costs can affect the price of goods to the consumer. Simulations can also provide a popular form of entertainment program. This chapter looks at how you can start to develop your own. Perhaps you can produce the next 'Sim City'.

Deciding how the interface operates

The way to offer the user control of the application varies more with a simulation (sim) than any other form. In a complex game there will be many dialog boxes and a complex variety of options provided via a menu. The program needs to provide constant feedback via the display. It is not the aim of this chapter to produce a finished game, rather to provide pointers along the way.

HOW DO THEY WORK? – 4:

Computer science

Computer science offers lots of clever tricks for the serious student. If sims are your main interest then you would benefit enormously from a concentrated study of the areas of computer science and mathematics covering graph theory and networks. You will be surprised at how many times the problem that faces you has already been solved, often long before computers were even available.

Modelling problems can include:

- *Map Colouring* – Colouring a map with a minimum number of colours. It has now been proved that any plane drawing can be coloured with four colours or less.
- *Network connections* – There are algorithms for determining the minimum number of vertices and edges to remove to separate a network into two parts. Many use ideas pioneered by Euler.
- *Routes* – Finding the path to take around a network to visit each vertex only once, or go down each edge only once.
- *Flows in networks* – Finding the maximum possible flow in a network.
- *Assignments* – Assigning work to individuals to achieve the maximum speed for a complex task.

It is beyond the aims of this book to teach the techniques involved, but if you are interested then explore the web for information on Hamiltonian cycles, Eulerian trails, Hungarian, Kruskal and Prims algorithms, the travelling salesman problem and the Königsberg bridges problem. You will benefit enormously from the information that you will find.

Example Ex11A

In the sim presented as an example, you are given the unwelcome task of being Prime Minister. You can tax the workers and choose to spread this over four different areas: defence, health, education and law and order. The example is a very simple model and I chose to have the relationships between the variables have the following effect.

- Defence: Spend too little on defence and you may be attacked losing some or all of the population.
- Health: Spend too little on health and your citizens will suffer, particularly the youngest and oldest.
- Education: The income of your workers depends on their educational attainment and a random factor. So if you spend too little on education you'll find that, in a few years' time, the amount you acquire through tax will go right down.
- Law and Order: Your citizens accumulate wealth and pensions to keep them in old age. If you spend too little on law and order this could be lost, their health will suffer and you will then need to spend more on health to make up.

As you can see, all the variables are connected. The first problem is how to provide a user interface and the visual display.

User interface design

I wanted to keep things simple. So I restricted the interface to spin controls. You met these earlier and they provide an easy way to alter details by discrete amounts. The design uses six controls. One each for the overall tax level and borrowing amount, and four to choose how to divide the gross taken between defence, health, education and law and order. The display is divided into four rows: the first row shows the population who are at work, the next row shows the home, then health and leisure and finally education. The people who are shown grow from babies to pensioners and, finally, as happens to us all, die.

This picture shows all the possible frames that a cast member can be:

Let's look at how the main variables are declared in the code.

```
(General) – (declarations)
Option Explicit

Private Type Person
  Sex As Integer
  Age As Single
  Frame As Integer
  Index As Integer
  X As Integer
  Y As Integer
  MoveX As Integer
  MoveY As Integer
  Income As Long
  Count As Integer
  Health As Single
  Married As Boolean
  Law As Integer
  Pension As Long
  Wealth As Long
  Education As Single
End Type5

Dim Cast(40) As Person
Dim IntPopulation As Integer
Dim LngBorrowing As Long
Dim IntBudget(4) As Integer
Dim BlnPlaying As Boolean
Dim SngTaxTake As Single
Dim LngGameDate As Long
Dim LngStartDate As Long

Const TOO_MANY = 41
Const TOO_FEW = 3
Const MAX_POPULATION = 40
Const MALE = 0
Const FEMALE = 6
Const OFF_SCREEN = −200
Const BABY = 0
Const CHILD = 1
Const TEENAGER = 2
Const ADULT = 3
Const PENSIONER = 4
Const DEAD = 5
```

```
Const ANNUAL_HEALTH_COST = 700
Const ANNUAL_EDUCATION_COST = 1000
Const ILL = 10
Const DYING = 2
Const SAFE_PENSION_LEVEL = 1000
Const WORK_ROW = 15
Const HOME_ROW = 115
Const HEALTH_ROW = 215
Const EDUCATION_ROW = 315
Const KEEP_JOB = 0.01
```

As you can see the 'Person' type is a complex data type storing lots of useful information for later use.

Debugging technique

Before we examine the code any more fully I thought it would be useful to discuss a number of options for debugging.

Visual Basic 5.0 now provides greatly improved debugging facilities over previous versions. Using the Immediate, Local and Watch windows you can get detailed information on the operation of your application. When the program is in break mode, you can enter commands in the Immediate window and print information to this window. By opening the Local window using the menu option 'View | Local Window' you can immediately see the values in the variables of the procedure where the program was halted. This is a great time saver; it is often unnecessary to use the Watch window since if your code is highly modular (as it should be) then the Locals window will provide all the feedback you require. The Watch window is also opened using a menu command 'View | Watch Window'. You add the names of variables that you wish to check to the Watch window. The scope of the variable is also of importance. Sometimes, however, the use of the more extensive debugging available from Visual Basic 5.0 is still not enough. If you are still using Visual Basic 4.0 then you will definitely benefit from the techniques that are described below.

When you are using Visual Basic 4.0, and you run the program, a window is opened that is referred to as the Immediate window. This is divided into two sections. The upper section is where the watch variables are displayed. You can add a watch to this by using 'Tools\Add Watch' from the main menu.

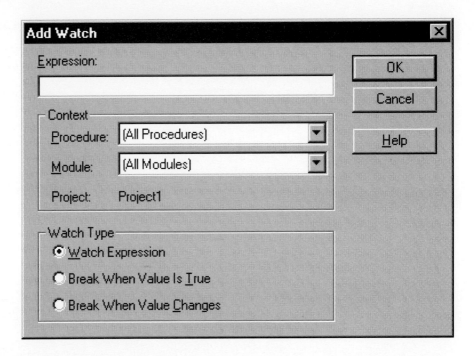

You enter the name of the variable that you are considering in the top box, then make sure that the scope for that variable is correctly set using the 'Procedure' and 'Module' combo boxes. If you fail to set the correct values for the scope then error messages will often appear in the debug window.

The lower section of the debug window has two purposes: Firstly, you can use it to run immediate code; that is, if you type 'print $2+3$' then 5 will be displayed. If you are using the 'Sprite.ocx' control and you wish to replace the background while the program is running, then break the program. You can use control break or the break button on the toolbar to break into the program. (The break button looks like a vertical equals sign). Now if you type 'Sprite1.LoadBackground App.Path + "\newbg.bmp", TRUE' then the background that is called 'newbg.bmp' will be loaded and the existing sprites will be retained.

The alternative way to use the debug object is to view the results of 'Debug.Print' statements. These are always displayed by the Immediate window.

Sometimes the use of watches, immediate mode code and 'Debug.Print' statements is not enough to fully examine the state of your program while it is running. If you move on to other languages then you will often see that a great deal of effort by the developers of the programming compiler and environment has gone into the debugger. With Visual Basic you will sometimes need to develop debug techniques of your own. One that works for me is a to create a dump file; that is, you create a disk file and send details of the current state of the program to this file as the program is running.

Here is a section of code that I used while developing this program.

```
Sub DumpCast(blnAdd As Boolean)
  Dim i As Integer, intFileNum As Integer
  Dim strTemp As String
  intFileNum = FreeFile
  If blnAdd Then
    Open App.Path + ''\dump.dat'' For Append As intFileNum
  Else
    Open App.Path + ''\dump.dat'' For Output As intFileNum
  End If
  Print #intFileNum, ''''
  Print #intFileNum, Format(LngGameDate, ''Medium Date'')
  Print #intFileNum, ''Budget LngBorrowing Tax Defence Health
Education Law and Order''
  Print #intFileNum, GetTotalIncome + LngBorrowing; Tab(8);
LngBorrowing; Tab(19); SngTaxTAke; Tab(25); IntBudget(1);
Tab(34); IntBudget(2); Tab(41); IntBudget(3); Tab(52);
IntBudget(4)
  Print #intFileNum, ''i Sex Age Frame Income Kids Health Wealth
Pension Education''
  For i = 0 To MAX_POPULATION
    Print #intFileNum, i; Tab(6); Cast(i).Sex; Tab(9);
Cast(i).Age; _
      Tab(15); Cast(i).Frame; Tab(19); Cast(i).Income; _
      Tab(26); Cast(i).Kids; Tab(31); Format(Cast(i).Health,
''.##''); _
      Tab(39); Cast(i).Wealth; Tab(46); Cast(i).Pension; Tab(54);
Cast(i).Education
  Next
  Close intFileNum
End Sub
```

It is easy to create or open disk files using Visual Basic, but it can be a little confusing. I remember when I first started I found it totally bewildering. So without trying to blind you with science, here is how you do it.

The first part of the code statement is really easy: 'Open'. Then you give the full name of the file, which could include the path-name if the current DOS directory is different from the one that includes the file in which you are interested. If you are new to DOS then don't even consider learning how to use it. Instead always include the full path. Then put 'For'. This is where things start to become more complicated. The next part of the statement can be 'Input', 'Binary', 'Append', or 'Output'. Any one of these will cause the subsequent code to behave differently with this disk file. Usually 'Input' and 'Output' are used with text files and 'Binary' with files that do not include text conversion. What does that mean? Let us take a number 234; this is a number that can be stored in many ways. Firstly, it could be stored in one byte of information. Remember that ultimately computer information breaks down to a switch that is either on or off – that is, one of two possible states. Two switches can have four possible states: switch 1 can be on or off, and switch 2 can be on or off, giving four possible states. Eight switches have 256 possible states. So 234 could be stored as the binary information 11101010 or $128 + 64 + 32 + 0 + 8 + 0 + 2 + 0$. This is the binary technique. But, an alternative way to store this information would be to store the code for 2 followed by the code for 3 followed by the code for 4, which is the technique used by text files. The advantage of a text file is the ease with which it can be displayed using Notepad or any word processor.

The final part of the statement is the number used to identify the file. It is best to select this number using the 'FreeFile' statement that is part of Visual Basic. Use FreeFile to assign a number to an integer variable. (Does that make sense? If so, then think about how you would have felt about that sentence when you first started to read this book. Hopefully you are feeling a lot more comfortable with the idea of computer code.)

If you create a text file with 'Output' then you can add to this file by reopening the file in 'Append' mode. You write to the file by using the 'Print' statement. To distinguish between printing to the screen and to a file you add the number of the file that is open before any printing information – that is, the variable that was assigned a value with the 'FreeFile' statement. 'Print #intFileNum' works just like 'Print' when printing things to the screen or 'Debug.Print' when printing things to the debug window. Use the standard formatting techniques such as 'Str' and 'Format' to achieve the desired layout.

NOTE

'Str' converts a number into a string. 'Format' allows you to manipulate the conversion process.

When working with disk files always remember to close any file that you open. Disk files can be very useful in the debugging process, because code executes so quickly that it is often difficult to determine the overall condition of the program at one particular instance using any other technique.

Initialising the program

As usual the Form_Load event contains the once-only initialisation routines.

```
Private Sub Form_Load()
  Dim i As Integer

  Sprite1.AutoSize = True
  Sprite1.LoadBackground App.Path + ''\bg.bmp'', False
  Cast(0).Index = Sprite1.CreateSprite(App.Path +
''\people.bmp'', 68, 90)
  For i = 1 To MAX_POPULATION
    Cast(i).Index = Sprite1.CloneSprite(Cast(0).Index, 0, 0)
  Next
  Width = 640 * Screen.TwipsPerPixelX
  Height = 480 * Screen.TwipsPerPixelY
  Left = (Screen.Width — Width) / 2
  Top = (Screen.Height — Height) / 2
  Sprite1.Left = 0
  Sprite1.Top = lblTax.Height + lblStatus.Height
  lblStatus.Left = 0
  lblStatus.Top = lblTax.Height
  lblStatus.Width = Width
  For i = 0 To 19
    Cast(i).X = Int(Rnd * 600)
    Cast(i).Y = Int(Rnd * 4) * 100 + 15
    'Initialise cast
    If Rnd < 0.5 Then
      Cast(i).Sex = MALE
```

```
      Else
        Cast(i).Sex = FEMALE
      End If
      Cast(i).Age = Int(Rnd * 90)
      Cast(i).Frame = Cast(i).Age / 15 + (Cast(i).Sex)
      If Cast(i).Frame = ADULT + MALE Or Cast(i).Frame = ADULT +
FEMALE Then
        If Rnd > 0.1 Then
          Cast(i).Income = Int(Rnd * 30000)
        Else
          Cast(i).Income = 0
        End If
      End If
      Cast(i).Health = Int(Rnd * 100)
      Cast(i).Law = Int(Rnd * 100)
      Cast(i).Pension = Int(Rnd * 100)
      Cast(i).Wealth = Int(Rnd * 100)
      Cast(i).Education = Int(Rnd * 100)
      Sprite1.MoveSprite Cast(i).Index, Cast(i).X, Cast(i).Y,
Cast(i).Frame
    Next
    For i = 20 To MAX_POPULATION
      Cast(i).X = OFF_SCREEN
      Cast(i).Age = 0
      Sprite1.MoveSprite Cast(i).Index, Cast(i).X, Cast(i).Y,
Cast(i).Frame
    Next
    BlnPlaying = False
    IntPopulation = 20
    SngTaxTake = 0.3
    LngBorrowing = 0
    LngGameDate = Date
    LngStartDate = LngGameDate
    For i = 1 To 4
IntBudget(i) = 75
    Next
    #If LifeDebug Then
DumpCast (False)
    #End If
    lblStatus.Caption = ''Adjust the Tax take and how this is spent
using the arrows. See how good you would be as Prime Minister!''
End Sub
```

Since each sprite shares the same pictures, I used the 'CloneSprite' option. Firstly, a sprite is created and the index value returned by the function is saved. Then, in a loop, the other sprites are created by cloning. The 'Cast' array is used to save all the returned index values. The cast are initialised to male or female, age, and income level. The health level is set and details such as the overall wealth of the individual is established. Finally a call to 'MoveSprite' is made otherwise the changes to the pictures would not be displayed on the screen. Initially the population is set to 40, the tax taken by government is set to 30%. There is no government borrowing, the initial date is set to today's date and the share of the tax is distributed evenly among the four options: health, education, defence and law and order.

Notice the use of a conditional debug statement at the end of the procedure.

The main program loop

I used the sprite control's Timer event to provide the main loop for the program:

```
Private Sub Sprite1_Timer()
   Static IntTest As Integer
   Dim i As Integer, sngTemp As Single

   If BlnPlaying Then
     LngGameDate = LngGameDate + 10
     'Is there an invasion
     If Rnd + 0.1 < 10 ^ — (IntBudget(1) / 30) Then
       sngTemp = IntPopulation — IntPopulation * Rnd
       MsgBox ''You've just been invaded and lost'' + Str(sngTemp)
+ ''million people.''
       For i = 0 To sngTemp
         KillCast (i)
       Next
     End If

     For i = 0 To MAX_POPULATION
       UpdateCastMember (i)
       Sprite1.MoveSprite Cast(i).Index, Cast(i).X, Cast(i).Y,
   Cast(i).Frame
     Next
```

```
    If IntPopulation < 1 Then
       MsgBox ''Ooops they are all dead!''
       End
    End If
    IntTest = IntTest + 1
    If IntTest = 50 Then
       IntTest = 0
       #If LifeDebug Then
          DumpCast (True)
       #End If
    End If
    ShowStatus
  End If
  Sprite1.UpdateStage
End Sub
```

There is a Boolean variable called 'blnPlaying' that is used to check whether the user has started to play! This is set to True by clicking any of the spin controls.

Have we been invaded?

```
If Rnd + 0.1 < 10^ −(IntBudget(1) / 30) Then
```

'Rnd' returns a value between 0 and 1. This code checks whether the right-hand side of the equation is greater than .1 + x where x can have any value between 0 and 1. OK, but what does that other bit mean? The symbol $^\wedge$ means raised to a power. Now you know that $2*2$ can be written as 2 squared and $2*2*2$ can be written as 2 cubed. Because it is easier to show computer code with all text the same size, this mathematical version is replaced by a new symbol $^\wedge$. $2^\wedge 8$ means that 2 is being multiplied 8 times. The power does not have to be an integer value. $2^\wedge 4.567$ is valid. Also the power does not have to be positive, it can be negative. If it is negative then it is the same as the reciprocal. If the number is x then the reciprocal is $1/x$. So $2^\wedge -2 = 1/(2^\wedge 2) = 1/4$. 'IntBudget(1)' is the allocation for defence. As long as sufficient is allowed then there is almost no chance of an invasion, but if the allocation for defence falls to rock bottom then the likelihood of this statement evaluating as True increases dramatically. To give you some idea of how the budget for defence affects the right-hand side of the test, here is a little table:

Defence budget (%)	25	20	15	10	5	0
$10^{\wedge}-(Budget/10)$	.003	.01	.03	.1	.3	1

As you can see, if you keep the defence level above 10% then the statement will never evaluate to True. In a real world-modelling exercise, you would examine tables of possible outcomes and you would need to feel comfortable dealing with differential equations.

NOTE

An equation connects two or more variables. Perhaps the simplest possible equation is $y = x$. There are rules governing how the equation of a curve and the slope of a tangent to a curve at a certain point are related. A tangent is a straight line that touches the curve at the chosen point and gives the slope of the curve at that point. The translation process between a curve and its tangent is referred to as differentiating. The equation that results after differentiating is itself a curve that has tangents. This second equation can in turn be differentiated. This process can continue until a constant value is the result ($y = 2$, for example). A differential equation is an equation that connects variables using these differentiated equations. They are useful in many engineering and modelling situations and form the basis of most applied mathematics courses.

If you are invaded then the simplest possible model is used for the result. The population is reduced by a random factor. No account is made of your defence installations, intelligence or the many variables that would really be involved. Because in the code the cast sprite members come and go, I decided to create a sub-routine to look after killing a cast member. The call to 'KillCast(i)' is a call to that sub-routine.

Another useful sub-routine is the one to update a cast member. Hopefully you will see by the choice of name that the code is made easier to read, and by modularising the code it is easier to maintain. It is fair to say that Visual Basic often encourages the lone programmer to use more global variables than would be prudent for the safe running of a program. But, too much parameter passing can make the code confusing. If you move on to C++ in the near future then the issues of scope need to be carefully addressed. The perceived wisdom is to use the minimum scope possible for a variable, to initialise it just before using it, and never expect it to have a certain value. You should try, wherever possible, to create code that is of the black box variety. This type of code is transportable from one programming job to the next and is easier to maintain.

The details

Each of the 40 possible sprites share the same code. First a call is made from the sprite control Timer event to 'UpdateCastMember'. A single parameter is used, which is the index of the sprite concerned.

```
Sub UpdateCastMember(i As Integer)
  If Cast(i).X = OFF_SCREEN Then Exit Sub
  If Cast(i).Age Then Cast(i).Age = Cast(i).Age + 0.1
  Cast(i).Frame = Cast(i).Age / 15 + Cast(i).Sex
  'Assess health of cast
  SetHealthStatus (i)
  'ShowCastStatus (i)
  If Cast(i).Health < ILL Then
    If Cast(i).Health < DYING Then
      If Rnd < 0.05 Then
        KillCast (i)
        Exit Sub
      End If
    Else
      Cast(i).Y = HEALTH_ROW
    End If
  End If

  If IntBudget(4) < 30 Then
    LawAndOrderProblem (i)
  End If

  Select Case Cast(i).Frame - Cast(i).Sex
  Case BABY
    Cast(i).Y = HOME_ROW
  Case CHILD
    SetEducationStatus (i)
    Cast(i).Y = EDUCATION_ROW
  Case TEENAGER
    SetEducationStatus (i)
    Cast(i).Y = EDUCATION_ROW
    If Cast(i).Frame > 5 And Rnd < 0.0005 * Cast(i).Health Then
NewBaby
  Case ADULT
    Cast(i).Y = WORK_ROW
    SetIncome (i)
    If Cast(i).Frame > 5 And Rnd < 0.0005 * Cast(i).Health Then
NewBaby
  Case PENSIONER
    Cast(i).Y = HOME_ROW
    Cast(i).Pension = Cast(i).Pension * 0.9
    If Cast(i).Pension < SAFE_PENSION_LEVEL Then
      Cast(i).Health = Cast(i).Health * 0.9
    End If
  Case DEAD
```

```
      If Cast(i).Age = 100 Then
        KillCast (i)
      End If
    End Select
  End Sub
```

When a cast member is off screen it is effectively dead from the perspective of the code so the first line of the routine checks this, if it is off screen then the sub-routine is terminated. Then the current age of this cast member is increased by .1 of a year. The displayed frame is determined by the age of the cast member. Deciding on the Health of the cast member is left to a special sub-routine, 'SetHealthStatus'.

Having returned from 'SetHealthStatus' the current value of 'Cast(i).Health' can be tested against the constants for DYING and ILL. If the current health factor falls below these constants then the code is executed to decide whether the day of reckoning is at hand. If the cast member is dead then there is little point carrying on with the sub-routine so the sub-routine is terminated. If the level of funds for Law and Order fall below the threshold of 10% then the sub-routine 'LawAndOrderProblem' is executed. Note that the values in the code are three times the percentage level. 30 is equivalent to 10%. This is to enable an easy routine when the spin controls are used. Each adjustment of a spin control raises or lowers that type, be it defence, education or whatever. The adjustment is +3 or −3. If 3 is added to a type then 1 is subtracted from each of the other 3 types. It is just to enable integers to be used and to make sure that the total of all the types is displayed as 100, that the internal code uses integer values that are three times those displayed.

The next section of code uses a 'Select Case' construction to choose between several different options. Notice that special routines are again used in this section. Calls are made to 'SetEducationStatus', 'SetIncome' and 'NewBaby'. It is now time to look at each of these special routines.

Law and Order

If a call is made to 'LawAndOrderProblem' then the cast members may lose some health and wealth, or possibly even their lives.

```
Sub LawAndOrderProblem(i As Integer)
    If Rnd < 0.03 Then
        KillCast (i)
    Else
        Cast(i).Health = Cast(i).Health * 0.8
        Cast(i).Wealth = Cast(i).Wealth * 0.8
        Cast(i).Pension = Cast(i).Pension * 0.8
    End If
End Sub
```

Having babies

If the conditions are right – that is, the cast member is female and approximately the right age – then a random factor decides whether she is to have a baby. Interestingly in this model, no males are needed to produce a baby! So it is perhaps not quite as faithful to the real world as we could wish. If a new baby is required then this simple code is executed.

```
Sub NewBaby()
    Dim i As Integer

    Do While (Cast(i).X <> OFF_SCREEN)
        i = i + 1
        If i > MAX_POPULATION Then Exit Sub
    Loop

    Cast(i).X = Rnd * 550
    Cast(i).Y = HOME_ROW
    If Rnd < 0.5 Then
        Cast(i).Sex = FEMALE
    Else
        Cast(i).Sex = MALE
    End If
    Cast(i).Wealth = 0
    Cast(i).Pension = 0
    Cast(i).Education = 0
    Cast(i).Income = 0
    Cast(i).Frame = Cast(i).Sex
    IntPopulation = IntPopulation + 1
End Sub
```

Education

The wealth of the individual and, in turn, the total tax taken by government are heavily dependent on the educational attainment of the population. Spend money on education and it will return its costs with dividends.

```
Sub SetEducationStatus(i As Integer)
  Dim lngEducationBudget As Long, sngSpendPerCapita As Single

  lngEducationBudget = GetTotalIncome() * IntBudget(3) / 300
  sngSpendPerCapita = lngEducationBudget / IntPopulation * 1000
  Cast(i).Education = Cast(i).Education + (2 - (Cast(i).Age >
20)) * sngSpendPerCapita / ANNUAL_EDUCATION_COST
  If Cast(i).Education > 200 Then Cast(i).Education = 200
End Sub
```

Health

Nearly as vital in this model is the spending on health. This society needs to be clever and healthy to survive.

```
Sub SetHealthStatus(i As Integer)
  Dim LngHealthBudget As Long, SngSpendPerCapita As Single
  Dim Factor As Single

  LngHealthBudget = GetTotalIncome() * IntBudget(2) / 300
  If IntPopulation Then
    SngSpendPerCapita = LngHealthBudget / IntPopulation
  End If
  Factor = (SngSpendPerCapita / ANNUAL_HEALTH_COST - 0.5) * 0.1
  Cast(i).Health = Cast(i).Health + Factor + (Cast(i).Age > 60)
* 0.1
  If Cast(i).Health > 100 Then Cast(i).Health = 100
End Sub
```

Useful functions in the code

To decide at any time what the total tax intake is likely to be requires a knowledge of the current incomes of all the population. This simple function provides that functionality.

```
Function GetTotalIncome() As Long
   Dim i As Integer, lngTemp As Long

   For i = 0 To MAX_POPULATION
     If Cast(i).Frame = ADULT + MALE Or Cast(i).Frame = ADULT +
FEMALE Then
        lngTemp = lngTemp + Cast(i).Income
     End If
   Next
   GetTotalIncome = lngTemp - LngBorrowing * 0.1
End Function
```

When their time has come this function tidies up the loose ends:

```
Sub KillCast(i As Integer)
   Cast(i).Age = 0
   Cast(i).Frame = 0 + Cast(i).Sex
   Cast(i).X = OFF_SCREEN
   IntPopulation = IntPopulation - 1
End Sub
```

When setting the income level of an employed cast member notice that the education level is used in the equation.

```
Sub SetIncome(i As Integer)
   If Cast(i).Education < Rnd * KEEP_JOB Then
     Cast(i).Income = 0
   Else
     'Income is based on a random factor and educational status
     Cast(i).Income = Cast(i).Education / 50 * 20000 + Rnd * 20000
     Cast(i).Wealth = Cast(i).Wealth + Cast(i).Income * 0.1
     'Pension is based on income level and a random factor
     Cast(i).Pension = Cast(i).Pension + Cast(i).Income * 0.05 +
Cast(i).Income * Rnd * 0.05
   End If
End Sub
```

To help display the current status of the game this code is used.

```
Sub ShowStatus()
   Dim strTemp As String, intEmployed As Integer, intUnemployed As
Integer
   Dim lngTotalIncome As Long, i As Integer
```

```
    lngTotalIncome = GetTotalIncome()
    For i = 0 To MAX_POPULATION
        If Cast(i).Frame = ADULT + MALE Or Cast(i).Frame = ADULT +
FEMALE Then
            If Cast(i).Income Then
                intEmployed = intEmployed + 1
            Else
                intUnemployed = intUnemployed + 1
            End If
        End If
    Next

    If BlnPlaying Then
        strTemp = Format((LngGameDate - LngStarTDate) / 365,
''.##'') + ''years''
        strTemp = strTemp + ''IntPopulation:'' + Str(IntPopulation)
+ ''m''
        strTemp = strTemp + ''intEmployed:'' + Str(intEmployed) +
''m''
        If intUnemployed Or intEmployed Then
            strTemp = strTemp + ''intUnemployed:'' +
Str(intUnemployed * 100 / (intEmployed + intUnemployed)) + ''%''
        Else
            strTemp = strTemp + ''intUnemployed: 100%''
        End If
        strTemp = strTemp + ''Tax take: £'' +
Trim(Str(lngTotalIncome)) + ''b''
        strTemp = strTemp + ''Budget: £'' + Trim(Str(lngTotalIncome
+ LngBorrowing)) + ''b''
        strTemp = strTemp + Format(LngGameDate, ''Medium Date'')
        lblStatus.Caption = strTemp
    End If
End Sub
```

Visual Basic provides lots of useful tools for string manipulation and this section of the code shows some of them in action. Earlier chapters have explained them all, but this is another useful example of them in action.

As I wrote earlier, spin controls provide most of the user interaction. This short code shows how each of the controls is used. Similar code is used for the other spin controls.

```
Private Sub spnBorrowing_SpinDown()
    If Not blnPlaying Then
```

```
    blnPlaying = True
  End If
  If lngBorrowing > 0 Then
    lngBorrowing = lngBorrowing - 1
    lblBorrowing.Caption = ''£'' + Trim(Str(lngBorrowing)) +
''billion''
  End If
End Sub
```

Review

In this book so far we have seen some very simple maths that are required to move the sprites on the screen. Computer simulations can call on a much more sophisticated level of mathematics. You may have heard of the calculus techniques developed by Newton and Leibniz in the sixteenth century to help understand moving objects. The challenge broke down to finding the tangent to a curve and the area under a curve. Techniques later called differentiation and integration provided these tools. A mathematical function such as $f(x) = 3x^2 + 2x + 4$ differentiates to $f'(x) = 6x + 2$ and can be differentiated again to $f''(x) = 6$.

Equations can be developed that use a function and its derivatives. That is, $f(x)$, $f'(x)$ and $f''(x)$. These functions are called differential equations and form the cornerstone of what is called applied mathematics. A complex computer modelling program is likely to make use of this level of mathematics.

This is an extremely simple example of simulation. A proper game developed to allow the user interactivity is a very challenging undertaking. Visual Basic would provide all the flexibility that you would require. You may choose to incorporate a database structure into your model and to use complex maths. I am afraid this chapter can only offer an introduction. If it whets your appetite to move on to these greater challenges then remember the golden rule, have fun.

QUIZ

1. How many colours are needed to colour any map?
Answer: 4

2. How do you create a disk file to which you can write program data?
Answer: Open filename 'For Output As x' (x is a value stored after a call to FreeFile).

3. If you open a disk file what must you always remember to do with it?
Answer: Close the file using 'Close x' (x is the file number used to identify the file).

4. Using 'Sprite.ocx', what code do you use if you need to copy a sprite?
Answer: newindex = 'CloneSprite(sourceindex, x, y)' (x and y dictate the initial position for the new sprite).

Summary

In this chapter you learnt about using very simple computer modelling to simulate real world conditions. This is a very complex subject, the detail of which is beyond this introductory book. A very high level of mathematical skill is required to create a computer model that fairly reflects the changing circumstances as each variable is so tightly dependent on another. You learnt that a fully configured program would most likely make use of differential equations to manipulate the world data.

CHAPTER 12

Screensavers –
Make them fun!

Screensavers are great fun. Why have flying logos or stars when you can do so much more. Maybe you didn't realise that with Visual Basic you can create your own screensaver. In this chapter you will discover how. We will also look at two other issues. So far the animation has been displayed using special controls and libraries. It is possible with Visual Basic's own controls to display animation, and the methods used are covered here.

Creating a screensaver

When Windows launches your screensaver it passes a command line message. If you have ever used DOS then you will understand what command line messages are. For those lucky enough never to have touched DOS, here is an explanation.

Using DOS to change from the current directory to another you type 'cd newdir' where 'newdir' is the name of the new directory. 'newdir' is an argument passed to the command 'cd'. When a screensaver starts it is either passed '\s', in which case the screensaver should show itself, or it is passed '\c', in which case a dialog box that enables configuration of the screensaver is displayed. It is usual to use this dialog box to set up a password. There are three other arguments that can be passed, but we will not cover them in this chapter. Other issues to be aware of are the screensaver starting multiple times, as the system clock decides that it is time to restart the screensaver. The final confusing issue regarding screensavers is the curious feature of Windows that a 'MouseMove' message is sent to the application approximately every two minutes. This could have the effect of terminating your screensaver unless you deliberately check for it in the code.

When starting a screensaver you want your code to react differently, dependent on the command line arguments. To enable this feature you need to start the program using a module rather than a form.

An application doesn't have to start using a form from the project; you can start your application with any form or a sub-main procedure in a standard module.

Using a sub-main procedure

You add a module to your project using the 'Insert|Module' menu option. The module must contain a procedure called 'Main'. This is rather like standard C programming where code always starts with the 'main' procedure. The code contained in the 'Main' procedure can be any you choose, but for the result to be seen by the user it is normal to use the code to 'Show' a 'Form'.

When the project starts execution, 'Sub Main' is called immediately.

```
Sub Main()
   If App.PrevInstance Then End
   If InStr(Command, ''/s'') > 0 Then
     CursorOff
     Ex12AForm.Show
   ElseIf InStr(Command, ''/c'') > 0 Then
     SetPassForm.Show 1
   End If
End Sub
```

If the screensaver has already started there is no point in it starting again, hence the first line in this procedure. 'Command' is a Visual Basic statement that returns the details used by the command line. The rather curious code

```
InStr(Command, ''/s'') > 0
```

is used to extract the command line switch '/s'. 'InStr' is a useful function included with Visual Basic that looks through a string and compares it with another string. If the second string is found then the function returns to the position where it is found.

Suppose that strTemp = 'Another string comparison routine!' and strFind = 'str', the

'InStr(strTemp, strFind)' would return 8, the position where 'str' is found.

Here we are only interested in whether a search finds the string at all. So if the function is positive then the search must have been successful. If unsuccessful, then 'InStr' returns 0. If the search is successful then the screensaver starts after turning the mouse cursor off. The procedure 'CursorOff' is one of the routines in this module.

```
Public Sub CursorOff()
  Dim intCurrentCursorDepth As Integer
  intCurrentCursorDepth = ShowCursor(False)
  intCursorCounter = intCurrentCursorDepth + 1
  Do While intCurrentCursorDepth > −1
    intCurrentCursorDepth = ShowCursor(False)
  Loop
End Sub
```

Turning the mouse cursor on and off is rather tricky with Windows. There is a Windows API function called 'ShowCursor' but this uses a counter. When the value of the counter is negative the cursor is off, when the value of the counter is positive the cursor is on. Sending 'ShowCursor' the argument 'False' decreases the counter, and sending it the value 'True' increases the counter. In this example we want to be sure that the cursor is off or on while not upsetting other programs that may be setting and resetting the cursor counter. We use a global variable to store the value of the current cursor counter. 'ShowCursor' returns the value of the current cursor counter. This value is saved using 'intCursorCounter', then the program loops calling 'ShowCursor' with the argument 'False' until 'ShowCursor' returns the value -1. At this point the cursor must have finally been made invisible.

The complementary procedure 'CursorOn' uses the stored value to increment the value of the counter to the original value before 'CursorOff' was called.

```
Public Sub CursorOn()
  Dim intCurrentCursorDepth As Integer

  intCurrentCursorDepth = ShowCursor(True)
  Do While intCurrentCursorDepth < intCursorCounter
    intCurrentCursorDepth = ShowCursor(True)
  Loop
End Sub
End
```

When you are using Visual Basic you can send command line arguments using the 'Tools | Options' dialog box.

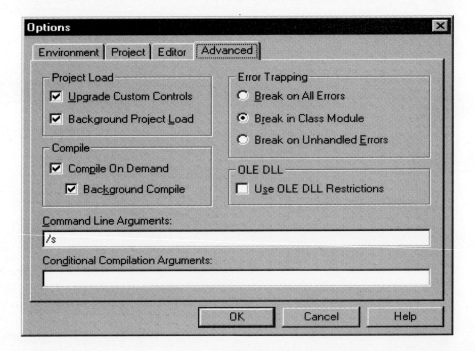

Clicking the 'Advanced' tab reveals an edit box that allows you to enter command line arguments. If you run 'Ex12a.vbp' then you will see that '/s' is entered in the command line arguments box, this allows you to test the program as it will run when the screensaver is launched.

The 'Project' tab lets you enter 'Sub Main' as the start-up procedure.

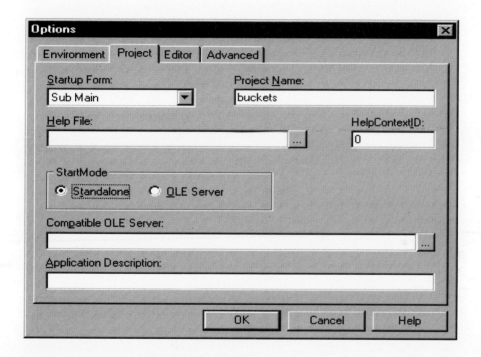

Windows API declarations

In this example we are looking to the Windows API calls for most of the functions. If you have not run the program already, then do so now. It will only run from within the design environment unless you pass the required command line argument, which you can do by using the 'Start | Run' option with Windows 95.

The program seems to animate on top of the Windows desktop. This is in fact a trick. Before we look at how it is done let's take a look at the declarations required.

```
(General) – (declarations)
Type RECT
   left As Long
   top As Long
   right As Long
   bottom As Long
End Type


Declare Function GetDesktopWindow Lib ''user32'' () As Long
Declare Function ShowCursor Lib ''user32'' (ByVal bShow As Long) As
Long                                                                    ↵
Declare Function ReleaseDC Lib ''user32'' (ByVal hwnd As Long, _
   ByVal hdc As Long) As Long
Declare Function GetDC Lib ''user32'' (ByVal hwnd As Long) As Long
Declare Function BitBlt Lib ''gdi32'' (ByVal hDestDC As Long, _
   ByVal x As Long, ByVal y As Long, ByVal nWidth As Long, _
   ByVal nHeight As Long, ByVal hSrcDC As Long, ByVal xSrc As Long, _
   ByVal ySrc As Long, ByVal dwRop As Long) As Long
Declare Function GetWindowRect Lib ''user32'' (ByVal hwnd As Long, _
   lpRect As RECT) As Long
Declare Function WritePrivateProfileString Lib ''kernel32'' Alias _
   ''WritePrivateProfileStringA'' (ByVal lpApplicationName As String, _
   ByVal lpKeyName As Any, ByVal lpString As Any, _
   ByVal lpFileName As String) As Long
Declare Function GetPrivateProfileString Lib ''kernel32'' Alias _
   ''GetPrivateProfileStringA'' (ByVal lpApplicationName As String, _
   ByVal lpKeyName As Any, ByVal lpDefault As String, _
   ByVal lpReturnedString As String, ByVal nSize As Long, _
   ByVal lpFileName As String) As Long


Global sngTwipsPerPixel As Single

Public Const SRCCOPY = &HCC0020
Public Const SRCPAINT = &HEE0086
Public Const SRCAND = &H8800C6
Public Const WALKRIGHT = 0
Public Const TURNLEFT = 1
Public Const CLIMB = 2
Public Const INTOCLIMB = 3
Public Const SMALLFALLRIGHT = 4
Public Const BIGFALLRIGHT = 5
Public Const POUR = 7
Public Const WALKLEFT = 8
Public Const TURNRIGHT = 9
```

```
Public Const SMALLFALLLEFT = 10
Public Const BIGFALLLEFT = 11

Global intCursorDepth As Integer
```

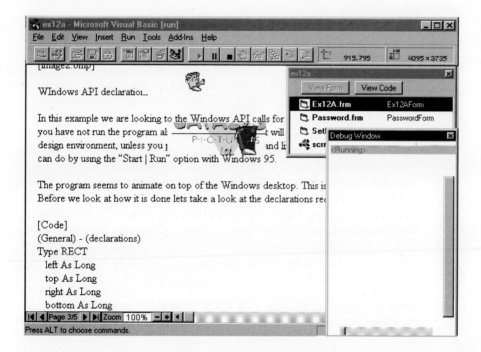

Most of these calls are used in the procedure that grabs the current screen. Let's look at the code.

```
Public Sub GrabScreen()
    Dim winSize As RECT
```

A RECT is a standard Windows data type. It contains four long integers that can store the pixel positions of the top, left, right and bottom.

```
Dim hwndSrc As Long, hSrcDC As Long, lngWidth As Long
Dim lngHeight As Long, lngResult As Long

'Assign information of the source bitmap.
'Note that BitBlt requires co-ordinates in pixels.
hwndSrc = GetDesktopWindow()
```

Now the long integer 'hwndSrc' contains a handle to the Windows desktop.

```
hSrcDC = GetDC(hwndSrc)
```

Windows programming for the C++ programmer is all about message maps and device contexts. A device context is an extended datatype that provides a storage point for information about a window. It can store information about the picture displayed, the current font and how lines are to be drawn, among other things. We only get at the picture that is being displayed on the desktop by getting the device context from the handle returned by the earlier call. I realise that this is very confusing, but if you really want to learn about this type of programming then there is no better source than Charles Petzold's book on programming Windows. Pass over the others, get that one.

```
lngResult = GetWindowRect(hwndSrc, winSize)
```

Here we call the function 'GetWindowRect' but we pass it two arguments: firstly, the handle to the desktop and, secondly, a pointer to a RECT data type. Windows will place all the details into the RECT. The 'lngResult' is just a dummy variable.

```
lngWidth = winSize.right    'Units in pixels.
lngHeight = winSize.bottom    'Units in pixels.
```

Now we know the size of the desktop in pixels. We also need to make sure that the copying that takes place will be persistent. Setting the AutoRedraw property to True ensures persistence.

```
Ex12AForm.AutoRedraw = True
```

Using 'BitBlt' you can copy the picture from one device context to another. Here the Windows desktop is copied to the background of the form used in the project.

```
lngResult = BitBlt(Ex12AForm.hdc, 0, 0, lngWidth, lngHeight, _
   hSrcDC, 0, 0, SRCCOPY)

'Release the DeskTop Windows' hDC to Windows.
'Windows may hang if this is not done.
```

Windows can only manage a limited number of device contexts, so
having used the desktop one it must be released to avoid horrible
crashes.

```
lngResult = ReleaseDC(hwndSrc, hSrcDC)

End Sub
```

The Ex12AForm

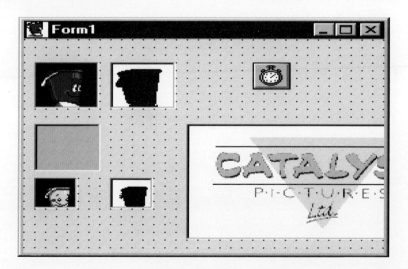

The form that provides the main display contains several picture
boxes. I deliberately wanted to show this alternative way of displaying
animation, partly as an attempt to show how much easier it is with the
sprite control! It is important with a screensaver to fill the screen and
to show no title bar or the controls to minimise, maximise and close
the application. To achieve this go to the forms properties and set the
following :

```
BorderStyle = 0 'None
MaxButton = 0 'False
MinButton = 0 'False
WindowState = 2 'Maximised
```

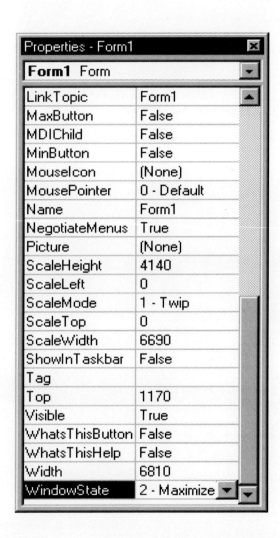

You should find that this will ensure the form fills the screen with no title bar.

The code for this screen makes use of two special datatypes that are declared in the '(General) – (declarations)' section of the form.

```
Private Type sprite
  X As Integer
  Y As Integer
  OldX As Integer
  OldY As Integer
  Width As Integer
  Height As Integer
  Row As Integer
  Col As Integer
  MoveX As Integer
  MoveY As Integer
  TargetX As Integer
  TargetY As Integer
  PicWidth As Integer
  PicHeight As Integer
  Action As Integer
  PicHDC As Integer
  MaskHDC As Integer
  Anim As String
End Type
Private Type dirtyrect
  X As Integer
  Y As Integer
  Width As Integer
  Height As Integer
End Type

Dim intNumOfBuckets As Integer
Dim Bucket(2) As sprite
Dim PaintRect(100) As dirtyrect
Dim intNumOfPaintRects As Integer
Dim intRow(100) As Integer
```

When the form is initialised the sprite datatypes are filled with relevant data.

```
Private Sub Form_Load()
  Dim i As Integer, j As Integer, b As Long

  intNumOfBuckets = 2

  picBigBucket.AutoSize = True
```

```
picBigBucketMask.AutoSize = True
picSmallBucket.AutoSize = True
picSmallBucketMask.AutoSize = True
For i = 0 To intNumOfBuckets - 1
  Bucket(i).X = Int(Rnd * 300)
  Bucket(i).Y = Int(Rnd * 300)
  Bucket(i).Row = 0
  Bucket(i).Col = 0
  Bucket(i).Action = 0
  Bucket(i).Width = 48 + 16 * (i = 1)
  Bucket(i).Height = 48 + 16 * (i = 1)
  Bucket(i).MoveX = 6 + 2 * (i = 1)
  Bucket(i).MoveY = 0
  Bucket(i).TargetX = Int(Screen.Width / _
    Screen.TwipsPerPixelX - Bucket(i).Width)
  Bucket(i).TargetY = Bucket(i).Y
  If i = 1 Then
    Bucket(1).PicWidth = picSmallBucket.ScaleWidth
    Bucket(1).PicHeight = picSmallBucket.ScaleHeight
    Bucket(1).PicHDC = picSmallBucket.hdc
    Bucket(1).MaskHDC = picSmallBucketMask.hdc
  Else
    Bucket(0).PicWidth = picBigBucket.ScaleWidth
    Bucket(0).PicHeight = picBigBucket.ScaleHeight
    Bucket(0).PicHDC = picBigBucket.hdc
    Bucket(0).MaskHDC = picBigBucketMask.hdc
  End If
Next i

left = 0
top = 0
Width = Screen.Width
Height = Screen.Height
picHidden.Width = ScaleWidth
picHidden.Height = ScaleHeight
picHidden.AutoRedraw = True
picHidden.Picture = picBackground.Picture
For i = 0 To Screen.Width Step picBackground.Width - 4
  For j = 0 To Screen.Height Step picBackground.Height - 4
    b = BitBlt(picHidden.hdc, i, j, picBackground.ScaleWidth, _
      picBackground.ScaleHeight, picBackground.hdc, 0, 0, _
SRCCOPY)
  Next j
Next i
```

```
    picBackground.Width = ScaleWidth
    picBackground.Height = ScaleHeight

    b = BitBlt(picBackground.hdc, 0, 0, ScaleWidth, ScaleHeight, ↵
picHidden.hdc, 0, 0, SRCCOPY)
    GrabScreen
End Sub
```

Notice the call to 'GrabScreen' that we looked at earlier. This places the current desktop into the form. The form now has a picture of the current desktop to work with.

The code that moves the sprites is very similar to the code that you have been using, only you have to work a little harder since the redrawing is your responsibility rather than a simple call to 'UpdateStage'

```
Private Sub MoveBuckets()
  Dim i As Integer
  'Replace background on hidden picture
  picHidden.AutoRedraw = True

  For i = 0 To intNumOfBuckets - 1
    b = BitBlt(picHidden.hdc, Bucket(i).X, Bucket(i).Y, ↵
Bucket(i).Width, Bucket(i).Height, _
      picBackground.hdc, Bucket(i).X, Bucket(i).Y, SRCCOPY)
    AddDirtyRect Bucket(i).X, Bucket(i).Y, Bucket(i).Width, ↵
Bucket(i).Height
  Next i
  'move bucket
  For i = 0 To intNumOfBuckets - 1
    Select Case Bucket(i).Action
      Case WALKLEFT:
Bucket(i).X = Bucket(i).X + Bucket(i).MoveX
If Bucket(i).X < Bucket(i).TargetX Then
  'change action
  Bucket(i).Action = TURNRIGHT
  Bucket(i).MoveX = 0
  Bucket(i).MoveY = 0
  Bucket(i).Row = Bucket(i).Height * TURNRIGHT
  Bucket(i).Col = 0
End If
'update frame
```

```
    Bucket(i).Col = Bucket(i).Col + Bucket(i).Width
    'cycle if at end of loop
    If Bucket(i).Col >= Bucket(i).PicWidth Then
      Bucket(i).Col = 0
    End If
    If Rnd * 100 > 98 Then
      Bucket(i).Action = SMALLFALLLEFT
      Bucket(i).TargetX = Bucket(i).X
      Bucket(i).TargetY = Bucket(i).Y + Int(ScaleHeight * Rnd)
      Bucket(i).Row = SMALLFALLLEFT * Bucket(i).Height
      Bucket(i).Col = 0
      Bucket(i).MoveY = 4
    End If
Case WALKRIGHT:
    Bucket(i).X = Bucket(i).X + Bucket(i).MoveX
    If Bucket(i).X > Bucket(i).TargetX Then
      'change action
      Bucket(i).Action = TURNLEFT
      Bucket(i).MoveX = 0
      Bucket(i).MoveY = 0
      Bucket(i).Row = Bucket(i).Height * TURNLEFT
      Bucket(i).Col = 0
    End If
    'update frame
    Bucket(i).Col = Bucket(i).Col + Bucket(i).Width
    'cycle if at end of loop
    If Bucket(i).Col >= Bucket(i).PicWidth Then
      Bucket(i).Col = 0
    End If
    If Rnd * 100 > 98 Then
      Bucket(i).Action = CLIMB
      Bucket(i).TargetX = Bucket(i).X
      Bucket(i).TargetY = Bucket(i).Y - 100
      If Bucket(i).TargetY < 0 Then Bucket(i).TargetY = 0
      Bucket(i).Row = CLIMB * Bucket(i).Height
      Bucket(i).Col = 0
      Bucket(i).MoveX = 0
      Bucket(i).MoveY = -4
    End If
Case TURNRIGHT:
    'update frame
    Bucket(i).Col = Bucket(i).Col + Bucket(i).Width
    'cycle if at end of loop
```

```
    If Bucket(i).Col >= Bucket(i).PicWidth Then
      'change action
      Bucket(i).Action = WALKRIGHT
      Bucket(i).MoveX = 6 + 2 * (i = 1)
      Bucket(i).MoveY = 0
      Bucket(i).TargetX = ScaleWidth
      Bucket(i).TargetY = Bucket(i).Y
      Bucket(i).Row = Bucket(i).Height * WALKRIGHT
      Bucket(i).Col = 0
    End If
  Case TURNLEFT:
    'update frame
    Bucket(i).Col = Bucket(i).Col + Bucket(i).Width
    'cycle if at end of loop
    If Bucket(i).Col >= Bucket(i).PicWidth Then
      'change action
      Bucket(i).Action = WALKLEFT
      Bucket(i).MoveX = -6 - 2 * (i = 1)
      Bucket(i).MoveY = 0
      Bucket(i).TargetX = 0
      Bucket(i).TargetY = Bucket(i).Y
      Bucket(i).Row = Bucket(i).Height * WALKLEFT
      Bucket(i).Col = 0
    End If
  Case SMALLFALLLEFT:
    If Bucket(i).Y > Bucket(i).TargetY Or _
      Bucket(i).Y > (ScaleHeight - Bucket(i).Height) Then
      Bucket(i).Action = BIGFALLLEFT
      Bucket(i).Y = Bucket(i).Y - Bucket(i).MoveY
      Bucket(i).MoveX = 0
      Bucket(i).MoveY = 0
      Bucket(i).Col = 0
      Bucket(i).Row = BIGFALLLEFT * Bucket(i).Height
    End If
    Bucket(i).MoveY = Bucket(i).MoveY + 1
    Bucket(i).X = Bucket(i).X + Bucket(i).MoveX
    If Bucket(i).X < 0 Then
      Bucket(i).X = 0
      Bucket(i).MoveX = 0
    End If
    Bucket(i).Y = Bucket(i).Y + Bucket(i).MoveY
  Case BIGFALLLEFT:
    'update frame
```

```
        Bucket(i).Col = Bucket(i).Col + Bucket(i).Width
        'cycle if at end of loop
        If Bucket(i).Col >= Bucket(i).PicWidth Then
          If Bucket(i).Row = (BIGFALLLEFT + 1) * Bucket(i).Height Then
            'walkright
            Bucket(i).Action = WALKRIGHT
            Bucket(i).MoveX = 6 + 2 * (i = 1)
            Bucket(i).MoveY = 0
            Bucket(i).TargetX = ScaleWidth
            Bucket(i).TargetY = Bucket(i).Y
            Bucket(i).Row = Bucket(i).Height * WALKRIGHT
            Bucket(i).Col = 0
          Else
            Bucket(i).Row = (BIGFALLLEFT + 1) * Bucket(i).Height
            Bucket(i).Col = 0
          End If
        End If
      Case CLIMB:
        Bucket(i).Y = Bucket(i).Y + Bucket(i).MoveY
        If Bucket(i).Y < Bucket(i).TargetY Then
          'change action
          Bucket(i).Action = WALKRIGHT
          Bucket(i).MoveX = 6 + 2 * (i = 1)
          Bucket(i).MoveY = 0
          Bucket(i).TargetX = ScaleWidth - Bucket(i).Width
          Bucket(i).TargetY = Bucket(i).Y
          Bucket(i).Row = Bucket(i).Height * WALKRIGHT
          Bucket(i).Col = 0
        End If
        'update frame
        Bucket(i).Col = Bucket(i).Col + Bucket(i).Width
        'cycle if at end of loop
        If Bucket(i).Col >= Bucket(i).PicWidth Then
          Bucket(i).Col = 0
        End If
    End Select
      b = BitBlt(picHidden.hdc, Bucket(i).X, Bucket(i).Y, _
    Bucket(i).Width, Bucket(i).Height, _
        Bucket(i).MaskHDC, Bucket(i).Col, Bucket(i).Row, SRCAND)
      b = BitBlt(picHidden.hdc, Bucket(i).X, Bucket(i).Y, _
    Bucket(i).Width, Bucket(i).Height, _
        Bucket(i).PicHDC, Bucket(i).Col, Bucket(i).Row, SRCPAINT)
      AddDirtyRect Bucket(i).X, Bucket(i).Y, Bucket(i).Width, _
        Bucket(i).Height
```

```
    Next i
End Sub
```

In addition to the form picture displayed there is a hidden picture that is exactly the same size. We draw to the hidden picture until the drawing is complete then show the results. This is a technique called *double buffering* and it has been going on in the background with all the code that you have been using. It eliminates the flicker from animation.

The interesting detail in the 'MoveBuckets' procedure is contained in the last few lines. 'BitBlt' is a very useful Windows call that allows you to do more than just copy pictures. You can combine them in weird and wonderful ways. The first call to 'BitBlt' takes the mask of the sprite and places this on the hidden buffer picture. But instead of a simple copy, the source and destination are combined using a Boolean And.

And	1	0
1	1	0
0	0	0

You know that deep down everything in your computer is behaving digitally. Well you can combine all those bits using Boolean logic. If the bits of A are 1 and the bits of B are 1 then the bits of the result are 1, but if either A or B have 0 bits then the result will have 0 bits.

How do we use this to make pictures?

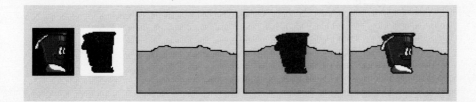

Calling 'BitBlt' using the mask picture and the command SRCAND, the result will be a picture where the pixel is preserved when the pixel in the mask is white and it will be black when the pixel in the mask is black. Looking at the diagram you can see that the mask is a silhouette version of the sprite. After calling 'BitBlt' using the mask and SRCAND, the background that you can see as the first box will have a silhouette of the sprite on it as in the second box. Now calling 'BitBlt' using the colour sprite picture and SRCPAINT combines the two images to give the result as required.

But remember that all this is taking place off screen, so the final call is to a new procedure: 'AddDirtyRect'.

```
Private Sub AddDirtyRect(x As Integer, y As Integer, Width As
Integer, Height As Integer)
   PaintRect(intNumOfPaintRects).X = x
   PaintRect(intNumOfPaintRects).Y = y
   PaintRect(intNumOfPaintRects).Width = Width
   PaintRect(intNumOfPaintRects).Height = Height
   intNumOfPaintRects = intNumOfPaintRects + 1
End Sub
```

Here we save the details of the box that has just been drawn to the hidden buffer. We want to know the left, top, bottom and right pixel positions for this area. We will use it to update the user's display.

The Timer event

Again the timing is achieved using a timer event procedure. Notice that after a call to 'MoveBuckets' the data stored in the 'DirtyRect' array for each call to 'AddDirtyRect' is used to repaint the user's screen. There is one extra feature: after every 3000 loops the screen is returned to the original desktop. Since the form picture was stored with the form's AutoRedraw property set to True, it is possible to return to this picture with a simple call to 'Cls'.

```
Private Sub Timer1_Timer()
   Static intCount As Integer
   Dim i As Integer, b As Integer

   picHidden.AutoRedraw = True
   intNumOfPaintRects = 0
   MoveBuckets
   AutoRedraw = False
   For i = 0 To intNumOfPaintRects - 1
      b = BitBlt(Ex12AForm.hdc, PaintRect(i).X, PaintRect(i).Y,
PaintRect(i).Width, _
         PaintRect(i).Height, picHidden.hdc, PaintRect(i).X,
PaintRect(i).Y, SRCCOPY)
```

```
      Next i
      If intCount > 3000 Then
        intCount = 0
        Cls
      Else
        intCount = intCount + 1
      End If
    End Sub
```

Closing down the screensaver

If a key is pressed or a mouse button, then closing down the
screensaver simply requires a call to the procedure.

```
    Private Sub Form_KeyDown(KeyCode As Integer, Shift As Integer)
      EndScreenSaver
    End Sub

    Private Sub Form_MouseDown(Button As Integer, Shift As Integer, x ↵
    As Single, y As Single)
      EndScreenSaver
    End Sub
```

But if the mouse is moved we need to check whether the mouse has
really been moved or whether Windows has sent a MouseMove
message. In this code 'Static' variables are used. These are variables
that keep their value from one call of the procedure to the next. The
'If' statement first tests whether they have just been created, in which
case they will both have the value zero. If they are both zero then the
screensaver is not terminated. The remainder of the 'If' statement
confirms that the mouse has actually moved by comparing the current
position with the previous position.

```
    Private Sub Form_MouseMove(Button As Integer, Shift As Integer, x ↵
    As Single, y As Single)
      Static intOldX As Integer
      Static intOldY As Integer

      If (intOldX > 0 And intOldY > 0) And (Abs(x - intOldX) > 3 Or
    Abs(y - intOldY) > 3) Then
        EndScreenSaver
      End If
```

```
        intOldX = x
        intOldY = y
End Sub
```

The 'EndScreenSaver' procedure

When the screensaver is used it must be configured to have a
password. You can do this using the 'Display | Screensaver' option in
the control panel. Here you will see a combo box that lists the
screensavers available and a button to set-up the screensaver. If you
choose to set-up the screensaver then the application starts with the
'/c' command line argument and a form is displayed allowing you to
enter a password.

The code that is used by this form is, in this instance:

```
Private Sub txtSetPass_KeyPress(KeyAscii As Integer)
   If KeyAscii = 13 Then
      WritePrivateProfileString App.Title, ''Password'',
txtSetPass.Text, ''buckets.ini''
      End
   End If
End Sub
```

Notice that the text box does not display your data, just a character '*'
as you type. This is achieved with no code. Simply setting the
'PasswordChar' property for the text box causes this operation.

Using ini files

The call to 'WritePrivateProfileString' is a Windows API call. This
writes data to a file that Windows can refer to later. The file can
contain several different options. The arguments for the call are

application name, Key name, Set to string, File name

Here the key called 'Password' has the text in the control 'txtSetPass' stored in it and the file to use is called 'buckets.ini' which will be in your Windows folder. It does not matter if the file does not exist; Windows will create it. The key press that is tested is a key press that has the ASCII value 13. This is the return key.

Now when the screensaver is terminated another dialog box is displayed. It is essential that you enter the password that you have previously used. The call 'GetPrivateProfileString' is the complementary function to 'WritePrivateProfileString'. This time the data stored is retrieved. You need to give the function a string variable. Windows will use this as the place to return the key requested. The third argument is a default string to return if the key cannot be found. Here this is used to check if the screensaver has been set up. If 'GetPrivateProfileString' returns 'none' then the function could not find the key name. The most likely reason for this would be that the screensaver set-up option had not been run.

```
Public Sub EndScreenSaver()
    Dim strTemp As String, strStatus As String, strEntered As String
    Dim lngResult As Long

    strTemp = Space(20)
    GetPrivateProfileString App.Title, ''Password'', ''none'',
strTemp, 20, ''buckets.ini''
    'Check to see if screensaver set-up has not been run
    If InStr(strTemp, ''none'') Then
        CursorOn
        End
    End If
    CursorOn
    PasswordForm.how 1
    strEntered = PasswordForm.txtPassword.Text
    lngResult = InStr(strTemp, strEntered)
    If lngResult Then
        End
    Else
        MsgBox ''Wrong password!''
        PasswordForm.txtPassword.Text =''''
        PasswordForm.Hide
        Exit Sub
    End If
End Sub
```

Instead of a direct comparison the 'InStr' function is used, since a direct comparison can result in confusion if trailing spaces are part of one string and not the other.

That completes the description of a fully functioning screensaver. You could easily use the Sprite.ocx to avoid the complexities of painting the animation, but, I thought that you might find it more interesting to learn about this alternative way of achieving animation displays. The link libraries that form the core of Windows offer many useful facilities. To learn more about them look out the many books that offer insight into the Windows API. Microsoft's web site can provide a great deal of information for the developer, and it would be of great benefit if you pointed your browser in their direction regularly.

QUIZ

1. Why can't you simply start your screensaver with a form?
Answer: Because you need to react to the command line arguments.

2. What is a device context?
Answer: A complex datatype that Windows uses to store device-specific information about bitmaps, line styles, etc.

3. If you wish to read from an initialisation file, how do you do this?
Answer: Use the Windows API function 'GetPrivateProfileString'.

4. How do you make a text box behave as a password box?
Answer: Enter a character such as '' in the PasswordChar option in the properties dialog.*

Summary

Experimenting with screensavers can be great fun. This chapter showed how to retrieve the Windows desktop so that you can draw directly onto it. The tricky subject of Windows device contexts was mentioned. You learnt how to use the 'Command' object to return command line arguments. Creating and reading an initialisation file is easy using the Windows API functions 'WritePrivateProfileString' and 'GetPrivateProfileString'.

CHAPTER 13

Ray casting – Using simple 3D in your games

So far our view of the world has been decidedly two dimensional. With good animation this can still give a very sophisticated display. But, I am afraid that, today, 2D alone is not adequate. You are going to need to get to grips with 3D.

NOTE

As your programming skills develop you will be able to make use of the new Windows libraries for real time 3D. Either DirectX or OpenGL offer great potential for the 3D programmer. They are both designed to make use of the extra 3D hardware that more and more users will find installed on their machines.

Before we break into the complex mathematics required to manipulate a true 3D world we are going to examine what is a half-way house. Ray casting is a technique that interprets a two-dimensional plan of a simple world and converts it into a three-dimensional view.

Phase 1

Open the project file 'RayCast1.vbp' or run the executable 'RayCast1.exe'.

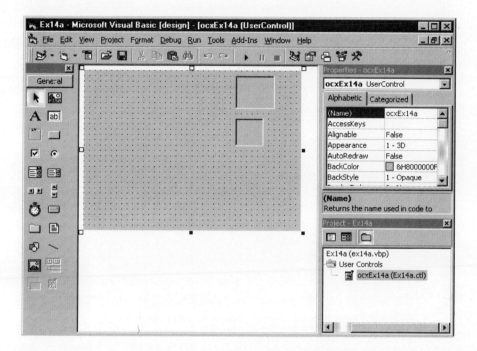

Click in the box and hold down the left mouse button. Drag a line, then release the button. First a grid is drawn, then several lines are drawn in the direction of the mouse. Dots are placed where the lines intersect with the grid. It might not look brilliant, but this is the clever idea behind ray casting.

Grid world

Ray casting at its simplest works in a very geometrical world. Imagine making a maze out of Lego. This is the kind of world that can work with ray casting. Before we introduce a way of describing the world for the computer, however, we need to understand how the computer can translate distance into height.

The mouse code

The interface uses a stretchy line. These are created by a little programming trick of inverting the current screen contents. If you draw a line twice with inversion then the screen returns to its original state. Think about drawing a black line on a white screen. The opposite of white is black, so if you are drawing with screen invert then drawing a line will result in a black line. But now if you draw the same line again the opposite of black is white, so you will be left with a white screen again. To do this with Visual Basic you use three mouse events, form scope variables and a flag.

Here is the MouseDown event

```
Private Sub picGrid_MouseDown(Button As Integer, Shift As Integer,
X As Single, Y As Single)
   intMode = 1
   ClearGrid
   picGrid.FillStyle = 0
   picGrid.FillColor = RGB(200, 0, 0)
   picGrid.Circle (X, Y), 2, RGB(100, 0, 0)
   picGrid.FillStyle = 1
   picGrid.DrawMode = 6
   picGrid.DrawStyle = 2
   intXPos = X
   intYPos = Y
   intXTarget = X
   intYTarget = Y
   lblStatus.Caption = ''Vector starts at ('' + Str$(X) + '', ''
+ Str$(Y) +''), now set direction.''
End Sub
```

The important issues here are the 'DrawMode' and 'DrawStyle' settings. A 'DrawMode' of 6 sets the drawing style to invert. The 'DrawStyle' option sets the line that is drawn to dashes. It could be solid, dots or dashes and dots. I used a flag called 'intMode' to indicate that a mouse event has occurred. The stored values for x and y positions and targets are also important. They are used when the MouseMove event is invoked.

```
Private Sub picGrid_MouseMove(Button As Integer, Shift As Integer,
X As Single, Y As Single)
   If intMode Then
      picGrid.Line (intXPos, intYPos) – (intXTarget, intYTarget)
```

```
      intXTarget = X
      intYTarget = Y
      picGrid.Line (intXPos, intYPos) - (intXTarget, intYTarget)
      lblStatus.Caption = ''(- + Str$(intXPos) + '', '' +
Str$(intYPos) + '') - ('' + ''_
        Str$(X) + '','' +      Str$(Y) + '')''
   End If
End Sub
```

This is not very complicated code. A line is drawn from the (x, y) position where the mouse was originally clicked to the (x.y) position stored as target. This inverts the line already drawn, having the effect of clearing the line. Then the value for target is updated with the parameters passed by the mouse event for X and Y. Now a new line can be drawn using these new parameters. Finally a few string commands are used to display a useful status feedback, indicating where the mouse was originally clicked and the current x and y positions. Once the mouse button is released, special actions need to be initiated.

```
Private Sub picGrid_MouseUp(Button As Integer, Shift As Integer, X
As Single, Y As Single)
   Dim sngDeltaX As Single, intXEnd As Integer, intYEnd As Integer

   If intMode Then
     intXTarget = X
   intYTarget = Y
   If Abs(intXTarget - intXPos) < 0.00000000001 Then
     sngDeltaX = 0.00000000001
     If intXPos > intXTarget Then
       sngDeltaX = -sngDeltaX
     End If
   Else
     sngDeltaX = intXTarget - intXPos
   End If
   intAngle = Int(Atn((intYPos - intYTarget) / sngDeltaX) *
RAD2DEG)
   If intYTarget > intYPos Then
     intAngle = intAngle + 180 - 180 * (intXTarget > intXPos)
   ElseIf intXTarget < intXPos Then
     intAngle = 180 + intAngle
   End If
   intDirection = Int((((intAngle + 45) Mod 360) / 90)
```

```
    picGrid.DrawMode = 13
    picGrid.DrawStyle = 0
    picGrid.Line (intXPos, intYPos)—(intXTarget, intYTarget), 0
    lblStatus.Caption = ''('' + Str$(intXPos) + '','' + _
      Str$(intYPos) +'') Angle '' + Str$(intAngle) +'' Dir Code:''
  + Str$(intDirection)
      RayCast1
    End If
    intMode = 0
  End Sub
```

What is 1000 divided by 0, or even 1 divided by 0? Well the truth is we don't know. It is impossible. Mathematicians call it undefined. Dividing by zero is something that you have to be careful to avoid in programming and in this case it just might happen. So the code tests for the difference in the x positions for the start of the mouse click and where the mouse is released. If these are the same then the difference is made to be as small as is practical, and to help with accuracy the sign is still considered. Now we enter the twilight zone.

Trigonometry

I can almost hear the sound of computer books closing and eyes glazing over.

Making it work for you

In a right-angled triangle the sides and angles are all related. It is usual to think of one angle as the defining angle. Since we know that one angle is a right angle, then knowing another angle defines the triangle. It is usual to call this angle theta (θ) as a homage to the great Greek geometricians who formulated all the details. But if it is easier for you, think of it as Fred. Now, knowing Fred is almost enough to know everything about this triangle. The only thing missing is the length of the longest side, this is usually called the hypotenuse, but it could be called Ginger. Fred and Ginger tell you everything you need to know about the triangle.

How is it all done?

The sides and angles are related as follows:

$$\sin \theta = \frac{\text{opp}}{\text{hyp}} \quad \cos q = \frac{\text{adj}}{\text{hyp}} \quad \tan \theta = \frac{\sin \theta}{\cos \theta}$$

which means that

opp = hyp * sin θ; adj = hyp * cos; θ tan θ = opp/adj

But, it gets worse. You have spent all this time feeling comfortable with a circle divided into 360 degrees. If you are like me, then you never really questioned why. Why not 432 or 234? The answer is that the Babylonians liked 60s. They liked it so much that they counted in 60: 360 is 6 times 60.

Now think about a circle. Can you recall that the circumference of the circle is related to the radius? Go on, dig deep. Yes, there is a number called π(pi). The relationship is that the circumference of a circle is 2 times the radius times π, $2\pi r$. It is helpful to divide a circle into 2π bits rather than 360 bits. You will find that, in programming languages, the trigonometric functions are all expecting to receive the information as radians rather than degrees. A full revolution using degrees is 360, a full revolution using radians is approximately 6.28, or 2 times pi. So if you used 90 meaning a right angle then the trig functions would think you meant more than 14 full revolutions. To make things easier to read in the code, and to help out when we finally get to real ray casting, I have used constant declarations and tables. These allow for simple conversions between degrees and radians. Here is the declarations code for the form:

```
(General) – (declarations)
Option Explicit

Dim intXPos As Integer, intYPos As Integer, intMode As Integer
Dim intXTarget As Integer, intYTarget As Integer
Dim intAngle As Integer, intDirection As Integer
Dim intRow As Integer, intCol As Integer

'Trig tables used
Const ANG360 = 360
Const ANG0 = 0
Const ANG30 = ANG360 / 12
Const ANG60 = ANG30 * 2
Const ANG90 = ANG30 + ANG60
Const ANG180 = 2 * ANG90
```

```
Const ANG270 = ANG180 + ANG90

Dim sngTan(ANG360) As Single
Dim sngInvTan(ANG360) As Single
Dim sngCos(ANG360) As Single
Dim sngInvCos(ANG360) As Single
Dim sngSin(ANG360) As Single
Dim sngInvSin(ANG360) As Single
Dim sngYStep(ANG360) As Single
Dim sngXStep(ANG360) As Single

'Useful constants
Const PI = 3.141592654
Const RAD2DEG = ANG360 / (2 * PI)
Const DEG2RAD = (2 * PI) / ANG360
Const GRIDWIDTH = 32
Const GRIDHEIGHT = 32
```

Notice the use of arrays with similar names to the trig functions and the conversion constants, RAD2DEG and DEG2RAD.

These are used by the Form_Load event:

```
Private Sub Form_Load()
  Dim i As Integer, sngRadAngle As Single

  picGrid.Width = 256 * Screen.TwipsPerPixelX
  picGrid.Height = 256 * Screen.TwipsPerPixelY
  For i = 0 To 8
    picGrid.Line (0, i * 32) - (picGrid.ScaleWidth, i * 32)
    picGrid.Line (i * 32, 0) - (i * 32, picGrid.ScaleHeight)
  Next i
  For i = 0 To ANG360
    sngRadAngle = i * DEG2RAD + 0.0003272
    sngTan(i) = Tan(sngRadAngle)
    sngInvTan(i) = 1 / sngTan(i)

    If (i >= 0 And i < ANG180) Then
      sngYStep(i) = Abs(sngTan(i) * GRIDHEIGHT)
    Else
      sngYStep(i) = -Abs(sngTan(i) * GRIDHEIGHT)
    End If
    If (i > ANG90 And i < ANG270) Then
      sngXStep(i) = -Abs(sngInvTan(i) * GRIDWIDTH)
```

```
      Else
         sngXStep(i) = Abs(sngInvTan(i) * GRIDWIDTH)
      End If
      sngInvCos(i) = 1 / Cos(sngRadAngle)
      sngInvSin(i) = 1 / Sin(sngRadAngle)
      sngCos(i) = Cos(sngRadAngle)
      sngSin(i) = Sin(sngRadAngle)
   Next i
End Sub
```

Here tables are made using the trig functions. This has the benefit that the code is faster and, hopefully, not as confusing. In the line

```
      sngRadAngle = i * DEG2RAD + 0.0003272
```

the strange use of 0.0003272 is to avoid division by zero at a later stage in the code.

Since we constantly redrawing the grid I decided to put this into a helpful sub-routine:

```
Sub ClearGrid()
   Dim i As Integer

      picGrid.Cls
      For i = 0 To 8
      picGrid.Line (0, i * 32) – (picGrid.ScaleWidth, i * 32)
      picGrid.Line (i * 32, 0) – (i * 32, picGrid.ScaleHeight)
   Next i
End Sub
```

Now we have a line pointing in a certain direction. We would like to find the points of intersection of this line and the grid. We know where the line starts and ends. From this information we can check for all the x intersections and all the y intersections.

You know that a graph is made up of x and y co-ordinates and that any 2D point can be defined using the x and y positions. Imagine a circle with its centre at the origin – that is, point (0, 0). This diagram shows how radians are usually defined: anti-clockwise from due east. The slope of our line can be positive or negative. The angle was stored in the form scope variable 'intAngle' for subsequent use. In determining the intersections we start from the original click position and work outwards. In looking for the Y intersections – that is, the intersections with vertical lines – we need to know whether to look from the current point to the left or to the right. If the angle is less than 90 degrees or greater than 270 degrees then we must be looking to the right. One thing we do know is the width and height of the grid, so updating the x value is easy. It is simply the width of the grid. But for every grid width move how much does the y value change? That is the interesting feature. This is where trigonometry is used.

```
sngYStep(i) = −Abs(sngTan(i) * GRIDHEIGHT)
```

When the tables were constructed they used the height of the grid and the value for tangent, together with a little altering to ensure that the sign was correct. Therefore, to get the Y move we simply look in the table 'sngYStep'. Now we can increment the x and the y values. The only problem is that we need to find the first intersection with the grid. Remember that the user can click anywhere within the grid. Here our old friend the Mod statement comes to our rescue. We are interested in the remainder after the (x, y) position has been divided by the grid width and height. That is exactly what Mod is for, and is a very useful tool. We need to keep this in mind, so store it in a variable.

Now look through this code and try to make sense of it.

```
Sub RayCast1()
  Dim intXOffset As Integer, intYOffset As Integer
  Dim dblXTemp As Double, dblYTemp As Double
  Dim dblDY As Double, dblDX As Double, intCastingAngle As Integer
  Dim i As Integer

'Find how far to the first grid lines
  intXOffset = intXPos Mod GRIDWIDTH
  intYOffset = intYPos Mod GRIDHEIGHT
'We are casting out rays in a fan
  intCastingAngle = intAngle − 30
'Negative angles are converted to positive by adding 360 degrees
  If intCastingAngle < 0 Then intCastingAngle = intCastingAngle ↵
+ ANG360
  picGrid.FillStyle = 0

  For i = 0 To 6
    'Cast out ray and find Y intercepts
    If intCastingAngle > ANG270 Or intCastingAngle < ANG90 Then
```

```
      'Must be heading right
      'First X intersection
      dblXTemp = intXPos - intXOffset + GRIDWIDTH
      'First Y intersection
      dblYTemp = intYPos - sngYStep(intCastingAngle) * (GRIDWIDTH
- intXOffset) / GRIDHEIGHT                                          ↵
      'The X increment
      dblDX = GRIDWIDTH
      'The Y increment
      dblDY = -sngYStep(intCastingAngle)
   Else
      'Must be heading left
      'First X intersection
      dblXTemp = intXPos - intXOffset
      'First Y intersection
      dblYTemp = intYPos - sngYStep(intCastingAngle) * intXOffset /
GRIDHEIGHT                                                          ↵
      'The X increment
      dblDX = -GRIDWIDTH
      'The Y increment
      dblDY = -sngYStep(intCastingAngle)
   End If
   picGrid.FillColor = RGB(0, 255, 0)
      Now iterate through the intersections drawing a circle where
they occur                                                          ↵
   Do
      picGrid.Circle (dblXTemp, dblYTemp), 2, RGB(0, 255, 0)
      dblYTemp = dblYTemp + dblDY
      dblXTemp = dblXTemp + dblDX
      'The loop terminates when the values of dblXTemp or dblYTemp are
off screen                                                          ↵
   Loop While dblXTemp < picGrid.ScaleWidth And dblXTemp > 0 And
dblYTemp < ScaleHeight And dblXTemp > 0                             ↵
   'Cast out ray and find X intercepts
   If intCastingAngle < ANG180 Then
      'Must be heading up
      'First Y intersection
      dblYTemp = intYPos - intYOffset
      'First X intersection
      dblXTemp = intXPos + sngXStep(intCastingAngle) *
intYOffset / GRIDWIDTH                                              ↵
      'The Y increment
      dblDY = -GRIDHEIGHT
```

```
        'The X increment
        dblDX = sngXStep(intCastingAngle)
     Else
        'Must be heading down
        'First Y intersection
        dblYTemp = intYPos — intYOffset + GRIDHEIGHT
        'First X intersection
        dblXTemp = intXPos + sngXStep(intCastingAngle) *       ↵
(GRIDHEIGHT — intYOffset) / GRIDWIDTH
        'The Y increment
        dblDY = GRIDHEIGHT
        'The X increment
        dblDX = sngXStep(intCastingAngle)
     End If
     picGrid.FillColor = RGB(0, 0, 255)
        'Now iterate through the intersections
     Do
        picGrid.Circle (dblXTemp, dblYTemp), 2, RGB(0, 0, 255)
        dblXTemp = dblXTemp + dblDX
        dblYTemp = dblYTemp + dblDY
        'Loop terminates when dblXTemp or dblYTemp are off screen
     Loop While dblYTemp < picGrid.ScaleHeight And dblYTemp > 0 And
dblXTemp < picGrid.ScaleWidth And dblXTemp > 0                  ↵
        'Finally draw line in current casting direction
        picGrid.Line (intXPos, intYPos) — (intXPos + 500 *   ↵
sngCos(intCastingAngle), intYPos — 500 * sngSin(intCastingAngle)),
RGB(255, 0, 0)                                                  ↵
        'Move to next casting angle
     intCastingAngle = (intCastingAngle + 10) Mod 360
   Next i

   picGrid.FillStyle = 1
End Sub
```

Now that is the principle. Send out a ray in a particular direction and use simple trigonometry to find where it intersects a grid. Using this idea can drastically reduce the number of checks needed to find the wall that eventually needs to be displayed. In addition, the technique allows you to determine how far away the wall is, and using this information you can draw an on-screen display that looks 3D.

Phase 2

We will now look at how to load a world from a text file. The code uses the file shown in Table 13.1

Table 13.1

```
20 World Rows
20 World Cols
11111111111111111111   1
1    111  1 1     1 1   2
1    1    1 1  111 1    3
1111    1111 1 1    1   4
1       1          1   5
1       1    1 1    1   6
1       1   11  11  1   7
11111  1 111     1 1    8
1  1 1  1      1 1      9
1          1 1111111   10
11111  1  1        1   11
1  1 1            1    12
1  1     1        1    13
1       1  1  111111   14
1  1  11111        1   15
11111  1   1111111 1   16
1  1 1  1         1    17
1          1  111111   18
11111  11111      1    19
11111111111111111111   20
12345678901234567890
```

Test World Data
Nik Lever
2 July 1996

Where there is a 1 we are going to place a wall. The numbers down the side and along the bottom are simply guides when creating the file. This file was created using the ever popular Notepad utility that is safely stored among your accessories. The first two lines provide information regarding the number of rows and columns.

Here is the code to read this file:

```
Sub LoadWorld(tFileName As String)
   Dim intFileNum As Integer, strTemp As String
   Dim i As Integer, j As Integer
'Get the number of a free file
   intFileNum = FreeFile
'Open the file for reading input
   Open App.Path + ''\'' + tFileName For Input As intFileNum

'Use the text file option of line input
   Line Input #intFileNum, strTemp
   intWorldRows = Val(strTemp)
   Line Input #intFileNum, strTemp
   intWorldCols = Val(strTemp)
   strTemp = Space(intWorldCols)
'Resize and clear the array that stores the world data
   ReDim intWorld(intWorldRows + 1, intWorldCols + 1)

   For i = 0 To intWorldRows - 1
'Read each line of the file
      Line Input #intFileNum, strTemp
      For j = 1 To intWorldCols
         'Store the value of each character in the current line
         intWorld(i, j - 1) = Val(Mid(strTemp, j, 1))
      Next j
   Next i
'Remember to close the file
   Close intFileNum
'If in debugging mode then call the DumpWorld sub-routine
#If RayCastDebug Then
      DumpWorld
#End If

End Sub
```

Disk files are very useful for storing data. Microsoft calls this persistence and refer to it as serialising data, but I think we would be better provided by keeping the amount of jargon to a minimum. Nevertheless, I hope you are now able to use disk files in your own programs. I have only shown very simple disk files in use, although Visual Basic offers superb database access. Databases is a topic that we need not discuss in detail in this book, but it is an area that you would do well to consider. The disk storage of a database is faster to sort and access than the simple text files that we have used.

I never feel happy with a section of code until I can see what it has done, so I wrote a simple dump routine. It is there to confirm that the array was correctly set when the file was opened.

```
Sub DumpWorld()
   Dim i As Integer, j As Integer

   Debug.Print
   Debug.Print ''World Data''

   For i = 0 To intWorldRows - 1
     For j = 0 To intWorldCols - 1
       Debug.Print intWorld(i, j);
     Next j
     Debug.Print
   Next i
End Sub
```

Now that the code involves world data, we need a way to clear and redraw this world. The 'ClearGrid' routine is extended to take care of this.

```
Sub ClearGrid()
   Dim i As Integer, j As Integer

   picGrid.Cls
   picGrid.FillStyle = 0
   picGrid.FillColor = RGB(100, 100, 100)

   For i = 0 To intWorldRows - 1
     For j = 0 To intWorldCols - 1
       If intWorld(i, j) Then
       'If the current grid cell has a value then draw a grey solid
box
       picGrid.Line (j * GRIDWIDTH, i * GRIDHEIGHT)-((j + 1) *
GRIDWIDTH, (i + 1) * GRIDHEIGHT), RGB(100, 100, 100), BF
       End If
     Next j
   Next i
End Sub
```

If you run program 'RayCast2.exe' then you can click and drag and see a maze that conforms to the text file saved as 'world.dat'. Try changing this file and observe the changes to the program as a result. You would be advised to back up the original file to allow you to return to the original for later programs.

Phase 3

So much for these simple overhead views, but I thought this chapter was about 3D. Yes, it is, and this is when you start to see where the code is leading. Once we can cast out a ray and detect an intersection with the grid, we can convert that position to the world data array. If the world data array has anything other than a space, then the ray has hit a wall. If it hits a wall then there is no point in casting the ray any further. In example "RayCast3.exe" the world data is loaded and the program pauses for user input. Click and drag as before. Now the overhead view is complemented by a 3D view.

How is the 3D view created?

In the previous two examples only seven rays were cast out, centred on the users click and drag line. In this example a ray is cast for every vertical line in the 3D display. This time the tables of trig values that were created are divided up into rather more than 360 parts to a revolution.

```
'Useful constants
Const ANG360 As Integer = 360 * 6
Const ANG0 As Integer = 0
Const ANG1 As Integer = ANG360 / 360
Const ANG10 As Integer = ANG360 / 36
Const ANG30 As Integer = ANG10 * 3
Const ANG60 As Integer = ANG30 * 2
Const ANG90 As Integer = ANG30 + ANG60
Const ANG180 As Integer = ANG90 * 2
Const ANG270 As Integer = ANG180 + ANG90
Const PI = 3.141592654
Const RAD2DEG = ANG360 / (2 * PI)
Const DEG2RAD = (2 * PI) / ANG360
```

Now 'ANG360' is a value of $360 \times 6 = 2160$. The reason for this is that the field of view is 60 degrees: 30 degrees to the right and left of the current direction. Using a table of 2160 different values makes for 360 values in the range 60 degrees. So we can draw a picture made up of 360 vertical lines using the tables.

If this is becoming confusing, let's take a look at the code.

```
Sub RayCast3()
  Dim intXOffset As Integer, intYOffset As Integer
  Dim dblXTemp As Double, dblYTemp As Double
  Dim sngCol As Single, sngRow As Single
  Dim intNextCol As Integer, intNextRow As Integer
  Dim dblDY As Double, dblDX As Double, intCastingAngle As Integer
  Dim i As Integer, blnFirst As Boolean, intCount As Integer
  Dim dXSave As Double, dYSave As Double
  Dim dblXDist As Double, dblYDist As Double
  Dim intTop As Integer, intBottom As Integer
  Dim intWallSize As Integer

  #If RayCastDebug Then
  'For debugging purposes a dump file can be opened and values stored
to it
    Dim intFileNum As Integer
    intFileNum = FreeFile
    Open App.Path + ''\data.log'' For Output As intFileNum
    Print #intFileNum, ''i intWallSize intTop dblXDist dblYDist''
    End If

  'In case of a divide by zero error checking is set to resuming at
the next command
  On Error Resume Next

  intXOffset = intXPos Mod GRIDWIDTH
  intYOffset = intYPos Mod GRIDHEIGHT
  'Translating between the current position and the world data
array
  sngCol = Int(intXPos / GRIDWIDTH)
  sngRow = Int(intYPos / GRIDHEIGHT)

  lblStatus.Caption = ''(Row:'' + Str$(sngRow) +'', Col:'' +
Str$(sngCol) + '') World:'' + Str$(intWorld(sngRow, sngCol)) + ''
Angle:'' + Str$(intAngle / ANG1)
  If intWorld(sngRow, sngCol) Then
    MsgBox ''Viewer is inside a wall!''
    Exit Sub
  End If
```

```
'The cast angle starts at −30 degrees from the current direction
intCastingAngle = intAngle − ANG30
If intCastingAngle < 0 Then intCastingAngle = intCastingAngle ↵
+ ANG360
picGrid.FillStyle = 0
pic3DView.FillStyle = 0
pic3DView.DrawStyle = 6
pic3DView.DrawMode = 13
pic3DView.DrawWidth = 2
'A graduated blue backdrop is drawn in the 3D view
For i = 0 To 255
  pic3DView.Line (0, i) − (400, i + 1), RGB(0, 0, i), BF
Next i
'The main loop
For i = 0 To ANG60
  'The distance to an intersection is set to a very large amount 1
with 20 zeros !                                                   ↵
  dblYDist = 1E+20
  dblXDist = 1E+20
  'Cast out ray and find Y intercepts
  If intCastingAngle > ANG270 Or intCastingAngle < ANG90
Then                                                              ↵
    'Heading right
    'Initial X position
    dblXTemp = intXPos − intXOffset + GRIDWIDTH
    'Initial Y position
    dblYTemp = intYPos − sngYStep(intCastingAngle) *  ↵
(GRIDWIDTH − intXOffset) / GRIDHEIGHT
    'X increment
    dblDX = GRIDWIDTH
    'Y increment
    dblDY = −sngYStep(intCastingAngle)
    'Because we are looking to the right we do not have to correct
the column value                                                 ↵
    intNextCol = 0
  Else
    'Heading Left
    'Initial X position
    dblXTemp = intXPos − intXOffset
    'Initial Y position
    dblYTemp = intYPos − sngYStep(intCastingAngle) *  ↵
intXOffset / GRIDHEIGHT
    'X increment
    dblDX = −GRIDWIDTH
    'Y increment
```

```
        dblDY = -sngYStep(intCastingAngle)
        'because we are looking left the column must be reduced by 1
        intNextCol = -1
    End If
    'The correction for the row is based on the increment value for
Y
    intNextRow = Abs(dblDY < 0)
    picGrid.FillColor = RGB(0, 255, 0)
    'Set flag for first iteration
    blnFirst = True
    'Loop for the cast ray
    Do
        'Set current array positions
        sngCol = Int(dblXTemp / GRIDWIDTH) + intNextCol
        sngRow = Int(dblYTemp / GRIDHEIGHT) + intNextRow
        'Test for a positive value for current array position
        If intWorld(sngRow, sngCol) And blnFirst Then
            'Update grid display for first time
            If (i Mod ANG10) = 0 And (optShowX.Value Or
optShowBoth.Value) Then
                picGrid.FillColor = RGB(255, 255, 255)
                picGrid.Circle (dblXTemp, dblYTemp), 10, RGB(0, 0, 0)
                picGrid.FillColor = RGB(0, 255, 0)
            End If
            blnFirst = False
            dXSave = dblXTemp
            Exit Do
        Else
            'Update grid display
            If (i Mod ANG10) = 0 And (optShowX.Value Or
optShowBoth.Value) Then
                picGrid.Circle (dblXTemp, dblYTemp), 10, RGB(0, 255, 0)
            End If
        End If
        dblYTemp = dblYTemp + dblDY
        dblXTemp = dblXTemp + dblDX
    'Repeat until off screen
    Loop While dblXTemp < picGrid.ScaleWidth And dblXTemp > 0
And dblYTemp < ScaleHeight And dblYTemp > 0

    'Cast out ray and find X intercepts
    If intCastingAngle < ANG180 Then
        'Heading up
        'Initial x position
        dblYTemp = intYPos - intYOffset
```

```
          'Initial y position
          dblXTemp = intXPos + sngXStep(intCastingAngle) *
intYOffset / GRIDWIDTH                                        ↵
          'Y increment
          dblDY = −GRIDHEIGHT
          'X increment
          dblDX = sngXStep(intCastingAngle)
          'Correction for array
          intNextRow = −1
      Else
          'Heading down
          'Initial y position
          dblYTemp = intYPos − intYOffset + GRIDHEIGHT
          'Initial x position
          dblXTemp = intXPos + sngXStep(intCastingAngle) *      ↵
(GRIDHEIGHT − intYOffset) / GRIDWIDTH
          'Y increment
          dblDY = GRIDHEIGHT
          'X increment
          dblDX = sngXStep(intCastingAngle)
          'No array correction
          intNextRow = 0
      End If
      'Array correction based on X increment
      intNextCol = Abs(dblDX > 0)
      picGrid.FillColor = RGB(0, 0, 255)
      blnFirst = True
      'Loop for x intersections
      Do While dblYTemp < picGrid.ScaleHeight And dblYTemp > 0   ↵
And dblXTemp < picGrid.ScaleWidth And dblXTemp > 0
          'Set current array position
          sngCol = Int((dblXTemp − intNextCol) / GRIDWIDTH)
          sngRow = Int((dblYTemp + intNextRow) / GRIDHEIGHT)

          If intWorld(sngRow, sngCol) And blnFirst Then
             'First wall
             If (i Mod ANG10) = 0 And (optShowY.Value Or         ↵
optShowBoth.Value) Then
                 picGrid.FillColor = RGB(0, 0, 0)
                 picGrid.Circle (dblXTemp, dblYTemp), 10, RGB(0, 0, 0)
                 picGrid.FillColor = RGB(0, 0, 255)
             End If
             blnFirst = False
             dYSave = dblYTemp
             Exit Do
```

```
        Else
          'Check next cell
          If (i Mod ANG10) = 0 And (optShowY.Value Or
optShowBoth.Value) Then
             picGrid.Circle (dblXTemp, dblYTemp), 10, RGB(255, 0,
255)
          End If
        End If
      dblXTemp = dblXTemp + dblDX
      dblYTemp = dblYTemp + dblDY
    Loop
    'Draw a line for every 10 degree angle
    If (i Mod ANG10) = 0 Then
      picGrid.Line (intXPos, intYPos) - (intXPos + 500 *
sngCos(intCastingAngle), intYPos - 500 * sngSin(intCastingAngle)),
RGB(255, 0, 0)
    End If


    'Calculate wallsize
    dblXDist = Abs((dXSave - intXPos) *
sngInvCos(intCastingAngle))
    dblYDist = Abs((dYSave - intYPos) *
sngInvSin(intCastingAngle))
    If dblXDist <= dblYDist Then
      'The small decimal is to avoid division by zero
      'sngFettle corrects the height of the slice to make sure that it
'doesn't look like
      a goldfish bowl
      intWallSize = 15000 / (dblXDist + 0.0000000001) *
sngFettle(i)
      intTop = 100 - intWallSize / 2
      intBottom = intTop + intWallSize
      pic3DView.Line (360 - i, intTop) - (360 - i, intBottom),
RGB(255 - intWallSize, 0, 0)
    Else
      intWallSize = 15000 / (dblYDist + 0.0000000001) *
sngFettle(i)
      intTop = 100 - intWallSize / 2
      intBottom = intTop + intWallSize
      pic3DView.Line (360 - i, intTop) - (360 - i, intBottom),
RGB(0, 255 - intWallSize, 0)
    End If
    #If RayCastDebug Then
      Print #intFileNum, i; intWallSize; intTop; dblXDist; dblYDist
    #End If
```

```
        intCastingAngle = (intCastingAngle + 1) Mod ANG360
    Next i

    #If RayCastDebug Then
      Close intFileNum
    #End If
    picGrid.FillStyle = 1
  End Sub
```

The trick here is having found where there is an intersection with the vertical lines where they form a boundary with a wall, and the intersection with the horizontal lines where they form a boundary with a wall. If the intersection with a horizontal wall is nearer than that with a vertical wall, then the horizontal wall is the one to consider. If, however, the intersection is with a vertical wall, then the vertical intersection is the one to consider. At this stage we know where the viewer is, and where an intersection occurred. Now we need to calculate the distance. Remember the trigonometry that we looked at earlier? Using this we can calculate the distance. We are considering the hypotenuse; we know the angle, the lengths of the sides adjacent to the angle and opposite the angle. So we can use this information to determine the length of the hypotenuse.

adj/hyp $= \cos \theta$ means that hyp $=$ adj/cos θ
opp/hyp $= \sin \theta$ means that hyp $=$ opp/sin θ

This is the code that checks the distances: 'Abs' is used to ensure a positive value. We are interested in the total length regardless of sign. Lengths can be negative. The tables created include 1/cos θ and 1/sin θ. Whenever something is at the bottom of a fraction it is called *inverse*. If you want to be very correct, you can say the denominator of a quotient, but no one would have any idea of what you were talking about. The inverse of cos and sin are termed 'sngInvCos' and 'sngInvSin'.

```
    dblXDist = Abs((dXSave − intXPos) *
  sngInvCos(intCastingAngle))           ↵
    dblYDist = Abs((dYSave − intYPos) *
  sngInvSin(intCastingAngle))           ↵
```

So now we know how far the current ray has to travel to hit a wall. Now we can use this information to decide how big to draw the current section of wall.

```
    intWallSize = 15000 / (dblXDist + 0.0000000001) * sngFettle(i)
```

Here 15000 is a scaling factor that works for the current dimensions of the screen. We use the distance away as an inverse scaling factor. Something further away results in a smaller wall; that is an inverse. The small decimal avoids the dreaded 'divide by zero'.

But what about the 'sngFettle'? This is because the graph of sin and cos forms a curve.

But our walls need to be straight. By multiplying the result by 'sngFettle' the fish-eye lens effect is reduced. So here we have the translation from a simple text file that is interpreted as a graph, to a 3D view.

Phase 4

This example allows you to explore the 3D world. Click on the buttons to move around.

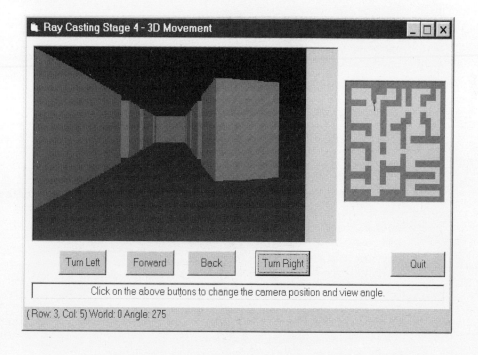

I would excuse you for being less than impressed by the speed. The problem here is partly the calculations involved, but much more the use of the 'Line' statement to draw coloured lines of such a variety of colours. To improve the speed we must link Visual Basic with another system.

Phase 5

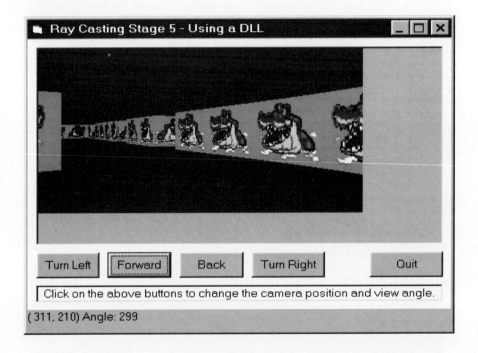

The final example in this chapter uses a dynamic link library written in C++. The functions available in the library are declared in the (General) – (declarations) section of the form.

```
Private Declare Function InitWorld Lib ''raycast.dll'' _
   (ByVal FileName As String, ByVal textureHdc As Long, ByVal
hiddenHdc As Long) As Boolean
Private Declare Function RayCast1 Lib ''raycast.dll'' _
   (ByVal Hdc As Long, ByVal XPos As Integer, ByVal YPos As Integer,
ByVal Angle As Integer) As Integer
Private Declare Function GetTable Lib ''raycast.dll'' _
   (ByVal TableType As Integer, ByVal Index As Integer) As Single
Private Declare Function GetWorldCell Lib ''raycast.dll'' _
```

```
    (ByVal Row As Integer, ByVal Col As Integer) As Integer
Private Declare Sub SetWorldCell Lib ''raycast.dll'' _
    (ByVal Row As Integer, ByVal Col As Integer, ByVal Value As
Integer)
Private Declare Function GetWorldRows Lib ''raycast.dll'' _
    () As Integer
Private Declare Function IsLeftMouseKeyPressed Lib ''raycast.dll'' _
    () As Boolean
Private Declare Function GetWorldCols Lib ''raycast.dll'' _
    () As Integer
```

Using the link library makes setting up the display easier. The Form_Load event is used to initialise the data. 'InitWorld' takes three parameters. A text file path for the world data file, a picture control handle to use for texture mapping and a picture control to use as a hidden buffer.

```
Private Sub Form_Load()
    Dim i As Integer, strTemp As String, b As Boolean

    b = InitWorld(App.Path + ''\world.dat'', picTexture.Hdc,
picHidden.Hdc)

    If b = False Then End
    picGrid.ScaleWidth = GetWorldCols() * 32
    picGrid.ScaleHeight = GetWorldRows() * 32
    picHidden.Width = pic3DView.Width
    picHidden.Height = pic3DView.Height

    intXPos = 130
    intYPos = 100
    intAngle = 30
End Sub
```

Take a look at the code on the CD to see how the other procedures are used.

Review

Ray casting is an interesting and useful technique, but it doesn't extend to allowing a full 3D view to be generated. Windows is moving to a position where 3D graphics will be easily available. A set of APIs can be called to generate and draw 3D views. DirectX is a library of functions available to the programmer for the manipulation of 3D views. At the moment it is only available to the C++ programmer, but there is plenty available to the Visual Basic programmer.

ActiveX controls can provide all the extra features that you will need when coding with Visual Basic. The powerful displays available using DirectX can be made available to the Visual Basic programmer using ActiveX controls. In the next chapter we will look at how you can create your own ActiveX controls using Visual Basic 5.0.

QUIZ

1. If you know the length of the hypotenuse and the length of another side, how can you find the angle between these two lines?
Answer: $adj/hyp = \cos\theta$. So using the information, we can find the required cosine. Having found the cosine, the angle involved can be found by using the inverse of the cosine function. This is usually called arccos, but on Visual Basic it is 'ACos'. So you need to use 'ACos (adj/hyp)'.

2. Ray casting works by checking all the intersections with vertical lines. True or False?
Answer: False. The checking needs to involve both vertical and horizontal lines.

3. What is 1 divided by 0?
Answer: Unknown; you will get an error message.

4. What is the name of Microsoft's new 3D library?
Answer: Direct3D which is part of DirectX.

Summary

This chapter forms a bridge between 2D games and 3D games. Using the ray casting link library you could create a fun maze-type game with texture mapping. But the real purpose of the chapter was to demonstrate the use of trigonometric functions in 3D display graphics. If you are feeling decidedly out of your depth using this level of maths, then Appendix E is intended to help provide the water wings that you need.

PART FOUR

Web Magic

CHAPTER 14

ActiveX controls – As easy as falling off your keyboard

Starting with release 5, Visual Basic allows you to create your own ActiveX controls. Previously you would have required another language such as C++. If you want to add interest to a web site, then an ActiveX control is an excellent technique to use. The development environment of Visual Basic has now been extended to allow the programmer to work on multiple projects. So far in this book we have looked at the single project approach, a technique that is suitable for both Visual Basic 4 and Visual Basic 5 users. In this final part of the book we concentrate on the techniques that are only available to the Visual Basic 5 user. In order not to restrict those Visual Basic 4 users who have yet to upgrade (and I highly recommend that you do so), the code can all be entered and debugged using the Visual Basic 5.0 Control Creation Edition that is included on the CD-ROM.

What is an ActiveX control?

Throughout Part 3 you used the sprite control, which is an ActiveX control. Many years ago Microsoft started to develop a common interface between 'objects' and 'applications'. This was a logical progression from the development of object-orientated code. A common interface was developed which allowed control objects to provide methods that the parent application could call; the object could itself generate events that the application could then respond to; and, in common with object-orientated code, the object had properties that could be manipulated to control the behaviour of the object. So that was the goal, an object with properties and methods which could generate events. This object could be inserted into an application. Remember that deep within the computer is a microprocessor that can deal with processing data in a routine manner. Extending the microprocessor, there are interfaces that can interrupt what the processor is currently doing. To exploit object-orientated ideas requires a common operating system that understands the demands of the objects.

Such ideas require a multi-tasking environment. Windows, in its more recent incarnation, is a multi-tasking environment in a sense as you do not require multiple processors to run more than one program. The code that allows you to switch from one program to another is rather clever. Windows looks good for the near future and Microsoft's vision of the computing future looks good for even longer. It is my conjecture that learning about ActiveX and how it extends the modularity of applications is well worth learning. We are now entering a new zone. Multi-tasking platforms are not the best environment for games programs, but the future requires you to incorporate code into multi-tasking environments. The web and browser technology are extending these ideas with a great drive. There are some great Active X controls already available, my favourite being 'Shockwave' which allows Director authors to include interactive content inside a browser. But your own controls can give you even greater flexibility.

HOW DO THEY WORK? – 5:

The World Wide Web

For much of this last section of the book we are concerned with the Internet. Most readers will have experienced the Internet in some way. The emphasis here is exclusively on the World Wide Web. The original specification allowed for hyper-text linking across a network; that is, certain sections of text, when highlighted, caused a jump to another section of text. This original specification was extended to incorporate pictures and was further developed to allow multiple pages to be used at the same time. If you feel comfortable with the concepts that you have come across so far, then developing for the web should provide no problems. You will, however, need to learn the basics of the code that is used. This code is written as a simple text file. Much of the text file is not displayed to the user; it describes the look and the interactivity of the page, not just the text content. You will be introduced to HTML (Hyper Text Mark-up Language) in the coming chapters.

Modular controls really came of age with OLE 2.0 (Object Linking and Embedding). But, although Visual C++ 4.0 made the creation of an OLE control a great deal easier than before, not everyone used or wanted to learn C++. That is no longer necessary as it is now available in Visual Basic 5.0.

Using Visual Basic 5.0 to create an ActiveX control project

When you start Visual Basic 5.0 you are confronted with a box that asks the type of project you are creating.

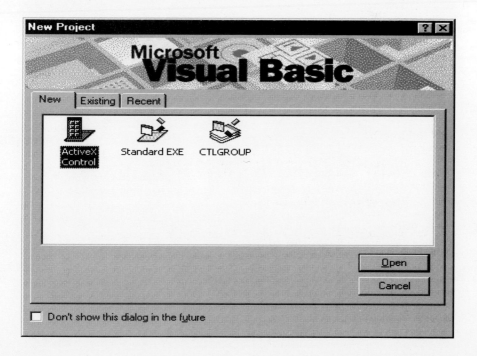

In the example we are about to create we avoid the use of external calls to methods and provide no events to which the parent application can react. The chapter concludes with a brief look at inserting the example in a web page. In the next chapter we use VBScript within an HTML file to call the methods within the sprite control and react to the events that the sprite control generates. In the following chapter we develop a control with methods and events and use VBScript to drive the control inside an HTML file.

NOTE

When you use a browser you are usually loading HTML files.

Example Ex14

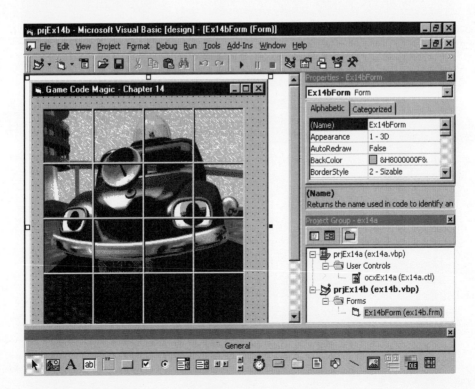

Open 'Ex14.vbg'. A '.vbg' file is a group of projects. Editing multiple projects is new for Visual Basic 5.0. In this group we have two projects. When you develop a ActiveX control you will always need to use more than one project. You will have a project that is the code used by the ActiveX control and another containing a Form that uses this new ActiveX control. To insert a control that you are developing into a Visual Basic Form it is important to follow this procedure.

1   Start the project as a new ActiveX control. Save the control and the project that created it.
2   Close the project but do not start a new project. Instead, use the option to add a project, under 'File|Add Project'. This time select the option to create a Standard Exe.
3   You should find that the default icon for a new control is added to the Toolbox. If the Toolbox is not currently displayed then select 'View|Toolbx' from the menu.
4   You should now be able to click on the Toolbox icon and draw the control to the Form using a left mouse click and drag.

This is the way the group project you have opened was created.

What does the example program do?

This illustrative program provides you with a tile puzzle. One of those puzzles where you can slide tiles into one blank square and you have to manipulate them to a certain formation.

Here are the declarations for the ActiveX control:

```
Private Type MoveTile
   X As Integer
   Y As Integer
   XMove As Integer
   YMove As Integer
   Tile As Integer
   Count As Integer
   Moving As Boolean
End Type

Dim intBoard(16) As Integer
Dim intBlankPos As Integer
Dim MTile As MoveTile
Dim intCurrentTime As Integer
```

The aim with this chapter is to show that you are able to use your existing knowledge in a totally new way. This time you will be able to use your code for more than just a stand-alone application using techniques with which you are already familiar.

Initialising an ActiveX control

Initialisation is not through the Form_Load event since a control does not use a Form. Instead it is through the UserControl_Initialize event.

```
Private Sub UserControl_Initialize()
  Dim intRow As Integer, intCol As Integer
  Dim i As Integer

  picWhole.AutoSize = True
  Debug.Print ''Control Size: ('' + Str(Width) + '', '' +
Str(Height) + '')''
  i = 0
  For intCol = 0 To 299 Step 75
    For intRow = 0 To 299 Step 75
      If i Then Load picTile(i)
      picTile(i).Width = 75
      picTile(i).Height = 75
      picTile(i).PaintPicture picWhole.Picture, 0, 0, 75, 75,
intCol, intRow, 75, 75
      picTile(i).Left = intCol
      picTile(i).Top = intRow
      picTile(i).Visible = True
      intBoard(i) = i
      i = i + 1
    Next
  Next
  intBlankPos = 15
  Debug.Print ''initialising control''
  End Sub
```

I have included debug statements in the code. These statements are intended to help illustrate the life cycle of the control. To see the results of the debug statements make sure that you have selected 'View|Immediate Window'. The Immediate Window is where you view the results of Debug.Print and where you can execute a line of code directly.

The initialising code for this example takes the picture stored in the picture control called 'picWhole' and slices it up into sections. Each section is loaded into a new control from the control array 'picTile'. At load time there is only one member of the control array, with index 0. As each new control is created with the 'Load' statement, it is resized and made visible after being loaded with the relevant section of the big picture. At the same time the position of the control is confirmed and the contents of an array that stores the current value of the board is decided.

Using an array to store information

The board array is the interface between the display and the computer understanding of the current status of the game. The use of PaintPicture has been covered earlier in the book; it allows the programmer to copy sections of a picture to other sections of a picture. The grid structure of the 'picTile' pictures has the following position values.

0	4	8	12
1	5	9	13
2	6	10	14
3	7	11	15

When the value of the board array is 5 then the 'picTile' with that index is at column 2, row 2.

intBoard(10) = 5 means that picTile(10) is in position 5. This is the correlation between the value of Board(index) and the position of picTile(index). All the tiles will be in the correct place when for each index value 0 to 15 the value of Board(index) = index.

Since initially the correct section of picture is loaded into the correct tile, the game starts with the tiles in the right place. Hence, the use of the command button. The command button on the main display has the caption 'Shuffle' and this is exactly what it does to the tiles.

```
Private Sub cmdShuffle_Click()
    intBoard(0) = 7
    intBoard(1) = 2
    intBoard(2) = 1
    intBoard(3) = 9
```

```
        intBoard(4) = 0
        intBoard(5) = 14
        intBoard(6) = 5
        intBoard(7) = 3
        intBoard(8) = 10
        intBoard(9) = 15
        intBoard(10) = 13
        intBoard(11) = 4
        intBoard(12) = 11
        intBoard(13) = 6
        intBoard(14) = 8
        intBoard(15) = 12
        intBlankPos = 12
        For i = 0 To 14
            picTile(i).Left = Int(Board(i) / 4) * 75
            picTile(i).Top = (intBoard(i) Mod 4) * 75
        Next
        picTile(15).Visible = False
        intCurrentTime = 0
        tmrTimer.Enabled = True
    End Sub
```

Repositioning the tiles is done as a two-pronged attack. Firstly, the main array of tiles, 'intBoard(index)', is updated; then the tiles are replaced using the data stored in the array. The control also includes a control scope variable called 'intBlankPos' which stores the current empty position.

User interaction

In the program the user can click on a tile. If the tile is adjacent to the blank position then the tile will move to the new square. I though it would be neater if this movement was done as a slide rather than a simple jump. So the control includes a timer. The picTile_Click event has the responsibility of controlling the way the Timer event behaves.

I have given comments in the code to help you understand what is going on.

```
    Private Sub picTile_Click(Index As Integer)
        'The MTile variable is a data structure declared in the
    declarations section of
        'the control. It stores all the information about the moving
    tile.
```

```
    'A test is made to determine if a tile is currently moving. If
'so then the sub terminates.
    'When the control is first created then timer is disabled.
  If MTile.Moving Or tmrTimer.Enabled = False Then Exit Sub
    'The value for the moving tile is set to the tile clicked using
'the Index property                                              ↵
  MTile.Tile = Index
    'The loop counter is set to 15
  MTile.Count = 15
    'To help illustrate what is being done by the control a debug
'statement extracts most useful information                      ↵
  Debug.Print ''intBlankPos='' + Str(intBlankPos) + _
    ''('' + Str(Int(intBlankPos / 4)) + '','' _
    + Str(intBlankPos Mod 4) + '') Index:'' _
    + Str(Index) + ''Pos:'' + _
    Str(intBoard(Index)) + ''('' + _
    Str(Int(intBoard(Index) / 4)) _
    + '', '' + Str(intBoard(Index) Mod 4) + '')''
  If intBlankPos = intBoard(Index) + 4 Then
    'Legal right move so set up the move variables
    MTile.XMove = 5
    MTile.YMove = 0
    MTile.Moving = True
  ElseIf intBlankPos = intBoard(Index) - 4 Then
    'legal left move so set up the move variables
    MTile.XMove = -5
    MTile.YMove = 0
    MTile.Moving = True
  ElseIf intBlankPos = intBoard(Index) - 1 Then
    'legal up move so set up the move variables
    MTile.YMove = -5
    MTile.XMove = 0
    MTile.Moving = True
  ElseIf intBlankPos = intBoard(Index) + 1 And (intBoard(Index)
Mod 4) < 3 Then                                                  ↵
      'It is important to avoid a legal down move from the bottom
'row. The ''Mod''                                                ↵
      statement checks for this.
    'Legal down move so set up the move variables
    MTile.YMove = 5
    MTile.XMove = 0
    MTile.Moving = True
  Else
      'No legal moves so set up variables
    MTile.Tile = -1
```

```
        MTile.Count = 0
        MTile.Moving = False
    End If
End Sub
```

Having set up the appropriate parameters in the picTile click event they all depend on an active Timer. The Timer is enabled using the 'Shuffle' button in the event code that we looked at above.

The Timer event

No rocket science here; just simple code to move the control in increments of 5 pixels, the direction being determined by the parameters set in the picTile_Click event. For each iteration the value of the counter is decreased. When the counter reaches zero the Move code is no longer executed. Instead a test is made for the value of the data structure member Moving which is a Boolean. If it is True then this must be the last iteration and time to transfer the position of the 'intBlankPos' and update the contents of the board array.

```
Private Sub tmrTimer_Timer()
  Dim intTemp As Integer

  If MTile.Count Then
    MTile.X = picTile(MTile.Tile).Left + MTile.XMove
    MTile.Y = picTile(MTile.Tile).Top + MTile.YMove
    picTile(MTile.Tile).Move MTile.X, MTile.Y
    MTile.Count = MTile.Count - 1
  ElseIf MTile.Moving Then
    MTile.Moving = False
    intTemp = BlankPos
    intBlankPos = Board(MTile.Tile)
    intBoard(MTile.Tile) = intTemp
  End If

  For i = 0 To 14
    If intBoard(i) <> i Then Exit For
  Next
  If i = 14 Then
    MsgBox ''Well done!''
    tmrTimer.Enabled = False
    picTile(15).Visible = True
    Shuffled = False
```

```
      End If
      intCurrentTime = intCurrentTime + 1
      lblTime.Caption = Format(intCurrentTime, ''000000'')
   End Sub
```

The next section of code in the Timer event checks to see if the user has successfully repositioned all the tiles. If so then the missing tile in the bottom right corner is made visible and a message box congratulates the player.

Finally, the 'intCurrentTime' variable is increased and a formatted value is sent to the displayed label control. This label control has its parameters set to make it include a border and green lettering on a black background.

The Resize event

Because this control must be displayed at a certain size I took control of resizing using this simple code. Notice that the control button and the label are repositioned using this short routine as well.

```
   Private Sub UserControl_Resize()
      Width = 300 * Screen.TwipsPerPixelX
      Height = 380 * Screen.TwipsPerPixelY
      cmdShuffle.Top = 310
      lblTime.Top = cmdShuffle.Top
   End Sub
```

Using the Tile Puzzle control

The UserControl that we have created will not run in the development environment as a stand-alone object. Remember, this is an object that can be used in other applications; it is not an application in its own right. It is for this reason that the multi-project environment of Visual Basic 5 was created. It is time now to look at the other project that was loaded when you opened the project group.

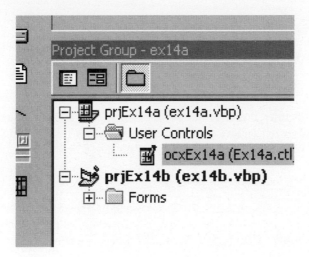

The project called 'prjEx14b' contains an instance of this new control. Using it is a simple matter of clicking on the icon in the Toolbox. Dragging a position for it on the Form and, hey presto, you have an ActiveX control on the Form.

Here is the Form_Load event

```
Private Sub Form_Load()
  ScaleMode = 3
  Width = 308 * Screen.TwipsPerPixelX
  Height = 380 * Screen.TwipsPerPixelY
  TestControl1.Left = 0
  TestControl1.Top = 0
  TestControl1.ZOrder 0
End Sub
```

Believe it or not that is the only code in the Form. All the functionality comes with the control.

Using the example in a web page

ActiveX controls can be embedded into a web page and viewed using Internet Explorer. The first step is make your development control into a true 'ocx' control. Make sure that the control is selected in the Project Window. Now select 'File|Make Ex14a.ocx'.

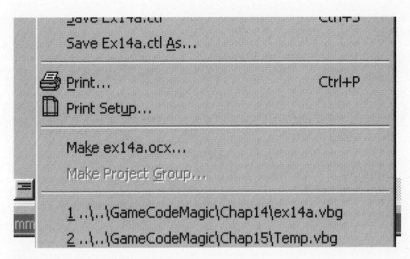

After the standard file dialog box appears, confirm the name and path for your control. You will now be able to insert this control into other applications. Using it in a web page involves writing an HTML file. You will need an application that allows you to insert an object into an HTML file. I use Microsoft's ActiveX Control Pad in this example but the principles are the same if you are using Frontpage or many other applications.

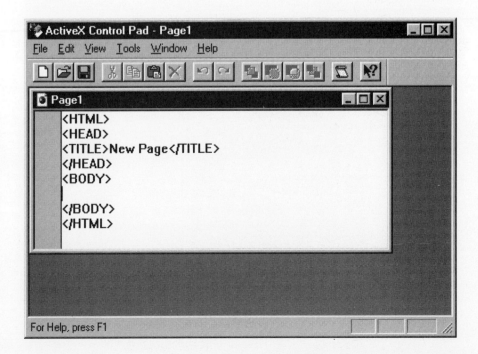

Inserting an ActiveX control

Select 'Edit | Insert ActiveX Control' from the menu. A pop-up menu appears listing the controls available on your machine.

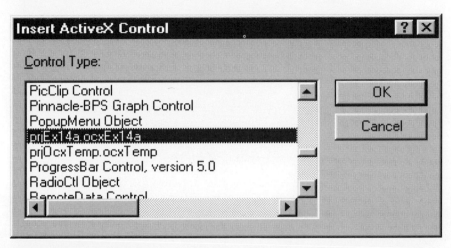

Select 'prjEx14a.ocxEx14a', which is a less than snappy title I agree, but you will learn in the next chapter how to give the control a more user friendly title. The program now creates a version of the control for you to view along with the properties for this control.

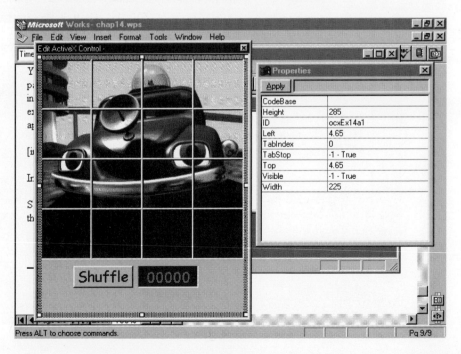

The HTML listing should now look like this

```
<HTML>
<HEAD>
<TITLE>New Page</TITLE>
</HEAD>
<BODY>

<OBJECT ID=''ocxEx14a1'' WIDTH=300 HEIGHT=380
CLASSID=''CLSID:D531CA32-4249-11D0-9227-444553540000''>
   <PARAM NAME=''_ExtentX'' VALUE=''7938''>
   <PARAM NAME=''_ExtentY'' VALUE=''10054''>
</OBJECT>

</BODY>
</HTML>
```

The complicated detail is the Class Id, which is a unique identification number for this control. Microsoft thought that as ActiveX controls were used more and more there would be many controls that had the same name, and to to avoid the operating system getting deeply confused they chose this unique identification number. It is because of this number that you really need to use an application that sources the details for you. If you are very keen to get your hands dirty, then you will find all the details in the system registry, but rather you than me!

If you save this listing as an HTML file, you can then run a copy of Internet Explorer 3 or above and use the 'File|Open' option to open a local file on your hard drive. The file will display your ActiveX control in all its glory.

To be really suitable for a web site you will need to consider getting the file size as small as possible and including interactivity beyond the control. That is what we will look at in the next chapter.

QUIZ

1. Can an ActiveX control run as a stand-alone application?

Answer: No, it must be added to a full application.

2. To initially add the control to a Visual Basic Form the control must be closed. True or False?

Answer: True. To display the icon in the Toolbox the control must be closed.

3. To add the control to a web page you simply need to know the name of the control. True or False?

Answer: False. The HTML file must include the unique identification number, the Class Id.

4. Can you add controls to a UserControl just as you would to a Form?

Answer: Yes. In developing the control almost all of the techniques are identical to those you have learnt when developing an application.

Summary

In this chapter you learnt how easy it is to create and edit an ActiveX control.

- You learnt how to edit multiple projects within the development environment.
- Inserting a developing ActiveX control into a developing application was covered.
- You learnt how to make the development control into a true ActiveX control.
- Finally, you learnt how to add the new control to a web page.

CHAPTER 15

Introducing VBScript – Make your web pages fun

This really is a hands-on chapter. You will need Internet Explorer 3 or later and a copy of the ActiveX Control Pad that is included on the CD. Working through this chapter, you will be introduced to just enough HTML to get you started and plenty of VBScript. If you are already a whiz with HTML just skip the next section. Jump in at Ex15b instead.

What is HTML?

HTML, or Hyper Text Mark-up Language, is a developing language to create interactive documents that can easily be transferred via the Internet. HTML is constantly developing and new capabilities are added at each stage.

To view HTML with the intended interactivity you will need a web browser. As you most probably know, Netscape Navigator is the most popular web browser at the time of writing, although, by the time you read these words, all the examples in this chapter will probably work with Navigator. As I write, Navigator is not yet able to incorporate

VBScript and ActiveX controls. I therefore recommend that you use Microsoft's browser.

Example Ex15a.htm

HTML is a simple text file formatted in a certain way that web browsers understand and can use to display in a graphic way with hyper-text links. To view the plain text of an HTML document use 'View|Source' from Internet Explorer. This opens Notepad and lets you view the document as it is written. I used ActiveX Control Pad for all the examples and I recommend installing this on your hard drive before you continue, unless you have some other authoring tool that is capable of inserting an ActiveX control into an HTML page. It's on the CD.

Here is probably the simplest web page with some interactivity.

```
<HTML>
<HEAD>
<TITLE>Game Code Magic – Chapter 15 Ex15a.htm</TITLE>
</HEAD>
<BODY BGCOLOR=''#FFFFFF''>
<H2>Introducing VBScript – Page 1</H2>
<HR> <BR>
This is a very simple HTML file.
<HR>
<A HREF=''Ex15b.htm''> Click here to continue </A>
</BODY>
</HTML>
```

Every HTML document starts with <HTML> and ends with </HTML>.

The header

A standard HTML document has two parts. The first part is the header. This contains information that is not printed to the screen; instead it is useful information for browsers to use to display the main caption or to use when you add a page to favourites. This short introduction to HTML is not intended to be comprehensive. If you wish to know more then download a reference document or get one of the many useful books on HTML.

The header is distinguished by the tags <HEAD> and </HEAD>. This technique of surrounding a section with an opening and closing tag is a standard feature of HTML. Closing tags are distinguished by the addition of the '/' character.

In this simple example the only use of the header is to store the title of the page. To tell the browser that the text is to be used as the title it must be in the header and it must be surround by <TITLE> ... </TITLE>.

The body

The printable main section of an HTML document is surrounded by the <BODY> ... </BODY> tags. The body tag can include additional attributes; in this case I have set the background colour by using BGCOLOR='#FFFFFF', which sets the colour of the page to white. You can use the name WHITE if you are using Internet Explorer. '#FFFFFF' is a hexadecimal value which simply means the value of red is set to #FF, the decimal equivalent being 255, the maximum level for red. Similarly the values of blue and green are set at maximum level, which results in the colour white. Palettes are covered in detail in Chapter 17, if you find converting between numbers and colours confusing.

Making text bigger

HTML includes many commands to alter the way that text is displayed. The simplest is the use of the <Hn> ... </Hn> tags, where n can be a number between 1 and 7. Here 1 is the biggest and 7 the smallest (which probably made sense to someone at some time!).

Forcing a line feed

HTML ignores the way that text is formatted in the original document. To cause a line feed to occur exactly where you want it, rather than leave that decision to the browser, requires the use of <BR>. If you wish to draw a horizontal rule, use <HR>.

Creating HyperText

To create text that causes a jump to another document or to a different place in the same document use the <A> ... </A> tags. A stands for anchor and to cause a jump to occur the browser needs to know the location of the intended jump. This is provided using the HREF attribute. (A word of warning here: Use relative addresses rather than particular addresses; in this way you can move an entire site easily providing all the relative addresses remain the same.) When I was creating the examples for this book they were at 'C:\AnimationMagic\Chap15\' but they are also at my company's web site, 'www.catalystpics.co.uk\book.htm'. If I had included the full path then moving the examples would require editing each address reference. By using relative addressing such as HREF='ex15b.htm', moving the files is easy.

Using frames

Click on the text that says 'Click here to continue'. The screen should look like this.

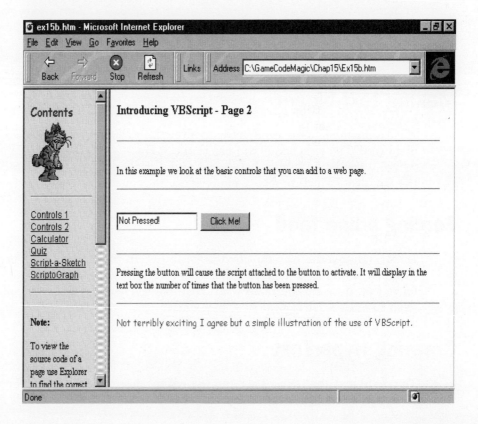

Frames are very useful for providing easy-to-use route finding. In this example a contents frame is open on the left. As the contents hypertext links are clicked, the right of the window changes, leaving the contents frame unaffected.

To use frames you create a page that sets up the FRAMESET for that page. The responsibility of this page is not to display an HTML document but to find one or more other HTML documents that are to be displayed. The <FRAMESET> ... </FRAMESET> tags surround the specifications of the documents to show. The window can be divided into columns (as in this example), rows, or a combination of rows and columns. In addition, the borders that by default surround the frame can be removed by setting the attribute FRAMEBORDER to NO. The COLS attribute takes one or more parameters. In this case it is set to 20% of the window for the first column and the remainder of the window for the others. It can be also be set by pixels by simply using an exact number without the % sign. Similarly, using three parameters would divide the area into three sections. The ROWS attribute works similarly; try writing a few samples to familiarise yourself with it.

Here I have put a frame with the name 'Contents' as the first to be displayed. The frame columns start at the left, rows start from the top. In addition to setting the NAME attribute the FRAME has also got a SRC, a source set to 'Contents.htm' this is the actual HTML document that will displayed in the left 20% of the window. The value of NAME is useful when navigating around the FRAMESET deciding which FRAME is used to display a new document.

```
<HTML>
<HEAD>
<TITLE>ex15b.htm</TITLE>
</HEAD>
<BODY>
<FRAMESET COLS=''20%,*''>
  <FRAME NAME=''Contents'' SRC=''Contents.htm''>
  <FRAME NAME=''Main'' SRC=''Ex15c.htm''>
</FRAMESET>
</BODY>
</HTML>
```

What does the Contents document look like?

Now that you have met the main HTML tags the majority of this document should be clear to you. I have added just three new tags.

<FONT> ... </FONT> is very useful for setting a font. You don't always get the font that is requested because it may not be available on the computer that is displaying the page, but your browser will make an excellent attempt to find something similar. I recommend checking Microsoft's web site for font information because the names that are available are regularly being updated. The FONT tag takes a NAME attribute, a SIZE attribute. With SIZE use ' +n' where n can be any integer from 1 to 7. This increases the size by a relative amount. Here 1 is the smallest increase and 7 the maximum. (By this stage the people who control HTML must have improved their maths!) Another new tag is IMG, which sets an image. This one is an 'animated Gif'. An animated Gif is really quite versatile. Each frame can have a transparent background and the duration of each frame can be set individually. They appear as a single file and are effectively compressed for low band width use on the web. The animated cat is just 19K, it contains 16 images and is set to loop for ever. It could be set to loop a certain number of times then stop. I used Microsoft Gif Animator to set up the Cat frames. This is available for free download; it may be on the CD, as we were seeking permission at the time of writing. The only other new tag is <ADDRESS>...</ADDRESS> which causes the text to be displayed in italics. It is usual to use it to encase an e-mail address or web site.

```
<HTML>
<HEAD>
<TITLE>Contents</TITLE>
</HEAD>
<BODY BGCOLOR=''#ddddff''>
<FONT FACE =''COMIC SANS MS'' SIZE='' +2'' COLOR=''GREEN''>
Contents</FONT>
< IMG SRC =''CAT.gif''> <BR>
<HR>
<FONT FACE =''ARIAL''>
<A TARGET =''Main'' HREF=''ex15c.htm''>Controls 1</A> <BR>
<A TARGET =''Main'' HREF=''ex15d.htm''>Controls 2</A> <BR>
<A TARGET =''Main'' HREF=''ex15e.htm''>Calculator</A> <BR>
<A TARGET =''Main'' HREF=''ex15f.htm''>Quiz</A> <BR>
<A TARGET =''Main'' HREF=''ex15g.htm''>Script-a-
   Sketch</A> <BR>
<A TARGET =''Main'' HREF=''ex15h.htm''>
```

```
    ScriptOGraph</A><BR>
</FONT>
<HR><BR><H4>Note:</H4>
To view the source code of a page use Explorer to find the correct
file. The name and path will be shown in the status bar as you move
your mouse over the hyper-text.
Selecting ''View|Source'' from the menu will only display the page
that includes the FRAMESET attributes.
<HR>
<ADDRESS>
<A HREF=''http://www.catalystpics.co.uk''>
Click here to view the authors web site </A>
</ADDRESS>
</BODY>
</HTML>
```

VBScript

If you skipped the HTML material then welcome back. If you worked right through then this is where the fun begins.

VBScript is a sub-set of Visual Basic, the major difference is the lack of graphics and file commands. Microsoft did not want to allow an HTML page to load and then wipe your hard drive, so all file controls are excluded. The other major difference is the lack of datatypes. In VBScript there is just one. So now you have learnt all the important details about datatypes and OOP. With VBScript some of these techniques are available, others are not.

Here's an easy VBScript to start with.

```
<HTML>
<HEAD>
<TITLE>ex15c.htm</TITLE>
<SCRIPT LANGUAGE=''VBSCRIPT''>
<!--
Dim intPressed

sub Pressed()
  intPressed=intPressed+1
```

```
    if intPressed > 1 then
      txtShow.Value = ''Pressed ''&CStr(intPressed)& '' times''
    else
      txtShow.Value = ''Pressed ''&CStr(intPressed)& '' time''
    end if
end sub
-->
</SCRIPT>
</HEAD>
<BODY BGCOLOR=WHITE>
<H2>Introducing VBScript – Page 2</H2><HR><BR>
In this example we look at the basic controls that you can add to a
web page.
<HR>
  <INPUT TYPE=TEXT VALUE=''Not Pressed!'' NAME=''txtShow''
SIZE=20>
  <INPUT TYPE=''BUTTON'' VALUE=''Click Me!''
ONCLICK=''Pressed''>
<HR>
Pressing the button will cause the script attached to the button to
activate.
It will display in the text box the number of times that the button
has been pressed.
<HR>
<FONT FACE=''COMIC SANS MS'' COLOR=''RED''>
Not terribly exciting I agree but a simple illustration of the use
of VBScript.
</FONT>
</BODY>
</HTML>
```

Most of this example has been covered in the HTML section. The
difference is the use of the <SCRIPT> ... </SCRIPT> tags and the
use of <INPUT ...> types. The default SCRIPT for the Internet is
JAVASCRIPT. You must have heard of JAVA. So if you are using
VBScript then you must specify the language. You can do this by
setting the LANGUAGE attribute to VBSCRIPT. You can include your
VBSCRIPT inline; that is, you specify the code as you define each
object, or you can put it all into the header. As I prefer to keep all
the code together, all my examples will use that approach. If you keep
all the code for a document in the header, it is then easy to find and
edit.

Where's the development environment?

At the moment your best development environment is the ActiveX
Control Pad. If you recall, I complained about the debugging facilities
offered by Visual Basic 4. Thankfully, VB5 is much better, now you
have local windows in addition to watch windows. With VBScript you
have no debugging information at all, and we will look at ways around
this problem in the next chapter. The development environment does
not include the syntax checking that is found in Visual Basic proper.
You can create VBScript documents with Notepad or an HTML editor,
but at first you may find it difficult to get out of the IDE (Integrated
Development Environment) way of working. Just get used to running
Internet Explorer and your text editor. To run your page use
'Open | File' in the menu options of Internet Explorer and select the
saved version of the file you are editing. Internet Explorer will load the
local HTML file. If there are errors then you will get an error message
that is probably totally unhelpful. Usually the message will state that
an error occurred at line n, where n can often be over 100. Counting
through the line numbers is a nightmare. I think that you will
probably have a better tool for the editing by the time you read this
because there are a lot of infuriated developers wanting a better
development environment for VBScript, so if you now have debugging
then spare a thought for those who have had to suffer.

In the SCRIPT section of this document, there is one variable defined
and one sub-routine. Here is one line of the sub-routine

```
txtShow.Value=''Pressed ''&CStr(intPressed)&'' times''
```

The object 'txtShow' is defined in the code

```
<INPUT TYPE=TEXT VALUE=''Not Pressed!'' NAME=''txtShow''
SIZE=20>
```

INPUT types include text boxes, buttons, radio buttons and check
boxes. The VALUE attribute varies from type to type; in this case it is
the displayed text. The above code defines a text box with 'Not
Pressed!' displayed and this box has the name 'txtShow'.

The sub-routine also includes 'CStr' which you have not yet met. Because every variable in VBScript code is a variant, it is sometimes necessary to convert this type to a specific type that is required. 'CStr' converts the variant to a string; 'CDbl' converts to a double; and 'CInt' converts to an integer. There are several others, and I recommend checking out the VBScript reference that is included with the ActiveX Control Pad.

```
<INPUT TYPE=''BUTTON'' VALUE=''Click Me!''
ONCLICK=''Pressed''>
```

You will notice that another object is created in the document in addition to the text box. This is a button. The value for a button again defines the displayed text. But the button includes an additional attribute. This is an event, the ONCLICK event. The standard controls have a selection of events associated with them that you can use to call sub-routines. Again for more detailed information use the online help included with the ActiveX Control Pad.

Notice that here the ONCLICK event includes the one word 'Pressed'. This must be the name of a defined sub-routine, otherwise you will receive an error message from Internet Explorer. Between the quotation marks you could include a complete listing of a sub-routine. If this was the case then the INPUT tag must include a LANGUAGE attribute. It is for this reason and others that I prefer to put all my code into the header and call each sub-routine from an event generated by an event.

If all the examples are as boring as that one, then you are at liberty to complain! Let's first look at another totally boring example that introduces most of the other INPUT controls that you can include with your code, then we will look at how you can use this new knowledge to much more interesting effect.

Lots of controls

Here I introduce two extra tags: <CENTER> ... </CENTER> where everything between the tags is centred in the window or frame and <TEXTAREA> ... </TEXTAREA> which behaves like a text input control except that it can be multi-lined and includes a vertical scroll bar. If text is longer than the size given for the width, then text is automatically transferred to the next line. The text between the tags is the initial value set for this control. This control can be given a NAME attribute like the INPUT types.

Using radio buttons

The radio buttons that are operating as a group must all have the same name. They can be referred to individually by referencing the Item(index) for that name. The indices are given automatically based on the order that the controls are created in the script.

```
<INPUT TYPE=''RADIO'' NAME=''radTest''> 'This will be index 0
<INPUT TYPE=''RADIO'' NAME=''radTest''> 'This will be index 1
```

The important information supplied by this control is the value of 'Checked'. Only one control in a group with the same name can have a value 'Checked'. You can iterate through the controls testing for 'Checked' as you go.

Other than this information, the remainder of the code is simply another example of VBScript in action.

```
<HTML>
<HEAD>
<TITLE>ex15d.htm</TITLE>
<SCRIPT LANGUAGE=''VBSCRIPT''>
<!--
Dim pi

pi=3.1415926535897932

sub ShowSin()
  Dim number

  number=CDbl(txtEnter.value)

  if cbxBox.checked then
    txtResult.value=CStr(Sin(number))
  else
    number=number/180 * pi
    txtResult.value=CStr(Sin(number))
  end if
end sub
```

```
sub ShowCos
  Dim number

  number=CDbl(txtEnter.value)

  if cbxBox.checked then
    txtResult.value=CStr(Cos(number))
  else
    number=number/180 * pi
    txtResult.value=CStr(Cos(number))
  end if
end sub

sub ShowLog
  Dim number

  number=CDbl(txtEnter.value)

  if number<0.00001 then
    status=''Number must be greater than zero''
    exit sub
  end if

  number=CDbl(txtEnter.value)
  txtResult.value=CStr(Log(number))
end sub

sub ShowColours
  Dim NL, strDisplay

  NL=Chr(13)&Chr(10)

  if radRadio.item(0).checked then
    strDisplay=''Red is selected''&NL
  else
    strDisplay=''Red is not selected''&NL
  end if

  if radRadio.item(1).checked then
    strDisplay=strDisplay&''Green is selected''&NL
  else
    strDisplay=strDisplay&''Green is not selected''&NL
  end if

  if radRadio.item(2).checked then
```

```
        strDisplay=strDisplay&''Blue is selected''&NL
    else
        strDisplay=strDisplay& ''Blue is not selected''&NL
    end if

    txtArea.value=strDisplay
end sub

sub ShowPassword
    txtPassword.value=pswPassword.value
end sub
-->
</SCRIPT>
</HEAD>
<BODY BGCOLOR=WHITE>
<H2>Introducing VBScript – Page 3</H2><HR><BR>
```

In this example we Introduce the standard controls that you can add to any web page

```
<HR>
    <BR>
    <CENTER>
    Answer <INPUT NAME=''txtResult'' TYPE=TEXT VALUE='''' >
    </CENTER>
    <P>Enter a number<BR>
    <INPUT NAME=''txtEnter'' TYPE=TEXT VALUE=''0''>
    <INPUT NAME=''cbxBox'' TYPE=CHECKBOX CHECKED>Radians
    <INPUT TYPE=BUTTON VALUE=''Sin'' ONCLICK=''ShowSin''>
    <INPUT TYPE=BUTTON VALUE=''Cos'' ONCLICK=''ShowCos''>
    <INPUT TYPE=BUTTON VALUE=''Log''
ONCLICK=''ShowLog''><BR><BR>
```

Clicking one of the maths buttons will convert the display in result to the correct value in radians or degrees depending on the checkbox.

```
    <HR>
    <P><FONT FACE=''Arial'' SIZE='' +2''
COLOR=''#ff0000''>Color</FONT>
    <INPUT TYPE=''BUTTON'' VALUE=''OK''
ONCLICK=''ShowColours''><BR><BR>
```

Clicking the OK button will cause the text area to display the selected radio button.

```
<BR><BR>
    <CENTER>
    <INPUT TYPE=''RADIO'' NAME=''radRadio'' CHECKED>Red
    <INPUT TYPE=''RADIO'' NAME=''radRadio'' >Green
    <INPUT TYPE=''RADIO'' NAME=''radRadio'' >Blue
```

```
<P>What did you choose?
<TEXTAREA NAME=''txtArea'' SIZE=''20,5''
ALIGN='RIGHT'>Click the OK button</TEXTAREA>
</CENTER><P><HR>
Reset will put everything back to the default.
<INPUT TYPE=''RESET'' VALUE=''Reset''><HR>
<CENTER>
<INPUT TYPE=''PASSWORD'' NAME=''pswPassword'' VALUE='It's a
secret''>
<INPUT TYPE=BUTTON VALUE=''Show Password''
ONCLICK=''ShowPassword''>
<INPUT NAME=''txtPassword'' TYPE=TEXT
VALUE=''''></CENTER><BR><BR>
Click the button in the middle to find out what is entered in the
password box.
<HR>
<FONT FACE=''COMIC SANS MS'' COLOR=''RED''>
That illustrates most of the standard controls that you can use with
HTML.
</FONT>
</BODY>
</HTML>
</BODY>
```

The INPUT with TYPE='RESET' puts the document back to the state when it is first loaded. The INPUT with TYPE='PASSWORD' is like a text box, but the display is simply the '*' character. The parameter stored as VALUE, however, is the same as a text box. In this example we transfer this to an actual text control to display the entered information.

Extending our knowledge

In this example we create a calculator. No new syntax. Try to work through the example discovering the techniques used to generate the display. Almost all of this code is simply standard Visual Basic with datatype conversion. It is very important that you feel comfortable with datatype conversions. I know that after many years of relying on nothing more than 'Str' to convert to a string, 'Int' to convert to an Integer and 'Val' to convert a string to a number, it was a trifle confusing to use a new type of syntax. But having programmed a great deal of C it was easier. I would guess that it could be one of the more difficult parts of using VBScript, which is made all the more difficult for the lack of a development environment.

```
<HTML>
<HEAD>
<TITLE>Calculator</TITLE>
<SCRIPT LANGUAGE=''VBSCRIPT'''>
<!--
Dim dblStored, intOperand, blnNewEntry
Dim PLUS, MINUS, MULTIPLY, DIVIDE

PLUS=1
MINUS=2
MULTIPLY=3
DIVIDE=4
intOperand=0

sub ButtonValue(index)
  if blnNewEntry then
    txtDisplay.value=''''
    blnNewEntry=0
  end if
txtDisplay.value=txtDisplay.value&index
end sub

sub UpdateValue()
  Select Case intOperand
  Case PLUS: dblStored=dblStored+CDbl(txtDisplay.value)
  Case MINUS: dblStored=dblStored-CDbl(txtDisplay.value)
  Case MULTIPLY: dblStored=dblStored*CDbl(txtDisplay.value)
  Case DIVIDE: dblStored=dblStored/CDbl(txtDisplay.value)
  Case Else: dblStored=CDbl(txtDisplay.value)
  End Select
  txtDisplay.value=CStr(dblStored)
  blnNewEntry=1
end sub

sub OnPlus()
  UpdateValue
  intOperand=PLUS end sub
end sub

sub OnMinus()
  UpdateValue
  intOperand=MINUS
end sub
```

```
sub OnMultiply()
  UpdateValue
  intOperand=MULTIPLY
end sub

sub OnDivide()
  UpdateValue
  intOperand=DIVIDE
end sub

sub OnEnter()
  UpdateValue
  intOperand=0
end sub

sub OnClear()
  dblStored=0 txtDisplay.value=''''
  intOperand=0
end sub
-->
</SCRIPT>
</HEAD>
<BODY BGCOLOR=WHITE>
<H2>Introducing VBScript – Page 4</H2><HR><BR>
In this example a simple calculator as part of a web page.
<HR>
  <CENTER>
  <INPUT TYPE=''TEXT'' VALUE='' '' NAME=''txtDisplay''
SIZE=30><HR><BR>
  <INPUT TYPE=''BUTTON'' VALUE=''0''
ONCLICK=''ButtonValue(0)''>
  <INPUT TYPE=''BUTTON'' VALUE=''1''
ONCLICK=''ButtonValue(1)''>
  <INPUT TYPE=''BUTTON'' VALUE=''Clear''
ONCLICK=''OnClear''>
  <INPUT TYPE=''BUTTON'' VALUE=''*''
ONCLICK=''OnMultiply''><BR>
  <INPUT TYPE=''BUTTON'' VALUE=''2''
ONCLICK=''ButtonValue(2)''>
  <INPUT TYPE=''BUTTON'' VALUE=''3''
ONCLICK=''ButtonValue(3)''>
  <INPUT TYPE=''BUTTON'' VALUE=''4''
ONCLICK=''ButtonValue(4)''>
  <INPUT TYPE=''BUTTON'' VALUE='' + ''
```

```
ONCLICK=''OnPlus''><BR>
  <INPUT TYPE=''BUTTON'' VALUE=''5''
ONCLICK=''ButtonValue(5)''>
  <INPUT TYPE=''BUTTON'' VALUE=''6''
ONCLICK=''ButtonValue(6)''>
  <INPUT TYPE=''BUTTON'' VALUE=''7''
ONCLICK=''ButtonValue(7)''>
  <INPUT TYPE=''BUTTON'' VALUE='' - ''
ONCLICK=''OnMinus''><BR>
  <INPUT TYPE=''BUTTON'' VALUE=''8''
ONCLICK=''ButtonValue(8)''>
  <INPUT TYPE=''BUTTON'' VALUE=''9''
ONCLICK=''ButtonValue(9)''>
  <INPUT TYPE=''BUTTON'' VALUE=''Enter''
ONCLICK=''OnEnter''>
  <INPUT TYPE=''BUTTON'' VALUE=''/''
ONCLICK=''OnDivide''><BR>
<HR>
Here we are using 17 input controls accesses by VBScript.
<HR>
<FONT FACE=''COMIC SANS MS'' COLOR=''RED''>
Use the contents to move on to the next example.
</FONT>
</BODY>
</HTML>
```

How are you doing so far?

To test your knowledge here is a simple quiz. This illustrates the use of arrays. You can still use these. Also, instead of putting the event into the INPUT statement, you can respond to an event by using the syntax.

```
object_OnClick()
```

The name used for object must be a current INPUT or TEXTAREA control. There are only 5 questions in the quiz. Notice the use of 'status' to write to the status bar.

```
<HTML>
<HEAD>
<TITLE>Quiz</TITLE>
```

```vbscript
<SCRIPT LANGUAGE=''VBSCRIPT''>
<!--
Dim strQuestion(20), intCurrent, intAnswer(20), NL, intScore

intScore=0
intCurrent=0
NL=chr(13)+chr(10)

strQuestion(0)=''How do you draw a horizontal rule in
HTML?''&NL&''A:Use HR''&NL&''B:Use RULE''&NL&''C:Use BR''
intAnswer(0)=0
strQuestion(1)=''What is the FRAMESET tag for?''&NL&''A:Setting
an animation frame''&NL&''B:Dividing the window into
sections''&NL&''C:Tennis games''
intAnswer(1)=1
strQuestion(2)=''Can you open a file with VBScript?''&NL&''A:Only
by using an ActiveX control''&NL&''B:Yes use Open as in Visual
Basic''&NL&''C:No never.''
intAnswer(2)=0
strQuestion(3)=''Can you use the Line drawing statement in
VBScript''&NL&''A:Yes if you use a form''&NL&''B:There is no
graphics support.''&NL&''C:Only by using ActiveX controls''
intAnswer(3)=2
strQuestion(4)=''This is a multiline text box, how is it
created?''&NL&''A:Using TEXTAREA tags''&NL&''B:Use a INPUT
TYPE=TEXT and set it to MULTILINE''&NL&''C:You need an ActiveX
control''
intAnswer(4)=0
strQuestion(5)=''How do you test a radio button?''&NL&''A:Test
for checked''&NL&''B:Test the radio.item(index).checked''&NL&''C:
Only possible using JavaScript''
intAnswer(5)=1

sub cmdEnter_OnClick()
  if cmdEnter.value=''Start'' then
    cmdEnter.value=''Enter''
    txtQuestion.value=strQuestion(0)
    exit sub
  end if
  if radChoice.item(intAnswer(intCurrent)).checked then
    status=''Well done!''
    intScore=intScore+1
    txtScore.value=CStr(intScore)
  else
```

```
      status = ''No the correct answer
is''&Chr(intAnswer(intCurrent) + 65)
   end if
      intCurrent = intCurrent + 1
   if intCurrent = 6 then
      status = ''That's all folks!''
      intCurrent = 0
      intScore = 0
   end if
   txtQuestion.value = strQuestion(intCurrent)
end sub
-->
</SCRIPT>
</HEAD>
<BODY BGCOLOR = WHITE>
<H2>Introducing VBScript – Page 5</H2> <HR> <BR>
In this example we test your knowledge
<HR>
   <FONT FACE = ''COMIC SANS MS'' SIZE = ''+3'' COLOR = ''#0f0''>
   You current score is</FONT>
   <INPUT TYPE = ''TEXT'' VALUE = ''0'' NAME = ''txtScore''> <HR>
   A<INPUT TYPE = ''RADIO'' NAME = ''radChoice'' CHECKED>
   B<INPUT TYPE = ''RADIO'' NAME = ''radChoice''>
   C<INPUT TYPE = ''RADIO'' NAME = ''radChoice''> <BR> <BR>
   <TEXTAREA NAME = ''txtQuestion'' SIZE = ''50,5''></TEXTAREA>
   <INPUT TYPE = ''BUTTON'' VALUE = ''Start'' NAME = ''cmdEnter''>
<HR>
Press the Start button when you are ready. Then use the Enter button
when you think you have got the right answer
<HR>
<FONT FACE = ''COMIC SANS MS'' COLOR = ''RED''>
I hope you do well with this quiz!</FONT>
<BR>
</BODY>
</HTML>
</BODY>
```

If you have been doing what I usually do, taking the examples and
tweaking them, then I am sure that you will have caused Internet
Explorer to complain on many occasions and found the reason for the
complaint difficult to identify. If you have, then this is the curve that
all VBScript users go through. You will come through it and start to
create complicated and useful interactive programs using VBScript.
Bear with it, you will find it useful.

Using an ActiveX control

To incorporate an ActiveX control into your web page at the moment involves retrieving certain information about this control, which includes a long and complicated number. It is highly recommended that you use a development tool for this task. I use ActiveX Control Pad, but you may have something better.

This example was created with Visual Basic 5.0 Control Creation Edition. It puts a silly little drawing game into your web page. The source for this control is included on the CD.

As this chapter is about VBScript, I don't intend to look at the code used for these two examples. It is fairly simple and I advise you to open the group projects in Visual Basic 5 to find out how they were created.

Script-a-Sketch

The ActiveX control used in this example does not expose any procedures. All the functionality is provided via mouse clicks on the control itself. Click on the white buttons and wobble the mouse and it will draw a black line in the grey area.

The HTML for this interactive page is remarkably simple because the functionality is provided by the control.

```
<HTML>
<HEAD>
<TITLE>Script-a-Sketch</TITLE>
<SCRIPT LANGUAGE='VBSCRIPT'>
<!--
Dim intBlank

sub blank()
end sub
-->
</SCRIPT>
</HEAD>
<BODY BGCOLOR=WHITE>
<H2>Introducing VBScript – Page 6</H2><HR><BR>
In this example a silly
<FONT FACE=''COMIC SANS MS'' COLOR=''BLUE'' SIZE=''+2''>
Active X</FONT>
control created with
<FONT FACE=''COMIC SANS MS'' COLOR=''BLUE'' SIZE=''+2''>
Visual Basic 5.0 CCE
</FONT>
<HR>

<OBJECT ID=''ScriptASketch1'' WIDTH=320 HEIGHT=240
CLASSID=''CLSID:0C64550D-4DB7-11D0-9227-444553540000''>
   <PARAM NAME=''_ExtentX'' VALUE=''8467''>
   <PARAM NAME=''_ExtentY'' VALUE=''6350''>
</OBJECT>

<HR>
Click on the knobs to draw a most excellent picture
<HR>
<FONT FACE=''COMIC SANS MS'' COLOR=''RED''>
So there we are from a simple HTML to Script-a-Sketch in 6 groovy
lessons. One more lesson to go: the fun ScriptOGraph.
</FONT>
</BODY>
</HTML>
```

ScriptOGraph

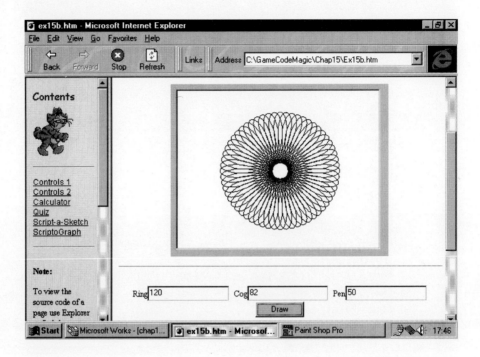

This final example includes the use of a sub-routine inside the control. The ScriptOGraph control draws the complicated patterns generated by the kids' drawing toy SpiroGraph. This toy uses a ring with cogs, a cog that fits into the ring and a pen that fits into one of many holes in the cog. This control includes a sub-routine with three parameters: the size of the ring, the size of the cog and the distance between the pen and the centre of the cog. The HTML document that includes the control must provide the user with input controls to provide these parameters. This example uses text boxes, but radio buttons could be used. The control becomes operational when the 'Draw' button is used. This calls the 'DrawGraph' sub-routine which provides some data checking since the size of the ring must be bigger than the cog, and the distance of the pen from the centre of the cog must be less than the size of the cog. Then it calls the ScriptOGraph Draw routine.

```
<HTML>
<HEAD>
<TITLE>ScriptOGraph</TITLE>
<SCRIPT LANGUAGE=''VBSCRIPT''>
```

```
< !--
sub DrawGraph()
  dim intRing, intCog, intPen

  intRing=CInt(txtRing.value)
  intCog=CInt(txtCog.value)
  intPen=CInt(txtPen.value)

  if intPen<=0 then
    intPen=1
    txtPen.value=CStr(intPen)
  end if
  if intPen>intCog then
    intCog=intPen+1
    txtCog.value=CStr(intCog)
  end if
  if intCog>intRing then
    intRing=intCog+1
    txtRing.value=CStr(intRing)
  end if

  ScriptOGraph1.Draw intRing, intCog, intPen
end sub
-->
</SCRIPT>
</HEAD>
<BODY BGCOLOR=WHITE>
<H2>Introducing VBScript – Page 7</H2><HR><BR>
In this example another silly
<FONT FACE=''COMIC SANS MS'' COLOR=''BLUE'' SIZE=''+2''>
Active X</FONT>
control created with
<FONT FACE=''COMIC SANS MS'' COLOR=''BLUE'' SIZE=''+2''>
Visual Basic 5.0 CCE
</FONT>
<HR>
  <CENTER>
<OBJECT ID=''ScriptOGraph1'' WIDTH=320 HEIGHT=259
CLASSID=''CLSID:0C6454DA-4DB7-11D0-9227-444553540000''>
  <PARAM NAME=''_ExtentX'' VALUE=''8467''>
  <PARAM NAME=''_ExtentY'' VALUE=''6826''>
</OBJECT>
<HR><BR>
  Ring<INPUT TYPE=TEXT VALUE=''120'' NAME=''txtRing''>
  Cog<INPUT TYPE=TEXT VALUE=''82'' NAME=''txtCog''>
```

```
        Pen<INPUT TYPE=TEXT VALUE=''50'' NAME=''txtPen''><BR>
        <INPUT TYPE=BUTTON VALUE=''Draw'' ONCLICK=''DrawGraph''>
        </CENTER>
<HR>
Press the Draw button. Nice? Now enter different values in the text
boxes. Then press the button to draw your own ScriptOGraph picture.
<BR>
<FONT FACE=''COMIC SANS MS'' COLOR=''RED''>
Note: that Ring should be greater than Cog which should be greater
than Pen.
The data is changed if this is not the case.</FONT><BR>
Never was such high technology so delightfully wasted. Instead of 2
pieces of clear plastic, £1000 worth of computer. Isn't technology
wonderful!<HR>
<FONT FACE=''COMIC SANS MS'' COLOR=''RED''>
I hope you enjoyed this quick demonstration of the delights of
VBScript. In the next chapter we look at incorporating the sprite
ActiveX control into a web page</FONT>
</BODY>
</HTML>
```

Review

Lots of new information was provided in this chapter. It is well worth
learning enough HTML to start to use VBScript; but it is worth even
more if you can use Visual Basic 5 to create ActiveX controls. These
controls, when added to an HTML page, provide an unlimited amount
of functionality. If it can be done on the Windows desktop it can be
part of a web page.

1. Can I open a file on the user's computer using VBScript?
Answer: Only by using an ActiveX control.

2. If I want to convert a VBScript variable to a string, what syntax do I use?
Answer: CStr(variable)

3. I want to let the user enter a short memo. What control should I use?
Answer: Use a multi-line text box using the following syntax:
<TEXTAREA NAME = "myName" SIZE = "50,5"> Enter text here </TEXTAREA>

4. I include an ActiveX control in my web page by using the name of the control. True or False?
Answer: False, You must include a long number called the CLASSID. This can be incorporated using an authoring program or by searching the registry. I recommend the authoring program technique.

Summary

In this chapter you learnt enough HTML to use VBScript.

- The basics of VBScript were covered, including how to use Active controls.
- VBScript differs from full Visual Basic by excluding file and graphic methods and functions. This is mainly for security reasons. If necessary the functionality can be added by creating your own ActiveX controls using Visual Basic 5.0.

CHAPTER 16

VBScript and sprites – Animation on your web site

Now that you have seen what can been done using VBScript it is time to extend this knowledge to fast animation techniques. The sprite control that you have used since Chapter 9 is suitable for inclusion on a web page. This chapter looks at ways in which you can add interactive animation to your web page using this control. Those who use your web page will need to download a version of this control, but at only 72K which is a very small download.

NOTE

You can include a copy of the control on your web site so that those viewing your site will automatically receive a copy of the control. The version of the control on the CD is the beta version that is not fully registered. Those viewing your pages will need to set up the options on Internet Explorer. Use the menu option 'View|Options' then select the security tab. Select the button labelled 'Safety level'. You will get a dialog box enabling you to choose a security level for

ActiveX content; select the medium option for experts
and developers only. Without doing this the content of
pages that you view while developing an ActiveX
control will not be shown.

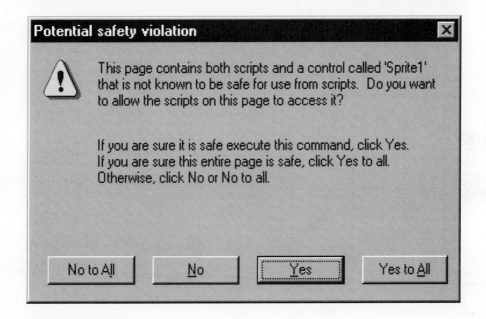

Professional development using VBScript

Your major problem is debugging. One of the central features of this
chapter concerns the techniques used to debug the code. To facilitate
debugging I open the page using a frame page. The following is the
HTML file that sets up the frames.

```
<HTML>
<HEAD>
<TITLE>Debugging Bucket.htm</TITLE>
</HEAD>
<BODY>
<FRAMESET COLS=''70%,*''>
  <FRAME NAME=''Bucket'' SRC=''Bucket.htm''>
  <FRAME NAME=''Debug''RC=''Debug.htm''>
</FRAMESET>
```

```
</BODY>
</HTML>
```

The main area is used by the HTML document "Bucket.htm". The remainder is used by the document "Debug.htm". Before we look at the main document lets look at the debug document.

```
<HTML>
<HEAD>
<TITLE>Debug Page</TITLE>
</HEAD>
<BODY>
<H3>Debugging Window</H3>
<HR> <BR>
  <FORM NAME=''DebugForm''>
  Bucket 1 info
    <INPUT TYPE=TEXT SIZE=30 NAME=''txtBucket1'' VALUE=''Not
Available''>
  Bucket 2 info
  <INPUT TYPE=TEXT SIZE=30 NAME=''txtBucket2'' VALUE=''Not
Available''>
  Bucket 3 info
    <INPUT TYPE=TEXT SIZE=30 NAME=''txtBucket3'' VALUE=''Not
Available''>
```

```
    Bucket 4 info
        <INPUT TYPE=TEXT SIZE=30 NAME=''txtBucket4'' VALUE=''Not
    Available''>
    Button info
        <INPUT TYPE=TEXT SIZE=30 NAME=''txtButton'' VALUE=''Not
    Available''>
    Platform info
        <INPUT TYPE=TEXT SIZE=30 NAME=''txtPlatform''
    VALUE=''Not Available''>
    <HR>
        <INPUT TYPE=BUTTON VALUE=''Update'' NAME=''btnUpdate''>
        <SCRIPT LANGUAGE=''VBScript'' FOR=''btnUpdate''
    EVENT=''onClick''>
    <!--
       Top.Bucket.DebugData
    -->
        </SCRIPT>
    </BODY>
    </HTML>
```

The main feature of this document is the event generated when the button called 'btnUpdate' is clicked. Here the procedure that is called is placed between the SCRIPT tags. The technique of using the attribute FOR and EVENT is an alternative syntax to the one used in the previous chapter. This is illustrated to show the option but I recommend the technique of placing all the procedures in the header for a document and calling them by name. This procedure is very simple, it calls the procedure 'DebugData', which it finds at location 'Top.Bucket'. Top is always available to a document displaying frames. It is the document that originated the frames. Bucket is the name given to one of those frames. DebugData is a procedure call found in that document.

The debug procedure in the document 'Bucket.htm'

In this example we are using forms within a document. Just as the window can be divided using frames, so an HTML document can contain forms. In the previous chapter we did not define a form, so reference to INPUT controls involved only the name of the control. In this example the controls are placed in a form. This is done by containing the controls within the Form tags. A form has a NAME attribute and it is this that is used to locate and refer to the individual controls that the form contains. In order to make the code more readable the form and its location can be placed in a variable. In this case we use the variable 'DrawForm', which is initialised to 'Top.Debug.DebugForm', that is the form called 'DebugForm' defined in the document called 'Debug' which is, in turn, defined in the document that created the frames.

The text box input controls, which were created when the Debug document was first created, are used to store important program information. This is a similar technique to using a Watch window with Visual Basic. I am afraid that, as it stands, it is not nearly as functional as the Visual Basic design and run time environment. You are now reaching the stage as developer where you will have to decide on your own way of creating and debugging code. You are better served by VBScript than by the development environments that many programmers have to use in their professional life. If you are programming the chips used in so many electronic gadgets the development tools are often no more advanced than the tools that you have when developing for VBScript. A sign of a good programmer is the ability to work around the limitations to make robust and effective programs.

```
Sub DebugData
  Dim DrawForm

  DrawForm=Top.Debug.DebugForm

  DrawForm.txtBucket1.Value=''(''&CStr(BucketX(0))&'',
''&CStr(Bucket
Y(0))
&'') Frame:''&CStr(BucketFrame(0))&''
Action:''&CStr(BucketAction(0))
DrawForm.txtBucket2.Value=''(''&CStr(BucketX(1))&'',
''&CStr(Bucket
Y(1))
&'') Frame:''&CStr(BucketFrame(1))&''
Action:''&CStr(BucketAction(1))
  DrawForm.txtBucket3.Value=''(''&CStr(BucketX(2))&'',
''&CStr(Bucket
Y(2))
&'') Frame:''&CStr(BucketFrame(2))&''
Action:''&C$tr(BucketAction(2))
  DrawForm.txtBucket4.Value=''(''&CStr(BucketX(3))&'',
''&CStr(Bucket
Y(3))
```

```
&'') Frame:''&CStr(BucketFrame(3))&''
Action:''&CStr(BucketAction(3))
  DrawForm.txtButton.Value=CStr(ClickButton)
if NextPlatform then
  DrawForm.txtPlatform.Value=CStr(NextPlatform-1)&'':
Type-''&CStr(PlatformType(NextPlatform-1))
  else
    DrawForm.txtPlatform.Value=''No platforms created!''
  end if
end sub
```

The debug code here is intended as a simple starter to suggest ideas of
how to generate your own debug and error messages.

Using the Sprite ActiveX control in a web document

The Sprite ActiveX control uses file commands to load bitmap
information and to play sounds. To use these techniques in a web
environment threatens the security of the system. Remember that
VBScript has been deliberately designed to exclude file procedures. To
use file commands involves generating a path to those files. To create a
path to the file you need to understand about the Scripting Object
Model.

Understanding the Scripting Object Model

Microsoft's Scripting Object Model allows the HTML programmer
access to several web-related objects. Here is a chart indicating the
design of the Scripting Object Model:

```
Window
    ├─Frame*
    ├─History
    ├─Navigator
    ├─Location
    ├─Script*
    └─Document
       ├─Link*
       ├─Anchor*
       └─Form*
          └──Element*
    (*Multiple objects allowed.)
```

The window object is always the top level. The window object contains a number of properties, methods and events.

Window		
Properties	*Methods*	*Events*
name	alert	onLoad
parent	confirmon	onUnload
self	prompt	
top	open	
location	close	
defaultStatus	setTimeout	
status	clearTimeout	
frames	navigator	
history		
navigator		
document		

Because the window object has global scope, to access a member does not require the syntax window.name; simply using "name" is sufficient. Consequently, the members of the window object are all reserved names and cannot be used as variable names. In order to generate a path to the files that the sprite control requires we will look at the 'location' member of the window object.

Location
Properties
href
protocol
host
hostname
pathname
port
search
hash

In this example I use the 'location.pathname' property.

NOTE

If you use the ActiveX Control Pad and open the Script Wizard either by clicking on the funny 'S' on the toolbar, or selecting 'Tools|Script Wizard' you can click on the word 'window' under the Insert Action list. This allows you to see the structure of the window object.

The pathname property includes the name of the current page. To use the property with the sprite control the value needs to be parsed further. The following is the code that is added to the window onLoad event.

```
Sub window_onLoad()
   Dim myForm, Path, Pos, OldPos

'Start by setting a variable to allow easy access to the BucketForm
   Set myForm=Document.BucketForm
'Put a message in the status bar
   status=''Loading please wait''
'Set the procedure that is called to clear the status bar
'syntax procedure name, time to call in milliseconds, script
language
   setTimeout ''ClearStatus'', 5000, ''VBScript''
'Set the variable Path
   Path=location.pathname
   Pos=0
'Remove any forward slashes
   Do (while left(Path, 1)=''/'')
     Path=right(Path,Len(Path)−1)
   Loop
'Find last back slash
   Do
     OldPos=Pos
     Pos=Instr(Pos+1, Path, ''\'')
   Loop While Pos
'Use information about last position of last backslash to remove
filename
   Path=Left(Path, OldPos)

   myForm.Sprite1.AutoSize=True
   myForm.Sprite1.LoadBackground Path & ''bg.bmp'', 0
```

```
'Initialise the platforms
for i=0 to 9
    if i then
      platform(i) = myForm.Sprite1.CloneSprite(platform(0), 0, 0)
    else
      platform(i) = _
        myForm.Sprite1.CreateSprite(Path&''platform.bmp'',70,102)
    end if
    myForm.Sprite1.MoveSprite platform(i), 1000, 1000, 0
next

'Initialise the buttons
for i=0 to 9
    if i then
      buttons(i)=myForm.Sprite1.CloneSprite(buttons(0), 0, 0)
    else
      buttons(0) =
      myForm.Sprite1.CreateSprite(Path&''buttons.bmp'',28,27)
    end if
    myForm.Sprite1.MoveSprite buttons(i), i*30+10, 273,
next

'Set up array of strings to use as user prompts
ToolBarTip(0) =''Click here to restart this level''
ToolBarTip(1) =''Click here to create a vertical pipe''
ToolBarTip(2) =''Click here to create a horizontal pipe''
ToolBarTip(3) =''Click here to create a ramp''
ToolBarTip(4) =''Click here to create a ladder''
ToolBarTip(5) =''Click here to create a lift''
ToolBarTip(6) =''Click here to create a spring''
ToolBarTip(7) =''Click here to create a soft landing''
ToolBarTip(8) =''Click here to pause the game''
ToolBarTip(9) =''Click here to enter a level password''

NumBuckets = 4
'Initialise Bucket sprites
for i=0 to NumBuckets-1
  BucketX(i)=CInt(rnd*400)
  BucketY(i)=CInt(STAGE_FLOOR) - 16*(i=SMALL_BUCKET)
    if i then
    if i=1 then
      BucketIndex(i) =
myForm.Sprite1.CreateSprite(Path&''sbucket.bmp'', 32, 32)
    else
      BucketIndex(i) =
```

```
myForm.Sprite1.CloneSprite(BucketIndex(0),0,0)
    end if
  else
    BucketIndex(i) =
myForm.Sprite1.CreateSprite(Path&''bbucket.bmp'', 48, 48)
    end if
    BucketAction(i)=WALK-RIGHT
    BucketWater(i)=1000
  next
  Bath=myForm.Sprite1.CreateSprite(Path&''bath.bmp'', 111, 83)
  BathWater=0
  myForm.Sprite1.MoveSprite Bath, 250, 100, 0 'Line 125
  DragBucket=0
end sub
```

Clearing the status bar using the 'setTimeout' method

Having set up a status bar message it is essential that it does not sit there for ever; a status bar message must be up to date to be useful. To synchronise the message with user actions, use the 'setTimeout' method. This useful method sets a timer, and a procedure call. The method takes three parameters: a procedure name, a duration in milliseconds and the language to use.

In this example the procedure 'ClearStatus' is called after 5 seconds.

setTimeout 'ClearStatus', 5000, 'VBScript'

```
sub ClearStatus
  status=''Animation Magic - Chapter 16''
end sub
```

The global variables and constants

The onLoad event sets up the global variables that are defined at the start of the HTML document. Many constants are used in this example. VBScript does not directly support constants so I declare a variable then set it to a value. To distinguish constants in the code I use upper case letters.

```
<HTML>
<HEAD>
<TITLE>Introducing VBScript </TITLE>
  <SCRIPT LANGUAGE=''VBScript''>
<!--
Dim BucketIndex(5), BucketX(5), BucketY(5), BucketAction(5),
BucketFrame(5)
Dim Platform(10), PlatformType(10), BucketWater(5), BucketMoveY(5)
Dim Buttons(10), Bath, BathWater, NextPlatform, BucketPlatform(5)
Dim NumBuckets, ClickBucket, DragBucket, ClickButton, DragPlatform
Dim ToolBarTip(10), PlatformX(10), PlatformY(10),
PlatformFloor(10), PlatformMoving(10)
Dim WALK_RIGHT, WALK_LEFT, TURN_RIGHT, TURN_LEFT, FALL_LEFT,
CLIMB, INTO_CLIMB
Dim POUR, SMALL_LAND_RIGHT, SMALL_LAND_LEFT, BIG_LAND_RIGHT,
BIG_LAND_LEFT
Dim RAMP, HORZ_PIPE, VERT_PIPE, LADDER, LIFT, LILO, SPRING,
STAGE_FLOOR, STAGE_LEFT
Dim STAGE_RIGHT, SMALL_BUCKET

SMALL_BUCKET=1

WALK_RIGHT = 0
TURN_LEFT = 1
CLIMB = 2
INTO_CLIMB = 3
SMALL_LAND_RIGHT = 4
BIG_LAND_RIGHT = 5
POUR = 7
WALK_LEFT = 8
TURN_RIGHT = 9
SMALL_LAND_LEFT = 10
BIG_LAND_LEFT = 11
FALL_LEFT = 13
FALL_RIGHT = 14

VERT_PIPE = 0
HORZ_PIPE=1
RAMP=2
LADDER=3
LIFT =4
SPRING=5
LILO=6
WALL=7
```

```
PlatformFloor(VERT_PIPE) =199
PlatformFloor(HORZ_PIPE)=251
PlatformFloor(RAMP) =247
PlatformFloor(LADDER) =192
PlatformFloor(LIFT)=185
PlatformFloor(SPRING)=247
PlatformFloor(LILO) =248
PlatformFloor(WALL)=164

STAGE_RIGHT = 350
STAGE_LEFT = 10
STAGE_FLOOR = 217
```

Differences between VBScript and Visual Basic

I found debugging to be the most difficult part. My method of working starts with writing down what I want the program to do, then I make the operations of the program more and more modular. The next stage is to consider each small module and how to implement it. I usually try to implement the code bit by bit, running small test routines if the current procedure requires a parameter that will be provided by another procedure that is not yet implemented. I rely on the watch window, the local window and the immediate pane to test each section. With VBScript the code can often fall over before the script starts and then the only feedback is a line number. Tracing back to the offending line was very difficult using the ActiveX Control Pad which did not allow a trace to a specific VBScript line by number.

I found the ability to trace variables via the debug frame very useful. I also wrote a parser using Visual Basic that allowed a jump to a specific line number. It is very basic, but if you would like to use it you will find it on the CD called "LineNo.exe". The following is the simple code that it uses

```
Private Sub cmdOpen_Click()
  cdgFile.ShowOpen
  sFilename = cdgFile.filename

  cmdRefresh_Click

  cmdRefresh.Enabled = True
  txtLineNo.Enabled = True
  cmdGotoLine.Enabled = True
```

```
      lstLines.Enabled = True
    End Sub

    Private Sub cmdRefresh_Click()
      Dim FileNum As Integer, stemp As String

      FileNum = FreeFile
      Open sFilename For Input Access Read As FileNum

      lstLines.Clear

      Do While (Not EOF(FileNum))
        Line Input #FileNum, stemp
        lstLines.AddItem stemp
      Loop

      Close FileNum

    End Sub
```

Clicking on the open file button triggers the cmdOpen_Click event. I
have used the Common Dialog box control and the ShowOpen method.
The properties for this control are set to show 'htm' files by default
and the default filename is 'Page1'. This is the current default for the
ActiveX Control Pad. After selecting a file, the Common Dialog control
will have a filename property that can be used to open a file for input.
A second button is on the screen, the refresh option, so that the file can
be updated as it is worked on. To avoid duplicating code the
'cmdRefresh_Click' sub-routine is called from 'cmdOpen_Click' event.
The open file is used to fill a list box line by line. Now that a valid file
is loaded the buttons can be enabled.

Displaying the required line number

To synchronise the list box and the line number, use this simple code.

```
    Private Sub cmdGotoLine_Click()
      Dim sLine As String, iIndex As Integer

      If Val(txtLineNo.Text) < 1 Then
      'Button clicked with no line number in display
      SetStatus ''Enter line number''
        Exit Sub
```

```
   End If

   iIndex = 1
   'Find the first occurrence of the SCRIPT tag
   Do
     sLine = lstLines.List(iIndex)
     iIndex = iIndex + 1
   Loop While (InStr(UCase(sLine), ''SCRIPT'') = 0 And iIndex
   < 10000)

   'Use a limit to avoid endless loop
   If iIndex = 10000 Then
     SetStatus ''No SCRIPT tag found!''
     Exit Sub
   End If

       'Now set the listIndex property to the line number required
 + the    line number of the
      'SCRIPT tag
   lstLines.ListIndex = iIndex + Val(txtLineNo.Text)
   End Sub
```

Finally, the status bar uses a sub-routine to reset the counter of a timer. Out of sync status bars are almost worse than none at all. Timer events are useful for clearing the contents.

```
   Sub SetStatus(sCaption As String)
     lblStatus.Caption = sCaption
     tmrStatus.Enabled = False
     tmrStatus.Enabled = True
   End Sub

   Private Sub tmrStatus_Timer()
     lblStatus.Caption = ''''
   End Sub
```

For the program to work effectively it is essential that all the script is put into a block. If your script is in line with your INPUT controls then this program will not be able to find the correct line number. I recommend placing all the code in a block.

More debugging tips

Finding the offending line can be very tedious. Use a method to isolate the problem. Try commenting out lines using the 'character. If a sub-routine calls another then comment out the new call. Use this approach until the script contains no errors. Then one by one remove the comments until the bug returns. VBScript is not case sensitive. Don't use variable names that differ only by case.

A more complicated example

Here is part of the listing of the Bucket program. A lack of user-defined datatypes makes the code a little more confusing. Much of this style of code will be familiar to you at this stage in the book.

The Mouse events

A Mouse Down event on the Bucket playing field could involve a click on a button, a platform or a bucket. The return value of the HitTest function is tested against the index value of the bucket, button and platform arrays.

If the Hit Test indicates that a button was selected, then the action is executed immediately in a Select Case construction.

```
Sub Sprite1_MouseDown(Button, Shift, x, y)
   Dim SpriteIndex, CurrentFps
   SpriteIndex=Document.BucketForm.Sprite1.HitTest(x, y)
   if SpriteIndex then
      DragIndex=-1
      for i=0 to NumBuckets-1
         if SpriteIndex=BucketIndex(i) then DragIndex=I
      next
      if DragIndex=-1 then 'Not a bucket must be a platform or a
button                                                          ⌋
         for i=0 to 9
            if SpriteIndex=Buttons(i) then
            ClickButton=i+1
            Document.BucketForm.Sprite1.MoveSprite
Buttons(i), i*30+10, 273, i+10                                  ⌋
            Select Case I
            Case 0:'Reset level
               for j=0 to 9

            Document.BucketForm.Sprite1.MoveSprite Platform(i),  ⌋
1000, 1000, 0
               PlatformX(j)=1000
```

```
        PlatformY(j) =1000
      next
      NextPlatform=0
      For j =0 to NumBuckets −1

        BucketY(j) =STAGE_FLOOR −16* (j =1)
        BucketWater(j) =1000
        BathWater =0
      next
    Case 8:'Pause

        CurrentFps =Document.BucketForm.Sprite1.Fps
      if CurrentFps =0 then
        CurrentFps =15

    Document.BucketForm.Sprite1.MoveSprite Buttons(i),
i *30 +10, 273, I                                        ↵
        else
        CurrentFps =0

    Document.BucketForm.Sprite1.MoveSprite Buttons(i),
i *30 +10, 273, i +10                                    ↵

    Document.BucketForm.Sprite1.UpdateStage
      end if

    Document.BucketForm.Sprite1.Fps =CurrentFps
    Case 9:'Tap
    Case Else: 'New platform
      If NextPlatform=10 then
        status =''No more platforms available''
        Exit Sub
      End If
      PlatformType(NextPlatform) =i −1

    Document.BucketForm.Sprite1.MoveSprite
Platform(NextPlatform), 180, 20,                         ↵
      PlatformType(NextPlatform)
      PlatformX(NextPlatform) =180
      PlatformY(NextPlatform) =20
      PlatformMoving(NextPlatform) =1
      NextPlatform=NextPlatform+1
    End Select
    status =ToolBarTip(i)
  end if
```

```
        next
        for i = 0 to NextPlatform − 1
          if SpriteIndex = platform(i) then
            DragPlatform = i + 1
            PlatformMoving(i) = 1
            Exit Sub
          End if
        next
        DragBucket = 0
        DragIndex = 0
      else
        status = ''You are dragging Bucket '' & CStr(DragBucket)
        DragBucket = SpriteIndex
      end if
    end if
  end sub
```

If dragging is enabled by the MouseDown event then the MouseMove event is used to keep the screen display updated. The user may be dragging a bucket or a platform; both options are included in the listing.

```
Sub Sprite1_MouseMove(Button, Shift, x, y)
  if DragBucket then
    Document.BucketForm.Sprite1.MoveSprite DragBucket, x − 24,
y − 24, BucketFrame(DragIndex)                                    ⏎
  end if
  if DragPlatform then
    Document.BucketForm.Sprite1.MoveSprite Platform(DragPlatform−
1), x − 10, y − 10, PlatformType(DragPlatform − 1)                ⏎
    PlatformX(DragPlatform − 1) = x − 10
    PlatformY(DragPlatform − 1) = y − 10
  end if
end sub
```

Having released the mouse button, the tidy-up operations simply involve resetting the DragBucket, ClickButton and DragPlatform global variables.

```
Sub Sprite1_MouseUp(Button, Shift, x, y)
  if ClickButton then
    ClickButton = ClickButton − 1
    if ClickButton < > 8 then Document.BucketForm.Sprite1.
    MoveSprite Buttons(ClickButton), ClickButton * 30 + 10, 273,
    ClickButton
```

```
       ClickButton=0
       end if
     end if
     if DragBucket then
       BucketX(DragIndex) = x — 24
       BucketY(DragIndex) = y — 24
       DragBucket=0
     end if
     if DragPlatform then DragPlatform=0
     ClearStatus
     end if
   end sub
```

The Timer event

As usual the animation is updated using the sprite control's Timer
event

```
   Sub Sprite1_Timer()
     for i=0 to NumBuckets—1
       if BucketIndex(i)<>DragBucket then
         select case BucketAction(i)
         case WALK_RIGHT: walkright(i)
         case WALK_LEFT: walkleft(i)
         case TURN_RIGHT: turnright(i)
         case TURN_LEFT: turnleft(i)
         case CLIMB: ClimbLadder(i)
         end select
         Document.BucketForm.Sprite1.MoveSprite BucketIndex(i),   ↵
   BucketX(i), BucketY(i), BucketFrame(i)
       end if
     next
     for i=0 to NextPlatform-1
       if PlatformMoving(i) then
         if PlatformY(i)<PlatformFloor(PlatformType(i)) then
           PlatformY(i)=PlatformY(i)+5
           for j=0 to NextPlatform—1
             if i<>j then 'Line 248
               if
       Document.BucketForm.Sprite1.CollisionCheck (Platform(i),
               Platform(j), —1) then
               PlatformY(i)=PlatformY(i)-3
               PlatformMoving(i)=0
             end if
```

```
      end if
            end if
        next
        Document.BucketForm.Sprite1.MoveSprite Platform(i),
          PlatformX(i), PlatformY(i), PlatformType(i)
       elseif PlatformY(i)>PlatformFloor(PlatformType(i)) then
          PlatformY(i)=PlatformFloor(PlatformType(i))
          PlatformMoving(i)=0
        Document.BucketForm.Sprite1.MoveSprite Platform(i),
          PlatformX(i), PlatformY(i), PlatformType(i)
            end if
    next
    Document.BucketForm.Sprite1.UpdateStage
end sub
```

Action sub-routines

Finally, the following are a few of the action sub-routines that are
called as the buckets are found in various locations performing diferent
actions:

```
sub walkright(i)
  BucketX(i)=BucketX(i)+4
  if BucketY(i)<(STAGE_FLOOR-16*(i=1)) then
    BucketMoveY(i)=BucketMoveY(i)+1
    BucketY(i)=BucketY(i)+BucketMoveY(i)
  end if
  BucketFrame(i)=(BucketFrame(i)+1) mod 8
  for j=0 to NextPlatform-1
    if Document.BucketForm.Sprite1.CollisionCheck (BucketIndex(i),
    Platform(j), -1) then
      BucketPlatform(i)=j
      Select Case PlatformType(j)
      Case VERT_PLAT
        BucketAction(i)=TURN_LEFT
        BucketX(i)=BucketX(i)-7
      Case HORZ_PLAT
        BucketY(i)=BucketY(i)-3
        BucketMoveY(i)=0
      Case RAMP
        BucketY(i)=BucketY(i)-4
        BucketMoveY(i)=0
      Case LADDER
        BucketAction(i)=CLIMB
        BucketFrame(i)=16
```

```
            BucketMoveY(i) = -3
         Case SPRING
         Case LIFT
            BucketY(i) = BucketY(i) - 5
            BucketX(i) = BucketX(i) - 4
         Case LILO
         End Select
      End if
   next
   if BucketX(i) > STAGE_RIGHT then
      BucketAction(i) = TURN_LEFT
      BucketFrame(i) = 7
   end if
end sub

sub ClimbLadder(i)
   BucketY(i) = BucketY(i) - 3
   BucketFrame(i) = BucketFrame(i) + 1
   if BucketFrame(i) > 23 then BucketFrame(i) = 16
   if (BucketY(i) + 30 + 16 * (i = 1)) < PlatformX(BucketPlatform(i))  ↵
then
      BucketAction(i) = WALK_RIGHT
      BucketFrame(i) = 0
   end if
end sub

sub walkleft(i)
   BucketX(i) = BucketX(i) - 4
   BucketFrame(i) = BucketFrame(i) + 1
   if BucketFrame(i) = 71 then BucketFrame(i) = 64
   if BucketX(i) < STAGE_LEFT then
   BucketAction(i) = TURN_RIGHT
      BucketFrame(i) = 71
   end if
end sub

sub turnright(i)
   BucketFrame(i) = BucketFrame(i) + 1
   if BucketFrame(i) = 79 then BucketAction(i) = WALK_RIGHT
      BucketFrame(i) = 0
        end if
end sub

sub turnleft(i)
   BucketFrame(i) = BucketFrame(i) + 1
```

```
    if BucketFrame(i) = 15 then
       BucketAction(i) = WALK_LEFT
       BucketFrame(i) = 64
    end if
 end sub
```

The body of the HTML file

The body of the file includes a reference to the Sprite ActiveX Control using the now familiar CLASSID (Class Id) number.

```
<CENTER> <H1>VBScript and Sprites</H1> </CENTER>
<BODY BGCOLOR=WHITE>
  <FORM NAME=''BucketForm''>
<CENTER>
    <OBJECT ID=''Sprite1'' WIDTH=445 HEIGHT=291
    CLASSID=''CLSID:9A438C83-0FC0-11D0-9227-444553540000''>
       <PARAM NAME=''_Version'' VALUE=''65536''>
       <PARAM NAME=''_ExtentX'' VALUE=''11783''>
       <PARAM NAME=''_ExtentY'' VALUE=''7691''>
       <PARAM NAME=''_StockProps'' VALUE=''64''>
    </OBJECT>
<BR> <BR>
    <INPUT LANGUAGE=''VBScript'' TYPE=BUTTON VALUE=''Rules''
ONCLICK=''Top.Debug.Location=&quot;Rules.htm&quot;''
    NAME=''btnRules''>
    <INPUT LANGUAGE=''VBScript'' TYPE=BUTTON VALUE=''Debug''
ONCLICK=''Top.Debug.Location=&quot;Debug.htm&quot;''
    NAME=-btnDebug->
</CENTER>
  </FORM>
</BODY>
</HTML>
```

The two buttons at the base of the frame are designed to switch the right frame between the debug window and rules.

Displaying on-screen rules

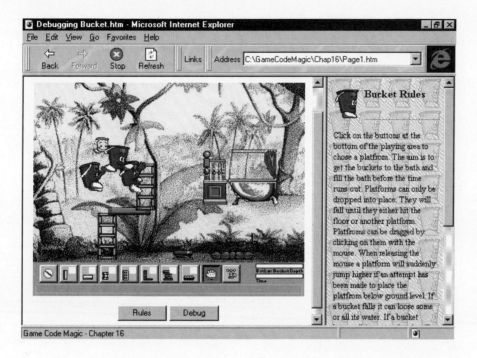

The way to play the game is displayed in the document "Rules.htm".

```
<HTML>
<HEAD>
<TITLE>Bucket Rules</TITLE>
<IMG SRC=''Bucket.gif'' ALIGN=Left>
</HEAD>
<BODY BGCOLOR=''#33bbff'' BACKGROUND=''BgTile.gif''>
<H2>Bucket Rules</H2>
<HR>
```
Click on the buttons at the bottom of the playing area to choose a
platform. The aim is to get the buckets to the bath and fill the bath
before the time runs out. Platforms can only be dropped into place.
They will fall until they either hit the floor or another platform.
Platforms can be dragged by clicking on them with the mouse. When
releasing the mouse a platform will suddenly jump higher if an
attempt has been made to place the platform below ground level. If
a bucket falls it can lose some or all its water.

If a bucket loses all its water then it will be removed from the play screen. Clicking on a bucket allows you to check the water level for that bucket. The two gauges at the bottom right of the play area are for you to check the level of the bath and the buckets. In later levels you will find that spilling any water will spoil your chances of filling the bath. Have Fun!

```
<HR>
</BODY>
</HTML>
```

Select 'Bucket.htm' to see a full listing of this file. Most of the details in the document are used in the techniques that we have considered throughout this book.

QUIZ

1. How can you find the path to the current page?
Answer: Use location.pathname. The location object is a member of the globally accessed window object.

2. When reporting an error, does the indicated line number start from the beginning of the document?
Answer: No it is the number of lines from the SCRIPT tag, including < !–. If the HTML document contains multiple SCRIPT tags then the number will only indicate the line numbers from the SCRIPT tag in the offending section.

Summary

The Scripting Object Model exposes many useful properties, methods and events for the web page programmer. In this chapter we looked at some tricks you can use. Debugging a VBScript document can be trying on the patience. In this chapter we looked at how you can use tricks to help out.

- Using a debug HTML file displayed in a frame of a multi-frame window.
- Isolating the problem with the line number tool.
- Using commenting out to pinpoint the problem.

As you get more confident with VBScript you will find that the limitations are not nearly the problem they at first seemed.

CHAPTER 17

Palettes – The mystery of the Windows Palette Manager

Nearly all the examples in this book require you to be using Windows with your display set to 256 colours. This is a very standard set-up, but one that is slowly being superseded by high-colour resolutions available with high-performance graphics cards. This chapter explains how Windows can present, on the same screen, several applications that require a different set of colours.

What is a palette?

Every colour that you see on your computer screen when it is set to 256 colours, or better, is defined by three byte-size numbers. As you know, a byte can store integer values from 0 to 255. The three different numbers are used to provide the level for the red, green and blue values of the colour. The following is a list of the first and last colours of a standard Windows palette:

Colour Index	Red	Green	Blue	
0	0	0	0	Black
1	128	0	0	Dark Red
2	0	128	0	Dark Green
3	128	128	0	Brown
4	0	0	128	Dark Blue
. . .				
254	255	255	0	Yellow
255	255	255	255	White

You first met this in Chapter 3. You may recall that Windows stores the three byte-colour values in a 32-bit Long integer. The highest level byte contains further information in the form of a flag. Usually this flag is set to zero, but this will be discussed later.

Example Ex17a

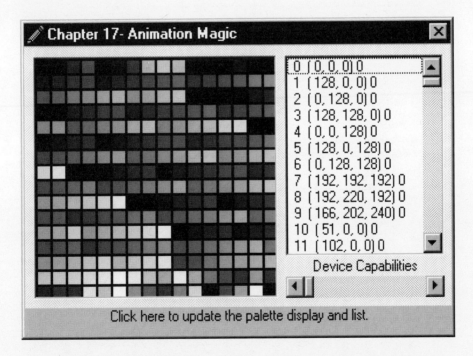

Now run the example program 'Ex17a.exe'. You will also require a running paint program and a few bitmaps with different palettes. I have included three small pictures with different palettes on the CD. They are 'Pal1.bmp', 'Pal2.bmp' and 'Pal3.bmp'. Run the paint program (I use Paint Shop Pro) and load all these bitmaps. As you switch from one picture to another, Paint Shop Pro changes the palette that is being used. You will see the palette change in the example program. If you want to retain this palette change then click in the status bar area where it says 'Click here...'. Notice how the pictures displayed in the Paint Shop Pro window always look at their best when they are the active picture with the highlighted caption bar.

Palette index versus RGB colour value

A Windows colour is always the 32-bit Long that we looked at earlier, but the information provided by a bitmap and sent to the display card when the display is set to 256 colours is just a single byte. How is this achieved? The answer is in the form of a look-up table. The information is provided by index values. Below is the colour table for a very simple 16 x 16 pixel bitmap:

Colour Index	Red	Green	Blue	
0	0	0	0	Black
1	128	0	0	Dark Red
2	0	128	0	Dark Green
3	128	128	0	Brown

The actual data for the bitmap is shown in Table 17.1

Table 17.1 16 × 16 bitmap

	0	1	2	3	4	5	6	7	8	9	A	B	C	D	E	F
0	0	0	0	0	0	0	0	0	0	0	0	0	0	0	0	0
1	0	2	2	2	2	2	2	1	2	2	2	2	2	2	2	0
2	0	2	2	2	2	2	1	2	1	2	2	2	2	2	2	0
3	0	2	2	2	2	1	2	2	2	1	2	2	2	2	2	0
4	0	2	2	2	1	2	2	2	2	2	1	2	2	2	2	0
5	0	2	2	1	2	2	2	2	2	2	2	1	2	2	2	0
6	0	2	1	2	2	2	3	3	3	2	2	2	1	2	2	0
7	0	1	2	2	2	2	3	3	3	2	2	2	2	1	2	0
8	0	2	1	2	2	2	3	3	3	2	2	2	1	2	2	0
9	0	2	2	1	2	2	2	2	2	2	2	1	2	2	2	0
A	0	2	2	2	1	2	2	2	2	2	1	2	2	2	2	0
B	0	2	2	2	2	1	2	2	2	1	2	2	2	2	2	0
C	0	2	2	2	2	2	1	2	1	2	2	2	2	2	2	0
D	0	2	2	2	2	2	2	1	2	2	2	2	2	2	2	0
E	0	2	2	2	2	2	2	2	2	2	2	2	2	2	2	0

```
F   0  0  0  0  0  0  0  0  0  0  0  0  0  0  0  0  0
```

It forms a red diamond on a green background with a black border. The centre of the picture is brown. Notice that the colours are referred to not as the full RGB value but by a reference to the index where the actual colour information is stored.

Windows device contexts

A Visual Basic application can have a palette attached to it; indeed each picture box can have its own palette. In Windows programming terminology each picture box is a device and each device is a complex data structure that Windows uses to store information about the Fonts, LineStyle, FillColor and other details for that control, or device. Windows thinks of plotters and printers as devices just as it thinks of the display, and realising the truly generic nature of the techniques can help to explain the complexity involved in the coding. This level of complexity is necessary to achieve the independence from hardware that is the goal of Windows. However, as a programmer you will usually only be scratching the surface of what is in fact available. In order to provide this degree of flexibility the Windows API calls can appear rather confusing.

The particular aspect of a device that we are considering in this chapter is the palette. Windows has two types of palettes: a logical palette such that if the device was the only one on the screen then that would be the palette available, and the system palette.

A logical palette

A Windows logical palette is declared in Visual Basic in the following manner:

```
Private Type PALETTEENTRY
  peRed As Byte
  peGreen As Byte
  peBlue As Byte
  peFlags As Byte
End Type

Private Type LOGPALETTE
  palVersion As Integer
  palNumEntries As Integer
```

```
palPalEntry(256) As PALETTEENTRY
End Type
```

Firstly, the PALETTEENTRY datatype is declared, then the
LOGPALETTE. Essentially the LOGPALETTE is simply an array of
PALETTEENTRY structures, with the addition of a version value and
the number of colours in the palette.

NOTE

**In the C version of this structure LOGPALETTE is
declared as an array of just one PALETTEENTRY.
This is because it is easy to reallocate memory and
adjust the size of the array at run time. While this
could be done with Visual Basic and some API calls I
thought it would just add to what is quite a difficult
chapter anyway, so I simply declared the
LOGPALETTE to have 256 PALETTEENTRY
structures.**

As a device becomes the main focus, the application is often written to
grab the system palette. You may expect that we could put all the
values in the logical palette into the system palette but unfortunately
this is not the case. Another application may have set some colours in
the system palette, to be reserved and unchangeable. Also it is very
much to be advised that the first and last ten colours of the palette
remain untouched. These colours, referred to as static colours, are the
colours that all applications use to display the main interface, icons
and toolbar buttons. If an application changes the palette values for
these, then the display can often become unusable.

NOTE

**Windows always keeps black and white in the palette.
Black is entry 0 and white is entry 255.**

You may have assumed that when an application wants the system
palette it simply updates all the values in the system palette to the
values in the logical palette; then index 100 of the system palette
becomes index 100 of the logical palette. This, however, is not what
happens. Firstly, there is the problem of reserved and static colours,
for which the process involves a translation layer. Each colour in the

logical palette is placed in the system palette at the first available slot, which usually means starting at slot 11. If there are not enough available slots in the system palette for all the entries in the logical palette then those colours will not be available. It is for this reason that palette ordering should have the most important colours at lower indices. If an important colour is in slot 220 then it is possible that Windows will be unable to make this colour available, particularly if another application has reserved some colours.

I can almost hear you ask 'how does this help when displaying 256 colour pictures?', and that is a good question. If you have spotted that the palette for your picture and the system palette are rarely the same then you are already beginning to understand Windows Palette Manager. Now you have a picture stored in memory that has a certain palette and a system palette that is different. To display the picture using the indices that describe the picture will result in garbage. The picture may think index 30 is a light green while the system palette has dark blue in slot 30. A translation layer is required to look at the colour the picture has as slot 30 and find the closest version of this colour in the system palette. There is a Windows API function to do just that.

```
Declare Function GetNearestPaletteIndex Lib ''gdi32'' Alias
''GetNearestPaletteIndex'' (ByVal hPalette As Long, ByVal crColor
As Long) As Long
```

Here the system palette is compared with the colour required and the best index is returned. The 'best' index is determined as the lowest value of

```
Square Root ((LogRed−SysRed)^2 + (LogGreen−SysGreen)^2 + (LogBlue−
SysBlue)^2)
```

Where 'Log...' refers to colours in the logical palette and 'Sys...' refers to colours in the system palette. If there is an exact value then this value will be zero. This algorithm finds the shortest *distance* between two points in 3D space. RGB colour values can be thought of as points in 3D space and the distance between two points defines the difference in colour.

If we consider (100, 20, 200) and (110, 18, 197), the difference is:

$$\sqrt{(100 - 110)^2 + (20 - 18)^2 + (200 - 197)^2} \simeq 10.63$$

If you guessed that this translation process is slow and unnecessary for the fast animation that we have used in this book, then you would be entirely correct. There is a work-around; that is, the logical and system palettes are identical. If this is the case then bitmaps can be pushed around without any translation at all. But how can we take a picture and make all the pixel values entries in the system palette? Well, the truth is that that is exactly what has been happening in the examples in this book. When the sprite control, for example, is initially loaded with a background, a logical palette is created from the colour values that are stored as part of a 'bmp' picture file. An attempt is then made to copy the logical palette into the system palette. Windows has functions called 'SelectPalette' and 'RealizePalette' to do just this. Then the entries that are now in the system palette are used to remap all the pixel values for the picture in memory. Finally the logical palette for the sprite control is made to be an exact copy of the system palette. Now, no conversion is necessary when a pixel is mapped from a hidden version of the picture in memory to the screen version of the picture. But if another application changes the palette, then the sprite control will display garbage. To fix this problem the sprite control needs to respond to a palette message – one of the many messages that Windows provides.

NOTE

A more robust version of the sprite control is available. Version 1.5 looks after the display as other applications make changes. It responds to the paint messages that are sent as one window overlaps the control. It also accommodates for displays of 16- and 24-bit colour. Bitmaps in the compressed Gif format can be loaded, making Internet downloads much faster. If you are interested in using the control in an application that you intend to distribute, then I recommend using this fully featured version. Details of availability are on the CD.

Enough of the theory, lets' look at how the simple example works.

The declarations

This example uses lots of Windows API calls. With Visual Basic you can use the API calls in much the same way that a C programmer would.

```
'Windows
API Types
Private Type PALETTEENTRY
  peRed As Byte
  peGreen As Byte
  peBlue As Byte
  peFlags As Byte
End Type

Private Type LOGPALETTE
  palVersion As Integer
  palNumEntries As Integer
  palPalEntry(256) As PALETTEENTRY
End Type

Private Type COLORREF
  red As Byte
  green As Byte
  blue As Byte
  flags As Byte
End Type

'Windows API constants
Const PC_EXPLICIT = &H2
Const PC_NOCOLLAPSE = &H4
Const PC_RESERVED = &H1
Const RASTERCAPS = 38
Const RC_PALETTE = &H100
Const SYSPAL_NOSTATIC = 2
Const SYSPAL_STATIC = 1

Const HORZSIZE = 4
Const VERTSIZE = 6
Const HORZRES = 8
Const VERTRES = 10
Const BITSPIXEL = 12
Const PLANES = 14
Const NUMBRUSHES = 16
Const NUMPENS = 18
Const NUMMARKERS = 20
Const NUMFONTS = 22
Const NUMCOLORS = 24
Const PDEVICESIZE = 26
Const ASPECTX = 40
Const ASPECTY = 42
```

```
Const ASPECTXY = 44
Const LOGPIXELSX = 88
Const LOGPIXELSY = 90
Const SIZEPALETTE = 104
Const NUMRESERVED = 106
Const COLORRES = 108


'Windows API declarations
Private Declare Function CreateSolidBrush Lib ''gdi32'' (ByVal
crColor As Long) As Long
Private Declare Function SelectObject Lib ''gdi32'' (ByVal hdc As
Long, ByVal hObject As Long) As Long
Private Declare Function Rectangle Lib ''gdi32'' (ByVal hdc As
Long, ByVal X1 As Long, ByVal Y1 As Long, _
   ByVal X2 As Long, ByVal Y2 As Long) As Long
Private Declare Function CreatePalette Lib ''gdi32'' _
      (lpLogPalette As LOGPALETTE) As Long
Private Declare Function RealizePalette Lib ''gdi32'' _
      (ByVal hdc As Long) As Long
Private Declare Function SelectPalette Lib ''gdi32'' _
      (ByVal hdc As Long, ByVal hPalette As Long, _
      ByVal bForceBackground As Long) As Long
Private Declare Function DeleteObject Lib ''gdi32'' _
      (ByVal hObject As Long) As Long
Private Declare Function GetDeviceCaps Lib ''gdi32'' _
      (ByVal hdc As Long, ByVal nIndex As Long) As Long
Private Declare Function SetSystemPaletteUse Lib ''gdi32'' _
      (ByVal hdc As Long, ByVal wUsage As Long) As Long
Private Declare Function GetSystemPaletteEntries Lib ''gdi32'' _
      (ByVal hdc As Long, ByVal wStartIndex As Long, _
      ByVal wNumEntries As Long, _
      lpPaletteEntries As PALETTEENTRY) As Long
Private Declare Function GetPixel Lib ''gdi32'' _
      (ByVal hdc As Long, ByVal X As Long, ByVal Y As Long) As COLORREF

Dim logPal As LOGPALETTE
Dim hPal As Long, hSysPal As Long
Dim sysPal As LOGPALETTE
Dim blnShowColour As Boolean
Dim blnShowCaps As Boolean
Dim strDeviceCaps(20) As String
Dim intDeviceCaps(20) As Integer
```

Finding details about a device

The Windows API call 'GetDeviceCaps' is used to receive many details about a device. The example program lets you use all these via the scroll bar and the status bar at the bottom of the screen. To enable this prompt to be updated at runtime two arrays are used. These two arrays, 'strDeviceCaps' and 'intDeviceCaps' are initialised in the Form_Load event.

```
Private Sub Form_Load()
  Dim i As Integer

'This array is used by the Device Capabilities scroll bar
  strDeviceCaps(0) = ''Width in millimetres''
  strDeviceCaps(1) = ''Height in millimetres''
  strDeviceCaps(2) = ''Width in pixels''
  strDeviceCaps(3) = ''Height in raster lines''
  strDeviceCaps(4) = ''Colour bits per pixel''
  strDeviceCaps(5) = ''Number of colour planes''
  strDeviceCaps(6) = ''Number of device brushes''
  strDeviceCaps(7) = ''Number of device pens''
  strDeviceCaps(8) = ''Number of device markers''
  strDeviceCaps(9) = ''Number of device fonts''
  strDeviceCaps(10) = ''Number of device colours''
  strDeviceCaps(11) = ''Size of device structure''
  strDeviceCaps(12) = ''Relative width of pixel''
  strDeviceCaps(13) = ''Relative height of pixel''
  strDeviceCaps(14) = ''Relative diagonal of pixels''
  strDeviceCaps(15) = ''Horizontal dots per inch''
  strDeviceCaps(16) = ''Vertical dots per inch''
  strDeviceCaps(17) = ''Number of palette entries''
  strDeviceCaps(18) = ''Reserved palette entries''
  strDeviceCaps(19) = ''Actual colour resolution''

'This array is used to set the value required by the GetDeviceCaps
function
  intDeviceCaps(0) = HORZSIZE
  intDeviceCaps(1) = VERTSIZE
  intDeviceCaps(2) = HORZRES
  intDeviceCaps(3) = VERTRES
  intDeviceCaps(4) = BITSPIXEL
  intDeviceCaps(5) = PLANES
  intDeviceCaps(6) = NUMBRUSHES
  intDeviceCaps(7) = NUMPENS
```

```
intDeviceCaps(8) = NUMMARKERS
intDeviceCaps(9) = NUMFONTS
intDeviceCaps(10) = NUMCOLORS
intDeviceCaps(11) = PDEVICESIZE
intDeviceCaps(12) = ASPECTX
intDeviceCaps(13) = ASPECTY
intDeviceCaps(14) = ASPECTXY
intDeviceCaps(15) = LOGPIXELSX
intDeviceCaps(16) = LOGPIXELSY
intDeviceCaps(17) = SIZEPALETTE
intDeviceCaps(18) = NUMRESERVED
intDeviceCaps(19) = COLORRES

'Initialising the form scope variable logPal
  logPal.palVersion = &H300
  logPal.palNumEntries = 256
  For i = 0 To 255
    logPal.palPalEntry(i).peRed = i
    logPal.palPalEntry(i).peGreen = 0
    logPal.palPalEntry(i).peBlue = 0
    logPal.palPalEntry(i).peFlags = PC_EXPLICIT
  Next

'Initialising the form scope variable sysPal
  GetSystemPaletteEntries hdc, 0, 256, sysPal.palPalEntry(0)5

  picPalette.ZOrder 0
  picPalette.AutoRedraw = True

'A handle to a palette is returned by CreatePalette
  hPal = CreatePalette(logPal)
'This handle is used to set the palette for the picPalette control
  SelectPalette picPalette.hdc, hPal, False
  RealizePalette picPalette.hdc
'The DrawSystemPalette is defined in this module
  DrawSystemPalette
End Sub
```

The important feature of the initialisation routine is the creation of the two logical palettes. One palette is used to keep information about the system palette. It is regularly updated by a Timer event. Since a Visual Basic application does not have an event generated by a change of palette this simple work-around keeps a version of the system palette, stored in the form scope variable sysPal. Without doing this it would not be possible to receive the palettes of another application since Visual Basic would restore the applications palette before any other event takes place. So when a call to find the contents of the system palette occurs, it would always find the same palette.

Displaying the system palette

The following is the sub-routine that displays the system palette:

```
Sub DrawSystemPalette()
    Dim brBrush As Long, brOldBrush As Long
    Dim intIncX As Integer, intIncY As Integer

'Replace the listing of the contents of the system palette
    lstPalette.Clear
    For i = 0 To 255
        strItem = Str(i) + ''('' + Str(sysPal.palPalEntry(i).peRed)
+ '','' + -
            Str(sysPal.palPalEntry(i).peGreen) + '','' + _
            Str(sysPal.palPalEntry(i).peBlue) + '')'' +
            Str(sysPal.palPalEntry(i).peFlags)
        lstPalette.AddItem strItem
    Next

    sysPal.palVersion = &H300
    sysPal.palNumEntries = 256
'Disable and enable the timer to reset its clock
    tmrStatus.Enabled = False
    tmrStatus.Enabled = True
    lblStatus.Caption = ''Entries in list updated.''

    picPalette.Cls
    picPalette.ScaleMode = 3
'Create a palette from the entries in the sysPal variable
    hSysPal = CreatePalette(sysPal)
'Make this palette the logical palette for the form
    SelectPalette hdc, hSysPal, False
    RealizePalette hdc

    intIncX = picPalette.ScaleWidth / 16
    intIncY = picPalette.ScaleHeight / 16
```

```
     i = 0
   For intRow = 0 To 15
     For intCol = 0 To 15
'Create a brush from the index value
       brBrush = CreateSolidBrush((i Or &H1000000))
'Select this brush into the picPalette control
       brOldBrush = SelectObject(picPalette.hdc, brBrush)
'Use the API function to draw a filled rectangle
       Rectangle picPalette.hdc, intCol * intIncX, intRow * intIncY,
(intCol + 1) * intIncX, (intRow + 1) * intIncY
       i = i + 1
'Restore the old brush
       SelectObject picPalette.hdc, brOldBrush
'Delete the new brush
       DeleteObject brBrush
     Next
   Next
 End Sub
```

Notice that a new handle to a palette is created from the contents of the sysPal variable. The palette entries are updated approximately every second as a result of the timer event.

The Timer event

The Timer event uses two Boolean variables to decide on the correct operation. If 'blnShowCaps' is True then the Device Capabilities scroll bar has just been clicked. The static variable 'intCount' is reset to zero and the test Boolean variable is set to False. The procedure is terminated.

The other Boolean variable is set when the mouse is clicked over the 'picPalette' control. If neither variable is set and the static variable 'intCount' is greater than 5 then the contents of the status bar is set to the 'Click here ...' message. Status bars need to be reset after being set by an event, otherwise their contents will be out of sync with events in the application. A Timer event is useful for this resetting.

```
Private Sub tmrStatus_Timer()
  Static intCount As Integer
```

```
    If blnShowCaps Then
        intCount = 0
        blnShowCaps = False
        Exit Sub
    End If
    intCount = intCount + 1
    If intCount > 5 And Not blnShowColour Then
        lblStatus.Caption = ''Click here to update the palette display
and list.''
        intCount = 0
    End If
    GetSystemPaletteEntries hdc, 0, 256, sysPal.palPalEntry(0)
End Sub
```

How the device capabilities scroll bar works

The scroll bar is very simple in operation. It uses the contents of the two arrays that were set during the Form_Load event. The Windows API function 'GetDeviceCaps' takes two parameters, a device context which Visual Basic provides via the hdc property of many controls. The other parameter is a Long value which the function uses to decide which capability to return. This parameter uses the value stored in the array 'intDeviceCaps'. When displaying the value returned by this function the value stored in the 'strDeviceCaps' array is used to inform the user of the meaning of this value.

```
    Private Sub hsrDeviceCaps_Change()
        blnShowCaps = True
        lblStatus.Caption = strDeviceCaps(hsrdevicecaps.Value) + Str(_
            GetDeviceCaps(hdc, intDeviceCaps(hsrdevicecaps.Value)))
    End Sub
```

Clicking on the picPalette control

I wanted you to be able to click on the palette display and receive information about the cell that you clicked. To do this I used the MouseDown, MouseMove and MouseUp events for the picPalette control. Firstly, the mouse x and y values are converted into the index value by simple arithmetic. The width of the control is given by the ScaleWidth. An integer value is set to the ScaleWidth divided by 16 since the palette grid is 16 x 16. Dereferencing the index involves dividing the x value by this 'intDeltaX' value and then adding to this the similar value for y multiplied by 16. As the grid moves down the box each row is 16 further in the index to the previous. By multiplying the y value by 16 this increase is catered for. The procedure also uses another very useful Windows API function, 'GetPixel'. This returns the colour value of a screen pixel, not the index value. By returning this 32-bit value in a COLORREF structure it is easy to dereference the individual components of the Long value.

```
Private Sub picPalette_MouseDown(Button As Integer, Shift As
Integer, X As Single, Y As Single)
  Dim Colour As COLORREF, intColorIndex As Integer
  Dim intDeltaX As Integer, intDeltaY As Integer

  intDeltaX = picPalette.ScaleWidth / 16
  intDeltaY = picPalette.ScaleHeight / 16

  Colour = GetPixel(picPalette.hdc, X, Y)
  intColorIndex = Int(X / intDeltaX) + 16 * Int(Y / intDeltaY)
  lblStatus.Caption = ''Mouse Position: ('' + Str(X) + '','' +
Str(Y) + '')'' + _
    '' Indexcolour:'' + Str(intColorIndex) + '' Colour: ('' +
_
    Str(Colour.red) + '','' + Str(Colour.green) + '','' + _
    Str(Colour.blue) + '')''

  blnShowColour = True
End Sub

Private Sub picPalette_MouseMove(Button As Integer, Shift As
Integer, X As Single, Y As Single)
  Dim Colour As COLORREF, intColorIndex As Integer
  Dim intDeltaX As Integer, intDeltaY As Integer

  intDeltaX = picPalette.ScaleWidth / 16
  intDeltaY = picPalette.ScaleHeight / 16

  If blnShowColour Then
    Colour = GetPixel(picPalette.hdc, X, Y)
    intColorIndex = Int(X / intDeltaX) + 16 * Int(Y / intDeltaY)
    lblStatus.Caption = ''Mouse Position: ('' + Str(X) + '','' 
+ Str(Y) + '')'' + _
      '' Indexcolour:'' + Str(intColorIndex) + '' Colour: ('' +
_
```

```
        Str(Colour.red) + '','' + Str(Colour.green) + '','' + _
        Str(Colour.blue) + '')''
    End If
End Sub

Private Sub picPalette_MouseUp(Button As Integer, Shift As Integer,
X As Single, Y As Single)
    blnShowColour = False
    lblStatus.Caption = '' ''
End Sub
```

Review

If Windows Palette Manager seems confusing then this is only to be expected. At this stage of your program learning curve you are ready to start to look at C++. With C++ you can do anything that is possible on a computer but much of the convenience of Visual Basic is lost. Providing an environment where 256 colours can be used to optimum effect by several applications is a great challenge, and the Windows implementation is one answer. Some of the ways that manipulation is effected may not be the same as the method you would choose to implement the same functionality. However, it is Windows that we are working with. As more users move to higher colour resolutions so the palletised displays will prove less of a problem. This change will be slow for the developer supplying business software. A large number of business customers have yet to move to 32-bit Windows. Nevertheless, over time True Colour will dominate, but until then you must learn to work with Palette Manager.

QUIZ

1. If you wish to guarantee that an area of colour is painted in a flat colour with no dithering, how can this be achieved?
Answer: Instead of using an RGB value use a palette index value using the following syntax (index Or &H1000000). Alternatively, a RGB value can be OR-ed with &H2000000 to guarantee that the nearest palette index will be used rather than dithering.

2. When an application uses its logical palette to set the system palette does it always get the palette requested?

Answer: No, hardly ever. The system static colours and the reserved colours of other applications restrict this.

3. When you use CreateSolidBrush to create a fill colour for a device context, what further two calls must be made?

Answer: The new GDI object must be selected into the device using SelectObject. After use the GDI object must be destroyed. GDI memory is limited and failing to delete the objects you create is a regular reason for memory problems.

4. If I wish to know the pixel resolution and colour depth of the display, how do I discover this information?

Answer: Call 'GetDeviceCaps' three times, with a handle to the device context and the values of the constants HORZRES, VERTRES, NUMCOLORS in turn.

Summary

In this chapter you learnt about Windows Palette Manager. The details of several Windows API calls were also included:

- 'GetSystemPaletteEntries' to find out about the current system palette.
- 'CreatePalette' to convert a logical palette into a handle to an actual palette.
- 'SelectPalette' to set the palette for a device context.
- 'RealizePalette' to ensure that the changed palette is reflected by the display.
- 'CreateSolidBrush' to create a solid colour for filling areas.
- 'SelectObject' to set parameters in a device context.
- 'DeleteObject' to restore the memory set aside when a GDI object is created.

CHAPTER 18

Introducing 3D Programming – Now you can move in and out

As computer hardware improves, the provision of real time 3D worlds becomes a reality for developers. You have seen earlier in this book how to use clever tricks to speed up the display, but those tricks despite being very ingenious restrict the 3D objects that you can display. In this chapter we look at the principles of 3D graphics and show how to implement it using just Visual Basic and three Windows API calls. Here we illustrate the techniques. For high-speed implementation C++ is recommended and the reader is pointed at Microsoft's DirectX SDK – a set of C libraries that make high-speed graphics easier to perform using the Windows platform and support additional hardware that the user may have. The other alternative is to use OpenGL libraries which share the same benefits of hardware support.

Such considerations are best left for another book; here we lay the foundations to make further study easier.

Describing a polygon

Before we launch into how to describe a 3D object, we will look at how to describe and move a 2D object. To allow full manipulation we need to be able to scale, translate and rotate the polygon.

First we need a way of describing the polygon that is suitable for a computer. Here is an example text file for storing data about a polygon, in this case a red square with sides of 200 pixels, drawn to the screen with centre at (340, 240) and rotation of 90 degrees.

```
4            'Number of vertices
1, 1         'First vertex
−1, 1        'Next vertex
−1, −1       'Next vertex
1, −1        'Next vertex
100          'Scaling factor
320, 240     'Position
90           'Rotation
255, 0, 0    'RGB Colour
```

You can see from the comments what each part of the file is used for.

NOTE

I like to store data in text files as it is easy to check and edit. It is for this reason that the code in this chapter will use text files for data storage. We could use binary files but viewing and editing them would then require a dedicated editor. By using a text file you can view and edit the files using Notepad.

Describing a simple polygon is quite complex. Imagine how much more complex is the data to describe a 3D world. We start simply in order that the more complex structures required in 3D graphics are easier to understand.

A routine to load the polygon

3D graphics is very suited to object-orientated programming. So in the examples in this chapter we are going to use Classes. Let us consider the polygon class. We will call it clsPolygon.

NOTE

If you were a C++ programmer then you would probably call it CPolygon. I prefer to distinguish Visual Basic code from C++, hence the choice to call it clsPolygon.

```
Public Sub Load(intFileNum As Integer)
   Dim strTemp As String, lngPos As Long, i As Integer, intIndex
As Integer
   Dim j As Integer

   Line Input #intFileNum, strTemp
   c_NumVertices = Val(strTemp)

   If c_NumVertices = 0 Then
     MsgBox ''No vertices or faces''
     Exit Sub
   End If

   ReDim c_Vertex(c_NumVertices)
   ReDim c_Screen(c_NumVertices)

   Do
     Line Input #intFileNum, strTemp
     strTemp = LCase(strTemp)
   Loop While (InStr(strTemp, ''vertices'') = 0)

   For i = 0 To c_NumVertices - 1
     Line Input #intFileNum, strTemp
     c_Vertex(i).x = Val(strTemp)
     lngPos = InStr(strTemp, '','')
     c_Vertex(i).y = Val(Right(strTemp, Len(strTemp) -
lngPos))
   Next
```

```
Do
   Line Input #intFileNum, strTemp
strTemp = LCase(strTemp)
  Loop While (InStr(strTemp, ''data'') = 0)

   Line Input #intFileNum, strTemp
   c_Scale = Val(strTemp)

   Line Input #intFileNum, strTemp
   c_Position.x = Val(strTemp)
   lngPos = InStr(strTemp, '','')
   c_Position.y = Val(Right(strTemp, Len(strTemp) − lngPos))

   Line Input #intFilcNum, strTemp
   c_Rotation = Val(strTemp)

   Line Input #intFileNum, strTemp
     c_Colour.Red = Val(strTemp)
     lngPos = InStr(strTemp, '','')
     c_Colour.Green = Val(Right(strTemp, Len(strTemp) − lngPos))
     lngPos = InStr(strTemp, '','')
     c_Colour.Blue = Val(Right(strTemp, Len(strTemp) − lngPos))

   Do
      Line Input #intFileNum, strTemp
strTemp = LCase(strTemp)
   Loop While (InStr(strTemp, ''end'') = 0)

   Transform
   Draw
End Sub
```

As you can see this code makes use of the class member variables that are declared in the (General) – (declarations) section. These are: 'c_NumVertices,' an integer value storing the number of vertices in the polygon; and 'c_Vertex()', an undimensioned array of the user datatype Point.

```
Private Type Point
   x As Single
   y As Single
End Type
```

'c_Screen(),' an undimensioned array of user datatype Point.
'c_Scale,' an Integer value used to size the polygon

'c_Position,' a variable of user datatype Point.
'c_Rotation,' an integer value storing the amount the polygon is
rotated anti-clockwise in degrees
'c_Colour,' a user datatype of style ColourRef.

```
Private Type ColourRef
   Red as Byte
   Green as Byte
   Blue as Byte
   mode as Byte
End Type
```

So you can see that a large part of the development of 3D graphics
programs involves designing good data structures and providing useful
functions to manipulate that data.

Displaying the polygon

Fortunately Windows provides some useful functions for displaying
coloured polygons. You will need to declare these functions in the
declarations section.

```
Private Declare Function CreatePolygonRgn Lib ''gdi32'' (lpPoint
As POINTAPI, _
    ByVal nCount As Long, ByVal nPolyFillMode As Long) As Long
Private Declare Function CreateSolidBrush Lib ''gdi32'' _
    (ByVal crColor As Long) As Long
Private Declare Function DeleteObject Lib ''gdi32'' (ByVal hObject
As Long) As Long
Private Declare Function FillRgn Lib ''gdi32'' (ByVal hdc As Long,
_
    ByVal hRgn As Long, ByVal hBrush As Long) As Long

Private Type POINTAPI
    x As Long
    y As Long
End Type

Const WINDING = 2
```

Using these functions provides you with a leap into full-scale Windows
programming. You learnt a good deal in the last chapter about
Windows palettes and about the GDI (Graphics Device Interface).
These functions are part of the many GDI functions that you can use

as a Visual Basic programmer. The following shows a section of code that illustrates their use.

```
Dim pt(c_NumVertices) as POINTAPI
Dim Rgn As Long, Brush As Long

For i =0 To c_NumVertices-1
  pt(i) =c_Screen(i).x
  pt(i) =c_Screen(i).y
Next
'Create region from point array
  Rgn = CreatePolygonRgn(pt(0), c_NumVertices, WINDING)
  Brush = CreateSolidBrush(RGB(c_Colour.Red, c_Colour.Green,
c_Colour.Blue))
  'Paint region with brush
  FillRgn PolygonForm.hdc, Rgn, Brush
  'Tidy up GDI objects
  DeleteObject (Rgn)
  DeleteObject (Brush)
```

Here we take the points in the screen array and convert them to POINTAPI types, storing them one at a time into the new array. Then we create a region using these points. Windows needs the first point only and the number of points.

NOTE

When passing variables to other functions Visual Basic usually passes the address of the variable; that is, instead of simply the number stored in pt(0) being passed it is the location in memory that is passed. Then the called function can retrieve all the point data that follows. This way of passing parameters is the default for visual Basic and is called *passing by reference*. The alternative passing by value can be achieved by putting ByVal in front of the parameter when the function is declared.

We must then create a brush. You may feel that a simple function that filled the region would be available, but in order to provide device independence you need to go through a few hoops to use the Windows GDI calls. One hoop is the use of brushes as data structures that describe how to paint a region. In this extract we use a solid brush.

This takes only one parameter: a colour reference. To Windows a colour reference is a 32-bit number that is split into 4 parts describing the RGB values and a final part that tells Windows how to use the colour on a palletised display.

You can now draw the polygon. I'm afraid if you copied the code and created clsPolygon and a PolygonForm then the code would not work since it uses the contents of the c_Screen array which, at the moment, is full of zeros.

Scaling

Scaling is easy, just take each point and multiply the x and y values by c_Scale.

Translating

Again translating is easy. Just add the current position and c_Position for the x and y parameters.

Rotating

This is much more complicated and needs trigonometry. Rotating any point about the origin (the point with co-ordinates (0,0)) you use sin and cos. Take, for example, the point (1, 1). We want to rotate this by 45 degrees anti-clockwise about the origin. This should put the new point on the y axis with $x = 0$.

The formula for the rotation is

$$NewX = OldX * Cos(angle) - OldY * Sin(angle)$$
$$NewY = OldX * Sin(angle) + OldY * Cos(angle)$$

You can use this formula to rotate any point about the origin.

So now you can write a program to load and display polygons saved as a text file description. The polygon can be rotated, scaled and translated. This is an exercise for you as there is no code on the CD. The example included on the CD is much more elaborate.

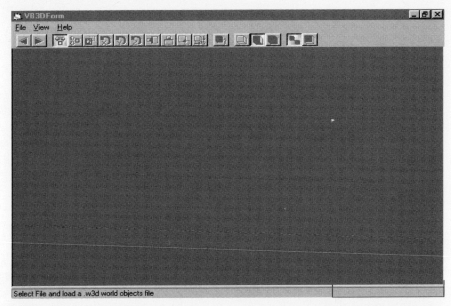

Run 'VB3D.exe' and the status bar prompts you to load a 3D world.
There are some simple examples on the CD; try 'Rhino.w3d'. The
arrow buttons allow you to move, rotate and scale the model. If you
linger over a button then you will get a Tool Tip advising of the
button's purpose. There are three draw modes – wireframe, solid and
shaded – and we will look at how the transformations and draw
methods are implemented.

How we store the data for a 3D world

The world data files are very similar to the polygon data files that we
considered earlier. Below is a simple file that includes two simple
cubes.

```
[Data file]
[VB3D-Number Objects on next line]
2

[Object]
cube1
8
6
[Vertices]
1,1,-1
-1,1,-1
```

```
-1,1,1
1,1,1
1,-1,-1
1,-1, 1
-1,-1,1
-1,-1,-1
[Faces]
0,1,2,3,0,255,0,0
4,7,1,0,4,0,255,0
1,7,6,2,1,0,0,255
4,0,3,5,4,255,255,0
3,2,6,5,3,255,0,255
5,6,7,4,5,0,255,255
[Data]
100,100,100
250,150,1000
100,100,100
[End]

[Object]
cube2 'Object name
8 'Number of vertices
6 'Number of faces
[Vertices]
1,1,-1 'First Vertex
-1,1,-1'Next vertex
-1,1,1
1,1,1
1,-1,-1
1,-1, 1
-1,-1,1
-1,-1,-1
[Faces]
0,1,2,3,0,255,0,0   'First face
4,7,1,0,4,0,255,0   'Next face
1,7,6,2,1,0,0,255
4,0,3,5,4,255,255,0
3,2,6,5,3,255,0,255
5,6,7,4,5,0,255,255
[Data]
200,100,100     'Rotation
150,350,1000    'Position
50,50,50        'Scale
[End]
[End data file]
```

When dealing with a 3D object we need to store information about the vertices that describe the object and how those vertices appear in the faces that build the object. A cube has 8 vertices. If you have a die then examine it now. Count the vertices, 8. Now count the faces, clearly a die has 6 faces. But we need to be able to describe each face using the vertex information. Ultimately we require a way to be able to tell whether a face is currently visible to the viewer. To use a very simple algorithm, to do this we require that each face describes the vertices in an order that is anti-clockwise when viewed from outside. This technique requires that the face is convex, that is, that there are no dimples. A triangle must be convex; there can be no dimples.

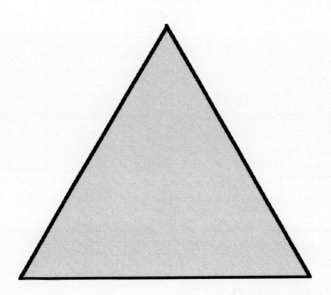

A four-sided polygon can be either convex or concave.

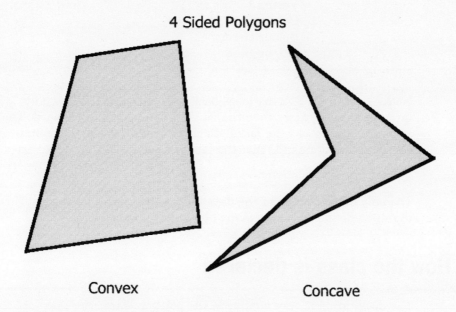

4 Sided Polygons

Convex   Concave

It is because triangles must be convex that most 3D graphics libraries use only triangular faces. The example program allows either 3- or 4-sided polygons. Using concave, a 4-sided polygon to represent a face of the object will result in a confused and almost certainly wrong display. I have deliberately allowed this to let you experiment with 3D routines. There is no better lesson than hands-on manipulation of data.

Each vertex in the list now requires three values: the x, y and z positions. Each face consists of a list of vertices.

The additional data are the scaling, position and rotation parameters.

The clsObject3D Class

The member variables of this new class must accommodate the addition of the face data. In the structure created, each face provides its own colour information. The list for a 4-corner polygon is as follows:

intIndex	Data
0	Vertex 1
1	Vertex 2
2	Vertex 3
3	Vertex 4

4	Vertex 1
5	Colour Red
6	Colour Green
7	Colour Blue

Notice how the vertex list loops back to the first. If the face only includes three vertices then the fourth intIndex will be unused. The software that checks the face data checks for a return to the first vertex and understands that the face is closed when the first vertex is repeated.

The only other change in the data file involves multiple objects. Now the same file can describe many objects.

How the class is declared

The declaration is very similar to the polygon class.

```
Option Explicit

Private Declare Function CreatePolygonRgn Lib ''gdi32'' (lpPoint
As POINTAPI, _
    ByVal nCount As Long, ByVal nPolyFillMode As Long) As Long
Private Declare Function CreateSolidBrush Lib ''gdi32'' _
    (ByVal crColor As Long) As Long
Private Declare Function DeleteObject Lib ''gdi32'' (ByVal hObject
As Long) As Long
Private Declare Function FillRgn Lib ''gdi32'' (ByVal hdc As Long, _
    ByVal hRgn As Long, ByVal hBrush As Long) As Long

Private Type POINTAPI
  x As Long
  y As Long
End Type

Const WINDING = 2

Private Type Point3D
  x As Single
  y As Single
  z As Single
End Type
```

```
Private Type Point
  x As Single
  y As Single
End Type

Private Type COLORREF
  Red As Byte
  Green As Byte
  Blue As Byte
  type As Byte
End Type

Dim c_NumFaces As Integer, c_NumVertices As Integer
Dim c_Vertex() As Point3D, c_World() As Point3D
Dim c_Screen() As Point, c_Face() As Integer
Dim c_Scale As Point3D, c_Position As Point3D, c_Rotation As
Point3D
Dim c_Name As String, c_Light As Point3D, c_Ambient As Single

Const DEG2RAD = 0.01745329251994
Const SCREEN_TO_EYE = 1000
Const VERTICES_IN_FACE = 4
Const FACE_SIZE = 8
```

I never trust any code without testing, so I included a Dump routine as
my next step in implementing this program. Dump routines are very
useful; you are encouraged to use them. Understanding the contents of
the member variables of a class is vital to effective debugging.

```
Sub Dump()
  Dim i As Integer, j As Integer

  Debug.Print ''========================''
  Debug.Print ''Dump of object:''; c_Name
  Debug.Print ''========================''
  Debug.Print ''Number of Vertices''; c_NumVertices
  For i = 0 To c_NumVertices - 1
    Debug.Print i; ''('' + Str(c_Vertex(i).x) + '','' + _
      Str(c_Vertex(i).y) + '','' + Str(c_Vertex(i).z) + '')''
  Next
  Debug.Print ''Number of Faces''; c_NumFaces
  For i = 0 To c_NumFaces - 1
    Debug.Print i; ''('';
    intIndex = i * FACE_SIZE
    For j = intIndex To intIndex + VERTICES_IN_FACE - 1
```

```
      Debug.Print Str(c_Face(j)) + '','';
    Next
    Debug.Print Str(c_Face(j)) + '') RGB('';
    For j = intIndex + VERTICES_IN_FACE + 1 To intIndex + FACE_
SIZE - 2
    Debug.Print Str(c_Face(j)) + '','';
    Next
    Debug.Print Str(c_Face(j)) + '')''
  Next
  Debug.Print ''Position ('' + Str(c_Position.x) + '','' +
Str(c_Position.y) + '','' + Str(c_Position.z) + '')''
  Debug.Print ''Rotation ('' + Str(c_Rotation.x) + '','' +
Str(c_Rotation.y) + '','' + Str(c_Rotation.z) + '')''
  Debug.Print ''Scale ('' + Str(c_Scale.x) + '','' + Str(c_
Scale.y) + '','' + Str(c_Scale.z) + '')''
End Sub
```

The next stage in the implementation of the class is persistence; that is, loading and saving or the serialisation of data.

Loading a 3D object

Here again the code is simply an extension of the code used to load a polygon.

```
Public Sub Load(intFileNum As Integer)
  Dim strTemp As String, lngPos As Long, i As Integer, intIndex As
Integer
  Dim j As Integer

  Line Input #intFileNum, c_Name
  Line Input #intFileNum, strTemp
  c_NumVertices = Val(strTemp)
  Line Input #intFileNum, strTemp
  c_NumFaces = Val(strTemp)

  If c_NumVertices = 0 Or c_NumFaces = 0 Then
    MsgBox ''No vertices or faces''
    Exit Sub
  End If

  ReDim c_Vertex(c_NumVertices)
  ReDim c_World(c_NumVertices)
```

```
ReDim c_Screen(c_NumVertices)
ReDim c_Face(c_NumFaces * FACE_SIZE)

Do
   Line Input #intFileNum, strTemp
   strTemp = LCase(strTemp)
Loop While (InStr(strTemp, ''vertices'') = 0)

For i = 0 To c_NumVertices − 1
   Line Input #intFileNum, strTemp
   c_Vertex(i).x = Val(strTemp)
   lngPos = InStr(strTemp, '','')
   c_Vertex(i).y = Val(Right(strTemp, Len(strTemp) − lngPos))
   lngPos = InStr(lngPos + 1, strTemp, '','')
   c_Vertex(i).z = Val(Right(strTemp, Len(strTemp) - lngPos))
Next

Do
   Line Input #intFileNum, strTemp
   strTemp = LCase(strTemp)
Loop While (InStr(strTemp, ''faces'') = 0)

For i = 0 To c_NumFaces − 1
   intIndex = i * FACE_SIZE
   Line Input #intFileNum, strTemp
   lngPos = 0
   For j = intIndex To intIndex + FACE_SIZE − 1
     c_Face(j) = Val(Right(strTemp, Len(strTemp) − lngPos))
     If j <> intIndex + FACE_SIZE − 1 Then lngPos =
InStr(lngPos + 1, strTemp, '','')
     If lngPos = 0 Then
       'Debug.Print ''Problem loading face information''
       Exit Sub
     End If
   Next
Next

Do
   Line Input #intFileNum, strTemp
   strTemp = LCase(strTemp)
Loop While (InStr(strTemp, ''data'') = 0)

Line Input #intFileNum, strTemp
c_Rotation.x = Val(strTemp)
lngPos = InStr(strTemp, '','')
```

```
      c_Rotation.y = Val(Right(strTemp, Len(strTemp) — lngPos))
      lngPos = InStr(lngPos, strTemp, '','')
      c_Rotation.z = Val(Right(strTemp, Len(strTemp) — lngPos))

      Line Input #intFileNum, strTemp
      c_Position.x = Val(strTemp)
      lngPos = InStr(strTemp, '','')
      c_Position.y = Val(Right(strTemp, Len(strTemp) — lngPos))
      lngPos = InStr(lngPos, strTemp, '','')
      c_Position.z = Val(Right(strTemp, Len(strTemp) — lngPos))

      Line Input #intFileNum, strTemp
      c_Scale.x = Val(strTemp)
      lngPos — InStr(strTemp, '','')
      c_Scale.y = Val(Right(strTemp, Len(strTemp) — lngPos))
      lngPos = InStr(lngPos, strTemp, '','')
      c_Scale.z = Val(Right(strTemp, Len(strTemp) — lngPos))

      Do
          Line Input #intFileNum, strTemp
          strTemp = LCase(strTemp)
      Loop While (InStr(strTemp, ''end'') = 0)

      'Dump
      Transform
      DrawWire
  End Sub
```

Notice how useful the ability to re dimension an array. Think what is going on in the background. The computer is freeing the memory previously used to store the array. You can then resize the array so that you can access any particular value simply using an intIndex. When using C++ you would almost certainly use a list to allow for the same functionality. You would gain flexibility. If you need to add a member in the middle of the array then a list is infinitely preferable, but you sacrifice clarity in the ease of understanding the code listing.

NOTE

If you move on to develop some code in C++, and particularly if you had little knowledge of programming before this book, then contact me. Try nlever@cix.compulink.co.uk. Also if you dirty your hands with some C++ then I recommend learning Microsoft Foundation Classes if you can't make up your mind which class library to concentrate on. For the same reason I would recommend Visual C++ as the compiler development environment.

To complement the load routine here is the save routine. Saving is always easier than loading since you are in control of the data. When loading you have to check for incorrect data. The load routine that I have shown does very little error checking to keep the concepts as obvious as possible. If you were creating a robust loading routine that was required to receive data from inexperienced users, then the code would need to consider how to respond to incorrect data at each stage.

```
Public Sub Save(intFileNum As Integer)
   Dim strTemp As String, lngPos As Long, i As Integer, intIndex As
   Integer
   Dim j As Integer

   Print #intFileNum,
   Print #intFileNum, ''[Object]''
   Print #intFileNum, c_Name
   Print #intFileNum, c_NumVertices
   Print #intFileNum, c_NumFaces
   Print #intFileNum, ''[Vertices]''

   For i = 0 To c_NumVertices - 1
     Print #intFileNum, Str(c_Vertex(i).x) + '','' + _
       Str(c_Vertex(i).y) + '','' + Str(c_Vertex(i).z)
   Next

   Print #intFileNum, ''[Faces]''

   For i = 0 To c_NumFaces - 1
     intIndex = i * FACE_SIZE
     For j = intIndex To intIndex + FACE_SIZE - 2
       Print #intFileNum, Str(c_Face(j)) + '','';
     Next
```

```
    Print #intFileNum, c_Face(j)
  Next

  Print #intFileNum, ''[Data]''
  Print #intFileNum, Str(c_Rotation.x) + '','' + _
  Str(c_Rotation.y) + '','' + Str(c_Rotation.z)
  Print #intFileNum, Str(c_Position.x) + '','' + _
  Str(c_Position.y) + '','' + Str(c_Position.z)
  Print #intFileNum, Str(c_Scale.x) + '','' + _
  Str(c_Scale.y) + '','' + Str(c_Scale.z)

  Print #intFileNum, ''[End]''

End Sub
```

The 'Print #intFileNum' statement is very useful for outputting to a text file and works similarly to printing to the screen. That is ';' causes no line feed, it simply puts a tab into the file.

Initialising the Object3D Class

When an instance of the clsObject3D is created it initially has no vertices or face data loaded. The module that created the instance will load the data into the class via an open file. To be sure that the class is initialised correctly, this simple code was added to the Class_Initialize event.

```
Private Sub Class_Initialize()
  c_NumFaces = 0
  c_NumVertices = 0
  SetPosition 0, 0, 0, False
  SetRotation 0, 0, 0, False
  SetScale 0, 0, 0, False
  c_Light.x = 600
  c_Light.y = -1000
  c_Light.z = 500
  c_Ambient = 0.2
End Sub
```

Each object can have its own light. This Point3D variable defines the position of a light and will be used in one of the routines that the class exposes for drawing the object.

Moving a vertex in 3D space

This is the fun part. Now we can load and save the data structure that is a simple 3D object. Before we can display the data we need a way to convert all those vertices to 2D points on the user's screen. We come back to scaling, translating and rotating and, just as in the 2D case, the complications are in rotation.

3D scaling

Scaling a vertex in relation to the origin, which is now the point (0, 0, 0) since there are three parameters to consider, is a simple exercise of multiplying the point parameters by the scale parameter. That is

```
New.x = Old.x * Scale.x
New.y = Old.y * Scale.y
New.z = Old.z * Scale.z
```

Translating

Translating an object is a simple task of adding the translation parameters to the current point. That is,

```
New.x = Old.x + Position.x
New.y = Old.y + Position.y
New.z = Old.z + Position.z
```

Rotation

This is a great deal more difficult and you may feel like simply taking the black box approach. That is, here is a batch of code that works; I'll copy it into my program.

Rotation comes in three varieties: there can be rotations about the x, y or z axis.

Rotation about the x axis
```
New.x = Old.x
New.y = Old.y * Cos(Rotation.x) + Old.z * Sin(Rotation.x)
New.z = Old.z * Cos(Rotation.x) - Old.y * Sin(Rotation.y)
```

Rotation about the y axis
```
New.x = Old.x * Cos(Rotation.y) - Old.z * Sin(Rotation.y)
New.y = Old.y
New.z = Old.x * Sin(Rotation.y) + Old.z * Cos(Rotation.y)
```

Rotation about the z axis

```
New.x=Old.x*Cos(Rotation.z) −Old.y*Sin(Rotation.z)
New.y=Old.x*Sin(Rotation.z) +Old.y*Cos(Rotation.z)
New.z=Old.z
```

Combining the rotations

In the code I have tried to speed it up a little by combining all these parameters into one set of coefficients. Notice how each rotation applies a combination of Sin and Cos to the Old (x, y, z) position. If you combine them all in a certain order you get the following:

```
New.x = −Old.x * Cos(phi) * Cos(rho) −Old.y * Cos(phi) * Sin(rho)
        +Old.z * Sin(phi)
New.y =Old.x * Sin(theta) * Sin(phi) * Cos(rho) + Cos(theta) *
        Sin(rho)-Old.y * Sin(theta) * Sin(phi) * Sin(rho) + Cos(theta) *
        Cos(rho) −Old.z * Sin(theta) * Cos(phi)
New.z =−Old.x * Cos(theta) * Sin(phi) * Cos(rho) + Sin(theta) *
        Sin(rho)+Old.y * Cos(theta) * Sin(phi) * Sin(rho) + Sin(theta)
        * Cos(rho)+Old.z * Cos(theta) * Cos(phi)
```

where theta is the x rotation, phi the y rotation and rho the z rotation.

Thankfully we only need to calculate most of this once for each movement of each object, not once for each vertex. If we strip the references to Old(x,y,z) out of the above equations then we have what are called the *coefficients*, i.e. the numbers by which *each* parameter must be multiplied. These coefficients are common for each vertex of the object.

NOTE

Most academic texts that consider 3D graphics in depth stress the use of matrices and, indeed, they provide an excellent way to write down the equations in a textbook. I feared that most of my audience would not feel too comfortable with matrices, inverses, determinates and homogeneous co-ordinates, so I have deliberately avoided that style of presentation. I would recommend, however, that if this chapter has captured your interest you should choose one of the 3D textbooks from the bibliography which I am sure you will find both useful and illuminating.

The Transform sub-routine

We are now ready to look at how all the scaling, translating and rotating is implemented in the code.

```
Private Sub Transform()
  If c_NumVertices = 0 Then
    Debug.Print ''No vertices to transform''
    Exit Sub
  End If

  Dim ax As Double, ay As Double, az As Double
  Dim bx As Double, by As Double, bz As Double
  Dim cx As Double, cy As Double, cz As Double
  Dim theta As Double, phi As Double, rho As Double, PF As Double
  Dim intCount As Integer, i As Integer
```

TIP

Trig functions take radians as their parameters. To convert from degrees to radians use the formula: Rad_Value = Degree_Value/180 * PI, where PI is 3.1415.

```
    'DEG2RAD is a conversion const for degrees to radians
    theta = c_Rotation.x * DEG2RAD
    phi = c_Rotation.y * DEG2RAD
    rho = c_Rotation.z * DEG2RAD

    'Calculate coefficients for this object
    ax = Cos(phi) * Cos(rho)
    bx = -Cos(phi) * Sin(rho)
    cx = Sin(phi)
    ay = Sin(theta) * Sin(phi) * Cos(rho) + Cos(theta) *
Sin(rho)
    by = -Sin(theta) * Sin(phi) * Sin(rho) + Cos(theta) *
Cos(rho)
    cy = -Sin(theta) * Cos(phi)
    az = -Cos(theta) * Sin(phi) * Cos(rho) + Sin(theta) *
Sin(rho)
    bz = Cos(theta) * Sin(phi) * Sin(rho) + Sin(theta) *
Cos(rho)
    cz = Cos(theta) * Cos(phi)
```

```
intCount = 0
For i = 0 To c_NumVertices - 1
  'Transform verteX
  c_World(i).x = (ax * c_Vertex(i).x + bx * c_Vertex(i).y +
cx * c_Vertex(i).z) * c_Scale.x + c_Position.x           ⏎
  c_World(i).y = (ay * c_Vertex(i).x + by * c_Vertex(i).y +
cy * c_Vertex(i).z) * c_Scale.y + c_Position.y           ⏎
  c_World(i).z = (az * c_Vertex(i).x + bz * c_Vertex(i).y +
cz * c_Vertex(i).z) * c_Scale.z + c_Position.z           ⏎

  'Convert to screen co-ordinates
  PF = 1 / ((c_World(i).z / SCREEN_TO_EYE) + 1)
  c_Screen(i).x = c_World(i).x * PF
  c_Screen(i).y = c_World(i).y * PF
  'Debug.Print i;''('' + Str(Int(c_Screen(i).x)) + '',''
  + Str(Int(c_Screen(i).y)) + '')''
Next

End Sub
```

Perspective

Surprisingly, converting the 3D co-ordinate to a 2D co-ordinate with perspective – that is, distant objects appear smaller than foreground objects – is a relatively easy exercise. Firstly we define a distance from the viewer to the screen, since the screen needs to be positioned in the same 3-dimensional space as the object. Now imagine a line extending from the viewer's eye to the vertex in question. We are interested in the point of intersection of the line from eye to vertex and the screen. This calculation is achieved using a very simple code.

```
PF = 1 / ((c_World(i).z / SCREEN_TO_EYE) + 1)
c_Screen(i).x = c_World(i).x * PF
c_Screen(i).y = c_World(i).y * PF
```

Here SCREEN_TO_EYE is constant, defining the distance between the screen and the viewer. First we calculate a coefficient that we can use for the x and y co-ordinates then we can simply multiply these co-ordinates by the coefficient and, hey presto, we have the object vertex in the right place. The total transformation requires two stages: first we take the vertex and place it in the 3D environment, then we convert this to the 2D plane where the screen is situated. For convenience the screen is located at $z=0$. Positive z values are behind the screen and negative values in front.

Drawing the object as a wireframe

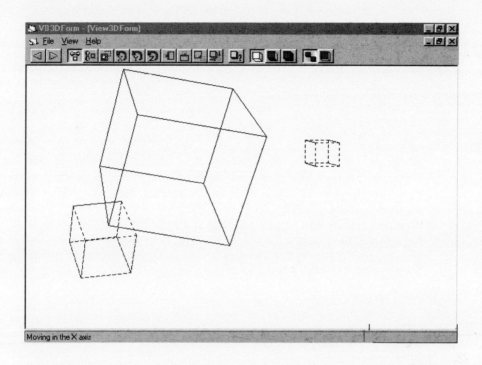

The simplest way to view the object on screen is to draw the object as a series of lines. This interpretation is called a wireframe. No consideration is made as to whether a surface is visible to the camera from the current position; it is drawn in any case. Also, the wireframe drawing as implemented in this code draws every line twice, because each edge is shared by two faces.

```
Public Sub DrawWire()
   Dim i As Integer, intIndex As Integer
   Dim intCount As Integer, intFirstVertex As Integer

   If c_NumFaces = 0 Then Exit Sub

   For i = 0 To c_NumFaces - 1
      intIndex = i * FACE_SIZE
      intFirstVertex = c_Face(intIndex)
      View3DForm.CurrentX = c_Screen(intFirstVertex).x
      View3DForm.CurrentY = c_Screen(intFirstVertex).y
      intCount = 0
```

```
      Do
        intIndex = intIndex + 1
        intCount = intCount + 1
        View3DForm.Line – (c_Screen(c_Face(intIndex)).x,
c_Screen(c_Face(intIndex)).y)
        Loop While (c_Face(intIndex) < > intFirstVertex And intCount
      <
VERTICES_IN_FACE)
    Next
  End Sub
```

The code simply loops through each face finding the value of each
vertex in the face. If the current vertex is the same as the first vertex
then this must be the final line for the current face. The code includes
a precautionary measure to protect against an infinity loop: if data has
been incorrectly edited in a text file then the face lists may not loop
back to the first vertex, so a counter is also tested against the value of
the constant VERTICES_IN_FACE; if the counter exceeds the value of
VERTICES_IN_FACE then the 'Do . . . Loop' is exited.

Drawing the object in solid colour

Unlike most of the programs in this book the code in this chapter
operates best if your computer is set up to have a 16- or 24-bit colour
display. The reason for this is the use of Windows API calls to draw
the coloured areas. They work very slowly on a 256 colour display since
they need to dither the colour to give it the correct appearance and this
is slow. Windows use of palettes, and GDI (Graphics Device Interface)
API (Application Programmers Interface) calls that relate to them is
covered in the previous chapter. If you are able to change your display
to 16 or 24 bit then now would be a good time. If you run the example
program, then select the toolbar button that selects Draw Solid.

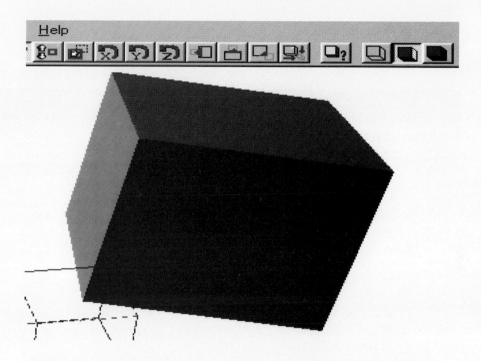

Notice the use of a Windows API data structure POINTAPI. This is simply two Long Integers, one for the x and one for the y. It was declared in the declarations section of the class.

When drawing a solid view of an object we need to decide whether a face is either on a side of the object that the viewer can see or at the rear of the object. Remember, earlier, that we made sure that the vertex information for each face was stored in a way that allowed us to determine the side of the face that we were viewing based on the order that the vertices appeared. If the vertices when transformed to screen co-ordinates, appear anti-clockwise then the face is visible; if the screen co-ordinates appear clockwise then the face is on the rear of the object, or the camera is inside the object in which case using the existing code the object would not be drawn at all.

Orientation

The procedure that checks for the order of the vertices is called *orientation*. First we obtain the point information for the current face based on the value passed as 'intIndex'. intIndex must point to the first vertex of a face. We then convert the vertex information into vectors. A vector can be thought of as an arrow that points in a certain direction. Using a little vector manipulation we can confirm the order of the vertices.

TIP

If you are interested in vector algebra then see Appendix E.

```
Private Function Orientation(intIndex As Integer) As Boolean
  Dim pt1 As Point, pt2 As Point, pt3 As Point

  pt1.x = c_Screen(c_Face(intIndex)).x
  pt1.y = c_Screen(c_Face(intIndex)).y
  pt2.x = c_Screen(c_Face(intIndex + 1)).x
  pt2.y = c_Screen(c_Face(intIndex + 1)).y
  pt3.x = c_Screen(c_Face(intIndex + 2)).x
  pt3.y = c_Screen(c_Face(intIndex + 2)).y

  'Debug.Print''('' + Str(pt1.x) + '','' + Str(pt1.y) +''  ↵
'('' +   Str(pt2.x) + _
  ' '','' + Str(pt2.y) + '') ('' +   Str(pt3.x) + '','' + ↵
Str(pt3.y) + '')'';

  pt1.x = pt2.x - pt1.x
  pt1.y = pt2.y - pt1.y
  pt3.x = pt3.x - pt2.x
  pt3.y = pt3.y - pt2.y

  If ((pt1.x * pt3.y - pt3.x * pt1.y) < 0) Then
    ''Debug.Print ''<<True
    Orientation = True
  Else
    'Debug.Print ''<<False''
    Orientation = False
  End If
End Function
```

The same Windows API calls are used as in the 2D version.

```
Public Sub DrawSolid()
  If (c_NumFaces = 0) Then Exit Sub

  Dim intFirstVertex As Integer, i As Integer
  Dim intIndex As Integer, intCount As Integer
  Dim pt(VERTICES_IN_FACE) As POINTAPI
  Dim Rgn As Long, Brush As Long

  For i = 0 To c_NumFaces — 1
    intIndex = i * FACE_SIZE
    intFirstVertex = c_Face(intIndex)
    intCount = 0
    'Get the vertices and store in point array
    If Orientation(intIndex) Then
      Do
        pt(intCount).x = c_Screen(c_Face(intIndex)).x
        pt(intCount).y = c_Screen(c_Face(intIndex)).y
        intIndex = intIndex + 1
        intCount = intCount + 1
      Loop While ((c_Face(intIndex) <> intFirstVertex) And
(intCount <= VERTICES_IN_FACE))                              ↵
      'Create region from point array
      Rgn = CreatePolygonRgn(pt(0), intCount, WINDING)
      intIndex = i * FACE_SIZE + VERTICES_IN_FACE + 1
      Brush = CreateSolidBrush(RGB(c_Face(intIndex), c_      ↵
Face(intIndex + 1), c_Face(intIndex + 2)))
      'Paint region with brush
      FillRgn View3DForm.hdc, Rgn, Brush
      'Tidy up GDI objects
      DeleteObject (Rgn)
      DeleteObject (Brush)
    End If
  Next
End Sub
```

Drawing the object with an apparent light source

The final version that is available in the example is the option to draw the object with shading. This introduces the idea of a face normal. Imagine a little arrow pointing out from the face at a right angle. Now imagine an arrow pointing in the direction of a light source. Examining the angle between these two arrows could give important information for the program to decide how brightly a face is lit by the light source. In order not to end up with objects that are black when pointing away from a light source I have also included a value for the level of ambient non-directional light. Both the light and the ambient values are included as member variables of the class. But I did not include a procedure that is callable from outside the class to manipulate these variables. Perhaps this is a useful exercise that you could do to see the results of playing with these variables. The value for ambient light is a proportion of the total light, so it should not exceed 1. But the interface to this could be regarded it as a percentage. This is the value of object-orientated programming. Since you only allow the manipulation of the data via procedures that you have written, you can provide data checking and conversion functions.

Calculating the direction of the normal requires the use of a vector cross product. This defines a new vector that is orthogonal, at right angles, to the other two vectors. But, this new vector can be of any length, and in order to use the result to find the level of illumination it is important that the vector has length 1. Length for a 3D vector is defined as the square root of the sum of the squares of the sides. This is simply the 3D version of Pythagoras's famous theorem. Converting a vector of any length to one of length 1 is called *finding the unit vector*. The following uses these special functions to find the cross product and the unit vector.

```
Private Function CrossProduct(vec1 As Point3D, vec2 As Point3D) As
Point3D
    CrossProduct.x = vec1.y * vec2.z − vec1.z * vec2.y
    CrossProduct.y = vec1.z * vec2.x − vec1.x * vec2.z
    CrossProduct.z = vec1.x * vec2.y − vec1.y * vec2.x
End Function

Private Function UnitVector(vec As Point3D) As Point3D
    Dim d As Double
    d = Sqr(vec.x * vec.x + vec.y * vec.y + vec.z * vec.z)
    UnitVector.x = vec.x / d
    UnitVector.y = vec.y / d
    UnitVector.z = vec.z / d
End Function
```

The procedure that calls these two functions is called 'FaceColour' and takes a face as a parameter. This is the number of the face, not the intIndex of the first vertex in a face. The function returns a COLORREF which again is a Windows API data structure. Fundamentally this is a 32-bit Long Integer.

```
Private Function FaceColour(i As Integer) As COLORREF
  'i is a face number
  Dim vec1 As Point3D, vec2 As Point3D, vec3 As Point3D
  Dim normalvec As Point3D, lightvec As Point3D, dblLightLevel As
  Double
  Dim Red As Byte, Green As Byte, Blue As Byte, intIndex As Integer

  intIndex = i * FACE_SIZE
  'Get first 3 points from face
  vec1.x = c_World(c_Face(intIndex)).x
  vec1.y = c_World(c_Face(intIndex)).y
  vec1.z = c_World(c_Face(intIndex)).z
  vec2.x = c_World(c_Face(intIndex + 1)).x
  vec2.y = c_World(c_Face(intIndex + 1)).y
  vec2.z = c_World(c_Face(intIndex + 1)).z
  vec3.x = c_World(c_Face(intIndex + 2)).x
  vec3.y = c_World(c_Face(intIndex + 2)).y
  vec3.z = c_World(c_Face(intIndex + 2)).z

  'make vec1 and vec3 vectors
  vec1.x = vec2.x — vec1.x
  vec1.y = vec2.y — vec1.y
  vec1.z = vec2.z — vec1.z
  vec3.x = vec3.x — vec2.x
  vec3.y = vec3.y — vec2.y
  vec3.z = vec3.z — vec2.z
  'Create unit normal vector
  normalvec = CrossProduct(vec1, vec3)
  normalvec = UnitVector(normalvec)
  'Create light vector
  lightvec.x = c_Light.x — vec2.x
  lightvec.y = c_Light.y — vec2.y
  lightvec.z = c_Light.z — vec2.z
'Make light vector of unit length lightvec = UnitVector(lightvec)
  'Combine with the light normal
  dblLightLevel = Abs(lightvec.x * normalvec.x + _
  lightvec.y * normalvec.y + _
  lightvec.z * normalvec.z)
'Correct for the ambient light level
dblLightLevel = c_Ambient + (1 — c_Ambient) * dblLightLevel
'Get the RGB values for this face from the c_Face array
```

```
intIndex = i * FACE_SIZE + VERTICES_IN_FACE + 1
FaceColour.Red = dblLightLevel * c_Face(intIndex)
FaceColour.Green = dblLightLevel * c_Face(intIndex + 1)
FaceColour.Blue = dblLightLevel * c_Face(intIndex + 2)

End Function
```

Now we are ready to look at the DrawShaded procedure which is very similar to the DrawSolid procedure. The only difference being the source of the colour is derived from the call to FaceColour.

```
Public Sub DrawShaded()
  If (c_NumFaces = 0) Then Exit Sub

  Dim intFirstVertex As Integer, i As Integer
  Dim intIndex As Integer, intCount As Integer
  Dim pt(VERTICES_IN_FACE) As POINTAPI
  Dim Rgn As Long, Brush As Long
  Dim fColour As COLORREF, lColour As Long

  For i = 0 To c_NumFaces - 1
    intIndex = i * FACE_SIZE
    intFirstVertex = c_Face(intIndex)
    intCount = 0
    'Get the vertices and store in point array
    If Orientation(intIndex) Then
      Do
        pt(intCount).x = c_Screen(c_Face(intIndex)).x
        pt(intCount).y = c_Screen(c_Face(intIndex)).y
        intIndex = intIndex + 1
        intCount = intCount + 1
      Loop While ((c_Face(intIndex) <> intFirstVertex) And
(intCount <= VERTICES_IN_FACE))
      'Create region from point array
      fColour = FaceColour(i)
      Rgn = CreatePolygonRgn(pt(0), intCount, WINDING)
      Brush = CreateSolidBrush(RGB(fColour.Red, fColour.Green,
fColour.Blue))
      'Paint region with brush
      FillRgn View3DForm.hdc, Rgn, Brush
      'Tidy up GDI objects
      DeleteObject (Rgn)
```

```
            DeleteObject (Brush)
         End If
      Next
   End Sub
```

Useful functions in the Object3D Class

To allow for the manipulation of the object in world space, three functions are included in the class. These functions allow the programmer to alter the position, rotation and scale in 3D space. Each function takes four parameters. In addition to the x, y and z values there is a final Boolean value which acts as a flag. If the value is True then the other parameters which are passed are considered to be relative to the current position. If the value is False then the other parameters are considered to be actual values.

```
Public Sub SetPosition(x As Integer, y As Integer, z As Integer,
relative As Boolean)
   If relative Then
      c_Position.x = c_Position.x + x
      c_Position.y = c_Position.y + y
      c_Position.z = c_Position.z + z
   Else
      c_Position.x = x
      c_Position.y = y
      c_Position.z = z
   End If
   Transform
End Sub
Public Sub SetRotation(x As Integer, y As Integer, z As Integer,
relative As Boolean)
   If relative Then
      c_Rotation.x = c_Rotation.x + x
      c_Rotation.y = c_Rotation.y + y
      c_Rotation.z = c_Rotation.z + z
   Else
      c_Rotation.x = x
      c_Rotation.y = y
      c_Rotation.z = z
   End If
   Transform
End Sub
```

```
Public Sub SetScale(x As Integer, y As Integer, z As Integer,
relative As Boolean)
   If relative Then
      If ((x) And c_Scale.x > 5) Then c—Scale.x = c_Scale.x + x
      If ((y) And c_Scale.y > 5) Then c_Scale.y = c_Scale.y + y
      If ((z) And c_Scale.z > 5) Then c_Scale.z = c_Scale.x + z
   Else
      c_Scale.x = x
      c_Scale.y = y
      c_Scale.z = z
   End If
   Transform
End Sub
```

In the application you can view the data in one of two ways. You can
view the data as a picture, where the various Draw routines are used.
Alternatively, I wanted a way to view the data in numeric format in
the application, and for this reason the Object3D Class includes a way
to show the data in numerical format.

```
Public Sub ShowData()
   Dim i As Integer, j As Integer, strTemp As String

   If DataForm.Visible = False Then Exit Sub
   With DataForm
      .lblName.Caption = c_Name
      .lstvertices.Clear
      For i = 0 To c_NumVertices - 1
         .lstvertices.AddItem Str(i) + '':'' + Str(c_Vertex(i).x)
+ '','' + Str(c_Vertex(i).y) + '','' + Str(c_Vertex(i).z)
      Next
      .lstfaces.Clear
      For i = 0 To c_NumFaces - 1
         strTemp = Str(i) + '':''
      For j = 0 To FACE_SIZE - 1
         strTemp = strTemp + Str(c_Face(i * FACE_SIZE + j))
      Next
      .lstfaces.AddItem strTemp
   Next
   .lblscale.Caption = Str(c_Scale.x) + '','' + Str(c_Scale.y)
+ '','' + Str(c_Scale.z)
   .lblrotation.Caption = Str(c_Rotation.x) + '','' + Str(c_
      Rotation.y) + '','' + Str(c_Rotation.z)
      .lblposition.Caption = Str(c_Position.x) + '','' + Str(c_
Position.y) + '','' + Str(c_Position.z)
```

```
      End With
   End Sub
```

Using the Object3D Class

This project is unusual in this book in that it uses a MDIForm. MDI stands for Multiple Document Interface. I simply wanted to include an example that used the Multiple Document Interface, and this seemed the perfect one to choose. I chose this simply to allow for alternative views of the data. The main view displays the world data as a 3D drawn view; the alternative view displays the object data in the numerical form that it is stored inside the instance of an Object 3D Class that is currently selected. It may be interesting to know that the DataForm can be extended to allow editing of the vertex positions. The following is the code that declares the variables for the parent form, VB3DForm.

```
   Option Explicit

   Dim Object3D() As clsObject3D
   Dim NumObjects As Integer
   Dim StatusText(10) As String
```

How LoadWorld calls Class Load

When you select the menu option to open a file, the sub-routine LoadWorld is executed. Here a text file is opened and checked that it is a valid VB3D file. This check involves scanning the first line in the file, which should include 'VB3D' as a line of text. If this is missing then the file is assumed *not* to be a VB3D file. The number of objects in the file is then stored, the Object3D array is redimensioned to this new value, and a loop is executed for the number of 3D objects in the file. This loop creates an instance of an Object3D and then asks the new object to load itself from the open file.

```
Sub LoadWorld()
  Dim intFileNum As Integer, strTemp As String, i As Integer

  cdlgfiles.Action = 1
  intFileNum = FreeFile
  Open cdlgfiles.filename For Input As intFileNum

  Line Input #intFileNum, strTemp
  If InStr(strTemp, ''VB3D'') = 0 Then
    MsgBox ''Not a valid VB3D file''
    Exit Sub
  End If
  Line Input #intFileNum, strTemp
  NumObjects = Val(strTemp)
  If NumObjects < 1 Then
    MsgBox ''No object total available''
    Exit Sub
  End If

  View3DForm.Show
  View3DForm.Cls
  View3DForm.DrawMode = 13
  ReDim Object3D(NumObjects)

  For i = 0 To NumObjects - 1
  Do
    Line Input #intFileNum, strTemp
    strTemp = LCase(strTemp)
  Loop While (InStr(strTemp, ''object'') = 0)
  Set Object3D(i) = New clsObject3D
  Object3D(i).Load (intFileNum)
Next
Close intFileNum
For i = 1 To 23
  Toolbar1.Buttons(i).Enabled = True
Next

  msbFile(3).Enabled = True
End Sub
```

Ultimately the objects are drawn and the toolbar is enabled.

Saving 3D worlds

The routine that looks after saving all the data of all the objects
becomes fairly trivial when the objects can save themselves to an open
file. Again the power of object-orientated programming shows itself.

```
Private Sub SaveWorld()
  Dim intFileNum As Integer, i As Integer

  cdlgfiles.Action = 2
  intFileNum = FreeFile
  Open cdlgfiles.filename For Output As intFileNum

  Print #intFileNum, ''[VB3D]''
  Print #intFileNum, NumObjects

  For i = 0 To NumObjects — 1
    Object3D(i).Save (intFileNum)
  Next
  Close intFileNum
End Sub
```

Using the toolbar

The toolbar control that comes with Visual Basic is useful for adding
Windows application functionality to your programs. It is rather
strange to set up since it requires a second control to get the images.
Why you cannot simply load in the pictures is a mystery, nevertheless,
to use it you need to add an ImageList control to your form. Use the
toolbar properties dialog box that pops up by right clicking the toolbar
to set up the control. First set the ImageList control as the ImageList
Property for the toolbar control.

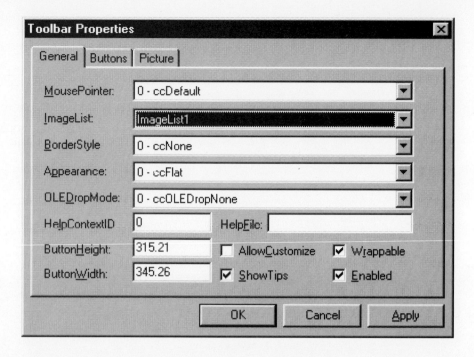

You can then set up the individual buttons using the insert button provided under the Buttons tab. For more information check the online help in Visual Basic.

Eventually you will have a toolbar that has the correct pictures. Each button can be either up or down. A button that is made part of a group operates like a check box in that only one member of a group can be pressed at the same time, and at least one member is always pressed. Each button can be referred to by its intIndex number or its key value. The key is a string value, and it is easier in code to identify a button by its key value. Just as the use of constants makes code easier to follow, so a key value of 'MoveZ' means much more than 7. The toolbar control provides this functionality.

In the code we only use the ButtonClick event, which has a Button object passed as a parameter.

```
Private Sub Toolbar1_ButtonClick(ByVal Button As Button)
    Dim MoveType As Integer, DrawType As Integer
    Dim SelectType As Integer
    Static MoveObject As Integer
    Dim i As Integer, x As Integer
```

```
For i = 5 To 14
  If Toolbar1.Buttons(i).Value Then MoveType = i
Next

For i = 18 To 20
  If Toolbar1.Buttons(i).Value Then SelectType = i
Next

For i = 22 To 23
  If Toolbar1.Buttons(i).Value Then DrawType = i
Next

Select Case Button.Key
Case Is = ''Dec''
  x = 10
Case Is = ''Inc''
  x = −10
Case Is = ''Select''
  MoveObject = MoveObject + 1
  If MoveObject > (NumObjects − 1) Then MoveObject = 0
  Object3D(MoveObject).ShowData
End Select
Select Case MoveType
Case 5: 'Move X
  Object3D(MoveObject).SetPosition x, 0, 0, True
Case 6: 'Move Y
  Object3D(MoveObject).SetPosition 0, x, 0, True
Case 7: 'Move Z
  Object3D(MoveObject).SetPosition 0, 0, x, True
Case 8: 'Rot X
  Object3D(MoveObject).SetRotation x, 0, 0, True
Case 9: 'Rot Y
  Object3D(MoveObject).SetRotation 0, x, 0, True
Case 10: 'Rot Z
  Object3D(MoveObject).SetRotation 0, 0, x, True
Case 11: 'Scale Z
  Object3D(MoveObject).SetScale x, 0, 0, True
Case 12: 'Scale Z
  Object3D(MoveObject).SetScale 0, x, 0, True
Case 13: 'Scale Z
  Object3D(MoveObject).SetScale 0, 0, x, True
Case 14: 'Scale All
  Object3D(MoveObject).SetScale x, x, x, True
End Select
```

```
      StatusBar1.Style = sbrSimple
      StatusBar1.SimpleText = StatusText(MoveType - 4)
      View3DForm.Cls
      View3DForm.DrawMode = 13
      For i = 0 To NumObjects - 1
        If i = MoveObject Then
          Select Case SelectType
          Case 18:
            View3DForm.DrawStyle = 0
            Object3D(i).DrawWire
          Case 19:
            Object3D(i).DrawSolid
          Case 20:
            Object3D(i).DrawShaded
          End Select
        Else
          View3DForm.DrawStyle = 2
          Object3D(i).DrawWire
        End If
      Next
    End Sub
```

Understanding how to extract information from this control should be quite easy for you at this stage. Notice how the functionality of the Object3D Class makes the code easy. I wonder if you spotted the weaknesses in the Object3D Class? Modularity should be total, but the class makes explicit calls to the two types of form that are included in the project. Taking the Object3D Class from this project and placing it in another program would generate errors if there were no versions of View3dForm and DataForm. To improve the situation you would need to use an initialisation routine to pass the information about the surface to be drawn. Also access to the class members should be offered as function calls. In this way the ShowData procedure would be replaced by functionality in the DataForm. This form would call the access members in the Object3D Class to update its content. I have deliberately presented the code in this form to help illustrate how you can endeavour to achieve fully modular code.

Review

This chapter covered the basics of 3D graphics programming. To extend these ideas you will need to use more complicated data structures. In my next book I will show how you can use and manipulate real time 3D worlds from Visual Basic 5. With the ability to load vrml worlds. 3d graphics is the future; learn the techniques and apply them in your code.

QUIZ

1. Briefly explain one way to avoid drawing hidden faces.
Answer: Use the orientation of the vertices to decide whether you are in front or round the back of the face.

2. Displaying 3D objects involves transforming the objects from their own co-ordinates to world co-ordinates and from there to screen co-ordinates. The screen is a flat object in this 3D space. What values for z does the screen have?
Answer: The screen is the plane where $z = 0$.

3. Windows supplies many useful graphics function calls. What calls are used to draw an irregularly shaped polygon?
Answer: CreatePolygonRgn together with FillRgn. Deciding how the region is filled will involve the use of CreateSolidBrush, CreatePatternBrush or CreateBrush calls.

4. When dealing with two vectors what does CrossProduct create?
Answer: A new vector that is orthogonal, at right angles, to the other vectors.

Summary

Anyone involved with computer graphics must understand 3D techniques even if they only use a 3D graphics library like Microsoft's DirectX. In this chapter the principles of 3D graphics programming were all introduced.

- Manipulating 3D objects involves creating a data structure within the computer.

- Displaying the object requires matrix manipulation and trigonometric techniques.
- In this chapter you learnt to draw wireframes, solid objects with hidden surface removal.
- Implementing lighting requires the use of surface normals and vector cross product.

Postscript

We have reached the end of this book, and I sincerely hope that I have passed on the enthusiasm that I have for code. I hope that the explanations broke through the computer science gobbledy-gook that is ever present in most documentation. I want coders to come from every background. If I offended those hardened professionals who know their code inside out, then I apologise; I simply wanted to share my experience with as many programmers as possible.

I am writing these words on a train from London to Manchester, England, on a 16-bit computer that is about the size of a bar of chocolate. A Psion Sienna with a battery life in excess of 50 hours, it puts my Pentium Laptop to shame. Such a miniature computer would have been unthinkable ten years ago. I write this simply to illustrate the development and diversity of the computer industry. It moves on every day, every month, every year. For some this very development is intimidating. Why learn techniques today when they may all change tomorrow?

The truth is that techniques are becoming more and more standardised. The techniques described in this book are the object-orientated programming techniques that have been the main concentration of computer science for the last 20 years. The specific implementation may very well change but the fundamental techniques will develop much more slowly. As syntax changes quickly, and techniques develop slowly, you are advised to learn the technique and get the syntax from online help. Never feel you need to know every parameter of every function call to say you are a programmer. If you have reached this stage of the book then, in my opinion, that is exactly what you are – a programmer.

Appendices

APPENDIX A

Introducing Visual Basic

This tutorial is intended for those new to programming or new to Visual Basic. To work through the tutorial you need to be at your computer with the book. None of the examples is included on the CD-ROM because you will probably learn much more by entering the code for the examples. The amount of typing involved is very small. The screen shots are from Visual Basic 5, but the techniques are equally suited to Visual Basic 4.

Visual Basic provides a convenient and very easy to use interface to Windows programming. Windows is a GUI (Graphic User Interface). The programmer must share the resources of the computer with other applications that may be running. To understand the techniques you must adopt I will introduce some terminology.

- *Controls* A window is full of small areas that are referred to as controls. A small area into which the user can enter text is a control. A button is a control.
- *Properties* Each control has certain properties. A button control has a property called 'caption'; this is used to store the text displayed on the button and guides the user on the button's purpose.
- *Events* As the user clicks the mouse or types at the keyboard, events are generated. The programmer can attach code to these events to add functionality to an application.

- *Methods* The programmer can use the functions that are built into a control in the programs. The control button has a method called 'Move' which has the following syntax:

object.Move left, top, width, height

Syntax is essential when programming. Although Visual Basic uses many English words, these words have to be used in a very specific way. The optional way that grammar is used in everyday speech is not echoed in the way program code is written. Visual Basic is precise about grammar and will correct you if you get it wrong.

In the Move example method, the word 'object' will be the name you have given to a button. Left, top, width and height are number values that define the position and size of the button on the Form.

What is a Visual Basic form?

A form is a window that is displayed when the program runs. You use the toolbox to add controls to the form.

Example 1

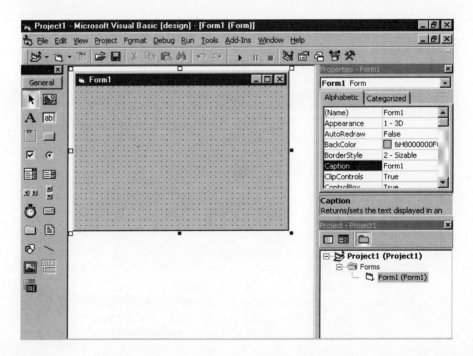

When you run Visual Basic, select 'Standard Exe' as the project type in the initial dialog box.

TIP

A dialog box is a window that is displayed to get specific user input. Usually it is a non-resizable window that locks out control to other windows until it is closed down.

This is the screen you will get. If the toolbox that you can see on the left is not displayed then select 'View | Toolbox' from the menu. Click on the command button icon on the toolbox.

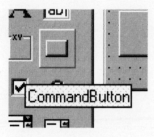

Now click and drag on the form in the middle of the screen. The button is placed and sized using the mouse click-and-drag technique. When you release the mouse button the button is drawn. Repeat this with the text box control.

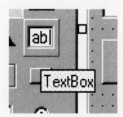

Now drag the corner of the form to resize it to fit neatly around the text box and command button. At this stage you should have a form that looks like this:

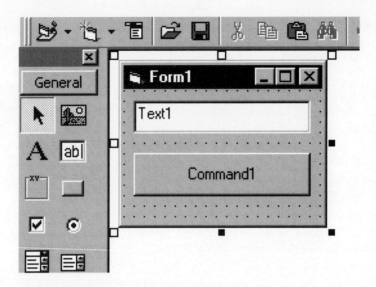

Try running the application now. To run the application you can press the toolbar button, which looks like this and has the tool tip 'Start':

Alternatively, you can also choose the menu option 'Run|Start' which has a keyboard shortcut F5. When the program runs you will be able to click the button and type into the text box. However, the program is not making any use of the contents of the text box or the event that is generated when the button is pressed. Stop the application by clicking the cross in the top right-hand corner.

Attaching code to an event

Double click the button on the form you have created, while Visual Basic is in design mode.

TIP

The Visual Basic development environment has a design mode and a run mode.

This will open the code window with an empty sub-routine like this:

```
Private Sub Command1_Click()
. . .
End Sub
```

The code that you enter goes between 'Sub()' and 'End Sub'.

NOTE

The first six chapters of this book introduce Visual Basic programming. In this tutorial we are interested in familiarising you with the development environment.

Enter the following code:

```
Text1.Text = 'Clicked!'
```

Now run the program again by pressing F5. When you click the button the text box displays 'Clicked!'. Stop the program again.

The text 'Command1' is not very instructive on the button. To change it you will need to alter one of the command button's properties. To alter a property of a control requires the 'Properties Window'. If this is not displayed press F4 or select 'View|Properties Window' from the menu. The top box is a combo box; by clicking the arrow on the right a drop-down list will be displayed. Select 'Command1' from this list.

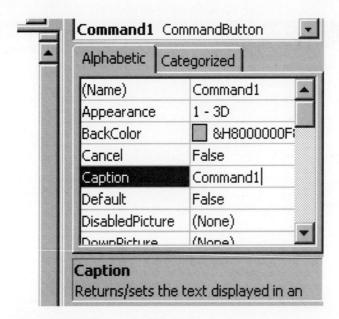

Select 'caption' as the property to change; click in the area to the right of the label 'caption'. Enter 'Click Me'. Now view the form again by selecting one of the 'View Object' icons at the top of the project window.

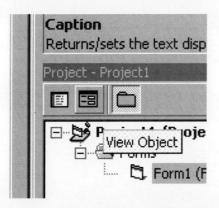

TIP

If the Project Window is not showing then select 'View|Project Explorer' from the menu or press the keyboard shortcut 'Ctrl R'.

Now the button has a more intuitive title.

Entering more code

Return to the code for the button by selecting the 'View Code' icon in the project window. Click the arrow to the right of the box 'Command1' and a drop-down list will show the objects that are available on this form, including the form itself. Choose '(General)'. The box to the right will now display '(declarations)'. These two boxes let you move around the code. As you attach more code to events there will be more and more sub-routines and you must get used to finding your way around the listing using these two boxes. The box to the left lists objects; the one to the right lists the events available to this object. If an event has code attached to it then it is displayed in bold type.

In the '(General)–(declarations)' section enter:

```
Dim intNumClicks As Integer
```

Details of variables and declarations are described in the first chapters of the book.

Now use the two boxes to return to the Command1_Click event. Notice from the event drop-down list that there are many other events involving the button that you can attach code to. This time add the following code to the Command1_Click event.

```
Private Sub Command1_Click()
  intNumClicks = intNumClicks + 1

  If intNumClicks = 1 Then
    Text1.Text = 'Clicked once.'
  Else
    Text1.Text = 'Clicked' + Str(intNumClicks ) + 'times'.
  End If
End Sub
```

In this example we are using the variable 'intNumClicks' that we declared in the '(General) – (declarations)' section. When Visual Basic first creates an integer (a number with no decimal place), it sets it to 0. When this routine is first called the value of 'intNumClicks' is increased by 1. Then we check the value of 'intNumClicks'. If the value is 1 then 'Clicked once' is displayed in the text box. If 'intNumClicks' does not equal 1 then 'Clicked *n* times' (where *n* is the number of times) is displayed in the text box. Every time we click the button this routine is run, and every time it increases the value of 'intNumClicks'. Try running the program and observing the result. Now stop the program and make a very small change. Where the variable 'intNumClicks' is declared put an apostrophe before the word Dim.

NOTE

To find where the '(General) – (declarations)' section is:
1. Click 'View Code' in the project window.
2. Select '(General)' in the object combo box on the left at the top of the code window.
3. Select '(declarations)' in the event combo box on the right at the top of the code window.

The line should now be listed in green.

```
'Dim intNumClicks As Integer
```

When text is green Visual Basic ignores it. The text is there for your guidance only. To add comments and notes to your code listing, place an opening quote (') and everything on that line after the quote will be ignored by Visual Basic. The code continues on the next line. Here we are using a technique called 'commenting out'; that is, by placing an opening quote before the code, sections of code can temporarily be eliminated from the program. This a technique often used when debugging (finding the big or small errors that often appear in a section of code). Now run the program again. Every time you click, the text box displays the same message, 'Clicked once'. Why?

Stepping through your code

Place the cursor on the line

intNumClicks = intNumClicks + 1

and press F9. The line should now be red. This signifies a breakpoint –
a point in the listing where execution will halt to enable you to
examine what is happening to your program. Run the program and
click the button. Execution halts and the code window shows the line
where the code stopped. From the menu select 'View | Watch window'
and 'Debug | Add watch' if 'intNumClicks' is not displayed in the
'Expression' text box, then enter it now to leave the other settings as
they are. The dialog box will look like this:

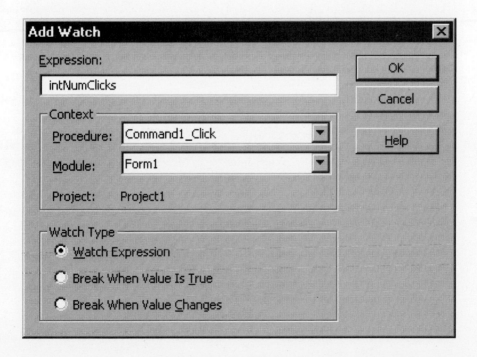

Click OK. Your screen should then look like this:

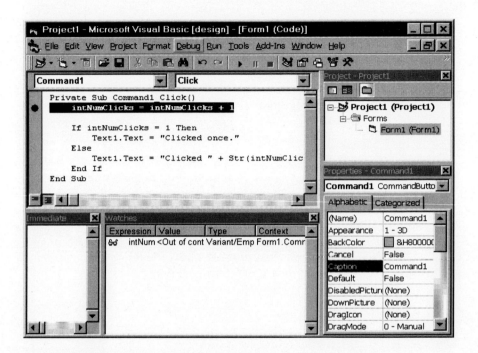

Notice the line in the watch window:

Expression	Value	Type	Context
intNumClicks:	<Out of context>:	Variant/Empty:	Form1.Command1_Click

Take note that the variable is 'Out of context', which indicates that Visual Basic cannot find it. It cannot find it because it does not exist. Also notice that it thinks it is of type 'Variant'. If Visual Basic is not given information about a variable then it creates one with type variant. But, the variable it creates is a local variable and as soon as this sub-routine is exited it will be deleted. So every time this routine is called, Visual Basic creates a variable called 'intNumClicks', initialises it to 0 and adds 1 to it. So every time the value of 'intNumClicks' is tested, it is always 1 leading to the display of 'Clicked once'. When 'intNumClicks' is declared in the '(General) – (declarations)' section, Visual Basic can find the variable and can update its contents. Another way to achieve the same ends while keeping the declaration of the variable local to the 'Command1_Click' sub-routine is to declare the variable as 'Static'. Change the subroutine to read like this:

```
Private Sub Command1_Click()
  Static intNumClicks As Integer

  intNumClicks = intNumClicks + 1

  If intNumClicks = 1 Then
    Text1.Text = 'Clicked once'.
  Else
    Text1.Text = 'Clicked' + Str(intNumClicks) + 'times'.
  End If
End Sub
```

When Visual Basic finds a variable declared as Static it creates the variable, and when the sub-routine finishes it does not delete it. Therefore, the next time the sub-routine is executed the variable is not recreated. If you run the program now by clicking the arrow button, pressing F5 or selecting 'Run|Start' from the menu, the code should behave as expected.

Using the Immediate window

At any time in the execution of your program you can break into the code by pressing the pause icon to the right of the Run arrow on the toolbar. The square to the right of the pause icon stops the program completely, returning Visual Basic to design mode. When the program is paused, 'break' will be displayed in the caption for the Visual Basic development environment. If the immediate window is not displayed then select 'View|Immediate window' or press Ctrl+G. You can enter single code lines in the immediate window. Try typing 'print intNumClicks'; the immediate window is not case sensitive so 'print intNumClicks' is the same as 'Print intNumClicks'. Press the enter key. The current value of 'intNumClicks' will be displayed.

You can also use the immediate window from your code by going to the 'Command1_Click' subroutine and entering the following line immediately after the line where 1 is added to 'intNumClicks'.

```
Debug.Print ''intNumClicks ='' + Str(intNumClicks)
```

Appendices

Now, as you run the code, the value of 'intNumClicks' is printed in the immediate window. You can use this technique to check on the values of your variables as your program runs. There are lots of examples of this trick in the book.

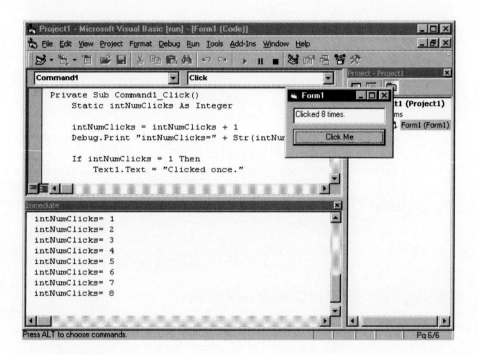

Other controls

The standard toolbox includes the following controls

Control	Purpose
Picture Box	To display pictures on your form
Label	To provide static titles
Text Box	To allow the user to enter text
Frame	To group controls together
Command Button	To provide a clickable button
Check Box	To provide options
Radio Button	To select one of a range of options
Combo Box	Editable text box and list box combined
List Box	Provides a location for lists of items
Horizontal Scroll Bar	Select values by moving a scroll bar
Vertical Scroll Bar	As above
Timer	Generates events at specific timed intervals

Control	Purpose
Control	*Purpose*
Drive List Box	To let a user choose a drive
Directory List Box	To let a user choose a directory
File List Box	To let a user choose a file
Shape	Simple shapes like circles and rectangles
Line	A line on the form
Image	Alternative to a Picture Box, less demanding on memory
Data Control	Manipulate databases
OLE Control	Insert an OLE object

As you work through the book you will use these controls and special controls created for this book. To insert a special control into your project select menu option 'Project|Components'. This brings up a dialog box that lists the extra controls that you can use with Visual Basic. Simply put a check in the box of the control you wish to use. When you close the dialog box an icon for this new control will appear in the toolbox. Selecting and placing the control on your form is exactly the same as for the standard controls. These extra controls will have properties, events and methods of their own. You will learn more about this as you work through the book. These extra controls are now called ActiveX controls and by the end of this book you will be writing your own.

Visual Basic provides good online help and excellent manuals. If there is something you need to know while working through the book, online help will provide the information you require.

What did we learn today?

This appendix is designed to get you up to speed on Visual Basic. You are not expected to be ready to write your own application, but you are expected to have some knowledge of the following:

- Where to find the toolbox.
- How to set a property for a control.
- How to add code to a controls event.
- How to find a sub-routine in the code listing.
- How to run your program in the development environment.
- The purpose of the immediate and watch windows.

APPENDIX B

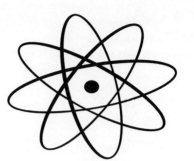

Visual Basic code conventions

What are coding conventions?

As you now know it is possible to write a program to achieve a certain objective in many different ways. You may write programs as a part of a team or alone. A program that you are familiar with today may seem difficult to understand if you need to alter it in a year's time. By adopting certain rules about the layout of your code you can make it easier for yourself and much easier for other people to understand the code you have written.

The conventions govern such issues as:

- Naming conventions for objects, variables and procedures
- Commenting conventions
- Text formatting and indenting guidelines

The main reason for using a consistent set of coding conventions is to standardise the structure and coding style of a script or set of scripts so that you and others can easily read and understand the code.

Using good coding conventions results in precise, readable, and unambiguous source code that is consistent with other language conventions and as intuitive as possible.

Naming conventions

Constant naming conventions

Constant names should be uppercase with underscores (_) between words. For example:

MY_FAVOURITE_THINGS

Variable naming conventions

For purposes of readability and consistency, use the prefixes listed below, along with descriptive names for variables in your code.

Subtype	Prefix	Example
Boolean	bln	blnFound
Byte	byt	bytRasterData
Date	dtm	dtmStart
Double	dbl	dblTolerance
Error	err	errOrderNum
Integer	int	intQuantity
Long	lng	lngDistance
Object	obj	objCurrent
Single	sng	sngAverage
String	str	strFirstName

Variable scope

Variables should always be defined with the smallest scope possible. Visual Basic variables can have the following scope.

Scope	Where variable is declared	Visibility
Procedure	Event, function, subroutine	Visible in procedure where declared
Form	General declarations	Visible only to form if declared private; visible globally if declared public
Class	General declarations	Declare private and provide member functions to access
Module	General declarations	As form

Class scope prefixes

The member variables of a class should be prefixed with a c_:

Class   c_   c_intWidth

Descriptive variable and procedure names

- The body of a variable or procedure name should use mixed case and should be as complete as necessary to describe its purpose.
- In general, variable names greater than 32 characters can be difficult to read.
- When using abbreviations, make sure they are consistent throughout the entire script.
- Randomly switching between 'Cnt' and 'Count' within a script or set of scripts may lead to confusion.

Object naming conventions

The next table lists recommended conventions for the various objects you may encounter while programming with Visual Basic.

Object type	*Prefix*	*Example*
Picture Box	pbx	pbxDisplay
Text Box	txt	txtUserName
Label	lbl	lblStatus
Image	img	imgPics
Command Button	cmd	cmdOK
File List Box	fle	fleFiles
Directory List Box	dir	dirDirectories
Drive List Box	drv	Drives
Common Dialog	dlg	dlgOpenFile
Timer	tmr	tmrTimer
Frame	fra	fraFrame
Check Box	chk	chkChoose
List Box	lst	lstWhichOne
Radio Button	rad	radJustOne
Horizontal Scroll Bar	hsb	hsbColour
Vertical Scroll Bar	vsb	vsbHeight
Line	lin	linVertical
Spin	spn	spnOneToEight
Shape	shp	shpCircle

Code commenting conventions

In an ideal world it is very useful if you include information about a procedure in a comment. Microsoft suggest the following: Procedure header comments should include the following section headings. For examples, see the section 'Formatting your code' that follows.

Section heading	Comment contents
Purpose	What the procedure does (not how).
Assumptions	List of any external variable, control or other element whose state affects this procedure.
Effects	List of the procedures effect on each external variable, control or other element.
Inputs	Explanation of each argument that is not obvious. Each argument should be on a separate line with inline comments.
Return Values	Explanation of the value returned.

Remember the following points:

- Every important variable declaration should include an inline comment describing the use of the variable being declared.
- Variables, controls and procedures should be named clearly enough that inline comments are only needed for complex implementation details.
- At the beginning of your script, you should include an overview that describes the script, enumerating objects, procedures, algorithms, dialog boxes, and other system dependencies. Sometimes a piece of pseudocode describing the algorithm can be helpful.

Formatting your code

Screen space should be conserved as much as possible, while still allowing code formatting to reflect logic structure and nesting. Here are a few pointers:

- Standard nested blocks should be indented four spaces.
- The overview comments of a procedure should be indented one space.
- The highest level statements that follow the overview comments should be indented four spaces, with each nested block indented an additional four spaces. For example:

```
Function intFindUser (strUserList() As String, strTargetUser As
Long) As Long
'**********************************************************
'Purpose: Locates the first occurrence of a specified user in the
'UserList array.
'Inputs: strUserList(): the list of users to be searched.
'strTargetUser: the name of the user to search for.
'Returns: The index of the first occurrence of the strTargetUser
'in the strUserList array.
'If the target user is not found, return −1.
'**********************************************************

    Dim i            'Loop counter.
    Dim blnFound      'Target found flag.
    intFindUser = −1
    i = 0
    Do While i &lt; = Ubound(strUserList) and Not blnFound
       If strUserList(i) = strTargetUser Then
          blnFound = True
          intFindUser = I
       End If
    Loop
End Function
```

APPENDIX C

Using the Sprite Dynamic Link Library

In the first part of the book you used a dynamic link library for many of the examples. You are welcome to use and distribute this library with your own programs. It is designed to work only with computers that are set up to have 256 colour displays, so you may prefer to use Version 1.5 of the Sprite ActiveX Control instead. Details of how to get a copy of Sprite ActiveX Control Version 1.5 are included in the Readme file on the CD.

The easiest way to use the dynamic link library is to ensure that a copy of the library is in your Windows\System folder. Then add the file Sprite.Bas to your application. This file is on the CD in the Extras folder.

The following shows how the file declares the various functions available in the sprite dynamic link library.

```
Declare Sub ShowDib Lib ''sprite.dll'' _
    (ByVal hdcDest As Long, ByVal strFilename As String, ByVal intX As
    Integer, ByVal intY As Integer)
```

```
Declare Function InitAnimation Lib ''sprite.dll'' _
  (ByVal hdcDest As Long, ByVal strFilename As String) As Boolean
Declare Sub CloseAnimation Lib ''sprite.dll'' ()
Declare Function InitSprite Lib ''sprite.dll'' _
  (ByVal strFilename As String, ByVal lngX As Long, ByVal lngY As
  Long, _ ByVal lngWidth As Long, ByVal lngHeight As Long) As Long
Declare Function ClearSprite Lib ''sprite.dll'' _
  (ByVal lngIndex As Long) As Boolean
Declare Function NewBackground Lib ''sprite.dll'' _
  (ByVal strFilename As String, ByVal blnKeepSprites As Boolean) As
  Boolean
Declare Sub MoveSprite Lib ''sprite.dll'' _
  (ByVal lngIndex As Long, ByVal lngX As Long, ByVal lngY As Long,
  ByVal lngFrame As Long)
Declare Function CloneSprite Lib ''sprite.dll'' _
  (ByVal Index As Long, ByVal X As Long, ByVal Y As Long) As Long
Declare Sub UpdateStage Lib ''sprite.dll'' ()
Declare Function GetSpriteActive Lib ''sprite.dll'' _
  (ByVal lngIndex As Long) As Boolean
Declare Function DrawFullStage Lib ''sprite.dll'' _
  () As Boolean
Declare Function CollisionCheck Lib ''sprite.dll'' _
  (ByVal lngSprite1 As Long, ByVal lngSprite2 As Long, ByVal
  blnAccurate As Boolean) As Boolean
Declare Function PasteSprite Lib ''sprite.dll'' _
  (ByVal lngIndex As Long, ByVal lngX As Long, ByVal lngY As Long,
  ByVal lngFrame As Long) As Boolean
Declare Function HitTest Lib ''sprite.dll'' _
  (ByVal lngX As Long, ByVal lngY As Long) As Long
```

How to use each function

- ShowDib hdcDest, strFilename, intX, intY

Here you can open and display a 'bmp' picture in the same way 'LoadPicture' works.

Parameters:

destHdc   A hdc from a Form or Picture Box control.
strfilename   A string to a valid 'bmp' file. The full path and filename must be given.

IntX   The left position on the destination device to begin the display.

IntY   The top position on the destination device to begin the display.

Return value: None.

- InitAnimation destHdc, strFilename

Before you can begin to display any animation you must pass the library a hdc for the destination device. This will be a form or a picture box. In addition you pass a background picture. This provides the colour palette for the animation and the size at which the animation is to be displayed.

Parameters:
destHdc   A hdc from a Form or Picture Box control.
strfilename A string to a valid 'bmp' file. The full path and filename must be given. This file will be the background picture.

Return value: True if successful; False otherwise.

- CloseAnimation

To tidy up memory. Before your application closes call CloseAnimation.

Parameters: None
Return value: None

- InitSprite strFilename, lngX, lngY, lngWidth, lngHeight

Before you begin to show sprite animations they must be loaded. A sprite gets its images from a 'bmp' file. The images must be arranged in a grid formation. The size in pixels of the grid is passed to this function.

Parameters:
strFilename The full name and path of the picture file to use for the sprites images.
LngX   The left position to display the sprite on the destination device.
lngY   The top position to display the sprite on the destination device.
lngWidth   The horizontal dimension in pixels of the sprite.
lngHeight The vertical dimension in pixels of the sprite.

Return value: The index value used to reference this sprite in the functions, MoveSprite, ClearSprite, CloneSprite, HitTest, CollisionCheck, GetSpriteActive and PasteSprite. You must store this index value to use the sprite. Zero is returned if the call was unsuccessful.

- ClearSprite Index

To remove a sprite that is loaded, pass the index for that sprite to this function

Parameter:
lngIndex   The index value of a loaded sprite

Return value: True if successful; False otherwise

- NewBackground strFilename, blnKeepSprites

Having initialised the animation, a new background can be loaded using this function.

Parameters:
strFilename   The name and path of a picture file to use as the new background image.
blnKeepSprites   When replacing the background you can choose to retain the loaded sprites or have them deleted. If retained they are automatically mapped to the new colour palette that is supplied with the new background picture. Choose True to retain the sprites and False to have them deleted.

Return value: True if successful, False otherwise

- MoveSprite lngIndex, lngX, lngY, lngFrame

Once a sprite is created or cloned the index value can be used in many functions. The Move function allows the programmer to place the sprite at a new pixel position on the destination device and choose to display an alternative frame.

Parameters:
lngIndex   The index of a loaded sprite.
LngX   The left position to display the sprite on the destination device
lngY   The top position to display the sprite on the destination device
lngFrame   The new frame to display. If the frame is out of bounds then the previous successful frame is used.

Return Value: None.

- CloneSprite lngIndex , lngX , lngY

If a sprite has been successfully loaded then it can be cloned. This uses very little memory since the images come from the parent sprite.

Parameters:

lngIndex   The index value of a loaded sprite. This could be a sprite that has been created by cloning.

LngX   The left position to display the sprite on the destination device.

LngY   The top position to display the sprite on the destination device.

Return value: The index value of the new sprite. Zero if unsuccessful.

- UpdateStage

Calls to MoveSprite are displayed to the user until a call to UpdateStage. The idea is that the programmer moves all the sprites as part of a control loop generated using a Visual Basic Timer control. Once all the moving is done the result of the changes is shown instantly by a call to UpdateStage.

Parameters: None.
Return value: None.

- GetSpriteActive lngIndex

If the programmer needs to check on the validity of a sprite (has it been initialised?), this function does that job. If the sprite is initialised then the function returns True.

Parameter:
lngIndex   A sprite index value

Return value: True if the sprite has been initialised; False otherwise.

- DrawFullStage

To facilitate fast redrawing the sprite library redraws the smallest areas possible. If a window is placed over the control and removed then the area beneath the window will be incorrectly displayed.

Place function in the Paint event of the Form or Picture Box being used as the destination device. Whenever the control has been covered by another window and revealed, DrawFullStage will redraw the total area.

Parameters: None.

Return Value: True if successful; False otherwise.

- CollisionCheck lngSprite1, lngSprite2, blnAccurate
  Tests if a collision has occurred between two sprites. The test can be done on the bounding rectangle or on the actual displayed pixels of the sprite.

  Parameters:
  lngSprite1   The index value of one sprite.
  lngSprite2   The index value of the second sprite.
  blnAccurate   If the test is for non-transparent pixels of the two sprites set this value to True. If a simple bounding rectangle is accurate enough then set this value to False. The simple test is much quicker.

  Return value: True if there is a collision; False otherwise.

- PasteSprite lngIndex, lngX, lngY, lngFrame

  This permanently adds the sprite image to the background. The sprite can then be moved and it will appear at both locations. The pasted image can only be removed by reloading the background. This function can be useful when creating a background screen at runtime from the images of a sprite.

  Parameters:
  lngIndex   The index value of a sprite.
  lngX   The left position to paste the sprite on the destination device.
  lngY   The top position to paste the sprite on the destination device.
  lngFrame The frame to use in the display.

  Return value: True if successful; False otherwise.

- HitTest lngX, lngY

  Using the values for x and y as co-ordinates, the return value is either zero or the index value of the sprite found there. Be warned: if multiple sprites are found at the same position this function will return the one with the lowest index value.

Parameters:
lngX   The x co-ordinate to use in the test.
LngY   The y co-ordinate to use in the test.

Return value: Index value of sprite found at that co-ordinate, or
zero if none found.

NOTE

Sprite index values all start at 1. Zero is a False value.

Using the Sprite ActiveX Control

To use the Sprite ActiveX Control select View|Components from the menu. Click the check box by Sprite OLE Control. An icon with two eyes will be added to the toolbox. Select this icon and drag a sprite control box onto your form.

Properties

The Sprite ActiveX Control has the following properties:

Name	The name you use in code to refer to the control.
Visible	The control is only visible when this property is set to True.
Enabled	The control is only enabled when this property is set to True.
AutoSize	If AutoSize is True then loading a background will resize the control to the size of the background.
Width	The control can be resized with Width when AutoSize is False
Height	The control can be resized with Height when AutoSize is False.
Left	The left position on the destination Form.
Top	The top position on the destination Form.

Fps   The frames per second that will be used by the sprite controls
           timer to generate timer`events.

Methods

Many of the methods are similar to the functions that you can use in
the dynamic link library.

- **UpdateStage()**

  Used to redraw the user's view of the stage.

  Parameters: None
  Returned values: None

- **CreateSprite(strPicName, intWidth, intHeight)**

  To create a new sprite you pass the picture that provides the
  images. The images must be placed in a grid pattern. The width and
  height parameters provide the size of the sprite. A picture that is
  300 pixels by 200 pixels and has the width and height set to 100,
  will have a total of 6 images to use.

  Parameters:
  strPicName   A string value providing the path and filename of the
               picture file to use.
  intWidth   An integer value used to set the width of the sprite
  intHeight   An integer value used to set the height of the sprite.

  Returned values: The index value of the new sprite as an integer.
  Zero if an error occurred.

- **HitTest(intX, intY)**

  Use this method to test if a sprite is to be found at a particular (x,y)
  co-ordinate.

  Parameters:
  intX   X position for test
  intY   Y position for test

  Returned values: The index value of a sprite if a sprite is found at
  this co-ordinate. Zero if none found.

- **MoveSprite(intIndex, intX, intY, intFrame)**

Once a sprite has been created the index value is used as a parameter in many other methods. This method allows the programmer to reposition the sprite at a particular (x,y) co-ordinate. The selection of which image to display takes any valid frame value. If the frame value is out of bounds then the previous image will be displayed.

Parameters:
intIndex   value of a sprite.
IntX   X position to display the sprite's top left corner.
IntY   Y position to display the sprite's top left corner.
IntFrame   The image to use for the display.

Returned values: True if successful; False if error occurred.

- **DeleteSprite(intIndex)**

This method removes the sprite from memory. The index value will no longer be valid.

Parameter:
intIndex   Index value of a sprite.

Returned values: True if successful; False if not.

- **CloneSprite(intSrcIndex, intX, intY)**

Once you have created a sprite it can be cloned. This allows multiple versions of a sprite that use very little additional memory since all the images come from the parent sprite.

Parameters:
intSrcIndex   Index value of a sprite.
IntX   Initial x co-ordinate of new sprite.
intY   Initial y co-ordinate of new sprite.

Returned Values: The index value of the new sprite

- **CollisionCheck(intSprite, intSprite2, blnAccurate)**

Parameters:
intSprite1   Index value of sprite.
intSprite2   Index value of sprite.

blnAccurate   A collision test can be based on the bounding rectangles of the two sprites or the visible pixels of both sprites. If this parameter is True then the pixel test will be done. The bounding rectangle test is much quicker.

Returned values: True if sprites overlap; False otherwise.

- **PasteSprite(intIndex, intX, intY, intFrame)**

Any image from a sprite can be permanently pasted onto the background. The image will stay there after the sprite is moved. To remove the image you will need to reload the background image.

Parameters:
intIndex   Index value of sprite.
IntX   X position of the top left corner of sprite image.
intY   Y position of the top left corner of sprite image.
intFrame   Image that is to be displayed.

Returned values: True if successful; False otherwise.

- **LoadBackground(strBgFilename, blnKeepSprites)**

Use this method to replace the background image. The second parameter determines whether the current sprites are retained. If the sprites are kept then their colours will be mapped to the palette of the new background.

Parameters:
strBgFilename   The name and path of a picture file that is used as new background image. The file must be a 256 colour 'bmp' file.
blnKeepSprites True if sprites are to be retained. False if sprites are to be deleted.

Returned values: True if successful; False otherwise.

- **PlaySoundFile(strSndFilename)**

Plays a Windows 'wav' file. The first time a file is used it is loaded into memory. When the file is used again it will normally be played directly from memory. If the file does not exist or is not a 'wav' file then no error will occur, but no sound will be played.

Parameter:
strSndFilename   Name and path of Windows 'wav' file.

Returned values: None.

- **PlayMusicFile(strMusicFilename)**

Plays a Windows 'mid' file. The first time a file is used it is loaded into memory. When the file is used again it will normally be played directly from memory. If the file does not exist or is not a 'mid' file then no error will occur, but no sound will be played.

Parameter:
strMusicFilename   Name and path of music midi file.

Returned values: None.

- **DrawFullStage()**

Allows the programmer to look after paint events. When a window covers the sprite control and is removed, the control will be incorrectly painted. Use a call to DrawFullStage to correct this.

Parameters: None.
Returned values: None.

Events

Click	Generated when the control is clicked.
DoubleClick	Generated when the control is clicked twice quickly.
KeyDown	Generated when the keyboard is used while the sprite control. has the focus.
KeyUp	Generated when a key is released while the sprite control has focus.
MouseDown	Generated when the mouse is clicked on the sprite control.
MouseMove	Generated when the mouse is moved over the sprite control.
MouseUp	Generated when the mouse button is released over the sprite control.
Timer	Generated periodically, dependent on the fps property value. A fps of zero pauses the control and no Timer events occur.

APPENDIX E

All the maths you need!

Most of the examples in this book need no more maths than you would come across at school. But, many of us have forgotten the maths we learnt in school and need a little reminder. In this short guide I hope to bring you up to speed on the maths you will need.

Scalars

A scalar is a single numerical value.

Vectors

It is often convenient to group numbers. A vector is one such grouping. A vector is an ideal way to store a point, for example; or a direction. You could have a vector with two values to store a 2D point and one with three values to store a 3D point or direction. You could implement a 2D vector in Visual Basic by creating a user datatype.

```
Type Vector2D
    x As Single
    y As Single
End Type
```

A vector is usually written as a column. The numbers are surrounded with elongated brackets.

$$\begin{pmatrix} 3.2 \\ 4.1 \\ 9.6 \end{pmatrix}$$

Matrices

Sometimes it is convenient to group numbers in a grid. The numbers form rows and columns. When manipulating 2D and 3D co-ordinates a matrix interpretation offers the simplest way of managing the numerical operations necessary.

A 3×3 matrix could be implemented in code as a user datatype:

```
Type Matrix3 × 3
    a1 As Single, a2 As Single, a3 As Single
    b1 As Single, b2 As Single, b3 As Single
    c1 As Single, c2 As Single, c3 As Single
End Type
```

A matrix is usually written using square brackets:

$$\begin{bmatrix} 1.0, 3.4, 8.9 \\ 3.2, 7.8, 9.2 \\ 7.1, 9.0, 4.5 \end{bmatrix}$$

A vector is simply a matrix with just one column.

Multiplying matrices

Matrix multiplication can only occur if the left matrix has the same number of columns as the right matrix has rows. Here is a guide to matrix multiplication.

$$
\begin{bmatrix} a1, & a2, & a3 \\ b1, & b2, & b3 \\ c1, & c2, & c3 \end{bmatrix} \begin{bmatrix} d1, & d2 \\ e1, & e2 \\ f1, & f2 \end{bmatrix}
$$

$$
= \begin{bmatrix} (a1\text{*}d1 + a2\text{*}e1 + a3\text{*}f1), & (a1\text{*}d2 + a2\text{*}e2 + a3\text{*}f2) \\ (b1\text{*}d1 + b2\text{*}e1 + b3\text{*}f1), & (b1\text{*}d2 + b2\text{*}e2 + b3\text{*}f2) \\ (c1\text{*}d1 + c2\text{*}e1 + c3\text{*}f1), & (c1\text{*}d2 + c2\text{*}e2 + c3\text{*}f2) \end{bmatrix}
$$

An interesting feature of matrix multiplication is that it is not commutative. If A is a matrix and B is another, then A * B is usually not the same as B * A.

Matrix addition

Numbers in the same position on both matrices are summed to give the new value.

$$
\begin{bmatrix} a1, & a2, & a3 \\ b1, & b2, & b3 \\ c1, & c2, & c3 \end{bmatrix} \begin{bmatrix} d1, & d2, & d3 \\ e1, & e2, & e3 \\ f1, & f2, & f3 \end{bmatrix} = \begin{bmatrix} a1 + d1, & a2 + d2, & a3 + d3 \\ b1 + e1, & b2 + e2, & b3 + e3 \\ c1 + f1, & c2 + f2, & c3 + f3 \end{bmatrix}
$$

Matrix subtraction

Numbers in the same position on both matrices are subtracted to give the new value.

$$
\begin{bmatrix} a1, & a2, & a3 \\ b1, & b2, & b3 \\ c1, & c2, & c3 \end{bmatrix} \begin{bmatrix} d1, & d2, & d3 \\ e1, & e2, & e3 \\ f1, & f2, & f3 \end{bmatrix} = \begin{bmatrix} a1 - d1, & a2 - d2, & a3 - d3 \\ b1 - e1, & b2 - e2, & b3 - e3 \\ c1 - f1, & c2 - f2, & c3 - f3 \end{bmatrix}
$$

The identity matrix for multiplication

A matrix that leaves the original matrix unaltered is called an identity matrix. It is a matrix that has 1 on the diagonal from top left to bottom right.

$$
\begin{bmatrix} 1, & 0, & 0 \\ 0, & 1, & 0 \\ 0, & 0, & 1 \end{bmatrix}
$$

Trigonometry

A circle can be divided into any number of segments. If you divide it into 12 segments then you have a design that is similar to a clock. A compass is divided into 8 main segments. North, Northeast, East, Southeast, South, Southwest, West, Northwest. The number of divisions can be any number you choose. If there are five for dinner you can cut the gateau into five pieces. When you are thinking about angles you probably think in terms of degrees. There are 360 degrees in a circle. I am afraid you need to get out of this way of thinking if you want to use computer trigonometrical functions. The computer wants you to divide a circle into approximately 6.283 segments. Why?

You may remember that the sin function can be defined as the opposite side from the angle divided by the hypotenuse (longest side) of a right-angled triangle. Another way of thinking of this function involves a circle with centre at the origin and radius 1.

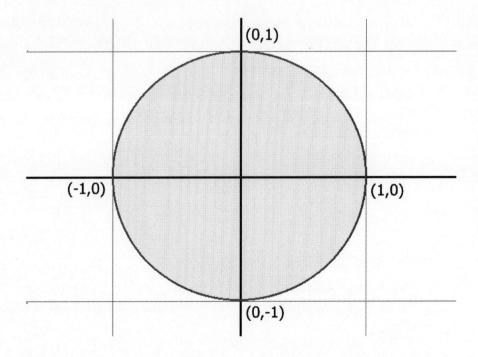

The co-ordinates of the points on the circle can be defined as (Cos θ, Sin θ) where θ is the angle between a line from the origin and the x axis. Remember that the total circumference of a circle can be related to its radius using the formula 2 * π * radius = Circumference. If the radius is 1 then the circumference is 2 * π. One of the reasons behind using 6.283 (2 * π) as the division of the circle is that reference is often made to the unit circle (the circle with radius 1, centred at the origin). Angles defined in this way are radians.

2D Co-ordinate transformations

The Visual Basic implementation uses a user datatype

```
Type Point2D
  X As Single
  Y As Single
End Type

Dim pt As Point2D, ptMove As Point2D, ptScale As Point2D, ptShear As
Point2D
```

Translation

When a 2D object is moved from one position to another. Each vertex needs to be converted to the new co-ordinate. The conversion is very simple

```
pt.X = pt.X + ptMove.X
pt.Y = pt.Y + ptMove.Y
```

Rotation

If the point is rotated about the origin by angle A the new position is given by

```
pt.X = pt.X * Cos(A) − pt.Y * Sin(A)
pt.Y = pt.X * Sin(A) + pt.Y * Cos(A)
```

This can be derived from the transformation matrix

$$\begin{bmatrix} \text{Cos(A)} & \text{Sin(A)} \\ -\text{Sin(A)} & \text{Cos(A)} \end{bmatrix}$$

Scaling

To resize the object in the X and Y direction requires a scalar multiple:

```
pt.X = pt.X * ptScale.X
pt.Y = pt.Y * ptScale.Y
```

The matrix representation is

$$\begin{bmatrix} \text{ptScale.X} & 0 \\ 0 & \text{ptScale.Y} \end{bmatrix}$$

Shearing

Distortion in the X direction is given by:

```
pt.X = pt.X + pt.Y * ptShear.X
pt.Y = pt.Y
```

Distortion in the Y direction is given by:

```
pt.X = pt.X
pt.Y = pt.Y + pt.X * ptShear.Y
```

3D Co-ordinate transformations

The Visual Basic implementation uses a user datatype:

```
Type Point2D
    X As Single
    Y As Single
End Type

Type Point3D
    X As Single
    Y As Single
    Z As Single
End Type

Dim pt As Point3D, ptMove As Point3D, ptScale As Point3D
Dim ptScreen As Point2D, ptShear As Point3D
```

Translation

When a 3D object is moved from one position to another, each vertex needs to be converted to the new co-ordinate. The conversion is very simple:

```
pt.X = pt.X + ptMove.X
pt.Y = pt.Y + ptMove.Y
```

```
pt.Z = pt.Z + ptMove.Z
```

Rotation

If the point is rotated about the origin by angle A the new position is given by:

About the negative Z axis

```
pt.X = pt.X * Cos(A) − pt.Y * Sin(A)
pt.Y = pt.X * Sin(A) + pt.Y * Cos(A)
pt.Z = pt.Z
```

The 3D equivalent of the 2D case.

About the positive X axis

```
pt.X = pt.X
pt.Y = pt.Y * Cos(A) + pt.Z * Sin(A)
pt.Z = pt.Z * Cos(A) − pt.Y * Sin(A)
```

About the positive Y axis

```
pt.X = pt.X * Cos(A) − pt.Z * Sin(A)
pt.Y = pt.Y
pt.Z = pt.X * Sin(A) + pt.Z * Cos(A)
```

Effects

Increase x rotation: The object tilts towards the camera.
Increase y rotation: The object's right side swings away from the camera
Increase z rotation: The object tilts in an anti-clockwise direction

The transformations can be multiplied together first. The order of the multiplication affects the result.

Scaling

To resize the object in the X and Y direction requires a scalar multiple.

```
pt.X = pt.X * ptScale.X
pt.Y = pt.Y * ptScale.Y
pt.Y = pt.Z * ptScale.Z
```

Perspective

D is the distance of the camera from the screen.

```
ptScreen.X = pt.X * D / (pt.Z + D)
ptScreen.Y = pt.Z * D / (pt.Z + D)
```

More vector and matrix manipulation

Vector length

The length of a 2D vector is given by

```
Sqrt(pt.X * pt.X + pt.Y * pt.Y)
```

The length of a 3D vector is given by

```
Sqrt( pt.X * pt.X + pt.Y * pt.Y + pt.Z * pt.Z)
```

Dot product

The dot product of two 3D vectors is given by

```
Function DotProduct( pt1 As Point3D, pt2 As Point3D) As Single
   DotProduct = pt1.X * pt2.X + pt1.Y * pt2.Y + pt1.Z * pt2.Z
End Function
```

Cross product

The cross product of two 3D vectors returns a vector at right angles to both the other vectors.

```
Function CrossProduct( pt1 As Point3D, pt2 As Point3D) As Point3D
   CrossProduct.X = pt1.Y * pt2.Z − pt1.Z * pt2.Y
   CrossProduct.Y = pt1.Z * pt2.X − pt1.X * pt2.Z
   CrossProduct.Z = pt1.X * pt2.Y − pt1.ZY* pt2.X
End Function
```

Unit vector

To create a vector of length 1 divide each member by the current length of the vector.

```
Function UnitVector( pt As Point3D) As Point3D
   Dim sngLength As Single
```

```
sngLength = Sqrt( pt.X * pt.X + pt.Y * pt.Y + pt.Z * pt.Z)
UnitVector.X = pt.X/sngLength
UnitVector.Y = pt.Y/sngLength
UnitVector.Z = pt.Z/sngLength
End Function
```

Trigonometric formulae

tan A = sin A / cos A
cot A = cos A / sin A = 1 / tan A
sec A = 1 / cos A
cosec A = 1 / sin A
cos A * cos A + sin A * sin A = 1
sec A * sec A = 1 + tan A * tan A
cosec A * cosec A = 1 + cot A * cot A

Addition

Sin(A + B) = Sin(A) * Cos(B) + Cos(A) * Sin(B)
Sin(A − B) = Sin(A) * Cos(B) − Cos(A) * Sin(B)
Cos(A + B) = Cos(A) * Cos(B) − Sin(A) * Sin(B)
Cos(A − B) = Cos(A) * Cos(B) + Sin(A) * Sin(B)
Tan(A + B) = (Tan(A) + Tan(B)) / (1 − Tan(A) * Tan(B))
Tan(A − B) = (Tan(A) − Tan(B)) / (1 + Tan(A) * Tan(B))

Double angles

Sin(2 * A) = 2 * Sin(A) * Cos(A)
Cos(2 * A) = Cos(A) * Cos(A) − Sin(A) * Sin(A)
Cos(2 * A) = 1 − 2 * Sin(A) * Sin(A)
Sin(A) * Sin(A) = .5 * (1 − Cos (2*A))
Cos(2 * A) = 2 * Cos(A) * Cos(A) − 1
Cos(A) * Cos(A) = 0.5 * (1 + Cos (2*A))
Tan(2 * A) = 2 * Tan(A) / (1 − Tan(A) * Tan(A))

Products

Sin(A) * Cos(A) = 0.5 * (Sin(A + B) + Sin (A − B))
Cos(A) * Sin(A) = 0.5 * (Sin(A + B) − Sin (A − B))
Cos(A) * Cos(A) = 0.5 * (Cos(A + B) + Cos (A − B))
Sin(A) * Sin(A) = 0.5 * (Cos(A − B) − Cos (A + B))

Sums

$$\text{Sin(C)} + \text{Sin(D)} = 2 * \text{Sin}(0.5 * (C + D))* \text{Cos} (0.5 * (C - D))$$
$$\text{Sin(C)} - \text{Sin(D)} = 2 * \text{Cos}(0.5 * (C + D)) * \text{Sin} (0.5 * (C - D))$$
$$\text{Cos(C)} + \text{Cos(D)} = 2 * \text{Cos}(0.5 * (C + D)) * \text{Cos} (0.5 * (C - D))$$
$$\text{Cos(C)} - \text{Cos(D)} = -2 * \text{Sin}(0.5 * (C + D)) * \text{Sin} (0.5 * (C - D))$$

APPENDIX F

ASCII character set

0	25	50 2	75 K
1	26	51 3	76 L
2	27	52 4	77 M
3	28	53 5	78 N
4	29	54 6	79 O
5	30	55 7	80 P
6	31	56 8	81 Q
7	32 [space]	57 9	82 R
8**	33 !	58 :	83 S
9**	34 "	59 ;	84 T
10**	35 #	60 <	85 U
11	36 $	61 =	86 V
12	37 %	62 >	87 W
13**	38 &	63 ?	88 X
14	39 '	64 @	89 Y
15	40 (	65 A	90 Z
16	41)	66 B	91 [
17	42 *	67 C	92 \
18	43 +	68 D	93]
19	44 ,	69 E	94 ^
20	45 -	70 F	95 _
21	46 .	71 G	96 `
22	47 /	72 H	97 a
23	48 0	73 I	98 b
24	49 1	74 J	99 c

100 d	139	178 ^{2}	217 Ù
101 e	140	179 ^{3}	218 Ú
102 f	141	180 ´	219 Û
103 g	142	181 μ	220 Ü
104 h	143	182 ¶	221 Ý
105 i	144	183 ·	222
106 j	145 '	184 ,	223
107 k	146 '	185 ^{1}	224 à
108 l	147	186 º	225 à
109 m	148	187 »	226 â
110 n	149	188 ¼	227 ã
111 o	150	189 ½	228 ä
112 p	151	190 ¾	229 å
113 q	152	191	230 æ
114 r	153	192 À	231 ç
115 s	154	193 Á	232 è
116 t	155	194 Â	233 é
117 u	156	195 Ã	234 ê
118 v	157	196 Ä	235 ë
119 w	158	197 Å	236 ì
120 x	159	198 Æ	237 í
121 y	160 [space]	199 Ç	238 î
122 z	161	200 È	239 ï
123 {	162 ¢	201 É	240
124 |	163 £	202 Ê	242 ñ
125 }	164	203 Ë	242 ò
126 ~	165 ¥	204 Ì	243 ó
127	166 ¦	205 Í	244 ô
128	167 §	206 Î	245 õ
129	168 ¨	207 Ï	246 ö
130	169 ©	208	247 ÷
131	170 ª	209 Ñ	248 ø
132	171 «	210 Ò	249 ù
133	172 ¬	211 Ó	250 ú
134	173 -	212 Ô	251 û
135	174 ®	213 Õ	252 ü
136	175 ¯	214 Ö	253 ý
137	176 °	215 ×	254
138	177 ±	216 Ø	255 ÿ

(If blank, those characters are not supported by Microsoft Windows.)
** Values 8, 9, 10 and 13 convert to backspace, tab, linefeed and carriage return characters, respectively. They have no graphical representation but, depending on the application, may affect the visual display of text.

Bibliography

There are many books that have informed and inspired the creation of this book. Here I list just a few that are especially useful.

Programming Windows 95 by Charles Petzold. If you intend to go beyond Visual Basic then this is the first book you should have in your library.
ISBN 1-55615-676-6. Microsoft Press 1996

Teach Yourself Visual C++ 4 in 21 Days by Ori Gurewich and Nathan Gurewich. If you intend to move into other programming languages then I recommend C++. The Visual C++ compiler and development environment is the only one I know well. It is robust and provides ample online help. The debugging tools leave Visual Basic standing. This introductory book is an excellent starter.
ISBN 0-672-30795-2. Sams Publishing 1996

Animation Techniques in Win32 by Nigel Thompson. Slightly predating Windows 95, this book introduces the reader to the 32-bit function calls available through Windows. The reader is guided through an implementation of a fast graphic library using Microsoft's Foundation Classes and additional code. The information is very accessible and the examples work well.
ISBN 1-55615-669-3. Microsoft Press 1995

Teach yourself Computer Graphics by John Lansdown. A concise but thorough introduction to 2D and 3D raster-orientated computer graphics. All the topics are here in a quick and easy to understand form. From Bresenham's line drawing algorithm to 3D transformations; it's all in here.
ISBN 0-340-40819-7. Hodder and Stoughton 1987

VBScript by Example by Jerry Honeycutt. I looked at about 6 VBScript books while writing this book and this is the best. It's not the biggest but it has everything you need to know, and the tutorial style gets you up to speed quickly.
ISBN 0-7897-0815-9. Que Corporation 1996

Bit-Mapped Graphics by Steve Rimmer. Without doubt the best book on bitmapped file formats. If you want to know how to work with a 'gif', 'pcx', 'tif', etc., then this is the book for you. It is written using the old style C, so you may need a copy of Kernighan and Richie's famous C Book.
ISBN 0-8306-4209-9. Windcrest Books 1993

The Illusion of Life by Frank Thomas and Ollie Johnston. The authors were two of the nine old men of Disney character animation. They worked on the films from *Snow White* through to *The Fox and the Hound*. As an animator I have read just about all the published books on the craft. Frankly, you can throw every other book in the bin. Just read this one book. A lifetime's experience at the craft of character animation is described in splendid detail and illustrated magnificently. I simply cannot recommend this book highly enough. Get a copy.
ISBN. Disney 19.

INDEX

BECOMING A PRENTICE HALL AUTHOR

Getting published with Prentice Hall

1. Can I do it?

It is easy to think of the publishing process as a series of hurdles designed to weed out would-be authors. That may be true of some publishing houses, but not Prentice Hall.

- We do all we can to encourage new talent.
- We welcome unsolicited manuscripts.
- We carefully examine every proposal we receive, and we always write back to let the authors know what we think of it.

Although many of our authors have professional or educational experience, we look first for a passion for computing. Some of our most successful books are written by first time authors. If you have built up expertise in any computing-related topic, please get in touch. You'll be surprised how easy it is to get through.

2. Is Prentice Hall a successful company?

Prentice Hall is a highly respected brand in technical and scientific publishing, a status reflected in our relationships with the book trade and various professional bodies. Our reputation has been made with classic computing titles such as Kernighan and Ritchie's *The C Programming Language* (over two million copies sold) and Bertrand Meyer's ground-breaking *Object Oriented Software Construction*.

We're part of Simon & Schuster, a $2 billion dollar global publishing company. Simon & Schuster is host to Macmillan Computer Publishing, home of renowned computer imprints such as Sams, Que, Waite Group Press, Ziff-Davis Publishing, Hayden and New Riders

Press (NRP). Simon & Schuster is itself owned by Viacom Inc, one of the world's largest entertainment and publishing companies. Viacom owns film and tv studios (Paramount Pictures), world-wide cable networks (MTV, Nickelodeon) and retail outlets (Blockbuster Video).

3. What sort of books does Prentice Hall publish?

The computing revolution in the office and home has prompted a massive and diverse market for computer books. That diversity is reflected in our approach. We are happy to consider book proposals on absolutely any computing topic.

Essentially, Prentice Hall publishes books for anyone whose job or hobby connects them to a computer. We are already familiar with your intended readership, whether your book is written for professionals, students, enthusiasts or beginners. Our progressive editorial policy encourages new authors and gives us the flexibility required in a rapidly changing technological environment. However, we do have a 'books wanted' list – contact the editorial department for the latest copy.

4. What are the rewards of writing a book?

Prentice Hall royalty rates are among the most competitive in the industry, and many of our authors earn considerable sums through royalties. Payments are calculated along industry-standard guidelines, i.e. the author receives a percentage of the publisher's net sales revenue. We always offer preferential royalty rates for senior figures within the computing industry, or for books on hot topics written by experts. For the right book at the right time, the financial reward to the author can be extremely generous. This is especially true of books aimed at professional software developers.

If you are a computer professional or an academic, your livelihood depends upon your professional reputation. Successful Prentice Hall authors enjoy a constant stream of business and employment opportunities as a direct result of getting published. A book works like a business card, advertising the author's talent across a vast network of potential contacts.

5. How do I know my ideas are good enough to publish?

In assessing the market-readiness of book proposals or finished manuscripts, Prentice Hall editors draw upon a huge database of technical advisors. All of our reviewers are senior figures in modern computing, and their role is to offer free advice to potential authors, highlighting both the strengths and weaknesses of proposals and manuscripts. The aim of the review process is to add value to your ideas, rather than just approving or rejecting them.

We understand that errors are inevitable when writing books, but as a Prentice Hall author you need not worry about the quality of your finished work. Many of our authors have not written a book before, so we are there to help – we scrutinise all our manuscripts for grammatical accuracy and style.

6. How much control would I have over my book?

We understand that a book is a highly personal statement from the author, so we invite your participation at all stages of the publishing process, from the cover design through to the final marketing plans. A Prentice Hall book is a co-operative venture between author and publisher.

7. Will I get any help with the technical aspects of book production?

Our highly professional staff will ensure that the book you envisaged is the book that makes it to the shelves. Once you hand over your manuscript to us, we will take care of all the technical details of printing and binding. Beyond the advice and guidance from your own editor, our 64-page *Author Guide* is there to help you shape your manuscript into a first-class book. Our large and efficient production department is among the quickest in the industry. We are experts at turning raw manuscripts into polished books, irrespective of the technical complexity of your work. Technical queries can be answered by your production contact, assigned, where relevant, to you at contract stage. Our production staff fully understand the individual requirements of every project, and will work with you to produce a manuscript format that best complements your skills – hard copy manuscripts, electronic files or camera-ready copy.

8. How quickly can you turn my manuscript into a book?

The production department at Prentice Hall is widely acknowledged to be among the quickest in the industry. Our turnaround times vary according to the nature of the manuscript supplied to us, but the average is about four months for camera-ready copy, five for electronic file manuscript. For time-sensitive topics, we can occasionally turn out books in under twelve weeks!

9. Where would my book be sold?

Prentice Hall has one of the largest sales forces of any technical publisher. Our highly experienced sales staff have developed firm business partnerships with all the major retail bookstores in Europe, America, Asia, the Middle East and South Africa, ensuring that your book receives maximum retail exposure. Prentice Hall's marketing department is responsible for ensuring the widest possible review coverage in magazines and journals – vital to the sales of computing books.

Our books are usually present at major trade shows and exhibitions, either on our own stands or those belonging to major retail bookshops. Our presence at trade shows ensures that your work can be inspected by the most senior figures within any given field of computing. We also have a very successful corporate and institutional sales team, dedicated to selling our books into large companies, user groups, book clubs, training seminars and professional bodies.

Local language translations can provide not only a significant boost to an author's royalty income, but also will allow your research/findings to reach a wider audience, thus furthering your professional prospects. To maintain both the author's and Prentice Hall's reputation, we license foreign language deals only with publishing houses of the highest repute.

10. I don't have time to write a book!

To enjoy all the advantages of being a published author, it is not always necessary for you to write an entire book. Prentice Hall welcomes books written by multiple authors. If you feel that your skills lie in a very specific area of computing, or that you do not have the time to write an entire book, please get in touch regardless. Prentice Hall may have a book in progress that would benefit from your ideas.

You may know individuals or teams in your field who could act as co-author(s). If not, Prentice Hall can probably put you in touch with the right people. Royalties for shared-author books are distributed according to respective participation.

11. Could my company benefit?

Many Prentice Hall authors use their book to lever their commercial interests, and we like to do all we can to help. If a well-written book is an excellent marketing tool for an author, then it can also be an excellent marketing tool for the author's company. A book is its own highly focused marketing channel, a respected medium that takes your company name to all the right people. Previous examples of marketing opportunities with our books include:

- free advertising in the back pages
- packaging in suitable corporate livery (book covers, flyers, etc.)
- mounting software demos in the back page on disk or CDROM

Although Prentice Hall has to keep its publications free of undue corporate or institutional bias, in general the options for cross-marketing are varied and completely open to discussion.

12. I have an idea for a book. What next?

We invite you to submit a book proposal. We need proposals to be formatted in a specific way, so if you have not received our guidelines, please contact the Acquisition Editor at this address:

Jason Dunne
Professional and Consumer Computing
Prentice Hall
Campus 400, Maylands Avenue
Hemel Hempstead, Herts.
HP2 7EZ
England

Tel: +44 (0)1442 882246
Fax: +44 (0)1442 252544

e-mail: jason_dunne@prenhall.co.uk

LICENSE AGREEMENT AND LIMITED WARRANTY
FOR ANIMATION MAGIC WITH VISUAL BASIC 5

READ THE FOLLOWING TERMS AND CONDITIONS CAREFULLY BEFORE OPENING THIS DISK PACKAGE. THIS IS AN AGREEMENT BETWEEN YOU AND PRENTICE HALL EUROPE (THE "COMPANY"). BY OPENING THIS SEALED PACKAGE, YOU ARE AGREEING TO BE BOUND BY THESE TERMS AND CONDITIONS. IF YOU DO NOT AGREE WITH THESE TERMS AND CONDITIONS, DO NOT OPEN THE DISK PACKAGE. PROMPTLY RETURN THE DISK PACKAGE AND ALL ACCOMPANYING ITEMS TO THE COMPANY.

1. GRANT OF LICENSE: In consideration of your adoption of textbooks and/or other materials published by the company, and your agreement to abide by the terms and conditions of the Agreement, the Company grants to you a non-exclusive right to use and display the copy of the enclosed software program (hereinafter "the SOFTWARE") so long as you comply with the terms of this Agreement. The company reserves all rights not expressly granted to you under this Agreement. This license is *not* a sale of the original SOFTWARE or any copy to you.

2. USE RESTRICTIONS: You may *not* sell or license copies of the SOFTWARE or the Documentation to others. You may *not* reverse engineer, disassemble, decompile, modify, adapt, translate or create derivative works based on the SOFTWARE or the Documentation without the prior written consent of the Company.

3. LIMITED WARRANTY: THE PROGRAM IS PROVIDED "AS IS" WITHOUT WARRANTY OF ANY KIND, EITHER EXPRESSED OR IMPLIED, INCLUDING, BUT NOT LIMITED TO, THE IMPLIED WARRANTIES OF MERCHANTABILITY AND FITNESS FOR A PARTICULAR PURPOSE. THE ENTIRE RISK AS TO THE QUALITY AND PERFORMANCE OF THE PROGRAM IS WITH YOU. SHOULD THE PROGRAM PROVE DEFECTIVE, YOU (AND NOT PRENTICE HALL EUROPE OR ANY OTHER AUTHORISED DEALER) ASSUME THE ENTIRE COST OF ALL NECESSARY SERVICING, REPAIR OR CORRECTION, NO ORAL OR WRITTEN INFORMATION OR ADVICE GIVEN BY PRENTICE HALL EUROPE ITS DEALERS, DISTRIBUTORS OR AGENTS SHALL CREATE A WARRANTY OR INCREASE THE SCOPE OF THIS WARRANTY.

The Company does not warrant that the functions contained in the program will meet your requirements or that the operation of the program will be uninterrupted or error-free. However the Company warrants the diskettes on which the program is furnished to be free from defects in material and workmanship under normal use for a period of ninety (90) days from the date of delivery to you as evidenced by a copy of your receipt.

Applicable law may not allow the exclusion of certain implied warranties or conditions, so the above exclusions do not exclude any implied warranties or conditions which may not under applicable law be excluded. THIS AGREEMENT DOES NOT AFFECT YOUR STATUTORY RIGHTS.

4. LIMITATION OF REMEDIES: The Company's entire liability and your exclusive remedy shall be: (1) the replacement of any diskette not meeting the Company's "LIMITED WARRANTY' and that is returned to the Company, or

(2) if the Company is unable to deliver a replacement diskette that is free of defects in materials or workmanship, you may terminate this agreement by returning the program.

ACKNOWLEDGEMENT

YOU ACKNOWLEDGE THAT YOU HAVE READ THIS AGREEMENT, UNDERSTAND IT AND AGREE TO BE BOUND BY ITS TERMS AND CONDITIONS. YOU ALSO AGREE THAT THIS AGREEMENT IS THE COMPLETE AND EXCLUSIVE AGREEMENT BETWEEN YOU AND THE COMPANY.

Should you have any questions concerning this agreement or if you wish to contact the Company for any reason, please contact in writing: Product Development Unit, Prentice Hall Europe, Campus 400, Maylands Avenue, Hemel Hempstead, Herts. HP2 7EZ.